Urban Land Use Policy:
The Central City

Urban Land Use Policy:
The Central City

Edited by
RICHARD B. ANDREWS

[Fp] THE FREE PRESS, NEW YORK
COLLIER-MACMILLAN LIMITED, LONDON

The Free Press
A Division of The Macmillan Company
866 Third Avenue, New York, New York 10022

COLLIER-MACMILLAN CANADA LTD., TORONTO, ONTARIO

Library of Congress Catalog Card Number: 70–169230

Printing number
1 2 3 4 5 6 7 8 9 10

Contents

	page
Acknowledgments	ix
The Contributors	xi
Introduction	xv
I. ZONING	1

Introduction to Zoning and the Land Use Control System

1. KEY ISSUES IN LAND USE CONTROLS William A. Doebele, Jr.	3
2. POMEROY MEMORIAL LECTURE: REQUIEM FOR ZONING John W. Reps	10

Economic Perspectives of Zoning

3. CONTROL OF COMPETITION AS A PROPER PURPOSE IN ZONING Daniel R. Mandelker	19
4. THE GENERAL WELFARE, WELFARE ECONOMICS, AND ZONING VARIANCES Lewis B. Merrifield, III	24
5. ECONOMIC ELEMENTS IN MUNICIPAL ZONING DECISIONS Otto A. Davis	41

Economics of Manufacturing and Residential Zoning

6. ZONING AND THE INDUSTRIAL DEVELOPER   51
   Dennis O'Harrow

7. THE ECONOMIC CONSEQUENCES OF INDUSTRIAL ZONING   56
   William M. Shenkel

8. PERFORMANCE STANDARDS IN INDUSTRIAL ZONING   64
   Dennis O'Harrow

9. PERFORMANCE STANDARDS IN RESIDENTIAL ZONING   74
   Frank E. Horack, Jr.

10. ZONING SKETCHES   81
    Charles Agle

11. ZONING FOR AESTHETIC OBJECTIVES: A REAPPRAISAL   83
    J. J. Dukeminier, Jr.

12. ELIMINATION OF INCOMPATIBLE USES AND STRUCTURES   92
    C. McKim Norton

Modern Zoning and Its Evolutionary Trends

13. THE NEW CHICAGO ZONING ORDINANCE   100
    Richard F. Babcock

14. EMERGING LEGAL ISSUES IN ZONING   110
    Charles M. Haar and Frank E. Horack, Jr.

15. PLANNING ABSORBS ZONING   123
    Carl Feiss

    SELECTED REFERENCES   130

II. BUILDING AND HOUSING CODES   131

Building Codes

16. PREPARATION AND REVISION OF BUILDING CODES   133
    George N. Thompson

17. POWERS AND PROCEDURES FOR ORDERING REPAIR AND
    DEMOLITION OF EXISTING BUILDINGS   140
    Gilbert R. Barnhart

18. CERTIFICATES OF OCCUPANCY   146
    New York State Department of Commerce

19. HOW CODE-ENFORCED WASTE CAN MAKE A $1,500 DIFFERENCE IN THE
    SALES PRICE OF TWO IDENTICAL HOUSES   148
    House and Home

Housing Codes

20. LOCAL DEVELOPMENT AND ENFORCEMENT OF HOUSING CODES   150
    Gilbert R. Barnhart
21. BUILDING CODES, HOUSING CODES AND THE CONSERVATION OF
    CHICAGO'S HOUSING SUPPLY   164
    Warren W. Lehman
22. HOUSING CODES IN URBAN RENEWAL   177
    Joseph Guandolo
23. MUNICIPAL HOUSING CODES IN THE COURTS   185
    Robert M. Oster
24. RENT WITHHOLDING, RENT STRIKES, TENANT UNIONS,
    MANDATORY STATEWIDE HOUSING STANDARDS   195
    Journal of Housing
25. TENANT RESPONSIBILITY, SHORT-TERM GOALS, SELF-HELP,
    NEIGHBORHOOD PRIDE   201
    Christopher J. Bellone

    SELECTED REFERENCES   206

III. TAXATION   207

Land Use Economics and General Taxation Policy

26. THE TAXING POWER AS A LAND USE CONTROL DEVICE   209
    Orlando E. Delogu
27. TAXATION AND DEVELOPMENT   217
    Mabel Walker
28. OPPORTUNITIES IN TAXATION FOR ACHIEVING PLANNING PURPOSES   222
    Charles Abrams
29. TAXATION AND DEVELOPMENT   227
    Myer R. Wolfe
30. EFFECTS OF PROPERTY TAXATION ON SLUMS AND RENEWAL:
    A STUDY OF LAND-IMPROVEMENT ASSESSMENT RATIOS   236
    A. H. Schaaf
31. CONTROLLING URBAN GROWTH:
    THE NEW ZEALAND AND AUSTRALIAN EXPERIMENT   242
    Robert O. Harvey and W. A. V. Clark

Land Value Taxation

32. TAXATION AND DEVELOPMENT   248
    Thomas J. Plunkett
33. LAND PLANNING AND THE PROPERTY TAX   253
    Mason Gaffney
34. HOUSING REHABILITATION AND THE PITTSBURGH GRADED PROPERTY TAX   260
    David C. Harrison

    SELECTED REFERENCES   276

Index   277

Acknowledgments

EDITORS OF BOOKS of readings face a virtually impossible task in trying to acknowledge the role of all participants in the drafting and collection of the articles and essays they present. Fortunately, the authors of the contributions in this volume have offered their own acknowledgments, most of which have been preserved in the individual readings. It is to these authors that my thanks are principally directed. Too, the journals, magazines, and professional associations that originally published these articles have been most gracious in extending publication rights. And mention is due the agencies of the federal government, whose research offerings were of particular value in preparing sections on building and housing codes.

The readings in this book have been subjected to the critical editing of upperclassmen at the University of Wisconsin for thirteen years. As a result of this constant reviewing, a selection has resulted which appears to be adequate for wider consumption. Hence, I duly acknowledge the substantial help from this source.

The graduate students who helped directly in the location and selection of the present readings include Robert Stanton, Robert Marquardt, Karel Clettenberg, and Clyde Richey. Generous research funds and typing assistance from the School of Business are also gratefully acknowledged. Finally, special thanks are due Jean and Stephen Zorn, who have either presided over or performed the arduous clerical and editing duties connected with producing this kind of book.

Richard B. Andrews

The Contributors

NOTE: Although this list was as accurate as the editors could make it at the time of this book's publication, changes in the status and/or location of individual contributors inevitably will obsolete the data provided here that relates to them.—R.B.A.

Authors

Charles Abrams
Chairman, Division of Urban Planning
Columbia University

Charles Agle
Ping Consultant
Princeton, New Jersey

Richard F. Babcock
Lawyer
Chicago, Illinois

Gilbert R. Barnhart
Administrative Regulations Specialist, Technology Branch
Division of Housing Research, U.S. Housing and Home Finance Agency

Christopher J. Bellone
Administrator, Division of Housing Improvement
Department of Safety and Permits, City of New Orleans

W. A. V. Clark
Lecturer in Geography
University of Canterbury

Otto A. Davis
Graduate School of Industrial Administration
Carnegie Institute of Technology

Orlando E. Delogu
Associate Professor
University of Maine School of Law

William A. Doebele, Jr.
Associate Professor of City and Regional Planning
Harvard University

J. J. Dukeminier, Jr.
Professor of Law
University of Kentucky

Carl Feiss
Private Consultant, Planning and Urban Renewal
Washington, D.C.

Mason Gaffney
Professor of Economics
University of Wisconsin

Joseph Guandolo
Associate General Counsel
U.S. Housing and Home Finance Agency

Charles M. Haar
Professor of Land Economics, Department of City and Regional Planning
Massachusetts Institute of Technology

Dennis O'Harrow
Executive Director
American Society of Planning Officials

David C. Harrison
City Planner
Boston Redevelopment Authority

Robert O. Harvey
Dean, School of Business Administration
University of Connecticut

Frank E. Horack, Jr.
Professor of Law
Indiana University

Warren W. Lehman
Professor of Law
University of Wisconsin Law School

Daniel R. Mandelker
Associate Professor of Law
Indiana University

Lewis B. Merrifield, III
Law Review Staff (1965), Law Center
University of Southern California

C. McKim Norton
Vice Chairman
Regional Plan Association

Robert M. Oster

Thomas J. Plunkett
Municipal Affairs Consultant
Montreal

John W. Reps
Professor and Chairman, Department of City and Regional Planning
Cornell University

A. H. Schaaf
Associate Professor of Business Administration
University of California

William M. Shenkel
Chairman, Department of Real Estate and Urban Development
College of Business Administration
University of Georgia, Athens

George N. Thompson
Chief of the Building Codes Section, National Bureau of Standards
Department of Commerce

Mabel Walker
Executive Director
Tax Institute, Inc.

Myer R. Wolfe
Professor of Urban Planning
University of Washington

Publishers

JOURNALS AND MAGAZINES

The Appraisal Journal
Denver Law Journal
Duquesne University Law Review
George Washington Law Review
House and Home
Journal of American Institute of Planners
Journal of Housing
Land Economics
Law and Contemporary Problems
Northwestern University Law Review
Southern California Law Review
University of Chicago Law Review
Zoning Digest

ORGANIZATIONS AND AGENCIES

American Society of Planning Officials
Department of Housing and Urban Development
(formerly Housing and Home Finance Agency)
New York State Department of Commerce

Introduction

PROBLEMS OF LAND use in modern American cities are met with mixed degrees of success by a group of formal control devices which include zoning, building and housing codes, subdivision regulations, and property taxation. As the dense built-up city of the nineteenth and early twentieth century has grown, it has also spread out so that today we think of the city as a metropolitan area. Extension of the traditional formal control devices to the new dispersed city has been only moderately successful. As a consequence, other control and development ideas are being tried, including public ownership, purchase of development rights, tax differentials for active farm lands, and the new town concept. In metropolitan areas, control and development experiments sometimes operate in a broader context that involves comprehensive planning and reorganization of metropolitan government. Nonetheless, it is the control systems and development ideas that must deal directly with the arduous details of land use relationships, for which comprehensive planning usually provides merely the broadest sketch, and metropolitan government, where it exists, only the vehicle.

This book brings together the best of the technical literature on urban land use controls and development ideas that has appeared during the past twenty years in this country. Selections have been taken from the leading scholarly journals in the fields of planning, housing, and land economics. These have been amply supplemented by articles from university law journals, federal government reports, and the proceedings of conferences of professional planners. Article selection is aimed at providing a deeper understanding of the social, political, and especially the economic aspects and implications of the American land use control system.

Treatments of the system which appear in existing books are usually strongly oriented to the law and to city planning. The articles presented here do not disregard the legal-planning bias, but provide what is hoped to be a deeper perspective. The emphasis on economics also is intended, in part, to give a better appreciation of the role of urban land economics in the broad fields of urbanism and of urban land use controls in particular.

A function, if not an objective, of this book is to provide background for the hearings and research studies of the National Commission on Urban Problems. To reproduce here pertinent research monographs sponsored by this body and excerpts from Commission hearings is considered inappropriate in view of the as yet free availability of most of these publications and the great length of some of them. Selected References listed at the end of each part include the Commission publications that contain materials pertaining to those sections. References also include the titles of other appropriate major research monographs, such as those of the Urban Land Institute and the Advisory Commission on Intergovernmental Relations. Occasional papers not available for publication here, and portions of books that have a socioeconomic emphasis, also appear in the Selected References. The purpose of the Selected References is to provide the reader and the researcher with an adequate margin of expansion beyond the technical articles that are usually presented in full in this book.

The subject matter of these readings is primarily confined to those socioeconomic aspects of zoning, codes, and taxation that relate to the central city and the developmental and environmental problems of its land use. It is the editor's belief that, while there are substantial overlaps between land use control policy approaches to management of the central city and of the metropolitan area beyond, there also exist sharp distinctions among the problems peculiar to each area. These distinctions warrant separate treatment of the two urban areas, both with respect to different applications of the traditional land use controls and with respect to the creation of new, specialized controls. Central-city land use control articles in this volume attempt to give the reader adequate description of a use-control system, critical analysis of it, and discussion of its reform potential.

Legitimate questions may be raised about conspicuous omissions from the central-city land use control subject areas. Urban renewal, for example, is not included because several new and excellent books of readings are available dealing with the socioeconomic aspect of this subject. Capital improvement programming, comprehensive planning, and official mapping also have been excluded, either because they do not operate as formal control systems or because the land use economic analytic literature on them is in short supply. Likewise, urban poverty programs are omitted from the central-city readings despite the fact that they are sometimes closely linked to land use control systems, or that, in their comprehensive forms, they may result in some variety of control over land use. Our experience in this area is just too scanty, and our measures of socioeconomic impact too speculative to justify inclusion. And finally, while many studies have been made of the economics of annexation, nearly all of them are on an *ad hoc* and area-to-area basis. These studies, moreover, give little indication of the macro or metro effects and deficiencies, nor of the strengths of annexation as a broad central-city land use control policy. Thus the reason for their omission.

As is inevitable in a book of readings, there appear to be many duplications of ideas. However, an attempt was made by the editor to keep these to a minimum while offering a selective range of views on the same land use control system.

The level of sophistication of the articles in this book is high and assumes the reader has a fair amount of background knowledge of urban land economics and urban social issues. Nonetheless, few of the articles which have been included should be troublesome to the layman because of special vocabulary or mathematical notations.

Not all articles in the book are in complete form. Text and footnote omissions are, however, indicated. Cuts have been made to avoid duplication and unnecessary detail.

These central-city readings have been divided into three parts: Zoning, Building and Housing Codes, and Taxation. Each part has, in turn, been split into groups of readings that are given an order and emphasis which tries to develop the major subject area in a logical manner.

As is true of all books of readings, and, in fact, of all books concerned with highly dynamic situations, cutoff dates must be established. Consequently, by the time this book is published some points of view included may be either outmoded or proven wrong. The reader is asked to be tolerant of this unavoidable reality. He may even want to prepare his own loose-leaf additions to the text.

Zoning

THE PRINCIPAL PURPOSE of Part I is to present a set of perspectives on zoning as an urban land use control device. While the main perspective is that of economic analysis, or the economic implications of zoning, many of the contributions can easily be adapted to social and political problems of urban growth.

The first two readings present the reader with an evaluative overview of urban zoning as presently practiced. Many of the ideas found in these introductory essays are intended to serve as a basis for understanding and judging the objective materials that follow.

In the next three readings the strictly economic aspects of zoning are examined. Such fundamental topics as value, competition, and welfare economics are presented in both objective *and* subjective form. The style of approach to these economic concepts is not always that of the pure economist: two of the articles were written by lawyers.

The following seven readings concentrate on economic questions and on problems of manufacturing and residential land uses. It is unfortunate that a broader range of uses could not have been included, but appropriate high-quality articles simply were not available at the time this book was being prepared. There is fair scope, however, in the treatment given residential and manufacturing uses. For example, the discussions in the first two of this group of seven articles offer in-depth treatment of two questions: the position of manufacturing in an urban economy where an adequate assessment base is a problem; and performance zoning and exclusive zoning as they suit the production and distribution needs of industry. Performance zoning is also discussed from the viewpoints of both manufacturing and residential use in two succeeding well-known articles. The next-to-last article in this group is of particular interest to students of urban environment since zoning for aesthetic objectives is treated in a most capable manner. Although the emphasis in this selection is on residential use, there are substantial implications suggested for the other major uses. C. McKim Norton's incisive article on incompatible land use elimination concludes this group. Although his article was published in 1955, Norton's treatment of the subject remains one of the best in the literature and, like the discussion on aesthetics, has meaning for the entire gamut of land uses.

A brief but sound critical review of a modern zoning ordinance, as well as a look at the future of zoning, are provided in the final group of three articles. Richard F. Babcock, legal specialist in zoning, appraises Chicago's new zoning approaches, and a planner and two lawyers give us their views of things to come. It is up to the economist to adapt his views and analyses to these anticipations. Thus far no economist or sociologist has commented extensively on zoning in this particular perspective.

MANY PERSONS have had the awesome experience of flying over one of our great cities at night, a spectacle of startling beauty and dazzling complexity. Here we can see the living organism of the human community at a superhuman, almost godlike, scale. No one concerned with city planning can observe the city from the air without a sense of both wonder and dismay—a wonder at the richness and variety, a dismay from a vague sense of discontent, the nagging thought that the problems of the metropolis have somehow gotten ahead of us, that we are in the grip of forces greater than our comprehension and beyond our powers of control. As one views the urban region from this vantage point, the reflection automatically arises as to whether one mind or any organized group of minds can ever really grasp this restless entity as a whole, or, being grasped, whether human efforts can control it.

In considering such questions, one might recall the remark of Justice Holmes about Blackstone, that "he gave us a set of spectacles to look at the common law, and we have been looking through those spectacles ever since." In the case of controlling the development of cities, we have been given a set of spectacles by a group of extraordinary men who worked in the 1910's and 1920's, and for the most part we have been looking through their spectacles ever since.

The early pioneers of city planning legislation in the United States—the Alfred Bettmans, and Frank Backus Williamses, the Edward Bassetts, and all the rest that space does not permit me to mention here—gave us a way of conceiving land use problems in the city that was based on their own experience. Being the creative men that they were, they succeeded in translating that experience and those conceptions into a set of legal devices that have up to the present day dominated the way we have in fact applied the powers of government in the field of urban development.

The principles which we have inherited embodied a number of conscious and unconscious assumptions about what cities are, how they grow, and how they may best be controlled. Essentially these men were concerned with minimizing the abuses of the city of the nineteenth and early twentieth century

Key Issues in Land Use Controls

William A. Doebele, Jr.

This article appeared originally in Planning 1963, pp. 5–13, *published by the American Society of Planning Officials, 1313 East Sixtieth Street, Chicago, Illinois 60637. Reproduced by permission.*

—the city of noisy and dirty factories, of overcrowded tenements, of poorly lighted workshops and offices, and of devastating fires. Their chosen instrument for dealing with these abuses was the police power, as embodied in building codes, tenement laws, restrictions on the heights of buildings, and most of all, zoning and subdivision regulations. Their purposes were well stated in Section 3 of the Standard State Zoning Enabling Act, which reads:

> Such [zoning] regulations shall be made in accordance with a comprehensive plan and designed to lessen congestion in the streets; to secure safety from fire, panic, and other dangers; to promote health and the general welfare; to provide adequate light and air; to prevent the overcrowding of land; to avoid undue concentration of population; to facilitate the adequate provision of transportation, water, sewerage, schools, parks, and other public requirements.

In the 1920's, therefore, land use controls were seen as being directed toward several objectives: (1) the segregation of noxious activities out of residential areas and into their own districts; (2) the limitation of the density of building and the over-exploitation of land, particularly in central areas; (3) the improvement of the efficiency of public services; and (4) the protection of property values by the homogenization of uses in each district. In terms of these purposes that it was designed to serve, zoning proved to be a remarkably successful instrument, especially in the stabilization of property values.

Today, however, we stand more than thirty years—a full generation—removed from the conditions that produced zoning and subdivision controls. Perhaps through the very effectiveness of these controls, we have seen the conditions that led to them decrease in importance with the passing years. A new set of problems has arisen to plague us, quite different in nature from the problems that gave rise to the police power based controls with which we have become accustomed to work. Thus, while some of the old problems are still with us, and zoning ordinances and subdivision regulations remain useful devices in many circumstances, it is also true that they no longer occupy the center of the stage. The simple fact of the matter is that the police power devices, as we have come to know them for thirty years, are not the appropriate instruments to deal with the most troubling and important aspects of contemporary urbanization.

If we look at the city of 1916—the date of the first comprehensive zoning ordinance in New York—and compare it to the metropolis of today, we can identify at least four major characteristics underlying early thinking on land use controls that are no longer true today:

First, the city in those days still seemed to be an integral political unit. If there was suburban growth, it could be dealt with by annexation or incorporation, or at least by a responsible suburban government.

Second, it was assumed, and indeed seemed clear from a hundred years of American history, that the city was capable of absorbing all types of immigrants, and in one or two generations transforming them into solid citizens. While ethnic and economic differences were quite real, the melting pot was working, and in the thinking of the time it seemed reasonable to believe that everyone would be comfortably Americanized within a foreseeable future.

Third, it was assumed that there was little need or place for state and federal intervention in municipal affairs.

Fourth, it was assumed that cities and metropolitan areas were distinct and separate. The phenomenon of the linking of metropolitan areas which we have come to call megalopolis was still beyond the horizon.

I suggest that all of these assumptions have, in fact, been shattered by the actual course of events in the last three decades, particularly since the end of World War II in 1945. We have seen in this period a growing fragmentation of local government and a citizenry more and more indifferent to local problems. We have seen a racial metamorphosis in our central cities on a scale that frequently has swamped our institutions for social assimilation. We have seen the exodus of the middle classes to the suburbs. In a period of unparalleled national prosperity, we have seen our principal cities slip closer and closer to the edge of chronic bankruptcy. At the same time that cities have grown more and more feeble in their capacities to deal with their own problems, we have seen an ever greater federal and state commitment of both power and money to urban problems, a trend that has gained even greater momentum from the discovery of megalopolis, an urban organization so vast that only the highest levels of government seem appropriate for grappling with it.

In the context of these conditions, the traditional concepts of land use controls have become less and less relevant. Indeed, under the Balkan condition of municipal powers in suburbia, zoning and subdivision control have come to be viewed as key weapons in complicated struggles for local prestige and position. In the hands of undersized political units, zoning has been too often perverted from a device for rational land use allocation to a ploy in an elaborate game of municipal "oneupmanship." And the results today are beginning to limit seriously the possibilities for variety and mobility in American society. In more metropolitan areas than one cares to count, it is virtually impossible today to build a suburban house on less than a $\frac{1}{2}$-acre lot. We are told by the home builders that all Americans prefer the single-family isolated house. The fact of the matter is . . . an American family building or buying a house today very often has little *legal* choice in the matter. The aged, the single, the childless, and most important, the less affluent of our population, are being systematically excluded from more and more parts of our metropolitan areas. Our suburbs seem increasingly intent on carrying into practice the poet's prayer:

We thank thee, God, that thy grace
Hast brought us to this lovely place.
And now, Dear Lord, we humbly pray
Thou willst all others keep away.

At the same time, we read daily in the newspapers of municipal competition for a choice light industry or shopping center. Fundamental principles of zoning and rational allocation of urban land on a metropolitan scale have been known to bend very easily when the local tax base is at stake.

Zoning and traditional land use controls have also been relatively ineffective in dealing with the changing racial composition of the central city, for the problem of property values is no longer chiefly one of the introduction of noxious uses into residential areas, but of two simultaneous shifts of population on a grand scale: evacuation by middle-income groups and immigration by rural lower-income groups (be they Negro, Puerto Rican or Appalachian mountaineer) seeking a better life in the city. These are conditions for which the zoning device was not designed. In dealing with these problems, it has frequently not been a positive force. Instead, it has been used as a crude and, in the long run, ineffective cofferdam against the accommodation and assimilation of the new immigrants. In this connection it is worth recalling that zoning was born under the shadow of the race problem in the Chinese laundry cases in California in the 1890's—an unhappy episode in our civic history. It is indeed unfortunate that today zoning has again become one of the tools used to forge what has been called the Iron Ring against Negroes in our suburbs.

What I am suggesting is that large-scale social developments in our culture in the last generation have made many of our institutions of land use control obsolete. The set of spectacles that we have inherited from the past no longer gives an accurate vision of the problem confronting us. For example, the breakdown of the zoning board of adjustment seems to me to be less a matter of getting more effective standards than rethinking the fundamental concept. For in many situations, particularly in central cities, such boards are now being faced with problems that are simply beyond the institutional and jurisdictional context for which the board was invented and established. No men, no matter how able and conscientious, can operate effectively and legally within an institution that was designed for quite a different set of problems.

Planners have, of course, already made a response to the challenge of new conditions. A response that has been, in many ways, an extraordinarily imaginative one: urban renewal, which began with the rather simple (and what now seems naive) idea of total clearance, and has rather rapidly evolved into quite an impressive range of techniques and devices, many of them still in the experimental stages. All of these are rather ingenious reactions to the problems of central city blight, the changing racial composition of the city, and the opportunities of growing state and federal financial commitment. As is the case with almost all social and political experimentation, the proponents of urban renewal underestimated the complexity of the problem with which they were dealing. The program still has grievous growing pains, as Jane Jacobs (in her more perceptive moments), Herbert Gans, and others have made us uncomfortably aware. However, with a bit of optimism, one can hope that enough ferment is occurring in urban renewal that evolution will continue to occur, and that in spite of some very serious internal inconsistencies and paradoxes inherent in its present objectives, it will, after a certain number of missteps (some of which are happily—or unhappily—already behind us) eventually mature into a reasonably useful and perhaps exciting part of the American urban scene.

Granting, then, some prospect of progress on the rocky road of conservation, rehabilitation, and renewal in the central city, what of the suburbs?

Here is a pattern which must, it seems to me, be characterized as increasingly exclusionary and parochial.

On the other hand, one must face the fact that it seems almost equally true that the local governments, even in the highly fragmented form in which they exist in many metropolitan areas, serve very substantial human needs. They are a unit in modern life which is still comprehensible, and furnish one of the last stages on which the average individual can directly participate in political life and decision. Nevertheless, as in the case of any other institution, checks are necessary. (And it is interesting to note that though legislatures have not yet acted, some judges in some courts in several recent cases are becoming concerned with the formulation of limits on local autonomy in land use policy.) What is more important, many of the most perceptive local government officials themselves are beginning to understand that zoning, subdivision controls, indeed, even good local planning, are slender reeds on which to build a secure municipal future. And more and more ordinary suburbanites are comprehending that the destiny of their town is going to be shaped more by the pattern of metropolitan freeways, by statewide policies on educational support, by the nature of the property tax system, and by genuine progress in the integration of minority groups, than by anything their town itself can do, even under the broad powers of self-government normally exercised in the United States.

I would therefore like to try to describe a new set of strategies that might increase our control over the growth and development of the great sprawls of land uses we call metropolis and megalopolis.

First, I suggest a negative strategy: the abandonment of the struggle for metropolitan government except in certain particular situations where very favorable conditions for success exist. While it is always hazardous to generalize about the more than 200 metropolitan areas in America today, it now seems fairly clear that in spite of Miami

and Toronto (both born out of rather special circumstances) the experience of two or three decades of intensive effort in this direction has demonstrated that the political, economic, and human facts of American life in the mid-twentieth century are too strongly stacked against it. Indeed, in retrospect, it seems unreasonable ever to have expected people to give up a local government which they knew for a metropolitan government in which it must inevitably appear that their voices would be swallowed.

Second, I suggest that a major part of the solution to present problems must lie in the creation of a quite new type of *three-tiered federalism*: institutional arrangements in which local, state, and federal jurisdictions each have a clear but limited role to play. The federal government has the financial and technical resources, the state has the necessary political jurisdiction over the total urban area and its hinterlands (laying aside for the moment the special problems of interstate cities), and the local government has the machinery for creating public policies which in this day of bigness are still mindful of the human scale. One of the most pregnant developments of our time in the field of controlling urban growth has been, it seems to me, not urban renewal itself, but the new kinds of relationships that urban renewal is creating. While we are still doing a great deal of experimenting, and the *ad hoc* arrangements are different in almost every metropolitan area, a number of very interesting new three-tiered arrangements are coming into being—truly symbiotic relationships among all levels of government in the field of urban problems. The concepts of Section 701 planning, the Workable Program, the CRP, Section 134 of the national highway act (as amended in 1962), requiring a state-local cooperative and comprehensive transportation planning process as a condition for federal funds—these devices, with all of their limitations in practice, still imply quite new *institutional* ways of approaching urban problems.

What is lacking, however, has been any *systematic investigation* into the institutional aspects of urban renewal, and so we have had the bold entrepreneurs in the field, such as Edward Logue, who calmly rebuilt a considerable part of the city government of Boston into an institution capable of taking advantage of the new realities of federal participation. What is needed, however, is a much more careful and complete exploration of the frameworks under which the many federal, state, and local agencies now engaged in tearing down, building up, and otherwise pushing around cities and their populations might operate with a great deal less friction than today. One gets a very real sense these days that in spite of many traditional bureaucratic rivalries still lingering, most government agencies dealing with urban problems are running scared, and would welcome immediate improvement in their channels of communication with each other. What is needed, in short, is a new set of Federalist Papers, a dialogue by politically sophisticated men to explore the very subtle kinds of intergovernmental relationships into which our urban problems are inevitably pushing us. Robert Connery and Richard Leach, in their book *The Federal Government and Metropolitan Areas*, Theodore Hutchinson in his monograph on *Metropolitan Area Problems: The Role of the Federal Government* prepared for the University of Michigan Law School, the U.S. Commission on Intergovernmental Relations Report to President Eisenhower, the proposals of the Council of State Governments on *State Responsibility in Metropolitan Affairs*, and other publications have gathered valuable background material and suggestions in this area, but we must go well beyond these preliminaries before we have operative institutions for federal, state and municipal cooperation in each of the country's metropolitan areas. (In this respect it is quite significant, I think, that former Governor Rosellini of Washington has called attention to the growing importance of state activities in the field of urban problems, and the increasing number of states now actively considering formal Departments of Urban Affairs.)

In concluding this point, let me especially emphasize that the new federalism I am describing is a far cry—indeed, almost the antithesis—of the old search for metropolitan federalism. For metropolitan federation proposed to create a new level of government out of whole cloth, and to do it, moreover, by cutting away pieces of existing local powers. The new three-tiered federalism that I am suggesting (and that we are in fact seeing born whether we like it or not) is a redefinition of the rights and powers of existing governmental units in new ways. It need not involve the creation of any new powers, but of new relationships among what exists. If the existing programs of the federal government alone were to be coordinated and really brought to bear in an organized way on urban problems, we could begin to create even today almost any type of metropolitan configuration that we chose.

As a *third* strategy, let me suggest that we have been living in a fool's paradise with respect to suburban chauvinisms, and that the time is inevitably coming for a larger concept. Specifically, we must move toward a Common Market in the allocation of metropolitan land, that is, a situation in which any industry, any shopping center, and most important of all, any family of whatever size or income, can locate freely within the metropolis without concern for municipal boundaries that have become technologically meaningless.

Let us be very clear about this point. The achievement of the freedom of which I speak will involve a direct attack on our system for supporting local government and services. I suggest that one of the greatest villains of the metropolitan drama today is not fractionization itself, but an archaic system of taxation that inevitably leads to irrationality in the use of land. For reasons that are hard to ascertain, we have seemed to regard our system of real property taxation as immutable as the stars in their courses. In fact, the real estate tax is nothing more nor less than a very crude form of income tax invented in the 18th century when a man's wealth could be seen in his real property, and when there was no other means to tax the rich and poor according to their means. Under modern conditions, I suggest that perhaps more sins with respect to the allocation of land use are committed under the name of "protecting the tax base" than any other single cause. If industries, commercial uses, and above all people, are to be able to move freely and rationally in the metropolis, and if local governments are to be liberated from the fears which now cause them to throw barriers against the entrance of new human beings while kowtowing at the entrance of new industry—if we really mean business about orderly metropolitan growth—the financial support of municipalities must be put on a different basis. This is one of the most significant, yet least discussed, forces dictating land use today.

I do not have the time nor the scope here to suggest the specific devices that might be invented to create the common market I have suggested. Two things do seem clear, however: First, that like the Common Market in Europe, our metropolitan common market will come into being by a series of evolutionary steps, not a single grand reform. Second, that a common market in metropolitan land use need not imply that all local services fall to the lowest common denominator. Rather, it means that certain basic services be assured everywhere regardless of the amount of industry or number of school children the municipality contains. There is nothing in the concept that need prevent any locality from offering more and better services in any field, preferably financed by methods far more equitable and imaginative than those on which our local governments presently depend.

To summarize: the theme of this essay has been that our classic concepts of land use controls have been based on the police power —of limiting the use of the individual parcel by zoning, subdivision controls, and the like —for certain overriding public purposes. These controls were enormously important in their day, and still are significant today. Except for minor variations, however, they are coming to have less and less importance each year in what actually happens to the land in our cities. In fact, someone has stated that to be hard-boiled about it, zoning is not a control at all, but a thermometer that measures the total amount of economic heat on a piece of property at a given moment. As the heat goes up, sooner or later the zoning

will respond. While this view may be considered almost corrosively cynical, it contains an uncomfortable amount of truth.

The major urban problems of our time, I have suggested, are municipal fragmentation, municipal bankruptcy, the growing presence of particularly difficult minority pressures in our central cities, and the emergence of supercities we are beginning to call megalopolis.

I submit that zoning and all the police power based controls, no matter how refined with new gadgets and accessories, cannot come to grips with these problems, and, indeed, sometimes operate to aggravate rather than assuage them.

On the positive side of our current ledger, we see the very powerful political and financial intervention of the federal and state governments into urban affairs. Having rejected metropolitan governmental solutions, our municipalities have, it seems to me, made this development inevitable, since only these higher levels of government can effectively deal with the damaging consequences of municipal fragmentation, bankruptcy, minority pressures, and the megalopolis.

Whether or not we as individuals favor or oppose increased state and federal activity is by this time coming to be largely irrelevant. The trends of state and federal involvement are already too firmly established to be reversed.

I therefore suggest that the "growing edge" of land use controls lies not in more elaborate devices for planned unit developments but in experiments like the Penn-Jersey Transportation Study (to mention only one of many) that are finding new mixtures of federal, state and local policy-making toward the whole metropolitan community.

The role of the intelligent man who is dedicated to the improvement of cities and the preservation of the best elements of local government in America, it seems to me, is to devote his talents to finding means by which the federal and state governments can help us achieve significant breakthroughs in controlling what happens in cities without these governments coming to dominate the whole show.

I believe that in devices like the workable program and the strong local development administrator, with his lines of communication both to the state capitol and to the major federal agencies, we are already beginning to see the emergence of institutions that will bring us the benefits of state and federal participation without destroying local independence. (Although local checks may also be needed to assure the political responsibility of the development administrator himself.) In the great metropolitan studies of the last few years, in Chicago, Detroit, Kansas City, Philadelphia, New York, St. Louis and elsewhere, these matters are being given more and more attention. But these are mere beginnings. We need a host of other devices. For example, we need new forms of the workable program for application to the state and metropolitan level, and dealing with the staging of development at a whole range of critical decision points including the strategy of highway location, the large-scale reservation of open spaces, the rationalization of property taxation, the coordination and equalization of educational opportunities between city and suburb, and the gradual but sure elimination of snob zoning. These policies might well be stated in quite new types of master plans, in the making of which federal, state and local units might all participate.

As in the past, the chief difficulty will be the snake's nest of local chauvinisms that have so long defeated metropolitan reorganization. But, unlike the past, there is now a totally new element of leverage in the picture —the increasing monetary commitment of the federal and state governments.

The stage is set as it has never been before for a restructuring of local-federal and local-state relationships. The definition of these new dimensions of intergovernmental relations will determine whether or not we can effectively control the use of land in our future urbanizing areas. It is in the invention of these new institutions that the Alfred Bettmanns, the Frank Backus Williamses and the Edward Bassetts of our generation must exercise their imagination and energies. Let us hope that the planners, lawyers and political scientists of our day are as successful as those who first laid down the institutions of land use control that have guided us so long.

2

Pomeroy Memorial Lecture: Requiem for Zoning

John W. Reps

This article appeared originally in Planning 1964, pp. 56–68, published by the American Society of Planning Officials, 1313 East Sixtieth Street, Chicago, Illinois 60637. Reproduced by permission.

THE YEAR 1966 was a significant one for American planning. It marked two anniversaries: the beginning of the fifth century of the oldest city in the United States and the ending of the fifth decade of comprehensive zoning. It is a nice question which is less obsolete—the St. Augustine plan of 1565 or the comprehensive zoning ordinances of this country based on the New York City Zoning Resolution of 1916. The quaint, narrow streets of the old Spanish town serve at least to attract the tourist dollar; the quaint, narrow provisions of our zoning ordinances, judging from current comments, attract only the lawyers.

Zoning is seriously ill and its physicians—the planners—are mainly to blame. We have unnecessarily prolonged the existence of a land use control device conceived in another era when the true and frightening complexity of urban life was barely appreciated. We have, through heroic efforts and with massive doses of legislative remedies, managed to preserve what was once a lusty infant not only past the retirement age but well into senility. What is called for is legal euthanasia, a respectful requiem, and a search for a new legislative substitute sturdy enough to survive in the modern urban world.

The powers of zoning and all of our other techniques for controlling urban development appear grossly inadequate when measured against the often radically different development patterns which modern metropolitan plans propose. I am not here judging the desirability of such alternative urban configurations as advocated by the Dutch in their Rim City plan, the Danes in their finger plan for Copenhagen, the British in their satellite city and greenbelt design for Greater London, or the radial corridor scheme for Washington, D.C. I am contending only that our existing system of development guidance permits us to hope for nothing better than partially controlled sprawl and that such bold plans now have little chance of success.

My concern is with only one of the means of planning implementation, but it is necessary first to view its position in the matrix of urban shaping devices. In another context I have suggested, as have others, that the mechanisms for directing the urban pattern might be regarded as a guidance system. Like the components of the machinery that places a satellite into a planned orbit, this urban guidance system comprises a number of subsystems that can be used to steer a metropolis through time to a predetermined goal.

Also, like the guidance system of missiles or satellites, mine takes its name from the acronym formed by the initial letters of its four groups of components. The word thus formed—ACID—is unfortunately not very inspiring, but it does tend to burn itself in one's memory.

What do those letters stand for? What are these methods by which the patterns of urban growth and change can be shaped? I suggest that all of our activities in this direction can be classified under one of the following: advice, controls, inducements, and development. The order in which I have listed them is roughly the order in which they have been employed in our attempts to assert greater public leverage in constructing urban patterns.

When the first public planning agencies were created, their sole power was that of advice: advice to governmental departments and officials, to other levels of government, to civic organizations, to individuals. Advice, and the closely related techniques of persuasion and inspiration, still play important roles in guiding development. Indeed, at the metropolitan scale this is the chief technique on which we rely. But the power of advice necessarily has its limits, especially where advice runs even faintly counter to the dictates of the marketplace.

Next in point of time came our inventions of various kinds of control devices—zoning, subdivision regulations, official map techniques, and building, housing, and sanitary codes. But controls are negative instruments —they can prevent but they cannot compel, and their usefulness proved limited.

We then turned to various types of inducements or incentives as a method of attracting private building of types and in locations and under conditions that contributed to the public good. Through low-interest loans, tax exemptions, aids in land acquisition, direct subsidy payments, guarantees against financial loss, and other techniques, public bodies began to influence the urban pattern by combining the carrot of inducements with the lash of controls. Early redevelopment projects resulted from programs extending such financial incentives. The cluster subdivision concept provides another example.

Finally, direct public development has now taken its place as an urban forming force. In one sense, of course, this is nothing new. Vast public construction of streets and utilities in advance of need during the 1920's made possible the land boom of those wild years and certainly influenced the form of cities. But acquiring, planning, and selling land in central redevelopment areas to reshape the city's core is employing public development powers in a new way. Expressways, rapid transit routes, trunk utility lines, and major public buildings have powerful influences on the growth patterns of cities, and coordinated planning of these and other city-shaping elements offers great promise as an effective guidance mechanism.

I would go much farther in the direction of public development and use some modification of redevelopment techniques at the urban fringe. To be specific, some public agency with metropolitan jurisdiction might acquire raw land, plan it, provide street, utility, park, and other needed improvements, and then convey lots, blocks, or neigh-borhoods to private builders for development as planned and as controlled by deed restrictions. This would accomplish three things: it would provide a public yardstick operation against which purely private land development activities could be measured, it would establish a more precise tool of environmental control and guidance, and it would, paradoxically enough, aid private enterprise and the competitive market by making it possible for small builders who cannot afford the uncertainties and costs of the modern scale of land development to stay in business.

I hope my position is clear that the incentives and public development components of the urban guidance system need much further examination and expansion. I am convinced that in the long run these are the areas in which much of our intellectual resources should be invested. It should also be clear that what I shall now have to say about zoning and its future deals with a minor, although far from unimportant, aspect of urban planning implementation.

Having narrowed the subject for discussion while at the same time placing it in its larger context, let me now attempt a working definition of zoning for purposes of analysis. I suggest the following: zoning is a police power measure enacted by units of local government under permissive state legislation. Zoning regulations establish, in advance of applications for development, groups of permitted uses that vary from district to district. These regulations are not necessarily related to other regulatory devices or to any community plan. They are administered by officials having only limited discretionary powers. Ultimate review of the regulations and the actions of administrative officials under them is by appeal only and is a judicial function.

Now let me challenge the wisdom of zoning as so defined. This is, frankly, an effort to eliminate whatever convictions one may have that our present system of zoning is somehow the only or the best method for controlling the bulk, use, intensity, location, and density of development. The sanctity of half a century of tradition stands between me and this goal, but let me make the attempt. A number of propositions will elaborate on the elements of my definition, against each one of which I will pose a question for consideration.

1. *Zoning is a police power measure*—It follows that the impact of zoning regulations must be reasonable and that their effect must not be so burdensome that they amount to a taking of property instead of a mere restriction in the interests of protecting or promoting the public health, safety, morals, or general welfare. Regulations found to be unreasonably burdensome are invalidated by court action. Constitutional rights are protected, but the community is stripped of this power to guide land development, and the public at large may suffer unfortunate consequences from the assertion of private rights in land. *Question:* Would it not be desirable to introduce a system of compensation to supplement the police power where severe limitations on land use are deemed essential or desirable to shape and guide community development?

2. *Zoning is permissive*—While much state legislation requires municipalities to carry out specified services or to provide certain facilities, the choice of regulating or not regulating land use is optional under American enabling statutes. *Question:* Would it not be desirable for state legislation to require all communities or those having certain characteristics to enact such regulations?

3. *Zoning is enacted by units of local government*—Zoning regulations are intensely parochial. Standards required in any single metropolitan area may vary enormously depending on the whims of local legislators. We make much of the principle that land similarly located must be similarly zoned within a given municipality, but this concept is cruelly violated when a homogeneous area is zoned for industry on one side of a municipal boundary line and for high-class, low-density residential uses on the other side.

Standards of enforcement vary equally widely. The possibility of achieving coordinated and balanced metropolitan development under such a situation, insofar as land use regulation is effective at all, can be written off as a mere fiction. *Question:* Would it not be desirable to deny zoning powers to the smaller units of government and place this responsibility at the county level, or as a duty of some metropolitan government or agency, or as a function of the state government?

4. *Zoning establishes regulations in advance of applications for development permission*—As Daniel Mandelker has so well put it, "One difficulty with American legal techniques is that they borrow constitutional trouble by making land use decisions with constitutional impact before the fact. Thus, exclusive agricultural zoning is restrictive immediately upon its enactment. It immediately raises a constitutional issue throughout its area of application regardless of the fact that many affected landowners would be quite happy with an exclusive agricultural restriction. But under the present system, an attack by a few will affect the entire ordinance."[1] *Question:* Would it not be desirable to have a method of control which avoided this difficulty and left the issue of legal validity to be raised when dealing with each application to develop land or to change its use?

5. *Zoning establishes groups of permitted uses that vary from district to district*—In our understandable attempt to simplify in a complex and bewildering world we have done three things. We have attempted to prepare detailed standards for development which are supposed to cover all conceivable situations. We have Balkanized our cities into districts with precise and rigid zone boundary lines. We have established categories of uses that have segregated rather than integrated functional portions of cities and which have often disregarded the interrelationships between rather widely separated categories of uses. *Question:* Would it not be desirable to do

[1] Daniel L. Mandelker, "What Open Space Where? How?" in *Planning 1963*, American Society of Planning Officials, Chicago, Ill., 1964, p. 25.

away entirely with, or at least place far less emphasis on, the creation of districts and lists of supposedly compatible uses?

6. *Zoning is not necessarily related to other regulatory devices*—Forget the theory here, and look at the facts. There is a multitude of regulatory measures—zoning, subdivision regulations, building codes, sanitary restrictions, housing ordinances, official map regulations, and others—enacted at different times, often by different bodies, enforced by different sets of officials, and reviewable by different administrative tribunals or courts. It is a rare zoning ordinance that does not in several ways conflict with the community subdivision regulations. It is a rare community that has not omitted some vital provision from both. It is a common necessity for the developers of all but the most routine and standardized projects to deal with several boards or officials and to secure amendments, approvals, waivers, or variances from the provisions of a number of ordinances and codes in order to proceed. *Question:* Would it not be desirable to consolidate all or most regulations dealing with control of urban growth into a single development ordinance that provided a sensible and efficient system of administration and enforcement, and which was purged of ambiguities, conflicting provisions, and redundancies?

7. *Zoning is not necessarily related to any community plan*—Again, forget the theory and look at the facts, including the depressing but understandable record of judicial review on this point. There are few communities that can claim with much justification that their regulations stem directly from any comprehensive, long-range plan. Charles Haar has demonstrated, in perhaps the most frequently court-cited law review article on zoning ever written, that whatever we think state legislation says about the necessity to ground zoning in a well-considered or comprehensive plan, the courts by and large have interpreted such a plan to be the zoning map itself.[2] This circular reasoning will prevail until new legislation changes the rules of the

judicial game. *Question:* Would it not be desirable for statutes to require any local development regulations or discretionary administrative decisions reached on development proposals to be clearly based on a community plan, expressed graphically and/or as meaningful statements of development policy?

8. *Zoning is administered by officials with limited discretionary powers*—I am not here concerned with the scandal of unwarranted discretionary decisions by boards of appeals or such comparative novelties as floating zones or site plan approval procedure, but with the amount of discretion normally exercised by administrative officials in reviewing applications for zoning or building permits. It is in the nature of controls by districts, use lists, and bulk and density standards that present administrative review is essentially mechanical and requires only a check-list mentality. *Question:* Would it not be desirable to construct a system of development controls in which, as is the case of subdivision review, informed discretionary judgment plays the dominant or at least a much larger role in the process of reviewing applications to build or develop?

9. *Ultimate review of the regulations and the actions of administrative officials under them is by appeal only*—Only a person who feels aggrieved and who has the ambition, time, and money to appeal can obtain some kind of review of the wisdom or legality of a zoning enactment or administrative decision. State governments, which have conferred regulatory powers on localities, have failed to provide any form of central review of the regulations as originally established or as amended or of administrative actions taken under them. There is no county or metropolitan review of local regulatory activities except the most peripheral. *Question:* Would it not be desirable to establish a system of state or metropolitan review of zoning-type regulations that could insure conformity with state or metropolitan development objectives and, in the case of local appeals

2 Charles Haar, "In Accordance with a Comprehensive Plan," **68**, *Harvard Law Review*, 1955, p. 1154.

situations, conformity with standardized fair procedures that would insure adequate attention to due process requirements and would curb both excessive restrictiveness and undue liberality on the part of administrative officials exercising wide discretionary powers?

10. *Ultimate review of zoning regulations and administrative action is a judicial function* —Courts are more and more being called on to decide issues which are increasingly technical and complex. Most courts have taken refuge in the doctrine of the presumption of legislative validity, but as the thrust of regulations becomes more vigorous it is unlikely that courts can refuse to decide issues on their merits. Yet, courts are ill-equipped to make decisions on technical matters, and it is far from clear that the adversary system provides the best approach to decision-making. *Question:* Would it not be desirable to create state administrative tribunals, assisted by an expert staff, authorized to obtain evidence in a variety of ways, and empowered to decide appeals or claims arising from the application of land use controls?

For my purposes I will assume that the answers to the foregoing questions are in the affirmative. What would be the broad outlines of that portion of a development guidance system replacing our present system of zoning? How would we approach the control of bulk, use, intensity, location, and density?

First, I think it highly desirable to combine such zoning-type restrictions with other related public controls into a set of what might be called Development Regulations. From the standpoint of procedure we have already moved some distance in this direction. The use of floating zones, increased reliance on special exception or conditional use devices, and the requirements of site plan review as a condition of zoning permit approval, to name three among several methods that are currently employed, have all brought the procedure for securing permits under the zoning ordinance closer to

that of subdivision control. I suggest that we pursue this approach much further and require most types of proposed development to be submitted to a local agency that would administer, through discretionary review, an ordinance combining at least zoning-type and subdivision regulations. This should simplify development control. Elimination of conflicting provisions and greater convenience for both administrative officials and land developers are but two of the advantages that would result.

Second, to guide administrative officials in reaching discretionary decisions, there should be a plan for community development and a comprehensive set of development objectives and standards. This plan should be made mandatory, it should be adopted by the legislative body, and review and readoption at fixed intervals should be required. Such plans should show generalized proposed future land uses, circulation systems, population density patterns, and community facilities.

Before adoption of the plan by the legislative body, hearings would be required. After adoption, provisions of the plan would be subject to review by a state agency that would also be empowered to hear appeals submitted by those opposing details of the plan. The state review agency would have final authority to confirm or modify the plan. All discretionary review of development proposals would be guided by this plan. Appeals from local decisions could be taken to the state review agency. Further appeals to courts would be permitted only on matters of procedure or on the scope of statutory power, not on matters of substance.

I realize that in this era of "ad hocmanship," advocacy of a community plan to serve as a guide to public decision-making sounds faintly antiquarian. But the use of a plan as just described provides fresh meaning to the planning process and thrusts the general plan forward to a position of new importance.

Discretionary action limiting development in such a way as to cause severe deprivation of property rights would be accompanied by some form of compensation. This would, in Haar's words, add "the money lubricant . . . to the machinery of land use controls in order to achieve greater flexibility."

Appeals to determine the amount of compensation, if an offer is declined, would lie to the state review agency. In reaching such determinations the state agency would consider the degree of regulation that would be upheld under the most severe exercise of the police power and the value of the land burdened by such restrictions. Compensation would be payable only for the difference between that value and the value of the land if further restricted as specified by the local administrative body. After the payment of compensation, the restrictions imposed would be registered as part of the title. If, in future years, more intensive development were permitted, the amount of the compensation would be repayable by the owner.

Parenthetically, I should add that a system of betterment charges should also be devised to permit public recoupment of part of any increased land value conferred by public activities. Such a system might prove unnecessarily complex if applied to all land, but as a minimum a somewhat wider view of our present benefit assessment techniques should be investigated. David Levin, in a recent exploration of offsetting compensation with betterment charges in connection with highway access limitation, suggests that this approach "could be expanded substantially, giving a much wider recognition to benefits that in fact exist."[3]

Third, while I have referred to the discretionary administrative review body as local, I envisage this body ultimately as one with a geographical jurisdiction more extensive than the present city, town or borough boundaries. The new pessimists from the left bank of the Charles River have lately been stating that multi-purpose metropolitan government is impossible to achieve and probably undesirable anyway. Perhaps they are correct, but as they point out, *ad hoc* metropolitan working agreements, authorities, special districts, and other single-purpose arrangements or agencies will be necessary as partial substitutes.

I suggest that sooner or later the general

[3] David Levin, "Aspects of Eminent Domain Proceedings in the United States," in Charles Haar, ed., *Law and Land: Anglo-American Planning Practice*, Cambridge, Mass., 1964, p. 238.

control of land use should be recognized as a responsibility to be located at the metropolitan level. In the absence of voluntary local action, the state agency previously mentioned should be empowered to establish broad guide plans in metropolitan areas and certain over-all land use control objectives and standards, against which local plans and land use objectives and standards would be reviewed. The next stage would be the creation of a metropolitan planning and discretionary control agency by action of the separate units of local government. Certain classes of development review might then well be left with smaller units of government, while other categories of development would be subject to metropolitan agency scrutiny. The alternative would be the direct exercise of land use controls by some agency of state government.

Fourth, the land use regulations themselves would need to differ substantially from those presently encompassed under zoning. Except as I will mention later, no district boundaries—no zoning map—would exist. The comprehensive plan, expressed in graphic form and in statements of development objectives, would be one guide to the discretionary administrative body, which might be called the Office of Development Review. While ultimately the plan itself might be regarded as a sufficient standard or rule of conduct to guide discretionary action, probably we shall need in addition rather detailed standards enacted by legislative bodies. These would be similar to those we now find in the better ordinances which authorize floating zones, conditional uses, and site plan approval permits. I suggest that these standards need to do more than merely specify the public good as a rule of conduct. In other words, the standards should be fairly specific and should relate to defined categories of land use. Such requirements should take the form of performance standards, rather than rigid specifications. Permissible ranges of height and bulk, for example, should be expressed in such measures as floor area ratios and angles of light obstruction. Emphasis should be placed on such

performance criteria as noise, traffic generation, smoke emission and air pollution, odor
production, vibration, and the like. Even so,
some specification standards would doubtless be needed.

Within this rather general framework of
plans, goals, and standards, the Office of
Development Review would exercise broad
discretionary power in granting or denying or
modifying requests for development permission. Such permits would be for both
tract development and single buildings on
individual sites. As in most current floating
zone procedures, approval would be for
specific uses and building designs as shown
on site plans, elevation drawings and as
described in supplementary text material.
This procedure, then, would not be at all like
present zoning, the effect of which is blanket
permission for any of a wide range of uses
permitted in the zoning district. The discretionary powers would be broad; the
development permit would be narrow in the
development rights that would be conferred.

Fifth, this type of discretionary review and
control would be most appropriate at the
urban fringe or applied to in-lying undeveloped areas. Some vestiges of the concept
of districts might have utility. We would
probably find it advantageous to establish a
skeleton list of uses that would be permitted
as a matter of right, along with a set of
simplified district boundaries. One advantage
of this approach would be to reduce the
volume of detailed review that would otherwise be necessary if we relied on a wholly
discretionary system. Another purpose would
be to clothe the new system in some of the
familiar garments of zoning to lend an air of
respectability in gaining both public acceptance and judicial recognition.

In areas largely built-up, where most new
construction would be on a discontinuous
lot-by-lot basis, more of the present zoning
techniques—district boundaries and use lists
—could be retained, although modernized to
incorporate many of the recent innovations
in zoning.

For redevelopment areas, major reliance

should be placed on deed restrictions as the
chief control mechanism. Former Urban
Renewal Commissioner William Slayton may
have been only partially overstating the case
when he recently asserted that zoning has no
place at all in redevelopment. Since the
redevelopment site passes through a period
of public ownership there is an opportunity
to condition the sale of such land with precise
and detailed restrictions. Police power controls can safely be suspended in such areas,
although held in readiness should some legal
flaws develop in the system of covenants, or
to be applied at the termination of the period
specified in the deed restrictions.

This approach to land use controls, set out
only in the broadest of outlines, appears to
me the most likely and desirable of several
alternatives to the present system. Doubtless,
one can recognize its similarity to the land
control process operating in Britain since
1947. It thus has precedents in a country not
wholly dissimilar to our own. Moreover, if I
read the trends correctly, it seems to be a
direction in which we are already heading.
The land planning and zoning code prepared
by Carl Feiss for Bratenahl, Ohio, is a first
step along the lines I have suggested.

Yet there are serious objections which can
be raised and with which, in conclusion, I
would like to deal. Seemingly this approach
to land use control violates the cherished
principles of certainty and predictability that
are supposed to be the virtues of our present
system of districts, use lists, and elaborate
development standards. This theory, however, is deeply undercut by the multitude of
zoning amendments, improper variances,
special exception permits, floating zone
approvals, and unenforced violations. What
remains is the structure of certainty without
the substance—a mere facade of respectable
predictability masking the practice of unguided administrative and legislative discretion.

Would a system such as I have proposed,
with discretionary judgments firmly based on
an official plan serving as Haar's "impermanent constitution" and guided by stated
development goals and standards, fundamentally reduce the degree of certainty that
now prevails? I submit that it would not, and
that it would be more honest to present the

meat of reality rendered of its semantic fat.

Further, I suggest we have little to fear from courts reviewing the legislative basis of such an approach to land development control. The little band of radicals in 1916 pushed the judicial clock further ahead in their time when they introduced comprehensive zoning than we would do in ours by pressing for additional discretionary powers. Perhaps I betray a naive faith in judicial liberalism, but recent decisions in our higher courts seem to leave little to fear in this respect.

My reservations concerning the wisdom and practicality of adopting the system I have proposed lie in other directions. Are planners, as those who would be charged with exercising such discretionary authority, ready to accept the responsibility inherent in such an approach to development control? Are they confident that they possess the informed judgment to make intelligent decisions when granting or withholding development permission? Are they certain that they could withstand the inevitable political pressures that would be brought to bear on them? Does the present status of planning suggest that legislators would be willing to grant them such powers in the first place? Is there any clear evidence that the adoption of such a system would lead to development patterns significantly different or markedly better than we are currently achieving or which might be brought about by some less drastic modification in our traditional techniques?

Finally, could we produce personnel of the quality and in the quantity that would be demanded to provide careful review of development proposals in a period of rapid urban growth and change? The new breed of planner seemingly has less interest in and knowledge of the micro-physical environment than in the novelties of new analytical methods based on a computer culture, more applicable to macro-planning at the metropolitan scale. Can we safely trust site plan review to this new generation of urban scientists?

Although we may now answer these questions in the qualified negative, that does not mean we should reject the alternative control system I have described. The same questions could have been posed in 1916. The answers

then would surely have been equally discouraging. Who could have predicted, for example, the almost indecent haste with which state lawmakers clutched to their legislative bosoms the Standard State Zoning Enabling Act of 1922?

While I think it extremely doubtful that that episode of almost revolutionary legislative history will be repeated, we should not lose hope in evolutionary progress. If large increments of discretionary powers seem called for eventually, we should begin now to prepare the legislative and professional basis for the future.

Fortunately, there are grounds for optimism. The last ten years have witnessed the adoption and judicial approval of many techniques to ease the rigid Euclidian bonds of zoning districts, use lists, and precise standards. There are new signs of life in the corpse of state planning that was laid to rest in the 1930's. The experiment with statewide zoning in Hawaii promises to teach us some new lessons. A committee of the American Law Institute, aided by a substantial foundation grant, is now at work on a reassessment of American planning legislation. The proposals before Congress for broadening federal aid for such programs as open land acquisition, metropolitan planning, advance provision of neighborhood facilities sites, and the development of new towns will require new legislative responses at the state and local levels.

At this stage of our urban development we badly need imaginative experimentation in our fifty legislative laboratories. Where are the states that have placed metropolitan decision-making power at the metropolitan level, that require state or metropolitan approval of local plans, that provide for state or metropolitan review of local appeal decisions, that have reorganized the fiscal systems of municipalities so that land use decisions can be freed from the shackles of tax and revenue implications, that permit zoning-type regulations based on a community plan instead of a zoning map? And where have been the planners who should have been in the front ranks of those demanding reforms at the metropolitan and state levels?

For half a century we have engaged in a kind of legislative Shintoism, worshipping at the shrine of the Standard State Zoning Enabling Act. Zoning served us well during a period when urban life was simpler and less dynamic. We should honor those who were responsible for its birth and early care—the Bassetts and the Bettmans and, later, the Pomeroys of our profession—all of whom demonstrated a fertility of intellect that we have failed to imitate. But we do these men, and ourselves as well, ultimate honor not by tending their legislative monuments at the end of the by now well-worn legal road they constructed but by carving new trails toward new frontiers to serve an emerging new urban America.

A PLANNER stands before his county commissioners in a suburban county that is part of a fast-growing metropolitan area. A commercial rezoning for a dry cleaning plant is under consideration. The planner is opposed. "The issue," he says, "boils down to recognizing first that the County can support only a few regional shopping centers." Once these have been located, "heavy commercial uses . . . should be limited strictly to those areas." The dry cleaning plant, a heavy commercial use, had been proposed instead for a neighborhood shopping center.

In this instance, the county commissioners accepted the planner's recommendation. Should their refusal be taken to court, however, the outcome would not be certain. A reviewing court might reverse their denial on the ground that the control of competition is not a proper purpose in zoning.

In America, comparative land abundance has not yet compelled mutually exclusive choices in the location of competing land uses, and commercial overzoning has been typical. Recently, the limits of demand have been increasingly consulted as the basis for controlling the availability of land for commercial use. Shopping centers and filling stations are two cases clearly in point. Because of their potential impact on the land use plan, they have frequently been subject to variance, exception, or special rezoning procedures. Filling stations may proliferate until community demand has been met if not exceeded, and in this event an application for an additional station will be refused. A decision on the location of even one shopping center, particularly a regional shopping center, can have considerable impact on the commercial and residential development of the surrounding area. A shopping center application may then be refused if another center is close by, so that the distribution of shopping centers in the community will be held in balance.

In the kind of case under consideration, then, the effect of the proposed use on commercial competition is an element in the zoning decision. Two different types of cases will be treated under this heading. One type raises a proximity question. No question of fulfilling community demand is presented,

3

Control of Competition as a Proper Purpose in Zoning

Daniel R. Mandelker

This article appeared originally in Zoning Digest, Vol. 14, No. 2, February 1962, pp. 33–42, *published by the American Society of Planning Officials, 1313 East 60th Street, Chicago, Illinois 60637. Reproduced by permission.* © 1962 *by the American Society of Planning Officials.*

but an application is denied because another filling station or shopping center is located close by. Were the application granted, the service areas of the two stations (or centers) would overlap, and neither would be completely successful. The second type of case raises a demand question, and in this instance an application will be refused because the community already has a sufficient number of filling stations or shopping facilities. Our example is more complicated than most, and presents both a proximity and a demand question. The first step is to determine the number of regional shopping centers needed in the county. Having done this, the commissioners should see to it that heavy commercial uses, such as dry cleaning plants, should be located only in regional centers. They should not be placed at other nearby locations, where they would be unnecessarily competitive with dry cleaning plants located in the regional shopping centers.

A survey of the opinions reveals that the courts have been far from unanimous in the weight they have given to the competition factor, and that they have not differentiated between questions of proximity and of demand in their consideration of that factor. At least five approaches can be distinguished:

1. *Control of competition ultra vires or unconstitutional in zoning.* This is the extreme view. It has been adopted in several jurisdictions, and has been reiterated most frequently in lower court New York and Ohio decisions, although the New York cases have not been consistent. Usually, no reason is given for the objection, nor is it always clear whether a consideration of competition is merely ultra vires the enabling act, or is an unconstitutional exercise of the police power. In some cases, the objection is based on the point that the control of competition is a matter for the market, and not for the regulating agency.

Perhaps the most satisfactory explanation for this point of view is found in *Circle Lounge & Grille, Inc. v. Board of Appeal*, a Massachusetts case, in which the issue was raised obliquely. The Circle Lounge protested a variance which allowed the construction of a Howard Johnson restaurant across the street. Although the Circle Lounge lies in a commercial zone, the new restaurant would be located in a residential zone bordering part of the street. This case came up as a standing question. Did the Circle Lounge have standing to appeal the Howard Johnson variance?

In answering the standing question, the Massachusetts court indicated its attitude toward the role of competition in the zoning process. It found that competition alone did not give the Circle Lounge sufficient standing to appeal the variance. The purpose of zoning is to protect the conformity of uses. Residential owners in the residential zone might object to the intrusion of a commercial use. But a commercial use in an adjacent commercial zone may not object to the conversion of a neighboring residential zone to a commercial use which would be no less restrictive.

2. *Businesses may not be licensed under the zoning power.* Some of the decisions make an additional objection to the consideration of the competitive factor in a zoning decision. They point out that filling stations and

shopping centers are not sufficiently affected with the public interest to be subjected to utility-type regulation. Again, the cases are not clear whether a vires or a constitutional question is involved. As the issue arises in a zoning context, the point seems to be that the zoning power is not the licensing power, and so may be used to regulate but not to prohibit, whatever that differentiation may mean. This defect could be cured by statutory authority to license shopping centers and filling stations under utility-type regulations based on need. Whether a statutory licensing scheme would be upheld is another question.

Whatever the basis for the cases that make the licensing objection, they fail to note that the land use questions have been obscured by the presentation of the issue as a conflict between competitors. Nevertheless, land use questions have not necessarily been removed from the case.

3. *Control of competition may not be the dominant purpose in zoning.* In all of the remaining categories, the cases give control of competition some weight as a factor in the zoning process. A dominant purpose rationale was adopted in *Appeal of Lieb*, a proximity case, in which a competitor challenged a rezoning for a shopping center. The court admitted that under some circumstances zoning limits competition by restricting the area within which it can be conducted. This is but a byproduct of zoning, and does not make the regulation unlawful. But zoning is not like public utility regulation, and so the "purpose" of zoning may not be the restriction of competition. *Lieb* is sensible in its recognition of the practical impact of a zoning ordinance, but its approach seems a little unrealistic.

4. *Control of competition may be a factor in zoning.* In many of the cases in this category, the competitive factor is not the only reason advanced for rejecting the application. Particularly in the filling station cases, traffic and safety objections may be advanced. Asked to pass on the refusal of a variance (or exception) for a filling station, a court may uphold the denial, noting that lack of need for the station in the area may properly be one of the reasons for refusal. Most of the cases which take this position are filling station appeals. The New Jersey cases have

been most consistent in this point of view.

One problem with the filling station cases is that the application at hand may have been prompted by the presence of other stations in the immediate area. If there are many neighboring stations, the traffic and safety objections to the addition of one more station may not be too persuasive. In these cases, the absence of demand sufficient to support an additional station may be the dominant reason behind the refusal. But the court may avoid coming to grips with this issue by ostensibly shifting its approval of the rejection to a more conventional basis.[1] Particularly in a variance or exception case, the board can then be affirmed on the ground that it did not abuse its discretion.

5. *The monopoly rule: the California cases.* The problem under discussion has been presented in a slightly different context in a series of California cases. The California courts have now made possible a consideration of the competitive consequences of a zoning decision. But in the early and leading case, the suburban municipality of Atherton had zoned only $1\frac{1}{10}$ acres out of its approximately four square miles for commercial uses. This commercial district, if it can be called that, was fully occupied by a few existing businesses. A businessman who had been convicted of running a store in a residential zone challenged the ordinance. Although evidence in the case had indicated that there were ample commercial areas in nearby communities, the court invalidated the ordinance for having conferred a monopoly on existing businesses.

While the Atherton case has never been overruled, its rationale has not been followed in recent decisions. These cases invariably refuse to apply the reasoning of the Atherton case: 1) because there is no intent to confer a monopoly; 2) because the municipality is residential and may be kept that way; or 3) because adequate shopping is available in nearby communities. Some of the grounds of decision in recent opinions would have justified the original Atherton ordinance. In all

but one of the recent cases, an Atherton-type ordinance was upheld. In the exceptional case, the Atherton rationale was rejected and the ordinance invalidated as applied to the parcel in question only because the lot was found to be a residential island surrounded by business property. Finally, in some of the recent cases, vacant land was still available in the commercial district. Quite conventionally, these cases have upheld restrictive commercial zoning of the Atherton type on the ground that the availability of vacant land in the commercial district makes the wisdom of the restriction fairly debatable. The cases ignored contentions that the size of the community would justify the zoning of additional areas for business.

Ordinances of the Atherton variety are not really very far away from those ordinances which exclude all industry from a residential community, in order to preserve its residential character. Ordinances excluding industry have usually been upheld, with some reliance on the point that industrial sites in sufficient number are available elsewhere in the metropolitan area. Indeed, to take a slightly converse situation, ordinances which invariably protect nonconforming uses could be said to confer a monopoly to the extent that they protect the competitive position of existing businesses. For this reason they would also be vulnerable under the Atherton approach.[2]

Planners have long urged their communities to make more efficient use of the available supply of land. The application of demand and proximity controls to the loca-

---

[1] Unfortunately, an ideal solution to these problems is prevented when, as is so often the case, the zoning function is distributed among dozens of competing municipalities in a metropolitan area.

[2] Of course, I would not affirm zoning decisions which indicated bias or bad faith, nor would I affirm a decision obviously intended to discriminate in favor of one competitor over another. It is always possible to imagine the unlikely event in which one drug store chain, as an example, corners all the drug store locations in all the shopping centers in a particular community. I would leave these cases to the antitrust laws, where they belong.

Whether compensation should be payable to an applicant who is refused a commercial use for economic reasons is another subject. Short of an either-or holding on *vires* or constitutionality, intermediate modes of securing compensation to the landowner might be made available.

tion of commercial facilities helps secure this efficiency. The question is whether demand and proximity controls should be judicially accepted as a proper component of zoning regulations. I submit that they should.

Very often, demand and proximity considerations reinforce conventional planning objections. For example, a decision about the location of a shopping center, especially a regional shopping center, has a clear influence on traffic and highway patterns and on the distribution of residential areas. Filling stations have less of an impact on community land use patterns. Proportionately, they fill a much smaller commercial need, and the impact of any one filling station is seldom catastrophic. However, filling stations are almost always a depreciating intrusion in the environment, whether it is a residential area or an area devoted largely to retail stores. In these circumstances, lack of need merely reinforces other arguments that would lead to disapproval of a filling station application.

Yet the circumstances that permit the planning authority to raise the lack of demand argument may also make untenable the more conventional planning objections. This point has already been made. For example, a court may find it impossible to accept an argument that one more station will make the traffic problem unbearable when there are several previously existing stations in the immediate vicinity. Under these circumstances, the effect of the last of a line of filling stations is important only for its cumulative consequences.

Nor may conventional planning objections weigh very heavily in a shopping center case. If the center is to be located in an undeveloped area, and is on the periphery of a residential section, traffic objections may easily be overcome and the intrusion on the residential environment may not be serious. Again, the competition argument may remain as the only objection. I suspect that the more frequent approval of shopping centers in the face of the competition objection is prompted by the aesthetically satisfying features of the typical shopping center development.

The frequent absence of conventional land use objections in many of the shopping center and filling station cases often leads the court to a consideration of fundamentals when the competition argument is raised. A court may fall back on generalities. A California ordinance restricting the size of a commercial area will be sustained on the grounds that its policy is fairly debatable. A denial of a variance for a filling station will be affirmed because the board has not abused its discretion. When the court rejects the competition argument, it may provide valuable insight on its conception of the zoning function. Here lies the importance of the *Circle Lounge* case. By predicating the zoning power on the preservation of the conformity of uses and the protection of the more restrictive from the less restrictive use category, the court echoes the historic function of zoning in the separation of the incompatible in land use.

But the point is that zoning is moving away from this historic and primarily negative function. It is beginning to give legal sanction to decisions affecting more positively the structure of the community. From this perspective, the control of competition can be seen as a proper function of zoning, although not in the form in which it has usually been presented.

English practice affords a clue to developing American trends. As English planning is based on an absolute scarcity of land, it has had to prevent unnecessary duplication in competing land uses. If a community can support only one shopping center it will be allowed only one shopping center. A recent development plan for one community in East Sussex noted that shoppers had been taking their trade elsewhere, and planned the community accordingly. The addition of new shops was restricted. An application to build beyond the planned capacity will be refused, and the refusal will be upheld unless the applicant can establish that the assumptions lying behind the development plan have been altered. In filling station control the English are a bit more ambivalent, but need may be a factor to be taken into consideration when the "planning" arguments are balanced.

We are not yet running out of land for urban development, but we are developing land scarcities of a different order. As metropolitan centers expand, the competition for desirable sites becomes more intense as size forces increase attention to travel, distance, and locational factors. Because it does not make allowances for the community's point of view, the market cannot be relied upon to make the most economic use of available sites. Under conditions of comparative land scarcity, planning will have to see to it that the right choices are made. Commercial facilities should not be built if the community does not need them, and a proper locational balance should be maintained between competing commercial uses.

Land use decisions of this kind raise both questions of proximity and demand, as they have been defined in this paper. The planner will have to make these decisions, and his

solutions will have an undeniable effect on competitive positions within the business community. Nevertheless, secondary effects on competition are an inevitable consequence of land use decisions predicated on land scarcities. The courts should uphold these decisions if they are fairly supportable, and the business community will have to adjust itself accordingly.[3]

[3] A planner who has read this paper suggests that homeowners often have a hard time defending themselves against a commercial intrusion, especially when the commercial applicant can afford expensive counsel. This comment supports the recognition of the rival commercial interest, which will be in a stronger position to defend the community plan.

4

The General Welfare, Welfare Economics and Zoning Variances

Lewis B. Merrifield, III

This article appeared originally in a fuller form in the Southern California Law Review, Vol. 38, Summer 1965, pp. 548–593. *University of Southern California, Los Angeles, California 90007. Excerpt reprinted by permission.*

THE TERM "general welfare" is an overworked phrase in the judicial vocabulary. Because decisions are often justified by maintaining that the decided course of action increases the general welfare, it would be useful to define the term and inquire into possible methods to determine when the general welfare increases. A branch of economics called the New Welfare Economics has focused its attention on these tasks and therefore may be helpful in an operational analysis of the vague term "general welfare." In the first section of this paper, some of the concepts and techniques of the New Welfare Economics will be presented.[1] These concepts will then be applied to an analysis of the law of zoning variances. The purpose in analyzing variance problems in terms of the concepts is twofold: first, to

[1] The exposition of the economic principles will be brief, and from a layman's point of view. Since work in the area is extensive, the author was faced with a significant problem in confining the scope of the article. Thus, vital areas have been entirely omitted. It is hoped, however, that the material included is sufficient to suggest some new analytic tools for the solution of legal problems.

illustrate how the concepts can be applied to the formulation and criticism of a body of law and second, to suggest changes which might be made in the current approach to variances.

I

Individual Welfare

An individual's welfare is influenced by the goods and services which he and others consume, the aesthetic characteristics of his environment, the moral tone of the society in which he lives, and other variables. This is not to say that the total welfare of a person is composed of a number of separate and distinct types of welfare such as "economic welfare," "aesthetic welfare," and "moral welfare." Such a view would ignore the integrated character of human personality and the dependence of an individual's evaluation of any one characteristic of his environment upon the other aspects of his life. The view proposed suggests that an individual's welfare, though affected by numerous separate variables, is itself a unity incapable of separation into various types of welfare. When the term "economic welfare" or "aesthetic welfare" is used, it means the change in welfare due to economic or aesthetic factors.

Many attempts to give objective content to a person's welfare have been made. Numerous standards, such as working hours, nutritional level, and standard of living have been proposed. Economists conceive welfare as a state of mind. Such a conception, however, is not too helpful because it is subjective. The analysis thus looks to the behavior of the individual. If the individual chooses or would choose situation A over situation B, it is concluded that A is preferred to B, and that the actor's welfare is higher in A than in B. It should be noted that this is not an explanation, but rather a statement derived from the postulate of maximization. In all branches of the social sciences it has proved useful to introduce the postulate of maximization. According to this postulate, the alternative selected by the actor is the one expected to leave the actor in the highest net welfare position.[2] It is assumed that an individual attempts to manipulate welfare affecting variables in order to maximize his welfare. The postulate is consistent with a common sense view of human behavior.

II
General Welfare

A. ITS RELATION TO INDIVIDUAL WELFARE

It is assumed that the general welfare of the community is directly related to the welfare of the individuals constituting the community.[3] This relation must be assumed unless a paternalistic concept of group welfare is accepted. Under a paternalistic view the general welfare is thought to be unrelated to the welfare of the individuals of the group. The views of an authority as to group welfare are accepted as the concept of group welfare. Thus, if the authority says that group welfare has increased, this conclusion is accepted even if the individual welfare of every member of the group has decreased. Such a view seems untenable in a society espousing a strong preference for the worth, responsibility, and self determination of the individual. Therefore, it is concluded that the general welfare must respond positively to changes in individual welfare.

B. FROM INDIVIDUAL WELFARE TO GENERAL WELFARE

Since the general welfare is positively related to individual welfare, a transition

[2] The postulate of maximization is too general to be regarded as proved. It is accepted by the social scientist for lack of a better postulate, and as the basis for the construction of analytical systems. Of course, it is subject to criticism. Thus it can be argued that, due to imperfect knowledge, the individual thinks he is increasing his welfare, but in reality is decreasing it. This criticism, though, tends to ignore the satisfaction of psychological needs. Thus it may be that, although from the standpoint of the objective observer, the actor is decreasing his welfare, he may in fact be increasing his welfare, or at least maintaining the status quo, by indulging in escape mechanisms.

[3] This assumption is implicit in the New Welfare Economics and is most often formulated as a condition which the process of decision-making must satisfy. See Arrow, *Social Choice and Individual Values*, 1951.

must somehow be made from individual welfare to the general welfare. The effects of changes in individual welfare on general welfare must be determined. Numerous methods for making this transition have been proposed, some of which will now be examined.

1. *Sum of the Individual Utilities*—The method of transition having the longest history is the Bentham-Edgeworth sum of the individual utilities. According to this view, the welfare of a society is equivalent to the sum of the welfare of its members. It is assumed that the welfare of the individual consists of the difference between the total of pleasures and the total of pains. Both pleasure and pain, and thus welfare, are assumed to be measurable quantitatively, their values depending upon intensity, duration, probability, promptness, and fecundity. When deciding upon a course of action one must predict the resulting pleasure and pain, give them quantitative values, and subtract one from the other. Between two alternatives, that alternative which results in a greater difference should be chosen since it increases the general welfare more than the other alternative.

The sum-of-the-individual-utilities theory of group welfare is subject to numerous criticisms. The theory rests upon the assumption that individual welfare can be cardinally (quantitatively) measured. There is serious doubt as to the possibility of doing so. No expeditious direct measure of welfare has been developed. Thus, welfare can be measured only by its presumed effect on behavior, that is, on choice. Choice implies a greater or lesser relationship, the product or activity chosen causing more welfare than the one not chosen. Thus, the magnitude of welfare can be expressed only in an ordinal system. It can be said that since A was chosen, or would be chosen, over B, A increases the actor's welfare more than B. But it cannot be said that A increases welfare five times as much as B, or that A causes twenty units of welfare while B causes four units of welfare. Also, there is little meaning in comparing changes in welfare at different levels of well-being, just as it makes little sense to say that an increase from zero degrees to one degree is as intense as an increase from 100 degrees to 101 degrees. Even if individual welfares could be cardinally measured, there is little meaning in adding them. If individual welfares cannot be added, it is futile to discuss the welfare of the society as the sum of the welfare of the individuals.

Another objection to the sum-of-the-individual-utilities principle is that interpersonal comparisons of welfare cannot be made in an objective way. Any attempt to make these interpersonal comparisons involves a value judgment and cannot be derived from empirical observations.[4] It might be decided that X's welfare is more important than Y's welfare because X is a prominent citizen while Y is a criminal. The members of the group may conclude that A's welfare is more important than B's because A is already at a sub-standard welfare level while B is at a super-standard welfare level. In either case, a value judgment is required. This is not to say that value judgments are to be abandoned. When they are made, however, it should be clear upon what grounds the decision is made. The judgment should not be cloaked with an aura of empirical objectivity.

As a result of these criticisms, the sum-of-the-individual-utilities principle has been abandoned by most economists. The New Welfare Economics has attempted to devise other methods of passing from individual welfare to group welfare and to develop tests for determining whether the general welfare has been increased.

2. *Paretian Criteria*—The concept of the social optimum as developed by Pareto has had considerable influence in the development of the New Welfare Economics. A social optimum is defined as a situation in which it is impossible to increase the welfare of anyone without decreasing the welfare of

[4] Hicks, "Foundations of Welfare Economics," *Economic Journal*, 49, 1939, p. 629.

someone else. If it is assumed that preference is indicative of the individual's welfare, the situation in question is one in which it is impossible to move one person to a more preferred position without moving another person to a less preferred position. Conversely, the system is not at a social optimum if it is possible to move one person to a more preferred position without moving someone else to a less preferred position. There may be numerous optimum positions, depending upon varying wealth distributions. The Paretian analysis thus yields a range rather than a single point. It does not purport to define the *best* optimum position as this would necessitate the assumption that the welfare of different individuals is comparable.

Pareto developed the following criteria for a change:

1. Situation A has a higher group welfare than situation B if and only if every member of the group is at least as well off, and if at least one person is better off, in situation A than in situation B.

2. Situation A has a lower group welfare than situation B if and only if every member of the group is as well off, and at least one member is worse off, in situation A than in situation B.

3. Situation A has the same group welfare as situation B if and only if every member of the group is as well off in situation A as in situation B, and in situation B as in situation A.

These criteria are very restrictive as they do not allow comparisons between situations which evoke mixed responses, that is where some people are better off and some worse off in one situation than in another. Thus, if three people are better off and four people worse off in situation A than in situation B, the situations cannot be compared. This limitation stems directly from the assumption that interpersonal comparisons of welfare cannot objectively be made. It cannot be maintained that making the three people better off increases group welfare more than making the four worse off decreases group welfare and that thus there is a net increase in group welfare, unless it is decided that the welfare of the three is worth more than the welfare of the four. There may be a very strong ethical predisposition to take this stand. Such a position would have to be supported on ethical grounds however, not on grounds of economic efficiency. Before such an ethical judgment is used to justify coercive government action it seems that a strong community consensus supporting the values upon which the ethical judgment is made would be required.

3. *The Compensation Principle*—The compensation principle was originally developed to circumvent the limitations imposed by the Paretian analysis and allow comparisons between situations evoking mixed responses. The principle has taken two forms, the possibility of compensation and the payment of compensation.

a. The Possibility of Compensation. The possibility-of-compensation principle maintains that in comparing two social states A and B, state A should be chosen if there exists a method of compensation under state A so that everyone will be better off (or everyone will be as well off, and at least one person will be better off) after compensation than they are under state B, even if the required compensation payments are not actually paid. Assume that individual X is benefited by a change from B to A, but individual Y is harmed. X gains; Y loses. Now if X could return Y to his original welfare position while retaining a net gain, the possibility-of-compensation principle would assert that group welfare had been increased by the change. A concrete illustration, utilizing the familiar smoke-damage hypothetical, may serve to demonstrate the application of the principle. Assume that a factory adjoins a hand laundry. In its manufacturing process the factory emits considerable smoke which damages the laundry's wash. The damage to the wash is $100 a week. The proprietor of the laundry would be willing to pay up to $100 a week to avoid the damage. The owner of the factory could install a smoke precipitation device at an amortized cost of $50 per week. Under these conditions, if the smoke precipitation device were installed, the laundry proprietor would gain $100 per week and the factory owner would

lose $50 per week. The possibility-of-compensation principle would dictate that the smoke-precipitation device should be installed. The laundry proprietor could pay the factory owner $50 per week, leaving the factory owner as well off as before. At the same time, the laundry proprietor would save $50 a week due to the lessened damage to his wash, making him better off. Thus, at least one person would be better off and no one would be worse off if the change was made and compensation paid.[5]

If the compensation were actually paid, it could be concluded, under the Paretian criteria, that group welfare had increased since X (the laundry proprietor) is better off and Y (the factory owner) is as well off. The possibility-of-compensation principle, however, does not require the payment of the required compensation. Since compensation is not paid it can only be said that the change has benefited X at the expense of Y. In the absence of actual payments it could be concluded that group welfare had increased only if the computed necessary compensations (in commodities, services, or money) for the concerned individuals revealed something comparable about their well-being and the welfare of the community. Assume a change from A to B. Individual X could be taxed up to $100 and still remain as well off in situation B as in A. Y would require $90 of compensation to remain as well off in situation B as in A. Thus, adequate compensation could be paid, and if it were paid situation B would involve a higher group welfare than A. If the compensation is not made, it could be concluded that group welfare had increased only if we knew that X gained more welfare than Y lost and that on balance the group welfare had increased. This would be true, however, only if the $100 represented more

[5] The smoke damage situation is an example of an external diseconomy. The traditional solution, justified on resource allocation grounds, has been to impose a tax on the activity "causing" the external diseconomy. Recently it has been demonstrated that the solution is not as easy as it once appeared. See Baumol, *Welfare Economics and the Theory of the State*, 1951, p. 124.

welfare than the $90. This in turn would rest upon the assumption of interpersonal comparisons of utility since the potential compensation is measured in money terms and the social value of a unit of money is believed to be the same in the hands of a rich man as in the hands of a poor man.

The possibility-of-compensation principle thus contains the following two assumptions: that equal changes in income give rise to equal changes in the level of welfare of the individual, and that every individual's welfare is the same function of his income level, except for an additive constant. Neither assumption, however, is realistic. For the marginal utility of income to be equal for each individual, whatever the level of income, individual utility indicators in a cardinal system and an oversimplified notion of interpersonal comparisons of utility must be assumed. The fact that a rich gainer gained more than a poor loser lost, is meager evidence that there has been a "balancing between satisfactions and dissatisfactions." It is highly probable that the "same amount of money might well represent a much greater loss to the poorer (loser) than the corresponding gain to the richer (gainer)."[6] Even if the restrictive assumptions are accepted, the analysis is inadequate if we feel that changes in some person's well-being should be weighed more heavily than changes in the welfare of others.

Since compensation is not actually paid, the distribution of wealth before and after the change will be different. The possibility-of-compensation principle ignores this distribution effect. If group welfare is considered to be a function of the level of production *and* the distribution of welfare, the analysis is deficient. It assumes that changes in group welfare due to changes in production levels can be isolated from changes due to distributional changes and concerns itself only with changes in welfare due to changes in production levels. Many writers have expressed doubt whether the principle is relevant for social action, that is, whether it will

[6] Baumol, *op. cit.*, p. 124.

be helpful in evaluating social states and policies. Even if an ordering could be made on purely production terms, there is doubt that such an ordering would have any relevance in ordering social states in terms of all pertinent aspects, including distribution. The impact of the problem can be assessed by envisaging two hierarchies of social states, one ordered in terms of production levels and one ordered in terms of distribution of welfare. No major problem will be presented where a proposed change results in a social state higher than the initial state in both hierarchies, since the change will be considered desirable in terms of both criteria, production, and distribution. Where, however, the change results in a social state higher than the initial state in one hierarchy, but lower than the initial social state in the other hierarchy, a dilemma is presented for which the possibility-of-compensation principle offers no solution. The dilemma is caused by the redistribution of welfare from some individuals to other individuals brought about by the failure to pay the requisite compensation.

[See pages 556 to 571 of the original article for point 3b, "The Payment of Compensation," and subsequent discussions which have been deleted in this presentation.—Ed.]

III

Zoning Variances

In this part of the comment, an attempt will be made to apply some of the tentative conclusions reached in the foregoing discussion to a specific body of law. As previously noted, it may be more fruitful to develop a group of rules from the theories, rather than to rigidly apply the theories to each particular case. Such rules would be designed to effectuate, in each case, the principle or principles adopted. This procedure will be adopted in the analysis of norms relating to zoning variances. The series of rules surrounding the granting or denial of a variance will be set forth and then analyzed to see if they can be justified in the light of the previous discussion. An analysis of zoning variances has been chosen as a vehicle for the demonstration of potential applications of the various theories presented. This field was chosen because it is felt that the area of direct effects can be reasonably ascertained. It is also a field in which the effect of a change is primarily upon economic values; the effect on non-economic values is, for the most part, incidental.

Most state enabling acts provide for the granting of zoning variances, the varying of the restrictions imposed by the zoning ordinance upon a particular parcel of land. Provision for variances was made in the New York zoning enabling act, the first such act in the United States, and is included in the Standard Zoning Enabling Act. Zoning variances may be divided into two types: use variances and non-use variances. A use variance allows a use other than the one prescribed in the zone. A non-use variance permits the applicant to erect, alter, or use a structure for a permitted use in a manner other than that prescribed by the restrictions of the zoning ordinance. A variance permitting a commercial use in a residential zone is a use variance. A variance permitting a three story commercial building in a commercial zone restricting building height to two stories is a non-use variance. Although there is general agreement that the power to grant a non-use variance is included within the authorization to grant a variance, there is some doubt as to whether the power to grant a use variance is included in the authorization to grant variances. Although some state enabling acts specifically authorize the granting of use variances, and some statutes specifically deny the power, the statutes of most states are silent. The courts have differed in determining whether use variances are authorized. Some courts take the position that use variances may not be granted on the theory that the function of the zoning appeals board is that of correcting minor deficiencies caused by the operation of the ordinance relating to area, bulk, or density. These courts frequently state that the granting of a use variance is essentially a legislative function which may not be delegated to an administrative body. Other courts, taking a broader view of the function of the board of appeals, allow use variances.

A. RATIONALES FOR VARIANCES

Numerous rationales for the granting of variances have been advanced. It was early recognized that zoning maps must of necessity be drawn in a broad manner; it is impossible to provide a separate zone for each parcel of land. The community is divided into a number of use districts; all property lying within a district must conform to the same regulation. Within each area, however, there may be, and in most cases are, parcels of land having widely divergent characteristics. Thus, euclidian zoning divides the community into use districts and imposes similar limitations upon parcels of land which are in fact unique and different. On the other hand, it was thought to be impossible to create a separate use district for each parcel of property. As a result, the burden of a zoning regulation falls unequally upon property owners. Because of the physical characteristics of the land, improvements, and surrounding terrain, the burden of the restrictions will be heavier on some than on others. Many pioneers in zoning felt that a board of appeals, empowered to grant variances, could prevent the disturbance and maladjustment which might be caused by the literal enforcement of such an imperfect ordinance. It was felt that such a board could ameliorate the practical difficulties and unnecessary hardships which would otherwise result from literal enforcement of the zoning enactment. It was thought that provisions for variances would provide a flexibility of procedure.

Closely related to this rationale was a rationale arising from the issue of the constitutionality of the zoning variance. Some of the pioneers in zoning regulation thought that the prime function of the board of appeals was to prevent attacks on the constitutionality of the zoning ordinance. Variances were supposed to act as a safety valve to safeguard against constitutional objections. It was feared that if hardship cases were not disposed of by an administrative agency the ordinance would be declared invalid as to a particular parcel of land, leaving its use unrestricted. Decisions of this type would increase, leaving more and more land unrestricted; zoning would be rendered ineffective as a means of land use control.

Some of the pioneers also feared that the local legislature, unfamiliar with zoning and planning principles, would constantly rezone individual parcels of land in an effort to relieve individual hardship, resulting in a subversion of the comprehensive plan, and a return to pre-zoning chaos. They felt that the granting of variances in such cases would be more expeditious for the landowner and would safeguard the integrity of the community plan.

Numerous other justifications for variances have been expressed. It has been said that they are necessary to avoid unwarranted interferences with the right of private property, and to treat the owner fairly. It has also been suggested that variances are necessary to prevent the non-use of land.

Implicit in each objective is the realization that a variance should in some manner advance the value position and welfare of the society. Each justification, however, seems to concentrate upon a particular value or set of values to the exclusion of others, assuming that by doing so the general welfare will be increased. The rationale concentrating upon individual hardship looks to the adverse effect of the ordinance on the applicant for the variance. It tends to ignore the possible benefits to the applicant and the effect on other values. The rationale stressing constitutionality concentrates on the individual hardship, requiring a severe amount of hardship, and the effects of the ordinance on "health, safety, morals et al." The rationale stressing fairness to the owner is concerned with concepts of equality. The theory that variances are granted to prevent the non-use of land looks to resource utilization. The problem is thereby obscured. The welfare of the community is influenced by numerous factors. The problem is to so manipulate these factors that the welfare of the society is increased. In an environment of scarce

resources, concentration upon one factor usually necessitates decreased realization of another. The advancement of one value may preclude the advancement of another. Because of the interdependence of welfare influencing factors, stressing one factor to the exclusion of others may cause a decrease in welfare rather than an increase. Rather than concentrating upon a particular welfare influencing factor, it may be more advisable to look to the resulting welfare of the community, in an effort to determine whether it has been increased.

The justification and theory of zoning variances which this writer proposes is as follows. The granting of a variance is justified by its relation to the general welfare. This relation may take a number of forms. Due to the decrease in the welfare of the applicant, brought about by the restrictions placed upon his property, the original ordinance may not have unambiguously increased the general welfare at the time of its imposition. On the other hand, the imposition of the ordinance, as modified by the proposed variance, may have unambiguously increased the general welfare. Thus, the granting of the variance is a corrective device to cure the original deficiency. Even if the general welfare had not been unambiguously increased at the time of the effectuation of the ordinance and it is concluded that it would have been increased if the ordinance, as modified by the proposed variance, had been effectuated, the variance might not be recommended. Thus, one might adopt the status quo as the frame of reference, and determine whether the granting of the variance would increase the general welfare. The choice between these two alternatives, as between the choice of a method of testing increases in the general welfare, will presumably depend upon the value predispositions of the decision maker and of the group. Thus, one person might conclude that it is inequitable to force the applicant to suffer the burden of a change which did not unambiguously increase the general welfare. If the effects of granting the variance were not too detrimental, such a person might thus grant the variance. On the other hand, if the effect of the variance was to lower the welfare of others to a substantial degree he might recommend that the variance be denied. This is the writer's personal preference. Even if the original ordinance had increased the general welfare, the granting of the variance might further increase the general welfare, in which case everyone would presumably support the variance.

B. STATUTORY BASIS

Zoning ordinances differ as to the grounds upon which a variance may be granted. Three requirements, however, are common, running throughout a great number of the ordinances, and frequently mentioned in the decisions. It must be found: (1) that the literal enforcement of the ordinance would cause unnecessary hardship or practical difficulty, (2) that the hardship is peculiar to the applicant's property and (3) that the granting of the variance will not be contrary to the public welfare or to the spirit of the ordinance.

C. SOME TRADITIONAL REQUIREMENTS

1. *Unnecessary Hardship*—One of the chief findings which must be made to support the granting of a variance is that literal enforcement of the ordinance would result in unnecessary hardship to the applicant. This provision was included in the original New York State Enabling Act, has been repeated in enabling acts from coast to coast, and is the most often mentioned in the cases. The applicant carries the ultimate burden of persuasion as to this element. It is, of course, necessary to develop sets of operative facts to which the conclusionary phrase "unnecessary hardship" will be applied as well as a theory or set of principles directing the application of this outcome-determinative phrase. In an effort to do so a considerable body of case law, much of it conflicting, has been developed. The circumstances under which unnecessary hardship may be found have been variously expressed. Many cases state that the applicant must show that the property will not yield a reasonable return if put to a permitted use. Other cases have said that the ordinance must result in rendering the property unsuitable for any reasonable use. Some courts have said that the restric-

tion must result in virtual confiscation. Still other courts have said that the restriction must be so unreasonable as to constitute a capricious and arbitrary interference with the right of private property, and that the hardship must be substantial, serious, and compelling. Despite the varying statements it can safely be said that the degree of hardship necessary to support the granting of a variance must be very high.

Every restriction on the rights and privileges to use land involves a potential hardship, as the restriction imposes upon the land owner a duty to refrain from performing certain acts in the use of his property. If the owner desires to do the particular act, and was able to do so prior to the restriction, the potential hardship becomes a real hardship imposed by the restriction.[7] It is assumed that the immediate effect of such restrictions decreases the welfare of the restricted person.[8] The restrictions applied to him, however, are similarly applied to others in his immediate neighborhood and in areas less proximate to him. The individual's welfare may be increased by these restrictions placed on others. If the benefits accruing to him are sufficient to compensate him for the decreased welfare due to the restrictions imposed upon him he will be as well off, or better off, than before the effectuation of the ordinance. Since he has been fully compensated, the welfare effects of the ordinance upon him do not prevent an unambiguous increase in the general welfare. The payment-of-compensation principle will have been satisfied, if it is assumed that the restrictions increase the welfare of some individuals. In

[7] If the owner could not previously perform the now-prohibited act due to personal disability, it cannot be said that the restriction has imposed a hardship on him. Likewise, if he has no desire to perform the prohibited act, it cannot be said that the restriction causes a hardship.

[8] It is possible, of course, that the owner may be of a philanthropic nature such that his welfare is a partial function of the welfare of others. Thus, an increase in the welfare of others may cause an increase in his welfare. If such is the case, one might inquire why he did not restrict his activity voluntarily.

such a case, compensation payments are automatically made by the exchange of benefits.

This view has frequently been expressed in cases dealing with attacks upon the constitutionality of an ordinance as confiscatory. It has been used to separate a permissible taking from a prohibited taking. This theory has been called "the average reciprocity of advantage" and the "correlative benefit" theory. Thus, it has been said:

> Indeed, it is to be presumed that a fully compensating individual advantage ensues from the general betterment.[9]
> Compensation for such interference with and restriction in the use of property is found in the share that the owner enjoys in the common benefit secured to all.[10]

Whether or not the applicant has been actually compensated will depend on numerous variables. Ultimately, of course, the payment of compensation depends upon the welfare effects on the applicant of the restrictions placed upon him, and the welfare effects of the benefits accruing to him. His wealth position, the amount of his loss, the proximity of other restricted property and the nature of the restrictions on such property will be relevant factors. The greater the loss is to the applicant the more improbable it is that he actually is being compensated.

Even if, at the time of the application for the variance, the petitioner has not been fully compensated, he may be fully compensated in the near future. If such is the case, it might be concluded that the necessary showing of hardship has not been made since any existing hardship will be rectified in the near future. Under such a view it might be permissible to temporarily deprive the property of any reasonable use; it would not be permissible to deprive the property of any reasonable use for a long period of time. If the deprivation of any reasonable use will continue for some time, such that the peti-

tioner will remain uncompensated, a temporary variance might be granted. The longer the period for which the applicant must wait for the benefits, however, the more difficult it is to say that the change has unambiguously increased the general welfare. The same objection will be encountered as was encountered when considering the Hicks justification of the possibility of compensation principle; over the long run both tastes and the composition of the group will change. Where tastes and the composition of the group have changed no valid welfare comparisons can be made within the framework adopted.

In determining whether the applicant is now, or in the future will be, fully compensated, a critical problem is deciding what shall be viewed as benefits accruing to him. Surely, the peculiar benefits which do not accrue to society as a whole will be included. Thus, where an area is zoned residential, each property owner in the zone derives, in return for the restriction imposed upon him, a special benefit flowing from similar regulation of his neighbors. Since other property owners will be unable to use their land for commercial or industrial uses, each owner is free from noxious odors, noise and sights, resulting in a more pleasant environment and a higher property value. Such benefits do not directly accrue to the society as a whole. A more difficult problem is presented in determining whether, and to what extent, common benefits accruing to the society at large shall be included in determining whether the applicant has been or will be fully compensated. If the common benefits flow from the advancement of common values, or common principles, such benefits should be included, since by definition they are shared by the applicant, and their advancement presumably benefits him. The issue is posited by zoning regulations which seek to control the spatial and temporal development of urban and suburban development. Such regulations benefit the community at large by decreasing the transverse costs of utility supply, and thus decreasing taxes.[11] The restricted owners,

[9] *Schmidt v. Bd. of Adjustment*, 9 N.J. 405, 88 A.2d 607 (1952).
[10] *Hendley v. City of Rochester*, 272 N.Y. 197, 5 N.E.2d 198 (1936).

[11] The alternative to zoning regulation is more accurate pricing of municipal services and more sophisticated taxing, so that there is a better relation of costs and benefits.

however, receive no benefits flowing from the restrictions imposed upon others. They may, however, receive benefits due to the advancement of values which they hold in common with other members of the society, and thus might assent to the regulations in any case other than their own. Thus, regulations restricting development may free capital for investment in better educational and cultural facilities, advancing the goals of enlightenment and aesthetic satisfaction. They may also bring about a more rational allocation of resources such that an increase in net goal satisfaction is brought about. If such is the case, these benefits should be taken into consideration when determining if the applicant is fully compensated.

In addition to imposing a hardship, the hardship must be unnecessary. The courts usually do not separate the two elements of unnecessary hardship, but rather treat them together, determining if the facts indicate an unnecessary hardship. Although they sometimes specify the elements which must be shown to support a finding of unnecessary hardship, no theory has been proposed as to what generally constitutes an unnecessary hardship. Nor has it been fully explained why a showing of unnecessary hardship must be made. Of course, it can be argued that unnecessary hardship must be found because the statutes and ordinances so dictate. Since the statutes do not specify what constitutes an unnecessary hardship, it is left to the board of appeals and courts to give operational meaning to the term. In doing so a knowledge of why unnecessary hardship is required would be helpful.

A particular hardship may be unnecessary for a number of reasons. It may be of such a magnitude that it prevents an unambiguous increase in the general welfare resulting from the effectuation of the zoning ordinance. Even though the ordinance had increased the general welfare, a particular hardship imposed by the ordinance may be unnecessary if its removal would increase the general welfare still further.

a. Failure To Earn a Reasonable Return. The courts frequently state that in order to support a finding of unnecessary hardship, it must appear that if the applicant complies with the regulations of the ordinance he can secure no reasonable return from his property, or can make no reasonable use of the property. It is not enough that the property would be more valuable or would earn more profits if put to a non-conforming use. The line between failure to realize a reasonable return and failure to earn additional profits is fine. If the application of the ordinance completely destroys the value of the property, or greatly diminishes its value, a finding that a reasonable return cannot be earned usually will be made. On the other end of the continuum are those cases in which the only showing is that the applicant could make more money; here the variance will be denied. Between these two extremes, however, there is disagreement. At least one court has recognized that the question is a matter of degree. An examination of the cases reveal a tendency on the part of the courts to require increasingly high standards of proof, particularly where the variance has been denied by the board.

If the degree of financial loss and hardship to the applicant is very high, it is probable that the general welfare has not been unambiguously increased by the zoning ordinance, since the applicant is worse off than before. This result may obtain whether the possibility-of-compensation test or the payment-of-compensation test is used. Using the payment-of-compensation test, the applicant may not have been fully compensated for the decreased welfare caused by the imposition of the restrictions upon him. Whether compensation is actually paid to the applicant will depend upon a number of factors, only one of which is the decreased welfare due to the restrictions placed upon the applicant. The benefits accruing to the applicant and his valuation of these benefits are also important. Thus, it would seem that the nature of the surrounding uses, and the restrictions imposed upon them are valid matters of inquiry. Also, relevant is the use to which such land would have been put in the absence of the ordinance. If land surrounding the applicant's parcel is restricted such that it can no longer be put to uses which detrimentally affect the applicant's welfare, perhaps he has been adequately compensated. If, on the other hand, surrounding land has not been restricted, no benefits may accrue to the applicant. Viewed from this standpoint the failure in some cases to give weight to the presence on adjacent lots of the same type of use as that for which the applicant seeks to obtain a variance[12] seems ill advised. There is some indication, however, that where the applicant's property is surrounded by nonconforming uses which are, for all intents and purposes, permanent the board may grant a variance on the basis of such evidence. Probably, the larger the decrease in welfare due to the restrictions, the more improbable it is that the applicant is being compensated, and thus the more improbable that the general welfare has unambiguously increased.

If the possibility-of-compensation test is employed, the results will be approximately the same. If the loss to the applicant is very large, it would seem that the probability that those who benefit from the restriction could compensate him is lessened. Whether or not those who gain could compensate the applicant depends upon the welfare value of the benefits accruing to them from the restrictions placed on the applicant. If the use which the applicant is prohibited from undertaking would have been detrimental to those affected, it may be assumed that the neighbors are benefited by the restriction. On the other hand, if the prohibited use would not have been detrimental, the restriction does not confer a benefit upon them. Thus, it may make a difference whether the land which cannot be used for a rolling mill is next to other industrial sites (nonconforming uses), or next to an exclusive residential apartment house.

12 Similar adjacent uses may arise in three instances: (1) the adjacent uses may enjoy the status of non-conforming uses, which were validly maintained up to the time of the adoption of the zoning ordinance and which therefore have a vested right of continuance; (2) owners of adjacent lots may have been granted variances in the past; and (3) the applicant's property may border on a zone in which similar uses are allowed.

Little's modification of the Hicks justification of the possibility-of-compensation principle is relevant at this point. Over the long run, if the possibility-of-compensation principle is followed, all individuals affected may experience a net gain due to an averaging out of gains and losses. This is made more probable if the large losers are actually compensated. An alternative is to remove the large loser's losses, or at least to diminish them. This can be done by granting a variance in those cases where the restrictions would impose a very large loss to the applicant. Where his loss is not as large, however, the variance would be denied.

Where the loss to the applicant is large in proportion to the losses imposed upon others, it is also more likely that the Scitovsky criteria will be unsatisfied. Thus, we may have a situation where the gainers could bribe the applicant to support the effectuation of the restrictions and the applicant could bribe the gainers to support its removal. Such a result may obtain because of the different wealth distributions, before and after the imposition of the restrictions. The greater the uncompensated loss, the greater will be the disparity between the wealth distributions before and after the imposition of the restrictions.

Still another problem is presented where the loss to the applicant, or any group of applicants is large; the effectuation of the ordinance will result in a significant redistribution of welfare. The larger the redistribution of welfare, the more squarely the redistribution question must be faced. It may well be felt that small redistributions of welfare, incidental to the imposition of the restrictions, may be overlooked. Where a primary effect of the ordinance is a redistribution of welfare, however, it might be argued that the limits of the police power have been overstepped. Such redistributions may be better accomplished through taxing measures and social welfare programs. If this rationale is not accepted we are presented squarely with the necessity of making a value judgment as to whether the redistribution of welfare is to be approved or disapproved. It may make a difference whether welfare is being redistributed from the rich to the poor or vice versa.

The interdiction against "mere" loss of prospective profits sustaining a variance is difficult to explain. Inability to earn greater profits has welfare effects upon the applicant. The present welfare position of an individual depends not only upon his present income, but also upon his estimate of his future income. If the individual learns that his future income will be less than he had expected, it is reasonable to assume that his present, as well as future, welfare will be decreased. The "loss of profits" rule thus cannot be justified by contending that loss of profits have no effect on present welfare. It may be contended that the rule stems from a problem of measurement. However, the amount of the applicant's loss, if he cannot make a reasonable return, can be ascertained with some accuracy. This can be done by multiplying the reasonable rate of return by his invested capital. The difference between this value and the projected amount of earnings can thus be looked upon as the applicant's loss. It could be argued that we cannot, with any degree of accuracy, determine the amount of loss of profits since prospective profits vary greatly; thus, the amount of compensation which must be paid to the applicant is not readily ascertainable. This argument loses considerable force when it is realized that the problems of measuring lost profits may be no more difficult or numerous than that of measuring a reasonable return and prospective earnings. In addition, the problem of lost profits has been met in other areas such as contract and tort.

b. Benefit to Public. The cases frequently state that a mere benefit to the public is not sufficient to support the granting of a variance since a hardship to the public, by denying them a convenience or necessity, is not hardship to the applicant. This rule has been justified on the grounds that to grant a variance on the basis of the public benefit involves a value judgment more appropriately left to the legislative body. Such a justification seems of little merit since it assumes that granting variances on the basis of unnecessary hardship, in which possible detrimental effects to the public are considered, does not require a value judgment. It has also been said that the necessity of the proposed use to the public has no bearing on

whether the property can be used for a permitted use; if the use is really necessary it can be developed in a proper zone. Following this line of reasoning courts have held that the fact that the proposed use would alleviate a parking problem, be convenient for tenants and relieve traffic congestion, increase municipal tax revenue, or expand the services of a public utility is no substitute for a showing of unnecessary hardship. Other courts, however, have not chosen to follow this rule, stressing such factors as increased parking facilities, the necessity for a service station and reduction in the hazard of an intersection, the convenience of an extra gas pump to the tenants of an abutting owner, the necessity for the use by adjacent residential owners, the need for a second business in town, the need for a site adequate in size for commercial purposes, and the increased employment opportunities created by the proposed use. In some of these cases, unnecessary hardship was shown. In others, however, the prime consideration seemed to be the public benefit secured by the proposed use.

If the variance truly benefits the public, in the sense that the general welfare is increased unambiguously, it is difficult to see why it should not be granted. Thus, the granting of the variance may have only *beneficial* effects upon those whom it affects, in which case everyone affected would be better off. Alternatively, the variance may have no effects upon some, while benefiting others. Since some individuals are better off, while the rest are as well off, it would be concluded that the general welfare had been increased. In determining whether the individuals affected are better off we must consider the net welfare effect of all of the welfare influencing variables affected by the variance. Thus, the proposed use may decrease welfare because of harmful aesthetic characteristics, but it may also be welfare increasing due to added convenience. If the positive welfare effects of the benefits offset the negative welfare effects of the detriments, those who initially appear to be detrimentally affected by the variance may not be affected at all. It is also possible that the benefits outweigh the detriments, in which case those affected would experience a net increase in welfare. Thus, under any of the welfare tests discussed, there is no theoretical justification for denying weight to benefits to the public. The only value judgment implicit in considering benefits to the public is the judgment that it is good to increase the welfare of some people if the welfare of others is not decreased.

When the courts follow the "benefit to the public" rule they may be directing themselves to cases in which the proposed use is beneficial to some members of the public; but either these benefits do not accrue to those detrimentally affected by the variance or the benefits are not sufficient to compensate those detrimentally affected. If the rule is restricted to such cases, it could be justified by the payment-of-compensation principle, since the losers are not actually being compensated. The benefit to the public rule, in this restricted application, might not find a justification in the possibility of compensation principle, since those who are benefited might be able to compensate those who are detrimentally affected and still retain a net benefit.

Even though ignoring public benefits cannot be theoretically justified, it may be practically justified. Problems of measurement are significant. Where there is a purported benefit to the public, it may be more difficult to ascertain the people who are affected and the effects of the ordinance upon them than when the investigation is confined to unnecessary hardship of the applicant. However, when the inquiry is confined to unnecessary hardship suffered by the applicant, the *detrimental* effects on "the public" of granting the variance are considered. The problems of proof would not seem to be more difficult when considering *benefits* to the public.

c. Self Created Hardship. Another important rule often enunciated by the courts is that the hardship may not be "self created." It must not result from the applicant's own actions, nor must it be hardship which he

could have avoided. This rule may be invoked where the applicant has proceeded in disregard of the ordinance thereby creating a condition which is claimed as the basis of unnecessary hardship. Thus, where the applicant constructs in contravention of side line requirements, or set back requirements, expands a nonconforming use, constructs a prohibited use, or sells a portion of a lot meeting minimum area requirements so that the remainder is substandard, and subsequently applies for a variance, the variance will be denied. The "self created hardship" doctrine is applied by some courts where the applicant has purchased the property after enactment of the ordinance, with actual or presumed knowledge of the restrictions. In many of these cases, however, the unnecessary hardship was due to some act or omission of the applicant other than a mere purchase. In still other cases, there was not a sufficient showing that the property was not adapted to a conforming use. Thus, in some of the cases, the enunciation that the self created hardship rule applies to a purchaser was unnecessary. In other states a purchase with knowledge of the restrictions is an element to be considered but does not, in itself, prevent the granting of a variance.

A possible justification for the "self created hardship" rule is that the applicant has chosen his position. It may be inferred that he is in a preferred position since he has voluntarily put himself in the position he now occupies. Of course, when he purchased the property, or constructed the nonconforming building, he expected to obtain a variance. If he had been acting rationally, and it is assumed that he was, he considered the risk of not obtaining the variance when deciding upon his course of action. If the granting of the variance will result in an unambiguous increase in the general welfare, however, it is difficult to see why the variance should not be granted, unless there is a strong value preference for applications to and approval by the board prior to undertaking action.

d. Uniqueness. The hardship of which the applicant complains must be peculiar to his property. The conditions resulting in the hardship must be unique to the property for which the variance is sought, not common to the area. It is often said that difficulties or hardship common to the area go to the reasonableness of the ordinance generally and are only a matter for legislative concern; an amendment or attack on the constitutionality of the ordinance is the proper remedy. The requirement of uniqueness is incorporated into many enabling statutes. Despite this seemingly uniform requirement of uniqueness, occasionally a variance is approved where the hardship and conditions are common to the area. In such cases, the board of appeals in granting the variance, and the court in approving the variance are cognizant of the plight of the applicant.[13]

When analyzing problems dealing with the uniqueness requirement, ideally it would be beneficial to distinguish between conditions common to the area and actual hardships common to the property owners within the area. Conditions common to an area may be potentially hardship causing, without imposing actual hardships upon all of the property owners in the area.[14] The hardship itself may be unique to one property owner. The courts, however, do not make this distinction, perhaps due to the difficulty involved in ascertaining whether the common conditions impose common hardships, and the probability that common conditions will impose common hardships.

If the distinction between common conditions and common hardships were made, perhaps the result in particular cases would be different. As was noted, one of the arguments against granting a variance where there are common conditions is that to do so would be invading an area of legislative or judicial activity. The assumption is that the legislature will act or that a court will declare the ordinance unconstitutional. If the hardship imposed by the ordinance is not common, despite the common conditions, the amount of force which can be exerted upon the legislative body to enact an amendment is sub-

stantially decreased. Few people will be motivated to lobby for the amendment. The same may be said of a judicial attack on the constitutionality of the ordinance; few people will desire to join with the one individual who experiences a peculiar hardship from a common condition. Thus, the force of the plaintiff's position is considerably weakened. In both cases, the person experiencing the hardship is at a disadvantage. Practically, his remedies of constitutional attack and amendment may be of little value where he experiences a peculiar hardship. Where, however, the common conditions impose a common hardship, the argument for legislative and judicial remedies is considerably stronger. All those suffering the hardship will be motivated to seek an amendment or judicial relief.

The distinction between common conditions and common hardships is also fruitful in estimating the cost of affecting the desired change. Where the common conditions create common hardships, it is likely that the total cost resulting from each individual obtaining a variance will be higher than if all those adversely affected joined in seeking an amendment or judicially attacking the ordinance; the desired change may be brought about at a lower cost if it is done so through an amendment or judicial action than if achieved by a series of individual variances. However, where the common conditions create peculiar hardships, few individuals will seek variances. Therefore, the cost of obtaining the desired change through variances may be less than if it were obtained through amendment or judicial action. If the suggested distinction is made, the common hardship rule may be viewed as a means of compelling the most efficient means of change.

If the conditions giving rise to the hardship are common to the area, it would seem more likely that the applicant is actually being compensated for his hardship by the benefits accruing to him from the similar restrictions placed on others. The assumption is, of course, that the extent of the benefits

[13] If the variance is denied, the applicant must either attack the validity of the ordinance or attempt to secure its amendment. Either procedure is laborious and apt to meet with little success.

[14] This would be the case if some of the individuals either did not desire to engage in the activity or were prevented from doing so by other than the common conditions.

accruing to other individuals is directly proportional to the extent of the restrictions placed upon the owners of land. This assumption is reasonable and, indeed, is implicit in all justifications for land use control. If a group of owners must conform to minimum setback requirements, and all are able to do so at approximately the same expense, it is probable that each is compensated for his hardship by the benefits accruing to him from the restrictions on the others.

If the applicant's hardship is unusually large in comparison to that of the other property owners in the vicinity, it is unlikely that he is being compensated by the benefits accruing to him from the restriction placed on others. This is the case because the restrictions placed on the others do not generate benefits sufficient to compensate the applicant for his disproportionate hardship. In the illustration above, while the benefits might be sufficient to compensate the owner for added expense, they would probably not be sufficient to compensate him for an inability to use his lot for any purpose. Thus, under the payment-of-compensation principle, the general welfare has not unambiguously increased. The results obtained by applying the possibility-of-compensation principle will be similar. If the hardship to the applicant is uniquely large it is unlikely that those benefited by the restrictions would be able to compensate him for his loss.

Where the hardship imposed upon a particular individual or group of individuals is significantly greater than that imposed on others, welfare redistribution effects are likely to be significant. Thus, the problems of the Scitovsky paradox and evaluating welfare redistributions becomes more acute.

2. *Effects of Variance on Others*—It is well settled that the board, when deciding whether to grant a variance, and the court in reviewing the board's determination, must consider the effects that the proposed use will have on the neighborhood. This recognition is expressed in two general propositions. It is often said that the variance must be in harmony with the general purpose and intent of the ordinance and must preserve its spirit. This requirement is often made explicit in the statutes. Many courts have interpreted this requirement to prohibit use variances, and the extension of nonconforming uses. It is also frequently stated that in granting the variance the public health, safety, and general welfare must be assured. Even where hardship is shown, the variance will be denied where granting it would transfer the hardship to surrounding property owners. Thus, variances have been denied where the proposed use would cause excessive noise, create traffic, fire, noise and sewage difficulties, engender fear and anxiety in the neighbors, or cause possible fire hazards, noise, fumes and traffic. Possible aesthetic objections are to be considered when the type of neighborhood warrants such objection. The boards and courts are sometimes influenced by the fact that abutting property owners do not object to the proposed use. Many zoning ordinances require an applicant for a variance to file consent statements of a specific percentage of nearby property owners with his petition. The courts have differed in their treatment of such provisions. Some cases hold the consent provisions invalid as a delegation of legislative power to adjoining owners without imposing standards governing the exercise of the legislative power. Other courts have upheld the consent provisions.

The effect on the public of granting the variance is relevant in two ways. Under the possibility-of-compensation principle, the benefits accruing to others from the restrictions imposed upon the applicant must be determined in order to see if those benefited by the restriction would be able to compensate the applicant for his loss resulting from the imposition of the restrictions. If the removal of the restrictions on the applicant, through the granting of the variance, will detrimentally affect others, it can be assumed that the imposition of the restrictions confers a benefit upon others. The effects on others of the imposition of the restrictions, indirectly revealed by effects if the restrictions were to be removed, are thus relevant in determining whether the general welfare has been unambiguously increased by the imposition of the ordinance. By a parity of reasoning, the effects on the public will be relevant in determining whether the imposition of the ordinance, as modified by the variance, would have increased the general welfare.

The effect of the proposed use is also relevant in determining whether the granting of the variance would cause an increase in the general welfare. Even if it is concluded that the imposition of the original ordinance did not unambiguously increase the general welfare, due to hardship imposed upon the applicant, and that if modified it would have increased the general welfare, it can be contended that the variance should not be granted. If the granting of the variance imposes hardships upon others, so that the general welfare would not be increased, it can be argued that the variance should not now be granted. Such a contention could be advanced on a theory of conservatism, or on the theory that the hardship should not be transferred to others. On the other hand, it could be contended that since the original ordinance had not unambiguously increased the general welfare, the applicant should not be forced to bear the burden of ill-advised action.

The granting of the variance can operate in one of three ways upon neighboring property owners; it may have no effect on them, it may work a disadvantage upon them, or it may benefit them. If the variance has no effect upon other individuals it is difficult to see why the variance should not be granted within the framework which has been employed. Since the variance presumably increases the welfare of the applicant, this would be a situation in which everyone is as well off, and at least one person is better off after the change. Such would be the case even if the applicant did not make the traditional showing of unnecessary hardship. Indeed, it could be said that any hardship was unnecessary if it prevented an increase in the general welfare. Despite this line of reasoning, the courts often state that the fact that the grant of the variance would do no great harm is insufficient reason for the grant of a variance in the absence of the traditional showing of failure to earn a reasonable return. In many of these cases, however, the

variance would have some detrimental effects on others. The fact that the proposed use will not be detrimental to others has been emphasized in many cases. The consent of neighboring owners or their failure to object to the proposed use is perhaps the best way of determining whether they will be affected by the variance.

If the grant of the variance is beneficial to others, the granting of the variance would increase the general welfare since this would be a case where everyone was better off. While a few courts have interpreted the public welfare language in the statute to sanction granting of variances when it is found that the community would benefit, most courts have not done so. Even if the proposed use were detrimental to some individuals, it could be contended that the variance would increase the general welfare. This would result if the possibility-of-compensation test were adopted, and it was found that those who would gain from the variance (the applicant and others benefited) could compensate those who would be harmed by the proposed use.

If the effect of the variance upon others is detrimental (welfare decreasing) a dilemma is presented. Under the payment-of-compensation principle, the variance could not be recommended, since those who are adversely affected will not be actually compensated for their losses. This case is apt to arise quite often. In many variance cases the proposed use will not significantly benefit adjoining land owners, but may harm them. If the possibility-of-compensation principle were adopted, its application would indicate that the granting of the variance would increase the general welfare if the applicant could compensate those adversely affected by the proposed use. Others who would benefit by the variance could also be included when determining if compensation could be paid. Where the gain to the applicant is large in comparison to the loss to the adjoining owners compensation will be possible. In many cases, however, compensation will not be possible. Ostensibly the question is then presented of whose welfare is more important, that of the applicant's or that of those adversely affected. It might well be contended that such a decision is essentially a political one, better left to a more representative body than the board of appeals or the courts. In many cases, however, the decision can be made on nonpersonal grounds. Thus, rather than being forced to make the decision as to whose welfare is more important, the problem can be resolved by applying certain values and principles held by the community. Even where such a resolution is available the determination of the values and principles involved and their application to the particular case may be a function which is better performed by a representative body, unless the values and principles are fundamental premises of the society and shared by all its members.

IV

Conclusion

In today's complex, interdependent society the conclusionary phrase "general welfare" is increasingly used to justify governmental action. Frequently the action taken has severe adverse effects on individual members of the society. These adverse effects are often cloaked behind the reassuring, objective sounding platitude "general welfare." All too frequently the term is employed to hide or obscure fundamental conflicts of values and interests; its aura of value-free objectivity often covers up basic choices.

This comment is an attempt to offer a perspective on possible methods by which an increase in the general welfare can be discovered. The effort has been to demonstrate the difficulties involved in constructing a value-free, objective criterion for testing the effect of governmental action on the general welfare and to suggest some possible methods of doing so. Of the methods analyzed the payment-of-compensation principle was suggested as being the most theoretically justifiable. It has not been contended that values should not enter into the process of decision, but only that the values and principles involved should be fully articulated. Where the payment-of-compensation principle fails to indicate whether a particular action will result in an unambiguous increase in the general welfare resort must be made to values and principles. It has been suggested that the values and principles relied upon should be common to the society and supported by a strong consensus.

The examination of zoning variances attempted to demonstrate the application of some of the principles developed to the analysis and criticism of a body of legal rules. Although some of the rules were found to be justified by the principles, many were not. It was seen that in many cases the rules would have been different if the suggested theories were applied.

Although there are considerable practical difficulties in applying the theories suggested and in discovering the common values and principles of a society, this writer believes that further inquiry in these fields would be extremely fruitful. The range of problems which can be analyzed in this manner and the degree to which the application of one or more of the theories will yield unambiguous and consistent decisions must be left as an open question at the present. This is unfortunate but not fatal. A tentative adoption and application of the analytical framework suggested may enable the law to continue sharing in the advances of the other social sciences. In this manner the concept of the general welfare may be given operational meaning.

SURPRISINGLY ENOUGH, the phenomenon of municipal zoning affords a rich and challenging area for both the application of economic theory and for the "economic approach" to political theory. Zoning is of interest to the economic theorist because of its relation to certain peculiarities of the urban property market. These peculiarities, external economies and diseconomies, have never been completely understood, although it is generally agreed that the presence of such uncompensated externalities means that the unrestricted market cannot function in such a manner as to achieve Pareto optimality.

On the other hand, it has long been recognized that the political process determines at least some of the rules under which any market mechanism is allowed to operate. These politically determined rules may or may not be viewed as "good" in some broad social welfare sense of the term; but it is seldom indeed that the economist has worried about the method of selecting constraints and has turned his attention to an analysis of the types of rules which the democratic process might tend to impose upon the market mechanism.

This paper represents a modest effort to theorize about the nature of the constraints which a democratic political process will tend to impose upon the operation of the market mechanism in urban property. In order to accomplish this we must make a brief analysis of the operation of the price system in the urban property market.

Economic Analysis

Despite various statements on the subject, it should be abundantly clear, at least to economists, that the desire for zoning restrictions arises because of the presence of external effects in the urban property market. In other words, if one happened to own a house in an exclusive residential district, the possible location of a glue factory, beer joint, or even a gasoline service station on the adjacent lot would no doubt be upsetting since possible odors, noises, congestion, etc., might act to lower the value of the residence. In fact, all zoning restrictions—use, height, area, and density regulations—can be viewed

5

Economic Elements in Municipal Zoning Decisions

Otto A. Davis

This article appeared originally in Land Economics, Vol. 39, No. 4, pp. 375–386. © 1963, *by the Regents of the University of Wisconsin. Reproduced by permission.*

as an effort to eliminate possible external diseconomies which the construction of "undesirable" property features might impose upon other properties in any given district. Thus this section will discuss briefly the effects of externalities in the urban property market.

An obvious effect of externalities is the following: An external economy will increase the capital value of affected properties, and an external diseconomy will decrease the value. The value of properties not directly affected by an externality may or may not change but this point need not concern us here. Without considering uses which produce externalities we may say that, as far as investment and urban growth is concerned, external diseconomies or even the danger of this phenomenon tend to reduce the psychological or monetary return from urban property. Thus capital outlays are lower in their presence than would be the case in their absence and "marginally productive" lots may remain undeveloped if the danger of external diseconomies is present. External economies, of course, have the opposite effect upon urban investment.

Having stated briefly some of the effects of externalities in the urban property market, the question naturally arises whether or not externalities can be expected to occur; or, in

41

other words, whether the price mechanism will function so as automatically to adjust for and eliminate externalities. This question can be answered, at least in part, by considering the effect of externalities upon location decisions.

Any given property feature may create an external economy, an external diseconomy, or be neutral in its effects upon other property. Considering only two properties at a time there are six relevant combinations to be discussed. If properties mutually create external economies upon each other, the profit or utility maximization criterion would indicate that they will be attracted to each other. As an example, witness the development of shopping centers or clusters of retail stores so that customers may "spill over" from one shop into another. By similar reasoning it may be concluded that properties which mutually create external diseconomies upon each other jointly repel and will not be motivated to locate on adjacent lots. If properties are neutral in their effects upon each other then neither attraction nor repulsion exists between them.

If property A creates an external economy for property B but B is neutral in its effect upon A, then granted a locational decision by A, B is motivated to locate nearby. The opposite is not true. A locational decision by B does not affect the decision of A. An example here might be a restaurant and a university.

Two possibilities remain. If A creates an external economy for B, but B creates an external diseconomy upon A, then granted a locational decision by A, B has motivation to locate upon an adjacent site. Such a choice by B would, of course, impose a capital loss upon A. On the other hand, granted a locational decision by B, A would not be motivated by externality considerations to locate nearby. Many examples of this particular combination exist, with "expensive" and "inexpensive" residential dwellings being very obvious.

Finally, if A is neutral upon B but B creates an external diseconomy upon A, then B might decide to locate near A if internal considerations warranted such a decision. An obvious example of this category is a single-family residence and a gasoline service station.

Of all these possibilities, zoning seems to be concerned only with the final two. Let us examine then how zoning tries to handle these two cases where external diseconomies might occur.

A Beneficent Dictator and the Zoning Method

In order to make sharp the distinction between the set of zoning constraints which are theoretically possible and the set of constraints which will be selected under our model of political action, let us assume that the city planner is a wise and beneficent dictator who has the authority to impose zoning ordinances without regard for the democratic process. How then would this wise and beneficent planner go about his task?

It would be necessary, of course, that the planner identify causes of external diseconomies. This is no simple task since the relevant external diseconomies seem to be caused by taste agreements among certain subsets of persons who happen to dominate the market for specific types of property. The planner must determine when these taste agreements are so significant as to cause an external diseconomy. Perhaps some examples will make this point clear. Consider first an exclusive, single-family, residential district. The planner might observe that the "representative purchaser" in the market for this particular type of residence preferred the quiet and the green open spaces associated with relatively large lawns and yards. Less expensive residences with smaller lots and yards would create an external diseconomy here since a person's enjoyment of his residence also has as a source the neighborhood. Similarly, apartment houses and businesses are considered not desirable in exclusive residential districts. This list could, of course, be extended but this does not seem necessary here. The main point is that the planner would have to classify various types of property and determine what property features might impose external diseconomies upon each type.

Having determined those property features which impose externalities upon each classification of property, the planner then has to decide district boundary lines for each classification. This task is somewhat simplified by observing what exists. The planner would then write the ordinance forbidding or "segregating out" those properties and property features which might impose external diseconomies upon the property in each classification. Supposedly, since this "segregation process" would be aimed only at the elimination of external diseconomies, this beneficent planner would set up a "base" district(s) of exclusive, single-family residences. This base district would have the most stringent restrictions in the form of minimum yard and lot requirements, allowable uses and maximum building heights, etc. The remaining residential districts and the various business districts could be ordered as minimum yard and lot sizes decreased, maximum building heights increased, and allowable uses increased.

It is easily seen that this beneficent planner would face a difficult task which would be complicated by dynamic considerations of transition. However, aside from these dynamic complications, he would never be able to eliminate altogether the probability of occurrence of external diseconomies due to the fact that specific district boundary lines cannot exclude completely those effects which might happen "near" the line. Yet, one might suspect that this beneficent planner would be able to reduce the probable occurrence of external diseconomies, and that, insofar as he was able to accomplish this reduction, persons might enjoy increased "security" and the urban property market would be moved "toward" Pareto Optimality. In fact, this simple segregation method alone cannot be said to accomplish this feat. The reason is that for certain uses "internal" profit considerations may be such that compensation theoretically could be paid for those external diseconomies which might be created. For example, it might be theoretically possible for a gasoline service station to locate in an exclusive residential district, pay compensation to those who suffer losses from the external diseconomies, and still make a profit.

On the other hand, if compensation were allowed or required, then this wise and beneficent planner might be able to make some appropriate adjustments in the rules although he would face difficult information problems since individuals affected by the external diseconomies might stand to gain by overstating their preferences. Yet, even without compensation, the zoning constraints which a truly wise and beneficent dictator would impose under the simple segregation method might be considered desirable since the probability of the occurrence of external diseconomies could be reduced.

Crucial Assumptions of the Political Model

Under modern zoning methods, either the planner or citizens may make proposals concerning a zoning ordinance. However, only the legislative body—the city council—has decision-making power. Legislative bodies, of course, consist of men who must make judgements based on practical politics in order to remain in power. Thus our present concern is to construct a model which might show how these matters of practical politics can alter the decisions from those which a wise and beneficent dictator might make.

Since political processes are complex and confusing, it is necessary that simplifying assumptions be made. Therefore, let us assume that every individual is able to perceive what is in his own self-interest and what is not and that he favors not those policies which might be considered "good" for the social entity but those policies which are in his own self-interest. Second, it is assumed that politicians act so as to be elected or re-elected; that is to say, they act so as to "maximize" the number of votes they can obtain in any election by "giving the people what they want." Finally, it is assumed that all councilmen are elected by the vote of all qualified voters in the city. This last assumption is made in order to avoid complicatory questions of legislative majorities under district representation. All these assumptions taken together mean that we may limit our attention to those policies which will be favored by simple majorities of the voters.

A Look at the Parts

Suppose that the zoning ordinance of some given metropolis is undergoing revision, that the planner has submitted his proposal to the city council, and that the politicians are contemplating changes and alterations which might please the body politic. In order to avoid complications it is assumed that some ordinance will be adopted and that the only question is what restrictions are to be imposed. The method of analysis will be to examine first given individual districts under differing conditions in an effort to determine the type of restrictions which a simple majority in the district would prefer. It will then be argued that the fact that the politician tries to maximize votes in the entire municipality instead of the individual districts does not change the results of the analysis.

As the first case, let us suppose that an entrepreneur is proposing a new subdivision at the time of the zoning revision. Assume that the subdivision is large enough to constitute a district. Now note that, if he is constrained to follow the simple segregation principle, profit maximization implies that he subdivide in such a manner that no external diseconomies are created. He would, of course, desire that the regulations fit his particular situation and, if there were no problems of external diseconomies extending across his boundary lines, the wise politician would be willing to grant the entrepreneur's wishes in order to obtain his vote and support. On the other hand, if the general zoning regulations allowed him also to obtain initial variances for the construction of those properties which might create external diseconomies but whose "internal" considerations made it still profitable, then his overall profit position might be improved by this departure from the simple segregation principle. This case may seem to be un-

interesting but it will turn out to be very important for policy purposes.

As a second case, consider a partially developed district. Suppose that the developer has constructed and sold residences on, say, one half the available land in the district. For the purpose of segregating out an entirely different problem let us make the unrealistic assumption that the boundary line cannot be changed. Now both the entrepreneur, who is assumed to own the undeveloped half, and the residents, who own and reside in the developed half, will wish to prohibit those property features and uses which might create external diseconomies. However, the resident property owners, as opposed to the developer, will desire to go one step further. If they are able to have the area "up-graded" or "over-zoned" (to get restrictions stricter than those which their property could meet) then any remaining construction in the area will have to be of a "higher" quality—more expensive, larger yards, etc. Since the value of any residential property depends upon the neighborhood in which it is located, then this higher quality construction will create external economies for the resident property owners and the value of their property will increase. There are several limiting factors here. The developer might refuse either to sell or allow further construction if he thought the ordinance might change in the future although the taste for the quiet of a semi-developed area on the part of the residents might make this alternative improbable. On the other hand, if no "favorable" change in the ordinance is foreseen, then the best that the developer can do is to continue construction or sell lots, since site values will bear the full effect of the ordinance-created external diseconomies.

In the above situation the wise politician, desiring to gain the support of as many voters as possible, would tend to favor the resident property owners, with the result that the area might be "over-zoned."[1] Note that the

[1] It should be noted that the term "over-zoning" has a different meaning here from that which it usually has in the planning literature. The planner often uses the term to refer to a situation where "too much" land has been placed in some particular category.

results of the above examples are not limited to the case of a subdivision. Assuming no renters to complicate the problem, "over-zoning" may occur in any type district if the number of resident property owners who consider their property as "developed" (meaning that they do not intend to invest in the development of alternative property in the given area at the time) outnumber those who do intend to develop additional property in the area if the politicians act so as to maximize votes and if the resident property owners do not choose to forego the possibility of a capital gain. The opposite does not hold true. If the developers outnumber the "statics," and if a change in the nature of the district—say, from residential to business—is not anticipated, then it can be expected that the area will be zoned "properly." Neither external economies nor diseconomies will be created.

Let us examine the more complicated case where renters are present. In order to avoid unnecessary complications, it is assumed that rents and values adjust "instantaneously" to externalities. Consider the subdivision example. Suppose that the developer has constructed and sold multifamily dwellings on lots comprising half the area of the district. Assume that the owners reside in the residences and have rented the several remaining apartments in each building to other families. Once again, both the resident property owners and the developer will desire to prohibit those uses and features which might create external diseconomies. Also once again, the resident owners will desire to have the area "over-zoned." The crucial element here is the renters. Supposedly, the renters know that, if the area is "under-zoned," uses and features which create external diseconomies may be constructed and rents may fall. On the other hand, if the area is "over-zoned" then their neighborhood may become nicer but rents may rise. Finally, if the area is "correctly" zoned, then the present situation will continue.

In order to determine which set of restrictions the renters will favor, it is necessary to examine the alternatives which they faced when deciding to choose apartments in this particular area. Supposedly, the renters

might have chosen apartments in a less attractive neighborhood at a lower rent or they might have chosen apartments in a more attractive neighborhood at a higher rent. However, these particular apartments in this particular area were chosen at given level of rents. There is no reason to suspect a change of tastes. The renters must be assumed to favor the "correct" zoning restrictions. Since in this example the renters plus the developer outnumber the resident property owners, the wise politician would favor the "correct" restrictions and the area would be properly zoned.

Once again this result can be extended. As long as the renters plus the developers outnumber those property owners who anticipate making no additional investment in property in the area, one can expect the "correct" restrictions to be imposed. If the situation is reversed, of course, then "over-zoning" can be expected to occur.

One word of caution is warranted here. It may be that in the real world residential renters are "transitory," meaning that they seldom expect to remain in the same location for a very long period of time. If, for example, they hold a lease which specifies the rent for the expected period of stay, they may be completely apathetic, not caring what restrictions are adopted. In such a case they would simply be left out of the counting process.[2]

Fortunately or unfortunately, the choice of zoning restrictions is not a "once and for all" phenomenon. Metropolitan growth and expansion imply that areas once suitable for one type of use may, granted the passage of time, become more suitable for other types of uses. This possibility means, of course, that the zoning ordinance may need to be changed. Accordingly, let us now examine the political problem of district transition.

Assume a single-family residential district near the center of the city. Suppose that at some time in the past when the ordinance was enacted, single-family residences were the most productive uses for the area. Assume

[2] Of course, even if renters are not transitory, the possibility that rents would not adjust instantaneously could alter our conclusions.

that the residences are still owner-occupied. However, let us suppose that a portion of the property owners have decided that, granted the time which has lapsed, the most productive use of their land is business; that is to say, a portion of property owners desire to demolish their residences and construct department stores, grocery stores, etc. These property owners will desire a change in the ordinance. However, the desired uses may create external diseconomies for those property owners who still consider the most productive use to be residential housing. A conflict of interest arises and there are two possibilities which might result.

First, if all the property owners who desire to re-zone are located in one area, then a new district might be created for that area and the remainder of the old district remain residential. This result is sometimes accomplished in the case of shopping centers. Second, if the property owners who desire to re-zone are scattered over the district, then the result depends upon which group is in the numerical majority. Since the wise politician is assumed to maximize votes by doing what the majority prefers, then if we depart slightly from one original assumption and business investments have really become the most productive for the area but a majority of the residents do not realize this fact, investment will be delayed until a majority becomes aware of this possibility. This assumes, of course, that variances are not granted.

Do renters make any difference in the transition case? Assume a situation similar to the previous example except that the residences are apartment buildings, and suppose that all property owners have decided that the most productive uses are no longer apartment houses but business uses. Thus property owners desire that the area be re-zoned from residential to business in order that apartment buildings may be demolished and business structures erected.

If the renters are not apathetic, their attitudes can be crucial. It must be assumed, of course, that given their incomes they have chosen the "type" of structures and "type" of neighborhood which they prefer. The most

extreme assumption which can be made is that equally desirable alternatives existed elsewhere for each individual at the time of his decision and that these alternatives still exist. However, granted the fact of having chosen to rent and having moved into the area and assuming no change in tastes, then the other alternatives can no longer be equally desirable since, if individuals are forced to rent elsewhere, they incur the expense of moving itself. Thus it would seem that if the renters outnumber the owners the district would not be re-zoned.

It might be argued that this conclusion is invalid since property owners can always evict their tenants. However, unless property owners agree to act as monopolists and evict their tenants either by direct action, by collusively raising the level of rents above the competitive rates, or by agreeing purposely to allow their property to deteriorate, individual profit maximization, granted the zoning restrictions, might require that none of the above take place with the result that tenants might remain "happy." It should be noted, however, that this situation gives rise to incentive for some individual to purchase all the property in the district so that tenants can be evicted and the area re-zoned.

Almost all of the above discussion assumed that district boundary lines were given and fixed. Of course, this is never the case. Whenever in any given district a group favors a set of restrictions not desired by the remainder of the individuals having "interests" in the area, then, if the members of this group are located in geographical proximity to each other, the possibilities exist that, if the sub-area in which this group is located is of a sufficient size and if the group is in a numerical majority in the sub-area, a special district may be created; or that, if the group is located near a boundary line of the given district, the boundary line simply may be changed. In either instance, granted the boundary line adjustments which a wise politician would make, the previous discussion still applies.

One important problem remains. It was earlier noted that the strict application of the segregation principle might result in the exclusion of uses which, although they might create external diseconomies upon other uses in the area, might be so profitable that, if it were possible to pay compensation, location in the area might still be warranted. However, in the absence of a mechanism with which the change in market values of the adjoining properties could be measured and in the lack of any type of compensation scheme, both property owners and renters would favor keeping such a use out of the district since the ordinance itself applies uniformly to all uses and the enactment of a zoning change for one use would allow other such uses to enter the area. The only possibility would be a variance which, under present rules, does not allow compensation.

The Total View

The "methodology" up to this point has been that of examining a single district and, assuming that the politician was considering only the given district, trying to determine whether or not a majority of self-seeking and non-apathetic persons would favor restrictions which would eliminate external diseconomies. Although this procedure may be appropriate for "minor" ordinance revisions, it might be suggested that for "major" revisions where the politician simultaneously must consider many districts or even the entire municipality the previous results do not hold. It will be argued here that, aside from adjustments that might be necessary because of multiple counting of property owners and others, the results of the previous analysis do apply.

Two arguments seem worthy of our examination. First, it might be suggested that "over-zoning" could cause investment which might have gone to develop sites within the city to be used to develop sites outside the jurisdiction of the municipality. Thus it might be held that the city, whose major source of revenue is the property tax, would be faced with a loss of revenue which it otherwise could have gained, that such an event would result in taxpayers having to bear a "greater burden," and that recognition of this fact would tend to mitigate the demands for "over-zoning."

Several points are relevant here. First, since returns from "over-zoning" are direct

and any possible burden would be indirect, one might suspect that individuals would tend to weigh direct returns more heavily. Second, insofar as expenditures are related to density as opposed to simple area, then a burden need not be created. Finally, and this is the important point, "over-zoning" need not discourage investment since, if owners of empty lots desire to see their property developed at all, site values will fall by an amount sufficient to compensate for at least a part of the ordinance-created externality.

Another argument why the previous political model might not be applicable to the case of a major zoning revision is that external diseconomies imposed upon properties in one area might not be neutral in their indirect effects upon property in other areas. If this were true, then it might be argued that, granted "adequate" zoning protection for his own property, any self-interest motivated property owner would favor either "under-zoning" or "no-zoning" for the remainder of the metropolitan area. Thus it might be stated that the direct result of our assumptions would be a zoning ordinance which left forty-nine percent of the property owners unprotected.

Fortunately, the above argument does not follow from the assumptions of the analysis. Assume any rental property which is "adequately" protected. The individuals who rent this property will desire to see all other areas zoned since any indirect external effects which caused a rise in the capital value of the protected property would also carry the implication of increased rents. Thus, as long as there are a significant number of renters, no wise politician would favor a policy which would result in zoning a part but not the whole. The previous analysis holds.

Rational Enactment

The previous analysis has suggested that zoning restrictions adopted through the democratic process need not be of an "ideal" type under which external diseconomies are simply eliminated. The possibility exists that an area may be "over-zoned" or that the ordinance may prevent transition. Thus the question arises as to whether or not it is "rational" for a metropolis to adopt a zoning ordinance at all. Let us briefly consider this question.

For any given metropolitan area individuals will know that the situation will not remain static, that the locational pattern will change, but the future development pattern will be unknown. Persons may have, of course, some expectations about future developments, but uncertainty will exist. Granted this situation, each individual, who is assumed to possess relevant knowledge, will compare the zoning with the non-zoning situation in an effort to determine expected gains or losses from the introduction of the ordinance.

Let us examine first the non-zoning situation. Any individual property owner will consider the following: First, he may gain in the municipal growth process either through development or re-development of his property, but, unlike the situation with zoning, he is always assured of being able to develop or redevelop in the manner which he considers most profitable. Second, if an external diseconomy is forced upon his competitors but not his own property, the result might be some gain in the form of an indirect pecuniary external economy. Third, an external diseconomy may be imposed upon his property with the result of a capital loss.

For the renter the non-zoning situation implies the following: First, if an external diseconomy is forced upon properties other than the one in which he is located, the result can possibly be a rise in his rent. Second, if an external diseconomy is forced upon the property in which he is located, he might or might not lose since the level of rents on property affected by the external diseconomy eventually must fall to a level where the "representative" renter is indifferent between that property and some alternative, but he could expect to be identical with the representative renter only by coincidence.

Let us now examine the situation with zoning. First, any property owner will know

that he can gain from the development or re-development of his property but with zoning he is not assured of being able to do so in the manner which he might consider the most profitable. Second, if he owns property which is already developed, he may gain from "over-zoning." Third, if he owns property which is undeveloped, he may lose from "over-zoning."

For the renter the zoning situation carries the following implications: First, if he happened to be located in a structure in a "semi-developed" area, he could conceivably lose since, if over-zoning occurred, the level of rents might rise. However, in all probability this possibility will be judged as unimportant since rental structures are usually grouped together and not interspersed with owner-occupied structures. Thus the renter might expect that the combination of renters and owners of undeveloped property would "out vote" the owners of developed property. Second, the renter might stand to gain in the transition case by so zoning that redevelopment is not allowed.

Persons are assumed to favor zoning if they stand to gain from the enactment of the ordinance. Examination of the above list suggests that renters would stand to gain and thus would favor zoning. Those property owners who would favor zoning since they might stand to gain but never to lose would be: (1) those who consider their property fully developed, and (2) those who consider the possibility of a loss from the imposition of an external diseconomy upon their property greater than the possibility of a gain in the form of an indirect pecuniary external economy caused by external diseconomies being forced upon others. Three groups of property owners might favor no zoning. These are: (1) those whose expectations are the reverse of those in (2) above. However, this group will probably be unimportant since losses are direct and gains indirect, and since it can be shown that aggregate losses are almost always greater than aggregate gains. Group (2) is composed of those property owners who feel that they might be prevented from developing their property in the manner which they consider most profitable and group (3) is composed of owners of undeveloped sites who feel that they might lose from "over-zoning."

If this breakdown of the body politic is relevant, it seems reasonable to suppose that those who favor zoning will almost always outnumber those who oppose it in any metropolitan area. However, the existence of those who would oppose zoning or the assured lack of unanimity among the populace suggests that zoning cannot be said to move a municipality toward the Pareto Optimality frontier in urban property.

Conclusions and Proposals

Insofar as the previous analysis is relevant to the real world, it has suggested that the democratic process may not always impose those constraints which simply result in the elimination of external diseconomies in the pricing system in urban property. Instead, a democratic political process sometimes may impose regulations which result in over-zoning and non-transition. Yet it has been argued that a rational electorate will almost always choose an ordinance. Since few of us would recommend turning the enactment of zoning ordinances over to dictators, beneficent or otherwise—it seems important that ways be found to improve the institution. Since the analysis which has been used in this paper has not been checked against the "facts," the following specific proposals are speculative, suggestive, and provisional. They are not positive recommendations for immediate adoption.

Let us consider the expansion of the metropolis. Any metropolitan area generally expands through the process of subdivision. It has been noted that, if the subdivider-developer is constrained by the segregation principle, it will be in his interest to so subdivide and develop his property that external diseconomies are eliminated. On the other hand, if he is able to initially depart from the simple segregation principle, it may be possible for him to improve his profit position by constructing, as variances or nonconforming uses, those properties which are warranted by "internal" considerations even though they might reduce the value of adjacent lots. It is to be emphasized that, if the

subdivider-developer operates in a competitive market, his maximum profit position is also optimal for society if "boundary line" externalities are ignored. The creation of external diseconomies becomes a "danger" only after the developed properties have been sold to various individuals.

In view of the above, it is proposed that the subdivider be required to draw up the ordinance for his subdivision subject to some constraints for boundary line externalities and that no change in the zoning restrictions for that area be allowed for a period of, say, ten years. The subdivider must be required, of course, to inform each prospective buyer of the restrictions and any possible nonconforming uses which he plans.

There are several arguments in favor of this method of initially adopting zoning restrictions. First, if the subdivider made a mistake in judging what constituted an external diseconomy, he would harm only himself since any prospective purchaser would know what the restrictions and plans for development were before buying and would be able to discount any allowable external diseconomies in deciding what he would be willing to pay for the property. Second, the danger of "over-zoning" would not immediately exist if the development of the subdivision were completed within the specified number of years.

In districts that are already zoned, the possibility exists that, if it were possible to measure objectively the effects of external diseconomies upon capital values and if a use were required to compensate for losses it imposed upon others, "internal" factors of cost and demand might still warrant locating in the area even though the strict application of the segregation principle would have forbidden it. The following is a brief outline of an attempt to construct a workable compensation scheme.

Suppose that the board of appeals were stripped of its power to grant use variances. Then suppose that the individual who desired such a variance was required to make detailed plans and was required to hold to these plans if a variance was granted. The variance could be granted only by a direct vote of property owners within the district. The rule for granting the variance might be, say, the unanimous consent of adjoining property owners and the consent of ninety percent of the remaining property owners in the area. Bribes would be legal, and compensation would be paid via bribes in order to obtain the vote of the required property owners.

This scheme is not, of course, perfect. It introduces a game element into the process of trying to obtain variances. It also overlooks possible effects upon renters. Its only virtue is that it does attempt to provide some sort of an approximation to a measure of the effects of external diseconomies and it does require compensation. Neither of these two proposals are concerned with the two problems, transition and "over-zoning," which might occur in the already "developed" portion of the metropolis. Accordingly, let us discuss briefly these two problems.

Once an area is partially developed, either through "original" development or re-development, in the absence of "over-zoning" which will push "empty" site values down to a point where the effect of external diseconomies is at least partially offset, uses upon which existing property in the area create external diseconomies will have extra incentive to stay away. Thus it seems unlikely that an area should ever be zoned "upward" within its own class unless urban renewal or complete re-development is to take place. Except for these events, it might be considered desirable to prohibit "up-grading" within given classes of property (residential, etc.). Property owners would have the choice of "down-grading" or changing classes, and the urban growth process can make the most profitable uses change in either of these two directions.

It was earlier suggested that one "danger" in transition is that renters prevent rezoning. However, if the transition problem were divorced from the usual political process, this danger might not exist. Thus it is proposed that for the purpose of transition only the question be decided by a vote of the property owners in the district.

It should be emphasized again that these proposals are tentative. They are not intended to be a panacea. Not only were they based on an untested model, but even considering only the model the proposals are incomplete. The problem of restrictions upon properties which may impose external diseconomies upon properties in other districts, for example, was not discussed here.

I AM SURE that every planner who has worked with a zoning commission or a city council has been asked one question—and he has probably had the question posed him in every city in which he has worked.

The question is: what percentage of the city's area should be zoned for industry?

I believe we should try to answer this question once and for all, with an answer that applies to all cities. The answer is simply that there is *no* definite percentage of the area of any city which *should* be zoned for industry. In short, I look with suspicion on any statement to the effect that "5 per cent" or "10 per cent" or any other percentage of the city "*should* be in industrial zones." I advise you to do likewise.

Rather than have you take this as a flat statement made on the basis of some unidentified scriptural revelation, I should like to describe the considerations which properly go into the process of designating the industrial districts in a city. Then I shall point out a few of the important problems that turn up in zoning for industry.

I would sort the factors determining the amount of industrial zoning into three groups. The first of these is *the suitability of the city itself for industry.*

It may seem elementary to say that some cities are more attractive to industry than other cities. But it is something that is easily overlooked by enthusiastic chambers of commerce and civic booster clubs. In the extreme cases it can lead to absurdity, such as the little western "cow town" that sets aside a thousand acres to permit the construction of an integrated steel mill—with not enough water in the area to wet down a postage stamp.

There is no way of measuring it, but I am sure that if you added all the land zoned for industry in little "cow towns," in depressed mining communities, in rural crossroad villages, in north woods communities—if you added all this land together, you'd have enough industrial land to take care of the national industrial growth for the next fifty years.

There are many factors that decrease the suitability of a community for industry, and consequently affect the amount of land in the community that should be set aside for

6

Zoning and the Industrial Developer

Dennis O'Harrow

This article originally appeared in Zoning Digest, Vol. 12, No. 12, Dec. 1960, pp. 393–399, published by the American Society of Planning Officials, 1313 East 60th Street, Chicago, Illinois 60637. Reproduced by permission. © 1960 by the American Society of Planning Officials.

industry. Some of these are obvious: shortage of water, shortage of labor, poor location in relation to markets, and poor transportation facilities.

Other factors are less directly connected with the industrial operation, but are still quite important. You might call these the "why-we-didn't-go-to" factors. I am sure you have seen at least one of the stories that has appeared during the past few years, in which an industrialist tells a town why his company picked another town, rather than theirs, as the site for a new plant. The reasons "why-we-didn't-go-to" your town include such things as bad housing, no decent hotels or restaurants, poor government, run-down schools, no airport, dilapidated churches, bad streets, even too-low taxes. If a city has enough of these "why-we-didn't-go-to" factors, it has no need for extensive industrial zoning.

I hope you understand that I am not trying to instruct cities as to what they should do to make themselves attractive to industry. I am trying to outline the considerations in arriving at the proper amount of land to be reserved for industrial use. The community that has two-and-a-half strikes against it obviously requires a smaller proportion of industrial land than you will find in Pittsburgh or Chicago or Detroit. I will admit, however, that the two-and-a-half strike towns often are not aware of these factors.

The second consideration is simply *the amount of land in the city that is suitable for industry.* In most cities this is probably the principal determinant of the amount of land zoned for industry. Most cities have, or can expect to have, sufficient water, enough labor for their size, good transportation, access to an adequate market, reasonably good government, hotels, restaurants, airports, schools, churches, housing—and usually no reason to complain that taxes are too low!

The criteria by which you judge whether or not land is suitable for industry are fairly clear and straightforward. To list some of them:

The topography should be reasonably flat.

The district should be fairly large, and the ownership in large parcels.

The district should be free from development of any kind at present, especially of residential development. (This, of course, does not apply to a site that is slated for demolition and redevelopment.)

There should be immediate access to a major throughfare, preferably to an expressway.

For heavier industries, there should be access to a railroad; and for certain special industries, access to a navigable waterway.

Electricity, gas, water, and sewers should be available at the site.

You can rapidly check a city for these factors. This gives you a starting point. But it is not necessarily true that every acre of land meeting these standards is suitable for industry. There are some other factors that are less definable—but probably more important. For want of a better term I will call these "community relationship." The relationship I refer to is a physical space relation to other tracts of land within the community used for other purposes—or even to other industrial areas within the community. I can illustrate this most easily with examples.

By all the criteria I listed, there are two first-rate industrial sites that no one would touch with a ten-foot pole. One is Central Park in New York. The other is Chicago's lakefront parks: Lincoln, Grant, and Jackson. Aside from the political impossibility of industrializing these areas, it is obvious to anyone that these open spaces are necessary to the health and life of the two cities.

It is clear that industrial development on the highest standards we could imagine, placed in these parks, would be disastrously injurious to adjacent residential development.

I must admit that the relation of proposed industrial districts to the remainder of the community and to the surrounding nonindustrial areas is not always as apparent and unambiguous as it is with Central Park and the Chicago lakefront parks. This is what leads frequently to discussions—sometimes to acrid and bloody disputes.

It is just about impossible to give any rules for community relationship. We can say that industry generates auto and truck traffic under even the best conditions; therefore, an industrial tract must be located so that none of the traffic is forced through a residential district. Until all industries are completely smokeless, dirtless, and odorless, those emitting smoke, dirt, and odor should be located down-wind from nonindustrial areas. Until rail switching is silent, it should be isolated beyond earshot of residences. This doesn't give the entire story on community relationship, but I think these examples give the general idea.

The third consideration in determining the amount of industrial land is simply *how much industrial development the city wants to have.* This is easy to understand when a city states that it wants all the industry it can possibly get. But it is not so clear to the industrial developer when the city states that it wants only a limited amount of industry, or that it has all the industry it wants, or particularly, when the city has no industry and states quite positively that it wants none.

I have no intention of lining up selling points for a city's having more industry, or, for that matter, any industry. In the first place there are few municipal legislatures that are not fully aware of industry's boost to the tax base.

In the second place, a graphic personal

example shows the danger of making sweeping statements about the value of industry on the tax rolls. The children from my own village of 4,500 population and the children in an adjacent village of about 12,000 population attended high school in two other neighboring cities, each with about 25,000 population. In both cities there is a great deal of heavy industrial development, including such plants as the Buda diesel engine factory and a $30 million Ford stamping plant. Both my village and the neighboring village are without industry and have only a token amount of commercial development.

We and our neighboring village wanted our own high school. The two present high schools were fast getting overcrowded; and our children were forced to travel long distances on buses. But we were told we were being foolish. We couldn't possibly support a high school—we had no industrial tax base, and we were purely residential.

Experts were called in from the University of Illinois to study the situation. They came up with the astounding finding that whereas one industrial city had a tax base of $50,000 per pupil and the other had a tax base of $58,000 per pupil, our two residential villages, without a stick of industry between them, had a tax base of $68,000 per pupil!

So you can see why I am careful about making general statements on the value of industry as a tax base.

The third reason why I do not offer reasons to persuade a municipality to zone for industry, even where it might be shown that industrialization is good for financial health, is that I am quite sure the tax support of local undertakings—and particularly of schools—will sooner or later be broadened.

* * *

Again, the most cursory study of the financial problem of metropolitan areas shows that the only solution is a broadening of the tax base to metropolitan financing. A good prototype is Toronto.

Finally, I come to the most important of all reasons for allowing municipalities to set limits—which may be zero—to their industrial zoning. This is that I believe in the democratic right of self-determination. I believe that the citizens of every municipality

have the right—and duty—to plot their own future.

I recognize that even if everyone were to accept my premise that a city has an inalienable right to determine the limits of its own industrialization, there are still points of discussion. Is the decision truly representative of the desires of the citizens? Are the citizens accurately informed of the meaning of their decision? Are the citizens familiar with the difference between modern industry or modern zoning control and the old industrial filth and ineffective zoning ordinances? Is the determination consistent with the welfare of the metropolitan area as a whole?

But if these questions can all be answered in the affirmative, I believe that no one has a right to upset the decision of the citizens through the use of legal technicalities.

I have mentioned the three general considerations that determine the industrial pattern of a city's land use: the suitability of the city itself for industrial development; the suitability of individual sections for industrial use; and the desires of the citizens for industrialization. In addition to these considerations, there are several problems connected with zoning for industry that do not classify easily.

There is the problem of time—a dimension that is particularly difficult to handle through a zoning ordinance.

For example, an industrial district should embrace a large tract of land. In most cities this has come to mean that it will be at the edge of the city or even beyond the city under county or suburban village control.

An industrial district must be kept clear and free of nonindustrial development. Complete prohibition of all use except industry renders the land valueless for any other use. If sale for industrial use doesn't take place pretty quickly, we may be charged with taking property without due process of law.

We try to ease the pain by permitting agriculture. This may work for a while, but even the most patient farmer gets restless when the shopping center promoter or the mass-production house builder starts waving money under his nose, after you have told him he'll have to wait for General Motors or

General Electric or General Dynamics. The plain truth is that when we zone for industry much more than five years in advance of development, there must be some special factors involved in the tract which assure us that we can hold it in an industrial zone. These would be such things as ownership by a corporation that wants it as a future plant site, or the obvious *unsuitability* of the land for anything except industry—such as the situation that exists around Lake Calumet in Chicago.

How do we handle this problem? What good is our land use planning if we can't carry it out? Why go to all the trouble of spotting future industrial sites if we cannot be sure that they are saved?

We always hope that the land use plan is carried out as we have indicated that it should be. In more cases than not, it will be carried out as we planned—if we planned well.

As for handling the problem, our best method is to zone the area for agriculture until the time is ripe for changing the zone without running afoul of due process. I am assuming, of course, that all the land we are interested in is under zoning control, a condition that I believe will soon be true of practically all land that *is* suitable for industrial development.

In spite of what we planners might wish to do, there will still be much zoning done by the free market. Land development today is in the hands of large developers using large hunks of land: home builders, department stores and retailing promoters, industrial developers—all with plenty of capital and big ideas. They are all competing for suitable land, and frequently the one that gets there first with the most is the one who gets the land—and calls the shot on the zoning. Occasionally, there is a fourth type of big developer competing. This is government itself.

In spite of all that I have said about a rational method of selecting industrial land, the bitter fact remains that a great deal of land is suitable for any one of a number of uses. I am sure that this does not come as news to most of you, nor is it news that you must compete in the free market for land.

This illustrates an aspect of the problem of time in zoning. If we were able to do a perfect job of allocating land to the various uses, it would be most regrettable to see our perfect planning subjected to these forces. But we readily admit that we cannot make a perfect distribution, nor that we can accurately foresee all of the changes in urban development that call for changes in the land use pattern. We are forced, therefore, to recognize that the free market must determine to some extent both the development pattern and the zoning. I do not mean that we should leave our land use planning and our zoning classification up to the developer with the greatest amount of money or the greatest power of persuasion. While I believe that, in many instances, land use can be determined by the free market, I also believe that we have, in many other instances, produced conditions that are most unhappy, errors that will take a long time to correct—if we *can* ever really correct them.

The free market is filling every crack and cranny, every nook and crevice, with one kind or the other of its developments. There is no space for relief, no place to breathe. The diffident fourth party in the free market, the people acting through their government, has been crowded out or has permitted itself to be crowded out.

Do we ever hear of *new* park and urban forest development on the scale of Lakewood, or Levittown, or Park Forest? Or on the scale of the Fairless works, or Appliance Park, or the Kaiser Aluminum plant at Ravenswood? Or on the scale of Northland, or Southgate, or Old Orchard?

The answer is, of course, no!

I believe that over the next ten to twenty years we shall have an increase in the strength of land use controls. I believe that cities are going to be reaching out farther and farther to control undeveloped areas, and that they will be controlling these areas with a firmer hand. They will be buying a great deal more land to retain for public open spaces. Much of this land that they buy, the industrial developer will think of as good industrial land—but it will be just as *verboten* as Central Park. As the years go on, I believe that there will be increasing difficulties in changing the land use plan, once it has been established.

It seems to me that the wise course for the industrial developer is to recognize this fact and to adjust to it—to work with the city and to offer his honest advice on the problems of industrial zoning.

7

The Economic Consequences of Industrial Zoning

William M. Shenkel

This article appeared originally in Land Economics, Vol. 40, No. 3, pp. 255–266, © 1964, *by the Regents of the University of Wisconsin. Reprinted by permission.*

TODAY, SPACE for industry is one of our principal urban problems. Colin Clark believes the most serious question facing America in the next twenty years will be "that of *location*, the distribution of industry and population between regions in the United States, and the apportionment of land for industry, housing, shopping centers and open space in the metropolitan area."[1] Indeed the shortage of suitable land zoned for industry is partly responsible for the migration of industry from urban centers. The importance of providing space for industry and the central role of industry in local communities is demonstrated by the various development commissions established in all states. Clearly providing suitable space for industry plays an important part in increasing the rate of industrial growth.

Yet despite the general importance of new industry—and its location—industrial zoning that affects locational decisions is often based on outmoded concepts—in most instances concepts that are founded on colonial nuisance controls. The needs of industry and the interests of the community are therefore in conflict with industrial zoning practices. This paper deals with several aspects of this conflict. First, to show the economic effects

of industrial zoning practices, which are usually quite archaic, the economic justification for zoning is reviewed. Secondly, objectives of zoning and their application to industrial land are given. Thirdly, preferred objectives of industrial zoning are then compared to current, mostly obsolete, industrial zoning practices. Finally, the economic consequences of misdirected zoning ordinances are suggested. The conclusion includes a discussion of industrial zoning measures that might better serve the community and claimed zoning objectives.

Urban land may be viewed as an economic resource that is relatively fixed, durable and, more significantly, relatively scarce. And because land also has utility, it has an economic value. The utility of urban land arises from its capacity to earn a return over costs. In the larger sense the concept includes public land since opportunity costs of publicly-owned land are evidence of economic value though the land is not devoted to private production.

To gain the maximum return (or satisfaction), land resources must be allocated rationally among the more urgent uses. To the economist, zoning is a device encouraging the distribution of land among those uses public, residential, commercial and industrial that result in maximum satisfaction, given the goals of the community.

Such a view goes beyond the popular view of planning. For instance, F. Stuart Chapin, Jr., states ". . . for land use planning purposes it would appear that the economics of use location can be given *crude recognition* by reference to the broad pattern of land values and trends of change in this pattern."[2] But if zoning is to serve the community, more than a cavalier treatment of urban land economics is needed. For many of the land use problems associated with industry, traffic congestion, depressed industrial areas, poorly maintained buildings, neighborhood obsolescence and the like have resulted from the "crude recognition" of the economics of industrial land use.

A controversy arises, however, over the conflict between zoning and the master plan. It is generally accepted that zoning is one of

[1] *Problems of United States Economic Development*, Vol. 1, New York, 1958, p. 289.

[2] F. Stuart Chapin Jr., *Urban Land Use Planning*, New York, 1957, p. 18.

the devices by which city plans may be carried out. The failure to coordinate the zoning ordinance with the master plan has produced three effects. It is contended that unplanned zoning (1) freezes development, (2) produces undesirable zoning, and (3) changes arbitrarily through ordinance amendments so that no comprehensive land use plan can be recognized. The record shows that the absence of community planning may soon be remedied. The latest study published by the International City Managers' Association showed that 645 cities of 1,227 cities recently surveyed used comprehensive plans. Another 406 cities were preparing master plans at the end of 1961.

Consequently the more universal adoption of planning may be expected to correct industrial zoning practices developed from nuisance laws. But as zoning is made subordinate to planning, as suggested, the economic effects of zoning would seem to deserve additional emphasis. In sum, planning is more than a means to create a satisfactory social life, it is a means to advance the economic and social goals of the community. Zoning can be used to serve economic objectives so that the limited supply of urban land is rationed among the most urgent uses. This concept also requires that each land use be given the optimum location leading to the maximum production of goods and services at the least cost.

If zoning is considered one means to implement the master plan, then we are vitally concerned with the efficiency with which zoning allocates scarce land resources among competing needs. And further, if zoning follows objectives of the master plan, zoning would appear adequate to accomplish the allocation function. Hence the effectiveness of zoning regulations may be measured by their contribution to the orderly development of the community as guided by the master plan.

The Demand for Industrial Land

The effect of zoning policies are understood more clearly by reviewing the characteristics of the demand for industrial space. It is then possible to identify requirements

that industrial zoning regulations must meet if industrial land uses are served. In the first place, industrial land is subject to a relatively low rate of utilization. Table 1 shows the projected demand for industrial land compared to the demand for other urban land uses in the San Francisco Bay area, 1960 to 2020.

Table 1—The estimated demand for urban land in the San Francisco Bay area: 1960–2020 (in square miles)

Property Type	1960	2020	Increase 1960–2020	Average Annual Increase
Total Urban	616	2,389	1,773	29.6
Residential and Commercial	518	2,079	1,561	26.0
Industrial	98	310	212	3.6

Source: Adapted from Office of Area Development, Business and Defense Services Administration, United States Department of Commerce. *Future Development of the San Francisco Bay Area, 1960-2020* (Washington, D.C.: Government Printing Office, 1959), pp. 63-71.

These data show an average increase in the demand for urban land of 29.6 square miles per year. The major part of urban land is required for residential and commercial purposes—26.0 square miles per year according to data of Table 1. But industrial uses account for only *3.6 square miles* annually. While it may be inappropriate to relate industrial land requirements with all other urban land requirements, these data seem consistent with other evidence. Even for industrial land uses that would be expected to show the highest rates of land absorption, observers have noted that investors in industrial land must be willing to hold vacant land over comparatively long periods. According to some investigators full utilization of an industrial park may take ten years or more.

The relatively low rate of utilization for industrial land places industry in an unfavorable bargaining position. The more intensive uses, residential and commercial, may absorb land that may have a higher comparative advantage for industrial purposes. Nonindustrial land uses that utilize a greater share of urban land will tend to use sites more appropriately reserved for industrial purposes. Later, it will be shown that industrial zoning weakens the bargaining power of industry compared to other businesses.

Yet another characteristic of industrial land use is worth mentioning: Purchasers of industrial land must acquire land for immediate and future needs. As industry expands, it is more economical (within limits) to enlarge an existing plant than to vacate an existing site. An expanding firm has the alternative of purchasing land beyond current needs or of buying the minimum space for immediate use and planning for later relocation. But under the typical zoning ordinance, industry, once sited, must compete for available land with commercial and sometimes residential uses. The result leads to a mixed, uneconomic allocation of land for either commercial or industrial purposes. Also price reservations among industrial landowners may increase to the point where relocation is the preferred alternative.

One other fact stands out in the case of industrial land users: they require a high level of municipal services. The relatively small firm is handicapped by the inability to invest in land improvements, *i.e.*, a water supply, a sewage disposal system, land grading, drainage and other utilities. For residential subdivisions, the necessary utilities may be readily supplied because the higher rate of land utilization decreases the cost of holding and risks associated with land development. Industrial zoning, therefore, that allows industrial land to be used for other uses contributes to the shortage of improved industrial sites. In addition, the utility services required by industry would seem to justify the allocation of sites that may be improved at the least expense. But in fact the zoning ordinance frequently relegates the land area with the lowest utility and the highest cost of development for industrial use.

And finally, industrial prospects require relatively low cost land. One reason accounting for the migration of plants to suburban areas is the cost of sites in areas of high population density. Because of the zoning

treatment of industrial land only the most intensive industries may compete successfully for centrally located space—in itself supporting the generalization that industry uses relatively low-cost land, *i.e.*, land that does not have a higher economic use.

If these characteristics of industrial land use prevail generally, it would seem that the zoning code would include regulations adapted to the unique demands of industrial land use. In the absence of other meaningful guides, the zoning code ideally would serve the following objectives: (1) to allocate industrial land according to anticipated industrial land needs; (2) to reserve industrial land for the exclusive use of industry and related businesses; (3) to reserve space for industries that use land extensively and for industries that generally lower the utility of surrounding land; (4) to provide areas for the development of prestige industrial districts (organized industrial districts); and (5) to conserve industrial real estate districts by regulating building bulk and height, building setbacks, parking and truck loading.

The first point constitutes recognition of the fact that industrial land is a limited resource. Under this assumption the problem facing the community is to reserve sufficient space of quality that seems most suitable for industrial purposes. In making the allocation, communities may be guided by the master plan, an expression of community goals. Then once the selection of land for industrial purposes is accomplished, it is most essential to reserve industrial land for only industrial and associated purposes. Flexibility may be provided by rezoning techniques presently used to change residential uses to commercial uses or other zoning revisions as provided by ordinance. But once land is zoned for industry, the community must be willing to enforce the exclusive use for industrial purposes.[3] Otherwise land zoned for industry may revert to commercial and other nonindustrial purposes if the second point is not observed in the zoning process.

The next two points are concerned with the sub-classification of industrial property. By segregating industrial uses on the basis of the

[3] Under this philosophy, zoning is viewed as an instrument to promote a rational land use plan.

intensity of use, many of the objections to industry may be removed. That is, by segregating the more extensive uses, *i.e.*, steel mills and the processing of bulk products to more isolated areas, the remaining industries may have a minor effect on the utility of surrounding areas. In this manner the utility of industrial space may be conserved even further. Furthermore, the final point suggests that reserving space for prestige industries is another way to classify industrial space demands. The industrial parks (or other special industrial districts in which landscaping controls, architectural controls, and structural coverage ratios meet the demands of the more discriminating industries) are a means to enhance the utility of industrial space and surrounding non-industrial space. The establishment of districts zoned for planned or organized industrial districts is further recognition of the need for quality industrial space. Performance standards that control the operation of industry are additional measures that conserve the utility of industrial space. The urgent need to revise industrial zones to meet actual industrial needs has been recognized in several leading sources.

If the goals of industrial zoning are accepted at least tentatively, it is then relevant to compare desired objectives with actual practice. For it is submitted that industrial zoning has developed, not from the analysis of the need for industrial space but from a desire to protect property owners from the assumed nuisances or dangers of industrial property. A re-examination of industrial zoning and its development shows how these early practices affect current zoning regulations.

The Development of Districts Zoned for Industry

Probably the first attempt to form industrial districts began with regulations banning gun powder mills and powder houses in residential districts. Such measures were common in colonial times. The early safety regulations against powder storage were broadened to control the location of wooden buildings, justified because of the fire hazard

of wooden buildings. A Wisconsin Act of 1889 authorized cities to designate zones for buildings and structures according to the fire risks involved.

Later, certain property uses were segregated from residential areas because of their nuisance classification. The laundry cases of San Francisco developed as a means of restricting the location of Chinese laundries in residential and in certain business districts. Such districting measures were defended because of fire hazards, poor drainage and the presumed moral hazards associated with Chinese laundries. Ordinances were subsequently enacted that restricted the location of dance halls, livery stables, slaughter houses, saloons, pool halls and other uses generally regarded as nuisances.

In 1916 Los Angeles enacted an ordinance that protected residential areas from commercial and industrial encroachment by establishing exclusive residential districts. Zoning at this time was merely a matter of protecting single family dwellings from the presumed nuisances of other urban land uses. Though districting tended to maximize the utility of residential space, it was not recognized that land must also be set aside for other urban, and equally necessary functions.

Comprehensive zoning, introduced by New York City in 1916 resulted in what has since been termed Euclidian zoning—zoning based on the establishment of use districts, building height and bulk controls and density regulations. The term comprehensive was used to describe the inclusion of other controls besides the establishment of districting. The comprehensive zoning of New York followed partly from the undesirable land use pattern documented by an investigation beginning in 1910. At the time it was claimed that the mixed commercial, residential and industrial uses developed because of inadequate land use (zoning) controls.

Thus zoning for industry started with the segregation of dangerous uses from residential areas. The principle was extended to include those uses not only dangerous but regarded as a nuisance to residential occupants. Until 1916 zoning was considered largely a means to protect residential property. The reforms introduced by the comprehensive zoning of 1916, though introducing intra-district regulations, did not change the philosophy of districting in favor of residential use. More recent zoning techniques have departed from the Euclidian concept by permitting districting flexibility.

Yet on analysis, zoning is still largely administered as a means of providing maximum protection to residential areas. It would seem that current industrial practices based on antiquated zoning regulations dating from colonial times violate objectives of the master plan. Some of the industrial zoning practices that appear inconsistent with (or directly opposed to) the master plan are covered next.

Industrial Zoning Practices

Of all zoning practices affecting industrial property, two practices stand out, selecting suitable industries on the basis of "prohibited" lists and making industrial districts progressively inclusive. The latter practice is illustrated by the typical ordinance that begins with single family dwellings—that district receiving preferred protection. Each district of the ordinance following usually permits all valid uses of the preceding district. Under this system typically, virtually all property uses permitted under the zoning ordinance are allowed in the final district—the industrial district. So then, residential districts are given *maximum* protection: industrial districts receive the *least* protection. The undesirable effects of the two issues warrant further discussion.

PROHIBITED INDUSTRIES

The zoning ordinance will usually state that land and buildings in the industrial districts may be used for any purpose *except* stated industries, the prohibited industries. Frequently the list of prohibited industries will end with the qualification that "any

further industry or use which creates corrosive, toxic or noisome fumes, gas, smoke, or odors, obnoxious dust or vapor, or offensive noise or vibration" is prohibited.

Prohibited lists are subject to three criticisms: They are obsolete; they are incomplete and they are misdirected. The obsolescence follows from the list of industries that are presumed to lower the utility of surrounding land. Technical advances in manufacturing, the preference for one story construction, modern industrial architecture and a tendency to increase the ratio of land to total floor area make prohibited lists, often copied from 1920 or 1930 ordinances, markedly out of date.

Prohibited lists are incomplete in the sense that the 77 pages of manufacturing industries listed in the *Standard Industrial Classification Manual*, any of which might conceivably lower site utility of surrounding land, cannot be incorporated into local zoning ordinances. In addition, many of the manufacturing industries not included in lists of prohibited industries may also be operated so as to lower the utility of surrounding land. An industry that uses public streets for loading and employee parking or permits outside storage of rubbish would fit in this category. It is virtually impossible to "protect" surrounding properties by limited lists of industries presumed offensive.

But the misdirection of prohibited lists constitutes their greatest weakness. For the acceptability of industry in reality is answered *not by the type* of industry in question but *by the operation* of that industry. Performance standards are based on the concept that if industries are operated in a manner that would not lower the economic usefulness of land, the industry should not only be accepted but encouraged. In fact, because of variations in the method of operation, industries that are omitted in most prohibited lists could seriously lower the utility of industrial land.

In sum, prohibited lists stem from the earlier practice of isolating industries from residential improvements. But if industries are desired as part of the program to implement the master plan—an expression of community goals—then prohibited lists are inconsistent with zoning objectives. The important issue here is that industry acceptability is judged by the effect an industry has on the surrounding environment. The list of *permitted* industries together with performance standards represents a preferred means to select industries in contrast to prohibited lists that follow from the "nuisance" theory of zoning.

PROGRESSIVELY INCLUSIVE DISTRICTS

Progressively inclusive districts started from the early practice of granting exclusive protection to residential districts. Zoning districts typically begin with the single family dwelling district in which uses other than residential are prohibited. With the addition of multiple family districts, commercial districts and industrial districts in the zoning ordinance, permitted uses are made cumulative so that the final district—usually industrial—permits virtually all uses.

Zoning ordinances based on this principle (and this includes the large majority) give virtually no protection to industrial uses. The one exception concerns residential uses which are now customarily excluded from industrial districts. To the extent that industry must compete for the available space with non-industrial users, three results may be anticipated: First, the competition for industrial space, increased because of non-industrial demands, may raise industrial land prices to a point above price reservations held by industry. Secondly, the industrial district is more comparable to a district with no zoning restrictions. The result is to create a mixed district—a district improved with businesses that have a low priority for land use. The effect produces land with the least possible utility for industrial purposes. Uncontrolled, non-industrial use in the industrial zone leads to traffic congestion, on-street truck loading, inadequate parking and, clearly, a supply of low quality industrial land. To the extent that commercial and recreational uses, *i.e.,* skating rinks, dance halls and the like, absorb industrial land, the master plan is not only ignored, but hindered.

A third consequence of progressively inclusive districts, and quite serious for cities with a shortage of industrial space, is the absorption of industrial sites by non-

industrial uses. If the supply of industrial space is critical and the industrial area represents the most appropriate use of given land area zoned for industry, then it would seem that maximum productive efficiency would be gained by giving industry the same exclusive protection afforded residential use.

Surely the importance of industry and its contribution to the local economy furnish even stronger arguments for exclusive protection relative to the specious reasons offered in support of exclusive zoning for residential property. If the goals of the master plan are to be realized, industrial districts and their regulation must conform more closely to *economic* reality. Industrial zoning characterized by obsolete, incomplete, misdirected prohibited lists and progressively inclusive districts gives little support to the master plan.

The Relative Elasticity of Demand for Industrial Space

The effects of industrial zoning practices are amplified by the relative elasticities of demand for industrial and commercial space. Industry is placed at a distinct disadvantage because of the highly *elastic* demand for industrial space in comparison to the relatively *inelastic* demand for commercial space. The highly elastic demand for industrial land follows because most manufacturers may choose among a wide range of sites. For industries that are market or raw material oriented, this selection is considerably narrowed but even here transportation advances are increasing industrial mobility. The availability of sites for the expansion of existing industries, the establishment of new industries, and plant relocation among competing communities leads to a highly elastic demand. In addition, the detailed study that many industries undertake before selecting a community and site also suggests a high demand elasticity for industrial sites.

In contrast to the demand for industrial space, the demand for commercial space is a derived demand dependent on potential sales.

In a given community, commercial enterprises would seem more restricted in the choice of sites than industry in general. Moreover the limits imposed by population and personal disposable income restrict the amount of land that can be used for commercial space. So for these reasons the demand for commercial space would appear relatively inelastic.

But the supply curve of industrial land is probably elastic only to the point where the available vacant land is absorbed. Beyond this point the marginal cost rises abruptly as the supply of industrial space is increased by conversion of existing non-conforming uses, the rearrangement of public improvements, the succession of commercial-residential land to industrial use and the like.

Given these facts the land use pattern may be distorted from the ideal allocation as follows: The demand for commercial space in industrially zoned areas will cause land prices to rise above offers submitted by industrial users. The resulting price will tend to discourage industrial use for only the most intensive industries with price reservations corresponding to commercial land values will site in the industrial district. Because of the higher prices bid by non-industrial businesses the best sites will be devoted to commercial use; the least usable areas will remain vacant or will be gradually purchased by industry at commercial land prices. For industry to compete successfully with commercial businesses, an additional condition is necessary: the demand for industrial land must increase substantially. But it is quite unlikely that the demand for industrial land in an area encroached by business would increase to the point where all land would be absorbed by industry. Yet another more serious result follows from the discriminatory effects of progressively inclusive districts: That is, in the long run further expansion of industry is possible only at points where the demand for industry intersects the rising portion of the supply curve since the commercial demand for low-cost space will probably absorb the available supply. In

other words, as the demand for urban land increases the industrial space tends to be used for non-industrial uses until vacant land is utilized. Communities that subscribe to progressively inclusive districts then have little opportunity to attract additional industry. With industrial land prices distorted upward by the demand for non-industrial space, it then becomes necessary to subsidize industry so that land costs are equal to alternative costs in other locations. Such subsidies are typical of urban renewal projects that redevelop mixed, industrial districts to exclusive industrial districts.

The latter effect has even more serious consequences when prohibited lists of industries are enforced by the local community. Then the result is to prevent entry of industry, further lowering the effective demand for industrial space under conditions in which commercial space demand distorts industrial land prices upward. Therefore, communities enforcing progressively inclusive districts and prohibited lists are relatively handicapped in attracting new industry. The remedy lies in constructing zoning ordinances more in accordance with economic objectives. But if zoning ordinances continue to be based on nuisance controls or Euclidian zoning, prospects for industrial expansion are considerably lowered.

Conclusion

Industrial zoning represents a paradox in community development. On the one hand, chambers of commerce, state development commissions, trade associations and the community in general, apparently favor new industry or the expansion of existing industry. The economic benefits of industrial expansion are widely accepted.

On the other hand, negative industrial zoning is without doubt inconsistent with community objectives. To the extent that the master plan is evidence of community intent and, if the enthusiasm shown for new industry is indicative of community desires (or even need), then industrial zoning not only fails to conform to public desires but may even retard community growth. The seeming conflict between industrial zoning practices and community desires follows from the continued observance of nuisance controls developed in colonial times. Yet nuisance controls violate claimed objectives of zoning controls and the master plan, even in view of the special land use requirements of industry.

The list of prohibited industries, a negative type of control, and progressively inclusive districts distort the land use pattern. Industry is unable to compete for scarce land more appropriately used for industrial purposes by reason of non-exclusive zoning. Prohibited lists bar industry that otherwise might use lower cost sites. In addition, progressively inclusive districts detract from the utility of sites supposedly reserved for industry and further result in increased industrial land prices.

If industrial zoning is to serve as a positive land use control, two zoning reforms would appear necessary: (1) the introduction of permissive lists of acceptable industries with performance standards as a substitute for prohibited lists, and (2) the extension of exclusive zoning privileges (usually granted only to residential uses) to industrial uses. The first point requires performance standards instead of prohibited lists of presumed nuisances. Performance standards have been criticized on grounds of administrative difficulties. However, the importance attached to industry surely justifies administrative expenses that would overcome the economic loss associated with inadequate zoning procedures.

The second point calls for a departure from existing zoning practices. But such steps have already been taken in part. The exclusive use of urban renewal sites for industrial purposes and the trend to exclusive zoning with limited court approval are steps in this direction. Special zoning districts, *e.g.*, planned industrial district zoning and governmental ownership of land reserved for industry are other developments supporting the need for the exclusive reservation of land for industrial purposes. Many of these land use practices, though necessary to overcome industrial zoning deficiencies, are a poor substitute for zoning that is consistently applied to all land uses, especially for industrial uses.

8

Performance Standards in Industrial Zoning

Dennis O'Harrow

This paper appeared originally in Planning 1951, pp. 42–55, *published by the American Society of Planning Officials, 1313 East Sixtieth Street, Chicago, Illinois 60637. Reproduced by permission.*

THE EXPRESSION "performance standard" is taken from building code terminology. Modern building codes are written more in terms of what materials and methods of construction will *do*—their performance under stated conditions—rather than in specific descriptions of materials and building methods. This change has been forced on building commissioners because of the great number of new materials and designs that have been brought out in the past ten or twenty years.

The situation in zoning is similar. Zoning administrators are asked to rule on new land uses, and on new—and improved—forms of old uses. Our factories are making new products, are using new production processes, and are taking on a new appearance. The buildings are kept to a single story. They are placed well back from the property lines. Factory grounds have neat lawns and beds of flowers. The buildings are windowless and air-conditioned. Many modern industrial plants would be an asset to many residential districts. Our zoning ordinances need re-working to catch up with our industrial techniques.

Our building codes have passed through three stages. In the first, or *primitive* stage, for example, the code said that a party wall

should be made of brick or stone. It was soon found that there are brick walls and brick walls. Some of them withstand burning and some do not. It was necessary to state *how* you wanted the wall constructed and how thick it should be. This was the second stage, the *specification* code. Then along came builders with new materials: monolithic concrete, cinder block, and so on. They were faster and cheaper to build, and the proponents claimed they would furnish all the protection we sought.

When we stopped to think, we found that we actually didn't care what the wall is made of—brick, concrete, steel or tissue paper—so long as it is fireproof. So we established a *performance* code. The party wall must be able to retain its strength and block off a fire produced under laboratory conditions. The fire reaches a temperature of 2,000° Fahrenheit in two hours. If the material holds up in this test, it is permissible to use it in building a party wall.

Some parts of our zoning ordinances have reached the *specification* stage—side yards, for example. We don't say "side yards must be furnished," which would be the primitive stage. Instead, we say "there will be two side yards, each of which will be not less than five feet in width." This is a *specification* standard, because we have specified a minimum acceptable width. It is not yet a *performance* standard. We haven't said what we want the house to do, which is to assure adequate light and air to its neighbor, nor have we set up an accurate definition of "adequate light and air."

While parts of our zoning ordinances have progressed to specification standards, there are still parts that are back in the primitive stage. Especially is this true of our method of handling industrial zoning. The clause that is best evidence of this primitive stage is probably somewhere in 99 per cent of existing zoning ordinances. It goes: ". . . and any other use that is not objectionable because of the emission of dust, odor, noise, excessive vibration or other nuisances."

It is not necessary to go into detail on the weaknesses of such clauses. All of us have recognized the weaknesses and we want to overcome them. Almost universally we have tried to overcome them by setting up groups of uses that we think have about equal powers of nuisance generation. We have outlined districts for "light" and "heavy" industry, but, for the life of us, we can't give a clear definition of "light" and "heavy." In some cases, we have limited the horsepower of individual machines—on what justification it has never been clear, except that someone else had done it before. Sometimes we have limited the number of employees, saying that a laundry employing five persons is a business and will be permitted in a business district, but that a laundry employing six persons is an industry and we cannot allow it.

In some places we have improved upon our primitive standards by granting conditional use permits. We shall permit the industry to locate in the district it requests *if* it fulfills certain conditions regarding the handling of dirty materials, off-street loading, paint spraying, sandblasting, and so on. Where discretion is vested in a zoning administrator, as it is in Los Angeles, we have been able to liberalize the unyielding provisions of our zoning ordinances in this manner.

It is not intended to leave the impression that our attempts to change from a primitive ordinance to a specification ordinance are without value. Although we can go a long way in writing performance standards into our zoning code, there are several fields in which we will have to continue specification standards for many years to come. Again we parallel the modern building code, which uses performance standards as often as possible, but still carries a list of specifications for items on which performance standards are either not available or not practical.

However, we can move out of the *primitive* stage at many points in our zoning regulations. This discussion will be confined to zoning for industrial uses, but industrial zoning is only one part of zoning control. We can do much to advance zoning by a critical re-examination of all parts of the ordinance.

We need a more complete definition of performance standard. The ideal zoning performance standard will substitute a quantitative measurement of an effect for the qualitative description of that effect that we have used in the past. It will not use the terms

"limited," "substantial," "objectionable," "offensive." Instead, it will establish definite measurements, taken by standardized methods with standardized instruments, to determine whether the effect of a particular use is within predetermined limits, and therefore is permissible in a particular zone.

This paper will review briefly the outlook for standards in those important fields in which they are lacking; state briefly what the performance zoning ordinances may do, and finally, suggest how we may advance toward making these performance standards available for our zoning ordinance revisions.

There are eleven fields in which we need to look for performance standards for industrial zoning. These are:

(1) Noise
(2) Smoke
(3) Odor
(4) Dust and dirt
(5) Noxious gases
(6) Glare and heat
(7) Fire hazards
(8) Industrial wastes
(9) Transportation and traffic
(10) Aesthetics
(11) Psychological effects

(1) NOISE

The possibility of setting up performance standards for noise appears both hopeful and difficult. It is hopeful because acoustical research has in the past few years come up with some new techniques for measuring noise, and with a new unit of noise called the "sone." Many of you have heard of the older unit, the "decibel." This is primarily a measure of the pressure created by sound waves, and will not be superseded in the measurement of the strength of individual tones. But the technical difference between "sound" and "noise"—particularly the difference between the decibel measurement of sound and the *loudness* of noise—is a subject that you want to approach only when you are in the pink of mental condition. The outlook is hopeful because of the work that is now being completed in Chicago by Professor G. L. Bonvallet of Armour Research Foundation. Professor Bonvallet has taken enough measurements of the kind of noise that we are interested in—street and traffic noise, industrial noise, transportation noise —so that he will soon be in a position to give us limiting spectra for noise.

The control of factory noise through zoning is also hopeful because the most effective means for the muffling of noise is a tool that we have used in zoning for some thirty-five years—setback. Noise is decreased approximately as the square of the distance. If the noise of a factory is a certain figure when you stand at the property line, move the factory twice as far away and the noise will be down to one-fourth the former density. (Don't be too quick to believe that objectional noise at ten feet has dropped to a whisper at twenty feet. Common sense tells us that isn't true. Noise measurements are on a logarithmic scale, and loudness drops slowly in the upper brackets.) But setbacks from property lines give us an extremely useful control for noise. And noise gives us another excellent excuse for setbacks.

The discouraging aspect of performance standards for industrial noise is that factory noise—the noise from industrial processes—is not the objectionable part of industrial noises in 95 per cent of our factories. This was first brought out in the famous New York City noise survey of 1930, in which factory noise was considered objectionable in only 1 per cent of the cases. This finding has been reaffirmed several times, most recently in the Chicago noise survey. Objectionable industrial noise is overwhelmingly due to traffic and transportation noises—trucks coming from and going to the plant, steam locomotives puffing and diesel engines thundering, box cars switching and gondolas banging, thousands of self-propelled employees changing shift. The chance of controlling this type of noise through a performance standard on noise generation is not good.

Nevertheless, we are going to have to approach our problem from all angles, and one of these angles is noise. At least 5 per cent of our factories *do* create objectionable production noise in addition to the traffic noise they spawn. Any factory noise adds to the overall noise pattern. It appears that we are ready to set up definite standards in this field.

(2) SMOKE

The second in the list of needed performance standards is a limit on smoke emission. Here we are in unusually good shape. Because of the strenuous work that has been done in smoke control over the past decade, we have excellent standards and simple methods of measurement.

There are two instruments for measuring smoke: the Ringelman chart and the umbrascope. The simplest and most popular is the Ringelman chart. On this chart are five designs, each representing a degree of smoke density. When you are far enough away from the chart, the designs merge into shades of gray, all except No. 5, which is solid black. The shades are numbered from 1 to 5. Multiply the number by 20 and you get the percentage density of the design. Thus, No. 1 is 20 per cent, No. 2 is 40 per cent, No. 3 is 60 per cent.

The model smoke control ordinance forbids the emission of dense smoke, and dense smoke is defined as equal to Ringelman No. 2 or darker. A few ordinances set the limit at Ringelman No. 3 or darker. We thus have our performance standard on smoke emission already worked out for us. All we have to do is to apply it.

There are, of course, some problems in bringing the smoke standards over into the zoning ordinance. For example, if our city smoke control ordinance forbids smoke more dense than Ringelman No. 2, we may want also an area in which we set No. 1 as the limit, or an area in which we specify no smoke whatsoever, requiring gas, oil or electricity as a fuel. However, there is no doubt that we are ready to drop smoke from the ubiquitous list of undefined nuisances and substitute the clear definition that we have available.

(3) ODOR

Thus far, there have been readily at hand some well-tested standards of measurement. In the field of olfactory offenses, we have to proceed cautiously.

Smell (and its concomitant, taste) is perhaps the most subjective of our sensations. You just can't measure odor. You can't even describe it, except to say that it smells like some other odor, or that it is pleasant, indifferent, or horrible. Odors have been classified in dozens of different ways. Numerous tries have been made to determine odor profiles, but none of them has quite come off. There are now some experiments under way to place odors in the electromagnetic spectrum. These experiments show promise, but results thus far are not usable.

One approach to odors is through measurements of the threshold of smell, which are available for a considerable list of compounds. These measurements show the minimum concentration to give the first sensation of odor. Measurements are made in ounces of the substance per thousand cubic feet of air. For example: .0011 ounces of hydrogen sulfide, the familiar "rotten egg" gas, in a thousand cubic feet of air, is the minimum concentration that can be smelled. Less than this concentration we cannot perceive. There is a wide variation in the amount of different substances needed for the threshold of smell. It takes .05 ounces of butylene beta, which is the warning odor used in illuminating gas. It takes only 18 millionths of an ounce of ethyl seleno mercaptan, which seems to hold some sort of position as the foulest of all smells.

A great many substances have had this odor threshold determined. A list of several hundred, mostly for polysyllabic organic compounds, included, however, only one of the compounds that constitute the peculiar odor that arises from a fish-processing plant. This investigation of odors has not exhausted current knowledge on the subject. At any rate, the list is too long to include, except by reference, in the ordinary zoning ordinance. Even if accurate measurement of odor is not now possible, it is only a question of time before it will be. In the meantime, we have some empirical methods open to us.

There are very few industrial activities in which offensive odor cannot be prevented from escaping. The odor from our old friends the glue factory, the slaughterhouse, and the fish cannery can be completely eliminated—at least as far as escape into the atmosphere is concerned. On the other hand, there seems to be no prospect, present or future, for the elimination of the odor nuisance from a stockyard. In the doubtful list we would also have to put petroleum refining, artificial gas manufacture, and rubber manufacture. Probably, our best approach to the odor problem is to bar no industry by name, because of its odor nuisance. Instead, we would specify that in a certain district, we shall permit no industry to locate that commits an odor nuisance. Then perhaps we should have a check-list of industries that have traditionally smelled bad. We would specify that these industries must present detailed plans to prove that they are going to eliminate the odor, or we won't let them operate in this district. Of course, we must not forget that if there are some industries not yet able to eliminate odors, they must be located *somewhere*. We must have a district permitting them to be erected in some, if not all, of our cities.

(4) DUST AND DIRT

The fourth in the list of needed standards is one for dust and dirt. The most frequent source of dirt from our industrial sections is the smokestack, blowing cinders and fly ash into the air. Here again, we have the work of the smoke abatement pioneers. They have definitely stated that they would not tolerate fly ash in excess of "0.3 grains per cubic foot of flue gas at a stack temperature of 500° Fahrenheit." This standard would not be difficult to incorporate into our zoning regulations. Again, we may wish to set different limits—such as .2 grain or .1 grain.

As for other kinds of dust and dirt, there are at present no standards to determine a permissible amount of pollution. Here, the solution may be the same as that suggested for odors. We would not list any industry by name. In those districts that we wish to keep free of dirt, we would require satisfactory proof that an industry will be able to keep all dust and dirt confined within the walls of the building. If there be any industry which cannot keep its dirt to itself, we'll need to find a district for it somewhere—down-wind. However, there is probably no industry conducted within a building that nowadays needs to pollute the air with dirt.

(5) NOXIOUS GASES

By noxious gases is meant those gases which are relatively odorless, but which can, in sufficient concentration, be dangerous to plant and animal life. Hydrogen sulfide, the rotten-egg gas that was mentioned previously, is quite poisonous. But, like the rattlesnake, it warns you before it strikes; the unmistakable smell telegraphs the presence of hydrogen sulfide in advance of toxic proportions.

When we are considering our standards for zoning ordinances, we should not forget that there is another body of law that is always in operation—the law of nuisance. While this research on the subject, to a layman, leads to the belief that it is all quite unclear as to what is nuisance and what is not nuisance, there is no doubt that the discharge of a poisonous gas in toxic quantities is definitely a nuisance. As such it will be promptly abated. Therefore, it is probably unnecessary to concern ourselves with clear nuisance in zoning.

One way of looking at our zoning regulation of some of these matters is to say that we are trying to regulate processes so that they never become nuisances. Standards for toxic concentrations of gases are easily available. Carbon monoxide, for example, is dangerous to human life at about 2,000 parts per million. The maximum safe concentration permissible in plants is set at 100 p.p.m. This is about the concentration found on a heavy traffic street.

Although we might prefer to forbid the release into the atmosphere of any noxious gas, it is unlikely that this can be accomplished. We may have to relegate the poison gas producers to the same district as the odor producers. The work we need to do here is to examine industries that are noxious gas producers, to see whether the escape of such gas can be completely eliminated. If it cannot, then we have at hand definite standards—that should be comparatively easy to adapt to zoning regulations.

(6) GLARE AND HEAT

The steel industry is the most spectacular producer of glare and heat. To watch a Bessemer converter blow off from some safe distance does not offend you. On the contrary, it fills you with awe and respect. Living close to it is not nearly so thrilling. The intensity of the light at night is great enough to make the neighborhood within several blocks as light as day. But the establishment of new blast furnaces and Bessemer converters is infrequent enough, and it presents so many special problems, that the glare and heat nuisance will never be a crucial consideration.

On the whole, this is a minor problem. It would probably arise most frequently from welding operations and acetylene torch cutting. Here we can get a performance standard—actually a prohibition. Such operations shall be performed so that they may not be seen from outside the property. This would mean that they would be inside a building where they could not be seen from outside. Or, if it is necessary to work outside, as it may be in scrap metal operations, the work will be behind a tight fence.

(7) FIRE AND SAFETY HAZARD

In most of our cities we have, in our building code or our fire code, a list of "special hazards," operations and processes that are held to be unusually dangerous. These uses are customarily forbidden anywhere within our first "fire zone."

If these special hazards were adopted into our zoning regulations, there might be some advantage in coordinating fire zones and land use zones. However, the disadvantages of using the typical "special hazard" list outweigh the advantages. For example, you will probably find "paint spraying" and "fireworks manufacture" on the same list. Although we may wish to prohibit both of these operations in our first fire district, we can't afford to treat them as equal in setting up our industrial zoning regulations.

What was in our minds when we wrote into our zoning ordinance that industries might be objectionable because of fire hazard? It wasn't to protect the hazardous industry from itself, because wherever it locates it will still be hazardous to itself and its own employees. The answer, of course, is that we wished to protect the neighbors, to offer assurance to any present or future manufacturer that he could locate in this area without fear of having a hazardous plant come in next door to him. How can we measure this potential danger?

In fire insurance ratings we have a great body of practical experience to draw on for the answer to this question. Fire insurance rates are established by experienced technicians using a schedule that is a kind of score card. There are several schedules in use throughout the country, but the best one is known as the "Analytic" schedule.

Briefly, in the Analytic schedule, the cost of insurance starts with a base rate for the individual city, to which rate are applied several factors in the form of percentage. Some of the factors increase the cost of the insurance and others decrease the cost. The factors fall in four major groups:

(1) Building construction
(2) Occupancy
(3) Exposure
(4) Condition

Of these, all but "condition" can be determined before the plant is built.

The effect of type of building construction on the insurance rating is well known. The completely fire-proof building carries the lowest rating—costs the least to insure— and frame construction carries the highest rating.

Occupancy factors, which are of particular interest to us in zoning, depend solely on the use to which the building is put, without regard to the type of building construction, or the exposure of the building because of surrounding hazardous conditions. These factors range from zero—i.e., nothing added because of the occupancy—for ordinary offices, to as much as 245 per cent additional for bottling acetylene gas, or even more for other occupancies. Occupancy factors also take into account special features in a plant, such as the use of inflammable gas, enameling operations and so on.

The third group of factors used to rate the fire hazard of a building covers the exposure of the building to nearby hazards. Since we are interested in settling a standard by which we can predetermine the acceptability of a given use, we are interested in the exposure hazard that the new plant brings in and not the one that it encounters when it gets there.

The rating factor applied for "condition" cannot be determined in advance of the construction and use of a building. It is based on housekeeping and general maintenance after the building is actually in use. Although it is important in arriving at the cost of insurance, it is not necessary to establish zoning standards.

In fire insurance rating, we have a method of setting up a definite numerical standard by which we can judge fire hazard. It is not going to be easy to set these numerical standards, but it does offer a chance to get away from naming names, and still be quite definite as to what we consider appropriate for our different industrial zones. We are interested in the hazard to other industries that our permitted uses will create. Therefore, we should recognize that there is no fire hazard we might create that cannot be eliminated by distance. We return to our old zoning tool —setbacks from property lines. Undoubtedly, the required setbacks to eliminate fire hazard caused by certain uses, such as gasoline tank farms, are going to be so great that economic necessity will force these uses to locate in our less valuable districts. This is as it should be, since it tends to direct the more intensive uses to the better locations.

There are some weaknesses in insurance rating schedules, but there is an opportunity to improve our zoning regulations by using them intelligently.

(8) INDUSTRIAL SEWAGE WASTES

A municipal sewerage system is, or should be if it isn't, planned for a long time in the future. In some rare instances it may be possible to expand the system—laterals, mains, interceptors, disposal works—easily for any part of the city. But in the majority of cities, the sewerage system is a miscellany of sections, some of which can handle more sewage than they are taking, others that are up to or over capacity, still other sections that cannot be expanded economically. So it is quite important that we plan our industrial areas with the present and potential sewerage system in mind.

Industrial sewage differs from the other subjects covered thus far, in that it is not necessarily a nuisance. Of course, industrial waste discharged raw into a stream can be a nuisance. However, it is assumed that state and local health laws are effective in preventing this. If they are not, the zoning ordinance cannot be a satisfactory substitute. Delineating industrial zones based on the capacity of the sewerage system is primarily a land planning problem. Still, the principal tool for carrying out the land plan is the zoning ordinance. Industrial sewerage standards should be in it.

Fortunately, we have excellent methods of measuring industrial wastes and in estimating them before the plant is built. For example: the production unit in a slaughterhouse is one hog. A steer is $2\frac{1}{2}$ hog-units. The amount of industrial waste accompanying the slaughter and preparation of one hog can be converted to a population equivalent. It is equal to the domestic sewerage waste of 2.43 persons. A slaughterhouse with a daily capacity of 1,000 hogs, or 400 steers, throws the same load on a sewerage system as would a population of 2,430 persons, or about six hundred families. The average cheese factory has a population equivalent of 2,000 to 3,000 persons; the average tannery has an equivalent of 18,000 to 20,000 persons; a beet-sugar factory equals 65,000 to 125,000 persons, depending on the process.

We have practically all the basic information that we need for industrial waste standards. When we set them up in our zoning ordinances, they will probably take the form of density regulations. Thus, for an area in which we have ample sewerage, we might permit industrial waste up to a population equivalent of 1,000 per acre. In another area we might have to limit the waste to a population equivalent of 50 persons per acre.

Again, we are setting a performance standard. Just as soon as a meat packer can demonstrate that his process causes industrial wastes with a population equivalent of only one person per hog-unit instead of two persons per hog-unit, then we can allow him to build on half the amount of land that we now think he needs.

(9) TRAFFIC AND TRANSPORTATION

As mentioned previously under the heading of "Noise," the largest part of industrial noise comes not from the factory itself, but from the various transport operations connected with it. For 95 per cent of our factories, the noise from machinery is not objectionable. In fact, it is probable that if we lumped together factories that might be objectionable because of plant noise, odor, fire hazard, industrial sewage, dust, noxious gases, glare and heat, we still wouldn't have over 20 per cent of our factories. But for factories that might be objectionable because of the traffic they generate, the figure is so close to 100 per cent that the difference is not worth worrying about.

A good illustration of the lag in our thinking about zoning is the infrequent mention of the traffic generating potential of a particular land use. In this we find that our lay citizens are ahead of us. All you need to do is sit in on the hearing of a request to extend the boundaries of an industrial zone. You will find that the possibility of increased traffic bothers the neighbors more than any other aspect of industry in the neighborhood.

Traffic and transport are not objectionable *per se*. Again, it is the effects of traffic that bothers us. It is the noise of roaring trucks and banging switch engines. It is the poisonous carbon monoxide pouring from the exhaust of motor vehicles. It is the smoke and cinders belching from steam locomotives. It is the street hazard created by autos of employees streaming to and from work. It is the pre-emption of parking space by those same autos. It is the driving hazard caused by improper loading berths. It is the dirt raised, even from concrete streets, by thousands of wheels. In fact, the effects of traffic include most of the annoyances for which we are trying to set up our industrial performance standards. In arriving at standards for traffic, we need some basic thinking. Performance standards, as we have talked about them heretofore, are one step removed from the problem. For example: we have studies that show doubling the number of motor vehicles will increase the noise level about 3 decibels, which corresponds to about a 40 per cent increase measured in sones. If the number of vehicles remains the same, but the percentage of commercial vehicles doubles, we get about the same increase—3 decibels or 40 per cent increase in sones. This gives us an idea of the overall effect of added traffic, and points up the annoyance power of commercial vehicles. It is hardly suitable, however, as a standard to write into a zoning ordinance.

Again, we have seen that we have quite definite standards on smoke production. These standards can be applied to railroad locomotives. But the control of locomotive smoke is not properly a responsibility of the industry served by that locomotive (unless it is an industrial locomotive owned by the plant).

From the viewpoint of semantics, it may be that our standards on industrial traffic will be called "specification" rather than "performance" but the distinction is not too important. The important point is to get *some* method of describing the limits in traffic generation that we wish to set up for a given district.

Our first step is to list the aspects of traffic and transport that we wish to recognize. There are probably a great many ways in which we could list these aspects. The following appears to be one for which we have background to set standards.

(a) Amount of employee traffic, based on number of employees and number of shifts.

(b) Amount of truck traffic, based on maximum daily truck-loads of raw materials in and finished products out.

(c) Railroad traffic, based on daily car-loads in and out.

(d) Off-street parking space, based on number of employees, and number of company vehicles.

(e) Off-street loading docks, based on daily truck-loads in and out.

For the last two of these, off-street parking and off-street loading, modern ordinances now include regulations. These are still rule-of-thumb provisions, but from experience and from the National Industrial Zoning Committee survey, we may be able to improve them.

With the other items in the list, we are going to have some trouble. In setting limits on number of employees, we run head-on into the weakness present in our attempts to limit industrial activity in commercial districts. It isn't reasonable to say that a plant with 100 employees is all right, but one with 101 employees is objectionable. We may be able to get around this by specifying *density of employment*—20 employees per acre of ground, for example. In this way we would spread out the focus of traffic generation.

A provision in the new residence-industry district in Cleveland is that industries locating in the district must operate only one shift and may not operate on Sundays, normal business holidays, or at night. This is an excellent method for reducing the objection to integrating industry into residence districts.

Standards for materials and products transportation are also going to be difficult to establish. A provision in the proposed New York City resolution states:

"Whatever merchandise is received and shipped has a high value in relation to its size and weight, so that very little trucking traffic will be generated."

This points toward one method of measurement. Here also, a density measurement may be possible—truck-loads or car-loads per day per acre.

The zoning ordinance is only part of the technique for handling industrial traffic. We must provide the industrial district with thoroughfares, proper truck routes and good mass transportation. The best way to keep a horde of auto-driving industrial employees off neighboring residential streets is to provide them with more attractive methods of getting to and from the factory, preferably in public transit, or at least on well-designed major thoroughfares.

(10) AESTHETICS

It may be questioned why aesthetics is included as one of the regulations that should be imposed on industrial buildings. Many new factories are handsome, intelligently-designed examples of functional architecture. They are set well back from the street in grounds that have been decently landscaped and that are carefully maintained. But not all new plants are built that way. In spite of the obvious advantages in employee satisfaction, as well as in company advertising and community relations, we still have industrialists who want to build an architectural monstrosity that covers every square inch of land. And, of course, they can always find an architect to help them.

The truth is that the great majority of our existing factories are eyesores—and unnecessarily so, in most cases. In spite of the fact that aesthetic control is not yet universally accepted, there are a number of legal decisions that recognize the right to control the appearance of buildings. If this were not enough, we need only note the voice of the people as expressed at zoning hearings and in aesthetic control ordinances. As usual, our supreme courts lag behind the wish of the citizens but they will eventually catch up.

If we are going to re-think our industrial zoning, we should recognize aesthetics. This is particularly true if we wish to bring industry up out of the dumps and wastelands and house it among more pleasant surroundings.

The more pleasant surroundings are now the domain of residences. Like Caesar's wife, industries are going to have to be completely without sin if they hope to live side by side with decent folk.

No attempt will be made to analyze aesthetic standards, partly because they are pretty hazy. For our purpose, they will call for simple regulations, specification standards pretty much the same as we now use in residence districts. We should have front yards, side yards, height regulations and prohibition of monstrous advertising signs. For those combined residence and industrial districts that we shall develop some of these days, we may need review of the plans by a municipal art commission. We should not have much difficulty writing these regulations, nor in getting them accepted.

The *avant garde* may think these are feeble suggestions for aesthetic control. Compared with the complete anarchy that we now permit in industrial zones they will be a long step forward.

(11) PSYCHOLOGICAL EFFECTS

When it comes to regulating uses on the basis of psychological effects, it is difficult to find a method of measurement. Even to illustrate, it is necessary to speak of definite uses. The clearest cases of land use objectionable because of psychological effects are those connected with the disposal of the dead. Crematoria have never been, and probably never will be, accepted as harmless. People just don't like the idea. They always express fear of odors. Yet for the past fifty years there does not appear to be one case of a crematorium having created the faintest suspicion of a nuisance. In all probability there will never be such a case in the future.

The same psychological distaste exists for funeral homes and cemeteries, although not to the same degree. There is also strong dislike for mental and contagious disease hospitals, and for prisons of all kinds. The dislike has no connection with any annoyance created by the uses.

The uses named are not industries, although some zoning ordinances have tried to relegate crematoria and mental hospitals to industrial districts. However, we are undoubtedly going to face the same psychological antipathy for certain industries. The recent struggle in Detroit shows that no matter how sweet and clean we make a slaughterhouse, a lot of people don't want it for a neighbor. There are some other industries that people don't like, including glue factories, breweries, distilleries, and tanneries.

It may seem that this worry is unnecessary; that these psychological nuisances are principally ones that create odor pollution and haven't shown much interest in cleaning up the smell. They will be permitted only in districts in which we allow a certain amount of odor to escape, and those districts will be as far down-wind as we can put them.

The concern is not, however, without grounds. In the first place, the example of the slaughterhouse is correct—slaughterhouses can be and are being cleaned up. Properly designed, they do *not* create an odor nuisance. In the second place, there are very few industries that seem hopeless in their efforts to eliminate odor. Some day only the hopeless ones will be allowed to perfume the air. Those uses mentioned are *not* among the hopeless.

Finally, if our zoning ordinance is to function as we should like it to function, industries will be judged only on the effects they produce, and *any* industry will be permitted to go into *any* industrial district—including a combined residence-industry district—if it can comply with our standards. This means that if the slaughterhouse meets the standards, it will be able to move into our combined district. You can be sure that this possibility will be pointed out by the citizens that are fighting the adoption of our modernized zoning ordinance.

As stated at the beginning, no method has been found of setting up standards to cover this subject. Perhaps we can assume that psychological hazards will be present in only the combined residence-industry district (but the Detroit slaughterhouse case contradicts that). For that combined district we may always have to prohibit certain industries by name.

This completes a brief coverage of the outlook for new performance standards. In

general, what can we expect in the zoning ordinance of the future?

The ideal regulation of industry would mention no industry by name. Of course, if the above analysis of psychological hazard is correct, there will be exceptions. Except for the exceptions then, our zoning ordinance will merely set up the standards for each zone, and any industry that can meet those standards will be permitted to locate in that zone. What we should work for is the elimination of named industrial uses for different zones. Our present ordinances truly smack of discrimination. The situation is quite similar to establishing separate residential zones for white, yellow and black; or for professional, white collar and labor.

A suggestion like this should not be left hanging in the air. It is about the same as making a city plan and not polishing it off with a capital improvement program. A specific recommendation is that either ASPO or the National Industrial Zoning Committee appoint a committee (or a sub-committee, as the case may be) which will be charged with the study of industrial zoning performance standards in detail. The committee should be small at first, perhaps three members. The three members would outline their objectives and methods. Then they would expand by appointing sub-committees to work in selected fields. On each sub-committee there would be at least one person familiar with zoning and at least one person technically qualified in the subject assigned to the subcommittee—in noise, or odors, or industrial waste, etc.

The sub-committee would report back to the parent committee, recommending standards; suggesting appropriate wording for zoning ordinances, or reporting the need for additional research, where that is necessary. The sub-committee reports could then be assembled to make the first manual of performance standards in industrial zoning.

Within a year, such a committee could undoubtedly make recommendations on industrial zoning that would revolutionize our procedure.

9

Performance Standards in Residential Zoning

Frank E. Horack, Jr.

This paper appeared originally in Planning 1952, pp. 153–161, *published by the American Society of Planning Officials, 1313 East Sixtieth Street, Chicago, Illinois 60637. Reproduced by permission.*

THE POST-World War I American city was composed typically of a central and antiquated business district, unattractive industrial areas, and residential zones of varying quality. Zoning was a governmental and legal infant as yet unblessed by the United States Supreme Court decision in *Euclid* v. *Ambler.*

In contrast, the medium size city of today finds its business district dispersing into neighborhood shopping centers, its residential housing overflowing into semi-rural communities, and its industry, by the elimination of smoke and noise, and through improved architecture, earning the right to locate on sites never before available to industrial use. Planning and zoning has come through its adolescence in a healthy state and now can afford to assess its actions and re-evaluate its principles. Currently, these principles are:

1. Residential land use, though of lesser economic value, represents the highest social and community value and must therefore be protected against all uses injurious to its full and complete enjoyment.
2. The protection of these values must be achieved by confining uses of greater intensity to specific and limited zones.
3. Within zones, and particularly within residential zones, the protection of one property owner from the unreasonable use of another's land can best be achieved by specific height, bulk, and area restrictions.

In short, the basis of the zoning process is the "zone" and the "intrazone restriction." In 1951, however, Dennis O'Harrow challenged this concept. In his brilliant paper *"Performance Standards in Industrial Zoning"* he observed that the history of building codes disclosed a steady development from specification standards, i.e. those which permit one and only one method of compliance to *performance standards*, i.e. those which permit any compliance consistent with the objectives of the code. He urged a similar development in industrial zoning standards and argued that industry should be permitted to locate on any site where its activity did not endanger the use of affected property or the orderly development of the community.

If this thesis is correct, as it appears to be, then it should be equally applicable to commercial and residential land use as well. Thus, each land use would be tested by its direct and indirect effect on adjacent land use, on governmental services, and on community growth. Under such a standard, industry, business, and homes could be located on any site in any zone so long as the intended use met adequate performance standards. Such a proposition requires a wholesale re-examination of the principle of the use district. Paradoxically, it could result in zoning without zones.

Challenging as this idea appears, it would not change materially the procedures by which planning is transformed into zoning regulation. For example, O'Harrow demonstrates the methods by which an industrial plant can be integrated into a residential district without injury to its residential character. If such integration is possible then certainly the apartment house, the two-family dwelling, and the single family residence can all live together in peace and harmony under proper circumstances.

An apartment or an industrial plant located in a single family residence area will intensify land use, noise, and traffic. Each in varying degrees will require additional utility services. Thus, the grant of a permit should depend upon the cost justification of extending oversize mains in an area which otherwise would not require such facilities.

An industrial plant may produce odor, heat and glare, dust and dirt, and noxious gases. The apartment will not. On the other hand, the industrial plant will not increase directly the burden on schools and recreational facilities at the site location. The apartment will. Thus, under performance standards, the industrial plant should receive a permit if it confines or fails to create injurious activities. In the same location, the apartment, though creating none of the conditions considered undesirable, should not receive a permit if school and recreational facilities are already overcrowded. An application for the same apartment at another site should be granted if the location of the apartment would conserve the capital invested in existing school facilities where children have grown beyond school age.

Under existing ordinances founded on the zone-principle, the application of both the industry and the apartment must be refused. Not infrequently, however, construction goes forward either by re-zoning or by less defensible procedures of the "special exception" or the "variance." The legal sufficiency of such practices are always in doubt, and rightfully, for intuitive judgments concerning injuries, benefits, and reasonableness should rest on firmer foundations. In contrast, if performance standards can be developed the zoning process can contribute to community growth without the burdens, aggravations, and legal uncertainties inherent in the case by case exception to the zoning pattern.

The factors necessary for adequate performance standards in zoning are much more complex than performance tests in building codes and thus there should be no optimism that zones will quickly be replaced by more realistic performance tests. Indeed, any attempt to apply such distinctions as have been considered above without extensive research will certainly bring deserved rebuke from the courts on the ground that such unguided discretion transcends all constitutional bounds. For the immediate future the basic three zone distinction will continue until reliable performance standards can be formulated. Even then, the business zone

perhaps should be retained if for no other reasons than to protect the over ambitious and inexperienced person from going into business in areas which will insure his bankruptcy.

The initial application of the performance approach is more likely to be successful in the field of intra-zone restriction. Height, bulk, area, and setback restrictions need thorough re-examination. The six foot side yard and a thirty per cent dedication of land to side yard purposes in single family districts is founded on very general assumptions as to the necessity of light and air, fire protection, security from noise, and aesthetic considerations. As a practical yardstick it may be justified in most instances; but the constant request for relief from its strict application suggests that a re-examination of its premises according to the performance approach may indicate its inapplicability to present day conditions.

Only a generation ago the most popular single-residence structure was the California type bungalow. Sub-dividers platted land accordingly. Fifty and sixty foot lots were considered more than adequate; forty foot lots were common and quite sufficient for the bungalow constructed with its narrow dimension facing the street. At the time the colonial type house superseded the bungalow its two story form permitted its easy accommodation on the lots of earlier sub-dividers. However, when the ranch type house became fashionable, earlier lot sizes became inadequate. Indeed, if the garage was integrated with the house, as it usually is, and the house is placed on the lot with its long dimension parallel to the street, the planner and the home-owner faced an insurmountable problem.

The problem today is—how to place a 1952 house on a 1922 lot.

Measured by performance the 30 per cent and 6 foot minimum side yard requirement, if it was ever justified for the bungalow, must now be re-judged in terms of the ranch house. In the first place the axis of the house and therefore the axis of residential living has been turned 90 degrees as fashion and home construction has changed. This change in axis in itself may suggest that the original

30 per cent requirements were insufficient to insulate the bungalow from its neighbors and may have contributed to the change in style in home construction. If the requirement is defensible in single family districts then what is the justification for the garden apartment and the row house? Does public health, safety, and welfare permit the double standard in home occupancy?

Applying O'Harrow's eleven tests to the ranch house it is apparent that some of the standards essential to the measurement of industrial activity have little applicability to residential housing. Smoke, odor, dust and dirt, noxious gasses, and glare and heat are not seriously intensified by single family land use. The remaining performance standards have much greater pertinence in determining the propriety of side yard requirements.

1. NOISE

In residential areas the number of persons per square feet of land, their age, their avocations, all determine the noise-creating potential of the neighborhood. Distance is one factor in reducing the impact of noise between adjacent families; but unlike industrial noise which may be determined with fair accuracy, the standards for the home and its occupants follow no fixed pattern. From the cradle to the grave noise is ever with us and ever changing. Of course, many of these risks must be accepted as the inevitable burden of community living and for the over-sensitive the choice must be the sound proof apartment or the secluded farm. The side yard requirements provide no iron curtain shielding one house from the noise of another. The architecture of the house may be much more important in noise prevention than the side yard. For example, two houses with living quarters adjacent to each other have with six foot minimum side yards only twelve feet protection. The same houses constructed with integrated garages on the side yard would be protected by the 12 foot strip plus the insulating quality of the garages, as a space of approximately 35 feet. If the inte-

grated garage occurs in only one of the houses the protected area would be approximately 25 feet. Yet in all three situations the zoning requirement of 12 feet is the same. If noise is the only factor, the side yard requirement should vary according to the architecture of the adjacent homes.

2. FIRE

Separation of inflammable structures by air space is an obvious fire prevention device. The only question is, what is the proper distance. But this is not an absolute standard as illustrated by apartment buildings and row houses where there is no air strip separation and fire protection is achieved by control of construction materials. Thus, the side yard requirement, if it is a fire prevention device, should depend as much on the type of materials used in home construction as on the distance between houses.

In single family districts, however, variation depending on structure becomes an extremely unmanageable concept because it leaves to the first builder the power to determine the side yard requirements of his neighbors. An ordinance sanctioning such a practice surely would be declared unreasonable by the courts.

3. WASTES

Side and particularly rear yard requirements are directly affected by the available means of disposing of residential wastes. Modern subdivision control ordinances frequently condition lot size on the absorption ability of the soil if sanitary sewer systems are not available.

These are performance standards of a high order; but the subdivision of land twenty or more years ago was not predicated on soil characteristics. Those lots therefore may be either too small or unnecessarily large for waste disposal purposes. Where the lot is too small, the integration of the garage with the house frees normal land areas for absorption fields.

4. AESTHETICS

Side yard and rear yard lines reflect many aesthetic considerations. Protection against a crowded, confined "feeling" is probably more important to most home owners than the commonly accepted legal justification for such restrictions. However, the size of the side yard necessary to achieve this result may depend considerably upon the district in which the structure is built. This principle is already recognized in front yard set back lines which may be averaged or indeed may be determined by the line of existing structures. If noise and fire are not predominant considerations there seems to be no reason why the flexible standard should not apply to the side yard so that the existing condition of the neighborhood in which the structure is to be built controls. In areas where the character of the neighborhood is already established, the character is seldom changed. Side yard and front yard restrictions are waived by Boards of Zoning Appeals so that the late builder need not meet standards more restrictive than those already existing in the neighborhood.

Although the Board of Zoning Appeals procedure provides a way of escaping specification standards and substitutes neighborhood norms when they are lower, it does not permit the enforcement of higher neighborhood standards. Currently, the only protection is the covenant running with the land. A performance standard would permit some enforcement of these norms by public agencies.

The aesthetic and psychological spaciousness of the side yard is affected by the height of adjacent structures. The height also directly affects light and air, noise and fire control. Thus, it seems reasonable to restrict building height not only by the usual maximum requirement but also by a height requirement dependent upon the average height of surrounding structures. This would prevent the "up-ended shoe box" effect occurring when a slant roofed English Tudor is built between two ranch type homes; and conversely avoid the pancake effect of a low ranch house wedged between two colonial style houses.

The desirability of architectural zoning must await more data and experience. The few cities that have adopted such restrictions seem satisfied. The prevention of incongruity appears to be supported by sufficient

economic, as well as social values, that courts may well reconsider their old antagonism to aesthetic standards.

But the difficulty for both courts and planner is that ours is a society of change. The ranch house of today will lose its popularity tomorrow. Thus, the court's resistance to aesthetic zoning instead of being a conservative or reactionary attitude as it is so frequently represented, is really a liberal one. It recognizes that what we do today will be unacceptable tomorrow; the difficulty is that in the interim the costs are great. But it is the planner's job, not the courts, to develop standards flexible enough to permit, indeed, encourage change and at the same time prevent the short term destruction of values.

5. PSYCHOLOGICAL EFFECTS

O'Harrow's last performance standard seeks to evaluate the psychological effect of the location of an industry on a particular site. Similarly the location of a particular house on a particular lot with given side yard, rear yard and setback lines will either make it a misfit in the neighborhood or integrate it into the community. But the bases for such determinations are not now present, and until they are, such requirements would certainly be considered as unreasonable restrictions on individual liberty.

Tested by O'Harrow's performance standards, the area and side yard requirements for single family dwellings appear capable of considerable improvement. The increase or decrease of the side yard depending on the integration of the garage has been extensively developed by this discussion. The examination of the other specification standards applicable to residential zones will no doubt suggest similar modifications.

Implicit in a reconsideration of zones and intra-zone specification standards is a re-examination of the administrative process by which zoning is enforced. After the adoption of a master plan classifying land use, zones are regulated through building and occupancy permits. Universally, however, ordinances recognize that in the transference of the general plan to a particular lot unreasonable hardships may result and a board of zoning appeals is authorized to grant variances or special exceptions. This authorization implies that the specific requirements of the zoning ordinance must on occasion be relaxed. Nevertheless, the board is condemned frequently for its spineless action in "granting every request for a variance that it receives." Before this judgment is accepted as absolute it should be remembered that each community continues to be or becomes the kind of community it wishes to be. That, for good or ill, the social judgment of the people has a way of over-riding the engineer's formula or the lawyer's ordinance.

Both professions should take heed, for the people have an uncanny way of being right. Perhaps not on short term issues but on long term policies. Consequently boards of zoning appeals decisions may speak for the citizen's intuitive understanding that the enforcement of a particular specification is neither necessary for the protection of the community nor will it contribute to the use and enjoyment of the affected property. At present the only relief is the slow, expensive and aggravating appeals procedure. If performance standards can permit that which is reasonable, and that which boards of zoning appeals now permit, without the currently attendant burdens, certainly it is not too soon to expand every effort in perfecting such standards.

Inherent in the performance test, however, is the weakness of the indefinite legislative standard. In industrial zoning this is not serious, for industrial construction is usually supervised by expert engineers and experienced architects. They are familiar with standards and measurements. In home construction the situation is otherwise. The prospective home builder and his contractor, at least in smaller communities, is unfamiliar with zoning ordinances. The specification standards provide him a definite answer. He can determine exactly what is expected. The performance standard is less satisfactory for its answer must be "it all depends upon the circumstances."

Likewise from the standpoint of the zoning official, particularly in the small community, the specification standard is preferable. His action is not discretionary; when he denies a permit he is less likely to be criticized for he can always point to an ordinance and say "your building does not comply. I can do nothing about it. Your remedy is to appeal to the Board of Zoning Appeals."

This supposed advantage of definiteness is defeated, however, if in too many cases specification standards produce unreasonable results. The performance approach will be more acceptable, even though more difficult to administer, if it can translate use, height, area, and bulk limitations into reasonable and flexible formulae.

Other administrative advantages are suggested by the performance approach. Currently, enforcement depends upon criminal prosecution or injunction. Neither are effective in the medium sized community. Criminal prosecution fails because the violation frequently is not considered harmful and the violator is not subject to community censure as a criminal. Injunction is more realistic because it does not imply criminality and insists only on compliance. But even the effectiveness of the injunction suffers from the common belief that the cost of removal or alteration of the structure is too heavy a price to exact from the violator.

Zoning enforcement is not best served by criminal prosecution or injunction. Preventative justice through administrative sanctions are more effective. Administrative control is exercised now through zoning and occupancy permits, required of the landowner, that is, the person for whom a structure is to be built. Unless he is a real estate developer he is almost certain to be ignorant of the building codes, zoning restrictions, and other construction requirements.

His ignorance places insurmountable burdens on enforcement. First, it means constant policing of all construction, an impossible task for the admittedly inadequate inspection services which most medium sized cities provide. Second, when violation occurs the liability rests on a citizen who legally may be presumed "to know the law" but who in fact does not. Enforcement is then in the unhappy position of prosecuting the decent citizen under circumstances which appeal to the community as bureaucratic entrapment.

In other words, the licensing device is good but the obligation is placed upon the wrong persons. The contractor, who holds himself out as a specialist, should be directly responsible for proper construction. The contractor should be licensed with bonds conditioned upon proper compliance with zoning and building ordinances. Enforcement even with the usual small staff of inspectors would be more efficient and effective because supervision would be required for a relatively small class of persons. Furthermore, the revocation of the contractor's license would be a more practical sanction than the abatement or removal of a non-conforming structure. Public resentment against enforcement would be eliminated if the obligation of compliance was placed on the contractor for it would be immediately recognized that the man who holds himself out as an expert should be expected "to know his business."

Special exception would of course be necessary for those who construct their homes personally. The percentage of such construction, however, is small, and the problem has been adequately met by special permits in most plumbing and construction codes.

The licensing of contractors will provide the single most effective step in establishing sound administrative procedures in the zoning field. Until this step is taken the enforcement of zoning ordinance will depend primarily upon public understanding and voluntary compliance. It is easy to say that planning officials and citizen commissions and boards should promote the public acceptance of planning and zoning by using all the media of mass communication, but this is a burdensome, time-consuming, and expensive undertaking and scarcely a guarantee of success when the public is seldom interested until a violation affects them directly.

Thus, the improvement in the zoning process depends first upon improved performance standards and second, upon a more effective licensing system. The first step cannot be undertaken without extensive research. This, few communities can afford; but through this Society the necessary studies can be undertaken. Several approaches can be

taken but the most reliable beginning would be the determination of the kind of performance communities actually permit under existing ordinances. The study of board of zoning appeals' cases in a number of typical cities will disclose those specification standards which citizen boards consider important.

Regional variation there will and should be, but pilot studies in a few areas will give guidance to later, more comprehensive researches. This is applying performance standards to governmental enforcement as well as to land use itself, an interrelation which, if ignored, will produce performance standards little better than those under which we now operate.

Finally, until performance standards are developed, present ordinances should be amended granting enforcement officials limited discretion to vary height, bulk, area, and setback requirements. In meritorious cases, the enforcement officer might reduce the requirements of the ordinance, by five or even ten per cent; in all cases the enforcement official could insist upon exact compliance and require the applicant to appeal to the board of zoning appeals.

Such an amendment would not solve all problems, nor is it a substitution for performance standards. It is proposed merely as an interim measure to avoid unnecessary appeals in obvious cases where even the most rigorous official knows that the application for a permit is reasonable, that it will be granted on appeal, but that if he issues the permit prior to appeal he will himself be violating the ordinance. It handles the case where the majestic old chestnut tree must be destroyed in order to build the ranch house or the side yard requirement must be slightly reduced. In such a case I think that anyone sitting on the board of zoning appeals would say "Zoner, spare that tree."

By a similar amendment many unnecessary appeals could be avoided if the height, area, and setback line requirements in areas already built up were conditioned by the average performance of structures already existing. This practice is authorized by ordinance in existing front yard setback requirements. Flexibility in all other specification requirements can be achieved only through board of zoning appeals procedure. Public acceptance of zoning would be furthered and administrative appeals reduced, all without reducing our actual standards, if we would confirm in the ordinance what we do in practice through appeal.

Indeed, the performance standard idea is such a good one we should apply it to our own performance.

10

PLANNER AGLE'S new approach to the zoning of low density urban residential areas includes these five revolutionary proposals:

1. Setback requirements and height limitations would be discarded in favor of controls on bulk based on the ratio of floor area to lot size.

2. Houses would be built—not on a straight line—but anywhere on the lots.

3. Building on the property line—front, rear or side—would be possible without sacrifice of privacy by relating building height and fenestration to land coverage.

4. Parking bays alongside the street would replace the costly garage and driveway and keep the cars off the lots.

5. Thus freed of parking space, street widths would be reduced from 26 feet to 20 feet and the distance between facing houses from 110 feet to 80 feet at substantial

Zoning Sketches

Charles Agle

Reprinted by permission from the July 1951 issue of The Architectural Forum (The Magazine of Building). Copyright Whitney Publications, Inc.

savings to the municipality, the builder and the buyer.

STREETS, TODAY AND TOMORROW

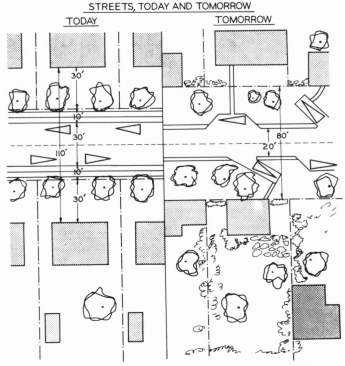

Figure 1: Typical result of today's obsolete zoning and wasteful land planning is the residential street at the left with its wide paving to accommodate parking, oversize public right-of-way, uniform setbacks. By comparison, the street at the right dramatizes several benefits of the proposed new kind of zoning: narrower street and right-of-way, off-street parking bays, absence of setback requirements. Bigger and better used building lots would be the result. Adapted from Agle art.

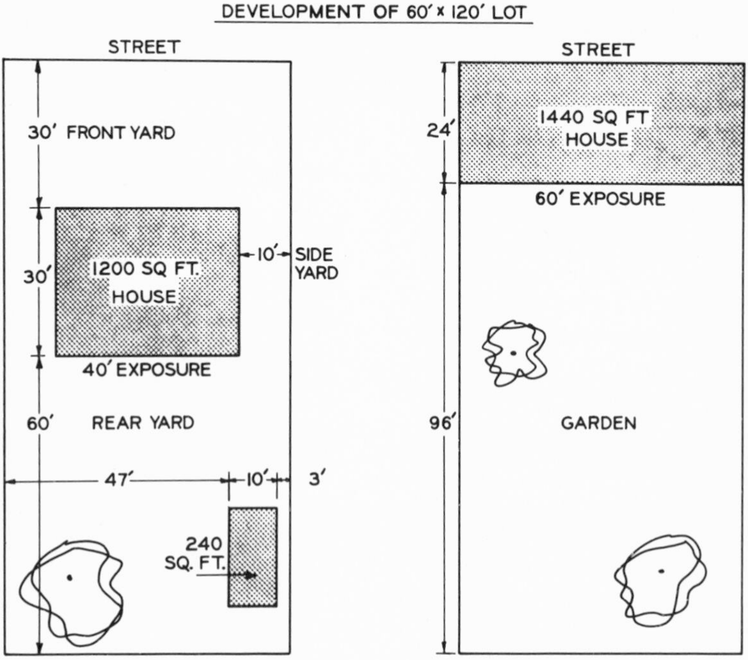

DEVELOPMENT OF 60' x 120' LOT

Figure 2: Today's subdivision (left) wastefully cuts lot up into four small yards with detached garage at rear. Proposed new zoning, with the same size house and attached garage built on three of the property lines of the same size lot, would give the home owner one big, useful yard 60' x 96'. Adapted from Agle art.

ZONING FOR aesthetic objectives is a perplexing problem. According to traditional
doctrine the community may not use the
police power to accomplish primarily aesthetic objectives, but planners and lawyers have
long had serious doubts whether in fact this
doctrine *describes* what courts have done in
the past in approving ordinances, whether it
may be used to *predict* what they will do in
the future, and whether it states a desirable
norm for decision. The problem has been
rather fully explored elsewhere along lines of
traditional legal analysis, and in view of the
previous studies perhaps a more fruitful
contribution can be made here by looking at
the problem and the doctrine from a different
perspective.

The primary object of this article will be to
examine contemporary doctrine as an instrument of community policy and to focus
attention upon its adequacy as an implement
of the sound judicial skepticism from which it
emanates. As will appear, the dearth of good
empirical studies in the field of aesthetics
seriously impedes the full consideration of
many facets of the problem of zoning for
aesthetic objectives, and the ideas and conclusions expressed herein are not comprehensively developed. Many of the ideas and
conclusions also are tentative and subject to
exception, although expressed without qualification. It is hoped, however, that this
article will stimulate more thinking about the
types of aesthetic control rational land
planning requires, which is the basic issue.

The Existing Confusion

The usual statement of doctrine is that the
police power cannot be used to accomplish
purely aesthetic objectives, but that aesthetic
objectives may be taken into consideration
where, for reasons of public health, safety or
morals the zoning regulation may be sustained as a proper exercise of the police
power. In order to view this formulation in
perspective it is necessary to make a short
detour here into history.

Early in this century, community officials,
responding to outraged popular sensibilities,
began to take action against billboards and
advertising posters which had in the eighteen

11

Zoning for Aesthetic Objectives: A Reappraisal

J. J. Dukeminier, Jr.

*Reprinted with permission of author and publisher from
a symposium, "Land Planning in a Democracy,"
appearing in* Law and Contemporary Problems, Vol. 20,
No. 2, Spring 1955, *published by the Duke University
School of Law, Durham, North Carolina.* © 1955 by
Duke University.

nineties suddenly mushroomed on most every
vacant lot. Ordinances and statutes were
passed regulating, and in some instances
entirely prohibiting, billboards. Most of these
regulations were quickly killed by the courts
which held that such regulations, having been
enacted for aesthetic objectives alone, were
without the scope of the police power. Yet
with the ever-widening desecration of the
landscape and with the public outcry against
billboards, it seems inevitable that the courts
would not long restrain the community
officials. And the courts did not.

The Missouri Supreme Court in 1911 in
St. Louis Gunning Advertising Co. v. St. Louis
provided the doctrinal shift by taking the
postulate that the police power might be
exercised to protect community health,
safety, and morals and then finding, as facts,
that billboards

> . . . endanger the public health, promote
> immorality, constitute hiding places and re-
> treats for criminals and all classes of mis-
> creants. They are also inartistic and unsightly.
> In cases of fire they often cause their spread
> and constitute barriers against their extinction;
> and in cases of high wind, their temporary
> character, frail structure and broad surface,
> render them liable to be blown down and to
> fall upon and injure those who may happen to

be in their vicinity. The evidence shows and common observation teaches us that the ground in the rear thereof is being constantly used as privies and dumping ground for all kinds of waste and deleterious matters, and thereby creating public nuisances and jeopardizing public health; the evidence also shows that behind these obstructions the lowest form of prostitution and other acts of immorality are frequently carried on, almost under public gaze; they offer shelter and concealment for the criminal while lying in wait for his victim; and last, but not least, they obstruct the light, sunshine, and air, which are so conducive to health and comfort.

The earlier cases had regarded aesthetic objectives as the predominating motive of billboard regulation and condemned the regulations for that reason; *St. Louis Gunning* initiated the deliquescence of earlier doctrine by regarding as primary the motives of safety, health, and morality and by sustaining the regulation for that reason.

From *St. Louis Gunning* and later cases following it emerged the postulates of contemporary doctrine:

(a) the police power may not be used to attain objectives primarily aesthetic; but

(b) the police power may be used to attain objectives primarily related to health, safety or morals;

based upon the following proposition of fact:

> Billboards and signs are primarily deleterious to health, safety or morals. Strictly speaking, this proposition is an unproven hypothesis, and there is strong reason to suspect that it is contrary to fact in most contexts. It is important to determine if the underlying proposition of fact is true, for if it is not true and if in deed (if not in word) the courts sustain regulation of billboards, then it will have to be admitted that the doctrine is an inadequate description of the factors that move decision in this context of fact.

It seems plain that the primary offense of billboards is ugliness. Any jerry-built billboard may of course be a menace to safety and a fire hazard, but the billboard regulations are not limited to keeping the signboard

screws tight. Limitations are placed upon size, positions, and frequency of placement. In some areas, billboards have been entirely prohibited, although the unsafe aspects might be easily obviated by proper construction requirements.

In business districts billboards and advertising signs have been prohibited unless the signs refer to business conducted or products sold on the premises. This provides a good illustration of the true objectives of community officials in acting against billboards and of the contrary-to-fact proposition of fact necessary under traditional doctrine to sustain this action. In the recent case of *Murphy, Inc. v. Westport*, the plaintiff billboard company asked for an injunction restraining the enforcement of the provision in Westport's zoning ordinance which prohibited "Billboards or advertising signboards . . . in all business districts except as they refer to business conducted on the property on which the billboards stand." The object of the exception in this sweeping prohibition is to make community action more palatable to local shopkeepers who wish to advertise their wares (and who are also sometime voters). The provision strikes primarily at billboard companies which erect billboards on vacant lots. For a city wishing to rid itself of all billboards, it is an expedient compromise. The Superior Court granted an injunction on the ground that this classification was unreasonable and "illegally discriminative"; it found the regulations contained "no provisions as to size, construction or site designed to insure the safety of the public; . . . the advertising matter appearing on the sign determines its safety to the public. Of course this is nonsense." It likewise dismissed the contention that the classification was reasonably related to public health or morals. The Connecticut Supreme Court of Errors reversed. It stated:

> In the earlier cases, courts apparently did not realize as clearly as they do now, as the result of *facts* found upon various trials, that billboards may be a source of danger to travelers upon highways through insecure construction, that accumulations of debris behind and around them may increase fire hazards and produce unsanitary conditions, that they may obstruct the view of operators of automobiles on the highway and may distract their atten-

tion from their driving, that behind them nuisances and immoral acts are often committed, and that they may serve as places of concealment for the criminal . . . .

As far as the record shows, the trial court did not have before it any adequate basis of *facts* upon which to determine that the invalidity of the provisions of the ordinance in question had been established. If we were to sustain its decision, we would in effect be holding that, as a matter of law, the legislative body cannot, with such exceptions as are provided in the ordinance before us, constitutionally prohibit billboards in the business zones of any of our towns, no matter what may be the circumstances or justification which existed in the particular case. We cannot so hold. . . .

As the trial court did not have before it sufficient *facts* to enable it to determine whether or not the plaintiffs were entitled to relief, we must remand the case for further proceedings. [Italics supplied.]

What kind of *facts* did the court want the trial court to consider? *Facts* tending to prove that the prohibition of all signs except those advertising goods sold on the premises promoted public safety and lessened traffic hazards? The Superior Court considered and rejected such evidence. *Facts* showing that the prohibited billboards created a danger to public health? *Facts* showing that billboards in open fields increased the danger of fire more than signs attached to buildings? *Facts* showing that nasty things go on behind billboards and that they afford hiding places for criminals and cops? Except in rare, isolated cases such *facts* are simply unattainable. For instance, a special master in the next-door state of Massachusetts, where the factual contexts should be fairly similar, after hearing evidence for 114 days found:

> In some isolated cases, certain signs and billboards in this Commonwealth have been used as screens to commit nuisances, hide law breakers, and facilitate immoral practices. Around some few filth has been allowed to collect, and some have shut out light and air from dwelling places. In and around others, rubbish and combustible materials have been allowed to collect, which to some degree tends to create a fire hazard. Those instances were all so rare, compared with the total number of signs and billboards in existence, that I am unable to find upon the evidence that signs and billboards, in general, as erected and maintained in this Commonwealth, have screened nuisances, or created a danger to public health

or morals, or facilitated immoral practices, or afforded a shelter for criminals, or created or increased the danger of fire, or hindered firemen in their work.

One of the more recent examples of community action against offensive advertising signs is the prohibition of signs overhanging the sidewalks in fashionable shopping areas. Although New York has long prohibited overhanging signs on Fifth Avenue, Park Avenue, and other East Side and downtown streets, only recently have other cities become interested in achieving the Fifth Avenue "uncluttered look" on certain of their main business arteries. In two recent cases the ordinances of Detroit and Minneapolis prohibiting overhanging signs on fashionable Woodward and Nicollet Avenues respectively were upheld. The city officials were pretty clearly not much concerned about safety, for if they were, signs hanging from the stores in a low-price district would also be prohibited. The practical result is that people who shop in the best stores have aesthetic preferences which may be recognized and protected by community officials.

While it is difficult to determine what is the primary offense of much land use, the simulation of blindness affords a simple rule-of-thumb; if a use is offensive to persons with sight but not offensive to a blind man in a similar position, the use is *primarily* offensive aesthetically. Applying this rule to the regulation of outdoor advertising, it seems clear that, except in certain areas where signs provide dangerous distraction to traffic, their offense is primarily their unsightliness. Is a well-constructed billboard or overhanging sign inimical to a blind man's safety, health or morals? Does it offend him in any way? The function of advertising signs is visual solicitation, and their offensiveness would seem to lie in the fact that their assault on the eyes in some contexts is most unpleasant.

Where courts have allowed community officials to prohibit what are in reality aesthetically objectionable land uses, their *language* indicates that they have closed their eyes to the real underlying facts. Yet what courts *say* and what courts *do* are two different things, and it is not proper to conclude from their language that courts do not know what is going on. Except in so far as the doctrine ensnares the unwary planner or judge who puts excessive faith in the plain meaning of words, it does not prevent any court from *holding* that community officials may zone for aesthetic objectives. But it seems to me that the doctrine may properly be criticized as meaningless theory, i.e., it does not describe past court response nor enable one to predict future court response. More will be said of this later. More important, and partly resulting from its aforementioned inefficacy, it appears to be an inadequate formulation of community objectives and an unnecessary hindrance to devising the most efficient means of achieving these objectives.

Clarification of Community Objectives

What are the community objectives? They must be clarified if the inadequacy of contemporary doctrine is to become evident and courts are to function as they should. It is difficult to know how far back toward basic value premises one must go in order to achieve the needed clarity. It is perhaps best to begin with some of what appear to me to be the merest truisms pertinent to the problem. These will sound very dogmatic, but I hope to elucidate and justify them in what will follow.

Among the strongest preferences of our society is for land use to be determined largely by private volition, and legal doctrine which implements this preference is a social hypothesis that goal values can more readily be achieved with a minimum of community intervention. The *St. Louis Gunning* doctrine is such an hypothesis. Individuals using their land as they desire are expected to increase total community wealth, encourage self-respect, and foster healthier and more beautiful surroundings. Thus we prefer that community officials should not intervene in the allocation and planning of land use

unless the privately determined use of land deprives other persons within the community of basic values, among which is the enjoyment of beauty by a wide number of people. Because the interests of particular individuals are not always compatible at the points of most intense reaction (e.g., a particular land use, such as a billboard, which increases the wealth of one person may be to others aesthetically offensive in certain contexts), community officials must sometimes intervene to secure the maximization of all community values. According to our basic social hypothesis, this intervention should occur only when community values are *seriously* damaged or threatened by specific uses of land. It is for the purpose of achieving the optimum use of its resources and deciding when individual use seriously impedes this achievement, that the community establishes planning boards and courts which shape land use practices and attendant legal doctrines. Precisely under what conditions community values are seriously damaged by individual action is a problem which seldom or never admits of a simple answer, but the answer is more easily reached if it is kept in mind that the ultimate objective of the community is to secure a use of land which promotes the most values for the most people and facilitates the harmonious functioning of residential, recreational, industrial and business areas.

Now it seems fairly clear that among the basic values of our communities, and of any society aboriginal or civilized, is beauty. Men are continuously engaged in its creation, pursuit, and possession; beauty like wealth, is an object of strong human desire. Men may use a beautiful object which they possess or control as a basis for increasing their power or wealth or for effecting a desired distribution of any one or all of the other basic values of the community, and, conversely, men may use power and wealth in an attempt to produce a beautiful object or a use of land which is aesthetically satisfying. It is solely because of man's irrepressible aesthetic demands, for instance, that land with a view has always been more valuable for residential purposes than land without, even though a house with a view intruding everywhere is said to be terribly hard to live in. Zoning regulations may, and often do, integrate aesthetics with a number of other community objectives, but it needs to be repeatedly emphasized that a healthful, safe and efficient community environment is not enough. More thought must be given to appearances if communities are to be really desirable places in which to live. Edmund Burke—no wide-eyed radical—said many years ago, "To make us love our country, our country ought to be lovely." It is still so today.

By assuming, however, that beauty is a matter neither subject to rational criticism nor capable of measurement by precise standards, courts say that although individuals may desire beauty, or, more accurately what they think is beautiful, community officials *qua* officials should not be allowed to force their own individual "subjective," "non-measurable," "irrational" aesthetic preferences upon others through use of the police power. This demand for precise criteria by which "beauty" can be measured, which is at the bottom of the judicial refusal to recognize openly aesthetics as a proper police power purpose, seems to be based upon a misunderstanding of the meaning of words. In any event, it needs some looking in to.

This demand assumes that aesthetic inquiries must begin by asking for the meaning of "beauty" and that only if this meaning is discovered can we possibly praise or condemn particular objects in our environment. Since beauty has in the past "proved notoriously refractory to definitive methods," it is easy to conclude that we cannot rationally appraise objects as beautiful. But by asking, "What is beauty?" courts have got themselves into the semantic bog which has long trapped the aestheticians, who too often start their intellectual meanderings in pursuit of that elusive will-o'-the-wisp: the true meaning of beauty. This same bog lies in the field of jurisprudence, except that judges rarely decide cases by inquiring first, "What is justice?"

Words simply do not have the kind of meaning that judges (and philosophers) are seeking when they ask, "What is beauty?" Words are neither "things" nor "ideas" that can be precisely measured; they have only uses or functions. The word beauty *means* nothing by itself. *To know the meaning of*

beauty is to know how to use it in an intelligible way to describe phenomena within a given context. One can meaningfully say, for instance, that Corot's "The Forest of Fontainebleau" is a beautiful painting or that the cathedral at Chartres is a beautiful building, but it is fruitless to ask if either is a correct use of beautiful. Philosophy has many revelations to offer but true meaning of word symbols is not among them.

That words have no single correct meaning points up that whether an object or a relation is beautiful (or "equitable" or "reasonable") hinges upon the perspective of the persons using the word. This semantic indefiniteness does not, however, force us to the very extreme position of Humpty Dumpty (as some judges assume it does in matters of beauty but not in matters of equity or reasonableness). Of course, if a word cannot be intelligibly used by persons in communication, then Humpty Dumpty is right, but there are good psychological and cultural reasons why the usage of words remains fairly stable, why people can and do meaningfully use the word beautiful.

What this adds up to is this: The cry for precise criteria might well be abandoned because it does not make sense. Beauty cannot be any more precisely defined than wealth, property, malice, or a host of multiordinal words to which courts are accustomed. Planners can give *reasons* for saying a particular arrangement of objects in the environment is beautiful based upon perspectives common in high degree among the people in a community, but they cannot *prove* it, and proof which is strictly unattainable should not be demanded. What is needed to decide whether beautiful can be used in an intelligible manner by planners is not a foredoomed search for precise criteria for its correct employment, but rather a clarification of some of the operations indicating how the general public and planners use the word, and an evaluation of these operations by reference to community goals. It will have to be admitted that a satisfactory set of operations describing what is beautiful in the varying contexts of land use is not easy to come by. The problem of contriving definitions that meet the operational test of meaning is a complicated, difficult business, for most of the relevant formal indices of beauty (such as symmetry, variety, uniformity, balance, rhythm, simplicity, intricacy, and quantity) will have to be further defined operationally. It is easy enough for planners to say, "Let beauty represent the ratio of formal indices to function," but it is hard to know what, if anything, they would be talking about.

Furthermore, in specifying and evaluating indices of attractive environments, it is important that community decision-makers —judges and planning officials—realize that they must promote land use which in time will succeed in appealing to people in general. In public planning, that environment is beautiful which deeply satisfies the public; practical success is of the greatest significance. In the long run, what the people like and acclaim *as* beautiful provides the operational indices of what *is* beautiful so far as the community is concerned. All popular preferences will never be acceptable to connoisseurs who urge their own competence to prescribe what is *truly* beautiful, yet it seems inescapable that an individual's judgment of beauty cannot be normative for the community until it is backed with the force of community opinion. History may be of some comfort to the connoisseurs: widely acknowledged *great* artists and *beautiful* architectural styles produced popular movements and not cults. A great age of architecture has not existed without the popular acceptance of a basic norm of design.

Planning attractive communities need not necessarily mean the uniform imposition of the dreary middle-brow tastes of the Philistines. To a large extent, artistic preferences are a result of conditioning (not entirely, of course, since even the marvelously adaptive human machine cannot become accustomed to everything). Preferences are formed through what the psychologists call canalization, a type of conditioning which eventually narrows the kind of stimulus that can satisfy a non-specific demand. The demand will at first be rather general but, through environmental conditioning, only one or two stimuli will bring satisfaction. Beauty, as one of the values sought by man, is one of his non-specific demands, and its satisfaction is conditioned by his environment. Objects in the individual's aesthetic continuum with which he identifies himself—to which he has become habituated—will more likely satisfy his demand than objects with which he is unfamiliar. Individuals do not like to impair the identifications of their personality structure, and, for that reason, resist new designs. For the same reason, other changes in the environment are resisted. Nevertheless lively perspicacious leadership in the arts, such as has been provided by the Bauhaus group, the Museum of Modern Art in New York, and other community art centers interested in improving contemporary design, can change —even "improve"—less educated "pedestrian" tastes (to use the jargon of art criticism). The real need is for those who want to influence community artistic preferences to examine, far more closely than has yet been done, the techniques by which contemporary aesthetic opinion is, and could be, manipulated.

When an individual responds to environmental stimuli by applying the word beautiful to particular objects, an enormous number of variables has influenced the response. These include the specific qualities of the objects perceived (shapes, colors, textures, arrangements, compositions, etc.), the physical and social context of perception, the entire physical and psychological history of the individual, and the values of the percipient and of the community. All these and infinitely more variables fuse into judgments of beauty. These judgments of beauty are like all other appraisals in that they are made by individuals. They will vary. There is no getting around the inherent limitations on man's power to reason which Kant demonstrated so many years ago. Still, it is necessary to conclude that because individuals are not *perfect* judging machines that *imperfect but rational* evaluations of what land uses are conducive to an attractive community cannot and ought not to be made? It is a pity that aesthetic disagreements cannot be resolved by reference to absolute standards, for we should all feel so much more secure in our judgments. What we need, however, to solve a value problem is not an illusion of an absolute standard but decision-makers whose thinking is sufficiently disciplined and whose technical training and knowledge of human beings are sufficiently extensive to qualify them to pass judgment on the particular problem, and to develop rational techniques for implementing our generalized, flexible, relativistic community values.

The Implementation of Values

Consideration of some specific land uses which have been widely thought to be aesthetically objectionable will show, perhaps, some types of aesthetic regulation rational community planning requires and how contemporary doctrine impedes the efficient implementation of community values. It will become apparent that the question of methodology of value implementation really needs far more extensive consideration than it has ever received in the past and far more than can be given it here. The following is intended to be more suggestive than comprehensive.

CONTROL OF BUILDING DESIGN

Many of the restrictions upon land use have, at one time or another, been said to be for aesthetic objectives. Indeed, many years ago it was thought by some that the main purpose of a city plan was to create a City Beautiful. Even today, claims that building restrictions (such as minimum lot size and minimum floor plan provisions) have mainly an aesthetic purpose are not unusual, but here it would seem almost impossible to separate considerations of beauty from considerations of health, safety, and other factors. Because these other objectives are so obviously involved, courts have usually sustained reasonable, minimum size provisions and have not recently struck down any provision of this type on the ground it was solely for an aesthetic purpose. If minimum size restrictions are without the police power, it is for

some reason other than that their objective is aesthetic. Thus a discussion of minimum size provisions is not directly pertinent here.

There are, none the less, certain community restrictions on land use which ruin the amenity of the neighborhood simply because it involves deviation from the neighborhood scheme and is considered unattractive. People expect and demand protection against deviations which they consider too ugly, and in new subdivisions protect themselves with private restrictive convenants, but in the older areas reliance necessarily is to a large extent on the intervention of community officials. Examples of these aesthetically motivated restrictions are requirements of two-story houses, of conformity to building line, and of larger front yards in the quieter, more exclusive residential areas with the least traffic.

Some cities with a distinctive architectural tradition have attempted to control the architectural design of buildings by establishing a public body to pass upon the design of private buildings. New Orleans, Williamsburg, Santa Barbara, and West Palm Beach are examples. Apparently the only reported court test of an *ordinance* of this type involved the West Palm Beach one, and it was held void as not related to "health, welfare, safety or morals." It is clear that restrictions on building design have aesthetic objectives in mind more than anything else; it also seems to me that in certain contexts such restrictions may be reasonable means of policy implementation.

Our communities need to achieve an environment that is emotionally satisfactory, that effects reduction in purposeless nervous and physical tensions of the inhabitants. When the inner life of an individual is out of balance, anxiety occurs, expressing itself in a number of socially destructive ways. Architecture, indeed every object in the individual's aesthetic continuum, has a direct effect upon the equilibrium of his personality and upon the happiness and richness of his life. Community officials need to become more aware of the significance design holds for each individual and thus for society.

Zoning restrictions which implement a policy of neighborhood amenity should be avoided, if at all, not because they are for aesthetic objectives but only because the restrictions are unreasonable devices of implementing community policy. Whether, I repeat, an ordinance of this type should be declared invalid should depend upon whether in the particular institutional context the restriction was an arbitrary and irrational method of achieving an attractive, efficiently functioning, prosperous community—and *not* upon whether the objectives were primarily aesthetic. It is obvious that the task of determining whether a restriction is arbitrary and unreasonable is not an easy one, but it certainly is not made easier by theory which turns a deaf ear to aesthetic effects. Before planners or courts can make a fully rational decision, they need to hear arguments as to the effect of a proposed decision on all community values. They need to know, *inter alia*, how the zoning ordinance will affect the distribution of community wealth, especially neighboring property values on which taxes and the financial security of the city depend, how the ordinance will affect the well-being of the community as a whole, including the effect upon physical and mental health and safety of the residents, and how the ordinance will increase the attractiveness of the community. They need to know about the matters which contemporary doctrine may exclude from evidence.

Undoubtedly courts do take aesthetics into consideration by smuggling aesthetic effects into the judicial ken by a kind of "judicial notice" and evaluating them by a mysterious and very inarticulate intuition. But too often this results in a court being fooled by its own Gestalt; too often it results in a decision as to the reasonableness or unreasonableness of an ordinance without careful consideration of extrinsic evidence of its aesthetic effect. Are not the defects of a legal system in which words do not match action, in which the gap between myth and decision is great, many and patent?

Conclusion

If we want our children to grow up in pleasant purlieus, we must give up something of the freedom of the individual to use his land as he chooses. This is inherent in the concept of land planning by community officials. Nevertheless, I do not wish to leave the impression that I think it either necessary or desirable that community officials be arbiters in all questions of aesthetic preference which crop up from the use of land. According to our basic social hypothesis, they should interfere only when individual use seriously hampers the achievement of community goals. If community officials instigate an artistic inquisition, it is certainly the court's duty to oppose it, but the cases do not suggest that community officials have acted rashly in attempting to improve appearances. In fact, they seem to have lagged far behind public execration of eyesores, and when they have acted extensive damage to community values has usually already been done. It is a pity, but it is not entirely their fault. Without frank judicial acceptance of beauty as a proper community objective attainable through use of the police power, the maximization of all community values is impossible and ordinances attempting to prevent eyesores generally become makeshift and piecemeal devices.

Zoning doctrine is still in its formative period; the complexion of our landscape for a long time in the future will be determined by our present attitudes toward zoning for aesthetic objectives. It seems to me that something more is needed than a case-by-case exception to the general rule, something approaching more closely to a systematic theory of planning which will cover the presently widely accepted doctrines as well as develop new ones to replace those which are now causing us trouble. A tabulation of differentiated factual situations in which restrictions were judicially approved gives community officials a more penetrating insight into the non-meaningfulness of our contemporary authoritative doctrine about aesthetics, but if we would have anything approaching a scientific method in law, we need a body of meaningful postulates and propositions, the efficacy of which is verifiable by case results and evaluated by community goals. Those courts which postulate that the police power may not be exercised for aesthetic objectives obscure the goals toward which community policy is directed and hinder a determination of what types of aesthetic regulation are required by rational community planning. An effective doctrine for aesthetic zoning may, probably should, provide for careful judicial supervision of the exercise of planning powers in this field. But whatever norm is adopted ought to be based upon an adequate recognition and description of the real factors which motivate decisions of planning boards and courts.

12

Elimination of Incompatible Uses and Structures

C. McKim Norton

Reprinted with permission of author and publisher from a symposium, "Land Planning in a Democracy," appearing in Law and Contemporary Problems, Vol. 20, No. 2, Spring 1955, *published by the Duke University School of Law, Durham, North Carolina.* © 1955 by Duke University.

GIVEN A reasonably suitable and extensive piece of open country, it is possible today to design and build a model town with "a place for everything and everything in its place." Recent examples of such developments are the new industrial town of Kittimat, British Columbia and the residential communities of Park Forest, Illinois and Levittown, Pennsylvania.

In such developments, incompatible uses are physically separated from each other. For the forseeable future, at least, a conventional zoning ordinance and its honest administration will maintain the desirable status quo and protect the town plan against encroachment.

The typical American community, however, was largely built in the period between the early concern over town layout of our colonial forebears and the reawakening of city planning in the twentieth century. Today an admitted cause of residential and commercial slums, traffic congestion, and other indicia of urban obsolescence is the haphazard mixing of incompatible land uses. A large part of the city planning problem today, therefore, is not how to design and build the perfect urban machine but rather how to take out the misfit parts of the machine which we have inherited.

Analysis of Incompatibility

The problem of incompatibility of land uses and buildings was well stated by Justice Sutherland when he wrote in 1926 in the Euclid decision:

Thus the question whether the power exists to forbid the erection of a building of a particular kind or for a particular use, like the question whether a particular thing is a nuisance, is to be determined, not by an abstract consideration of the building or of the thing considered apart, but by considering it in connection with the circumstances and the locality. . . . A nuisance may be merely a right thing in the wrong place—like pig in the parlor instead of the barnyard. In some fields, the bad fades into the good by such invisible degrees that the two are not capable of being readily distinguished and separated in terms of legislation.

Since 1926 the city planning profession has been trying, without as yet complete success, to develop standards of compatibility and incompatibility which are objective, scientific, and, as a practical matter, enforceable.

In the earliest days of zoning, it was thought that all uses could be classified very simply by a "hierarchy of uses" into three districts—residential, commercial, and manufacturing. Residential districts included nothing but "parlors," other than a few essential accessory uses such as churches, public schools, and suburban railroad depots. Everything allowed in residential districts was permitted in commercial districts. The manufacturing or pig-sty district was a catch-all for every kind of use including manufacturing, commerce, and housing (for people who could not afford to live elsewhere).

As a contrast to this primitive separation of uses and buildings, consider the proposed new zoning resolution for New York City. Here in the nation's largest and most complicated city, the planning consultants find the need for 15 zoning districts in which are permitted 18 different use groups (combinations of compatible uses). The use groups include: three groups of residential uses; two groups of community facilities which are properly associated with some or all residential districts; four groups of retail and commercial uses; three groups of wholesale and commercial amusement uses, one group of heavy commercial and automotive service uses; and six groups of manufacturing uses.

One of the manufacturing use groups includes office, laboratory and manufacturing uses which, when subject to adequate controls over bulk and landscaping, are appropriate in certain locations in low density residential areas if they comply with certain performance standards. In other words, it is even proposed to let a pig into the parlor provided it is a housebroken pig with a pleasing (preferably red brick colonial) face. The philosophy behind this attempt at classification according to standards of compatibility and incompatibility was most lucidly summarized by New York City Planning Commissioner Lawrence M. Orton when he stated:

> As has frequently been said, it isn't so much *what you do* as *how you do it*, that counts. Houses and apartments, stores and even factories, can be mixed harmoniously and advantageously, provided the design is right.

From the standpoint of residential areas, incompatibility of uses and buildings has generally been measured by the following factors (most of which are cited in the Euclid opinion to justify the separation of industry and high density apartments from a single-family district): (1) Danger to persons or property (such as fire, explosion, hazard, corrosive fumes, and auto, truck, railroad, airplane traffic); (2) danger to health, convenience, and comfort (such as excessive smoke, dust, odor, noise (including traffic noise), vibration, glare at night, industrial waste, garbage, obstruction to light and air, and overcrowding of people on the land); (3) danger to morals (such as commercial gathering places for drinking, gambling, amusement); (4) miscellaneous other factors (such as aesthetic, psychological and physical deterioration of neighborhood desirability due to factors including appearance of grounds and buildings, commercial signs, uses with unpleasant associations, decline of neighborhood homogeneity, prevalence of strangers on business visits, encroachment of commercial-visitor parking on residential streets, increased vehicular street traffic induced by commercial and industrial estab-

lishments, and parental fear of physical and moral danger to children).

From the standpoint of commercial areas, incompatibility of uses and buildings may be measured by "economic incompatibility factors" such as land uses and buildings which interrupt pedestrian traffic flow in retail areas. Such interruptions are created by: (1) "dead spots" where shoppers lose interest in going further; (2) driveways and other such physical breaks in the sidewalks; (3) cross traffic, either vehicular or pedestrian; and (4) areas characterized by hazards, noises, odors, unsightliness, or other unpleasant features. The new shopping centers are setting sensible standards of order and appearance, lack of which in existing business centers includes such nuisance factors as too many commercial signs, heavy vehicular traffic unrelated to the shopping center, and overcongestion of buildings in relation to streets and parking facilities.

Similarly, industry today recognizes the new design standards of modern factories and planned industrial districts and, in general, that residences should be excluded from manufacturing districts on the principle, no doubt, that if people live in the pigsty long enough, they eventually will send the pigs elsewhere.

Efforts To Achieve Compatibility

A. BY ZONING

The basic principles of comprehensive zoning were developed before the automobile era, the great expansion of metropolitan cities, and the technological revolution, still going on, in ways of housing people, business, and industry. A first tenet of comprehensive zoning was, and still is, that it is possible to map an urban land area into districts in which a class or classes of compatible uses are permitted and uses incompatible with them are prohibited. The first zoners, however, liked their districts "straight" with few or no accessory or mixed uses or building types. Thus single-family districts were considered as areas in which apartment houses were rigidly excluded.

Talented architects and new-town planners like Clarence Stein argued that row houses and apartments could quite properly be mixed with single-family houses and demonstrated the fact in developments such as Radburn in unzoned Fairlawn, New Jersey. They railed against the crudity of zoning classifications, but to little avail, since it was widely believed that the general improvement which zoning promised outweighed the admitted rigidities it imposed on design.

When zoning was first developed, its proponents hoped that existing incompatible uses and buildings (classified by the zoning ordinance as non-conforming) would gradually disappear. Thus zoning would act as a comb to straighten out the tangled kinks of past city development.

Zoning, one must remember, was a radical concept in 1916 even as regards regulating the future use of undeveloped land areas. During the preparatory work for the zoning of Greater New York, fears were constantly expressed by property owners that existing nonconforming buildings would be ousted. The demand was general that this should not be done. The Zoning Commission went as far as it could to explain that existing nonconforming uses could continue, that zoning looked to the future, and that if orderliness could be brought about in the future the nonconforming buildings would to a considerable extent be changed by natural causes as time went on.

Nonconforming buildings and uses, however, have shown great vitality in persisting because of the simple fact that most nonconforming uses (such as a store or a filling station in a residential district) have the high earning capacity of a well-situated monopoly created and protected by law.

Although most zoning ordinances permit, and a few state enabling acts require, that nonconforming buildings and uses continue when an ordinance goes into effect, their alteration or enlargement is generally prohibited, and their reconstruction after abandonment, discontinuance or destruction by fire, hurricane, explosion or other act of God is denied.

Furthermore, there is an accelerating trend towards the positive elimination of nonconforming uses without compensation under zoning regulations which require discontinuance after a reasonable period of time in which the nonconforming value of a building or use is deemed to be amortized.

Thus, for example, the city of Los Angeles requires that nonconforming buildings or structures in residence zones shall be completely removed or made conforming when they reach specified ages from the date of their erection (ranging from 20 to 40 years, depending on their building code class of construction). Nonconforming commercial or industrial use of a residential building or residential accessory building is to be discontinued within five years, where no buildings are employed in connection with such use, where the only buildings employed are accessory or incidental to such use, or where such use is maintained in connection with a conforming building. A nonconforming use of land which is accessory to the nonconforming use of a nonconforming building must be discontinued at the same time as the nonconforming use of the building is discontinued. Nonconforming signs and billboards are to be removed within five years. All nonconforming oil wells, including any incidental storage tanks and drilling and production equipment, must be removed within 20 years.

The Los Angeles ordinance has gained added interest because of a current court test. A wholesale plumber contested the validity of the provision. He resided on the property and had also been using his house and garage for office and storage purposes and the adjoining lot for storage in racks and bins.

The California District Court of Appeals, in its opinion, summed up the issues involved in compulsory amortization by zoning about as successfully as they have ever been stated:

> Exercise of the police power frequently impairs rights in property because the exercise of those rights is detrimental to the public interest. Every zoning ordinance effects some impairment of vested rights either by restricting

prospective uses or by prohibiting the continuation of existing uses, because it affects property already owned by individuals at the time of its enactment. . . . In essence, there is no distinction between requiring the discontinuance of a nonconforming use within a reasonable period and provisions which deny the right to add to or extend buildings devoted to an existing nonconforming use, which deny the right to resume a nonconforming use after a period of nonuse, which deny the right to extend or enlarge an existing nonconforming use, which deny the right to substitute new buildings for those devoted to an existing nonconforming use—all of which have been held to be valid exercises of the policy power. . . .

The distinction between an ordinance restricting future uses and one requiring the termination of present uses within a reasonable period of time is merely one of degree, and constitutionality depends on the relative importance to be given to the public gain and to the private loss. Zoning as it affects every piece of property is to some extent retroactive in that it applies to property already owned at the time of the effective date of the ordinance. The elimination of existing uses within a reasonable time does not amount to a taking of property nor does it necessarily restrict the use of property so that it cannot be used or any reasonable purpose. Use of a reasonable amortization scheme provides an equitable means of reconciliation of the conflicting interests in satisfaction of due process requirements. As a method of eliminating existing nonconforming uses it allows the owner of the nonconforming use, by affording an opportunity to make new plans, at least partially to offset any loss he might suffer. The loss he suffers, if any, is spread out over a period of years, and he enjoys a monopolistic position by virtue of the zoning ordinance as long as he remains. If the amortization period is reasonable the loss to the owner may be small when compared with the benefit to the public. Nonconforming uses will eventually be eliminated. A legislative body may well conclude that the beneficial effect on the community of the eventual elimination of all nonconforming uses by a reasonable amortization plan more than offsets individual losses.

Other cities which have outlawed nonconforming uses include New Orleans, which began in 1927 with a one-year discontinuance for all commercial and industrial uses in residential areas, changed to a 20-year period in 1929, and abandoned the principle in 1948; Boston, Massachusetts, which requires elimination of all nonconforming buildings and premises after April 1, 1961 or 37 years

after such buildings and premises first became nonconforming due to zoning action; Fort Worth, Texas, which requires certain nonconforming uses of land to be discontinued and all material completely removed by its owner within 3 years, and nonconforming commercial signs and billboards also to be removed within 3 years; Wichita, Kansas, which requires nonconforming commercial or industrial buildings located within specified dwelling districts to be either removed or converted to a conforming use on or before January 1, 1997 or within 60 years as to such buildings for which a permit was issued after January 1, 1937; Seattle, Washington, which requires in two residence districts any nonconforming use of premises which is not in a building to be discontinued within a period of one year; Chicago, Illinois, which requires discontinuance of nonconforming uses upon transfer of ownership or termination of the existing lease unless the nonconforming use is carried on in a building designed for the purpose, and in this latter event discontinuance is required upon expiration of the normal useful life of such building (which is fixed at 100 years for buildings of solid brick, stone or reinforced concrete with structural members of steel; 75 years for buildings of solid brick, stone or reinforced concrete with structural members of metal, reinforced concrete, masonry, timber or a combination thereof; and 50 years for buildings of all other construction); Tallahassee, Florida, which requires discontinuance of certain commercial uses in residential districts after 10 years; Richmond, Virginia, which requires discontinuance of nonconforming uses of land only within one year and discontinuance of nonconforming buildings in residence districts at different times, such as 3 years for boarding houses and 20 years for commercial and industrial buildings which were at least 20 years old at the time of the ordinance, or, if not 20 years old, then 40 years from the date of the issuance of the building permit. Other cities with amortization provisions in their zoning ordinances include Cleveland, Ohio, St. Petersburg, Florida, Kansas City, Kansas,

Richmond Heights, Missouri, Corpus Christi, Texas, and Akron, Ohio.

Compulsory amortization of nonconforming uses, as an exercise of the police power under zoning, seems to be a reasonable and useful method of eliminating three categories of incompatibility—namely: (1) most uses involving no structures or structures of an impermanent nature; (2) nonconforming structures of an impermanent nature or representing a relatively small investment; and (3) nonconforming uses in conforming structures. These include such developments in residential districts as: (1) commercial storage on open lots (junk yards, lumber yards, etc.); (2) filling stations, sheds for commercial use, and billboards; and (3) residential buildings used for commercial purposes.

In short, nonconformities which may be reasonably eliminated by up to ten years' amortization are properly disposed of by this method, especially when their incompatibility is so inherent in their operation that no reasonably enforceable performance standards could be devised to make them compatible. In many situations, for example, the commercial traffic essential to the nonconforming use makes its presence in a residential neighborhood a permanently deteriorating influence.

When the nonconforming structure represents such a large investment that more than ten years is required to eliminate it, the amortization method seems inadequate. To wait a generation or two before eliminating or even lessening the effect of an incompatible use is futile as a means of preventing the spread of the infection of incompatibility, unless the incompatibility is more imaginary than real.

B. BY ABATEMENT OF NUISANCE

Where an incompatible use or structure representing a major investment is a genuine menace to the area in which it is situated, it may be ordered discontinued or removed as a nuisance. Long before zoning, the courts sustained municipal regulations which re-quired the immediate elimination of uses and buildings which, while short of a common law nuisance, had definite, tangible, physical effects which menaced public health, safety, and welfare.

Thus a Los Angeles regulation requiring the discontinuance at once of the manufacture of bricks in a section of Los Angeles which was developed as a residential area was sustained by the Supreme Court of the United States in a leading case. In its opinion the Court said:

> It is to be remembered that we are dealing with one of the most essential powers of government, one that is the least limitable. It may, indeed, seem harsh in its exercise. Usually it is on some individual, but the imperative necessity for its existence precludes any limitation upon it when not exerted arbitrarily. A vested interest cannot be asserted against it because of conditions once obtaining. . . . To so hold would preclude development and fix a city forever in its primitive conditions. There must be progress, and if in its march private interests are in the way they must yield to the good of the community.

The same Los Angeles ordinance had previously been sustained by the state supreme court as applied to eliminate 110 Chinese laundries and a lumber yard. Subsequently, an ordinance prohibiting livery stables in residential areas was sustained by the Supreme Court of the United States, as have ordinances against other uses—for example, smoke nuisance and oil tanks.

The nuisance doctrine as applied to elimination of incompatible uses has had much less attention paid to it in recent years than it deserves. It generally has been felt that the use to be enjoined must be of a very tangible, crude and physical nature—a use so obviously detrimental to public health, safety, and welfare as to be a nuisance by common law reasoning, if not a common law nuisance (such as storage of gunpowder in a residential district). Perhaps this is because the early proponents of zoning, eager to make it palatable to land owners and investors, disassociated the harsh doctrine of nuisance from the broad regulation of future developments based on a community plan.

The courts are ready, however, to sustain regulations requiring discontinuance of practices which are demonstrated to be harmful to the public. In the often-cited case of Jones v. Los Angeles where the court refused to sustain a law which prohibited all sanatoria for nervous diseases outside of specified districts and would have required discontinuance of four such sanatoria, the court made it clear that it could find an "undoubted menace to public health, safety or morals." Similarly, in a case quite similar to the Hadacheck case, the court refused to sustain an ordinance requiring the cessation of gravel pit operations because it found the discomfort "more imaginary than real."

What makes an activity an abatable nuisance depends upon the facts of the situation. As our understanding of nuisance factors in urban development increases through medical, sociological and economic research, and as the city planners develop performance standards against which such factors can be measured, the nuisance doctrine will take hold in some situations where amortization under zoning would be ineffective. The cumulation of nuisance factors may at least justify the shortening of the period of grace given nonconforming uses. The zoning ordinance of Seattle, Washington, for example, requires certain nuisance-type industries (cement manufacturing, glue manufacturing, slaughter houses, etc.) in other than an industrial district to be discontinued within six months.

The county of Los Angeles has devised what appears to be a significant combination of the amortization and nuisance doctrines. By an ordinance adopted in 1950, existing nonconforming uses are granted an "automatic exception" to continue. Such exception remains in force for specified times, except that it may be revoked by the Regional Planning Commission if the Commission finds:

1. That the condition of the improvements, if any, on the property are such that to require the property to be used only for those uses permitted in the zone where it is located would not impair the constitutional rights of any person.
2. That the nature of the improvements are such that they can be altered so as to be used in conformity with the uses permitted in the zone in which such property is located

without impairing the constitutional rights of any person.

The basis for such findings includes the grounds that the use is exercised so as to be detrimental to the public health or safety or as to be a nuisance.

C. BY SPECIAL PERMIT

Throughout the history of zoning, there has been a quest for some formula which would enable law makers to establish a complete series of fixed regulations to guide logical urban development by rules of law. No such formula has ever been found.

The variance procedure, conceived originally as zoning's "safety value" to relax pressures arising from minor situations involving "practical difficulty and unnecessary hardship," has been much used and abused (thereby often adding new incompatible uses more rapidly than nonconforming uses were eliminated). Spot zoning, illegal but usually untested, has given the veneer of conformity to incompatible uses. Other devices such as the "legislative permit" and New Jersey's "variance recommendation" procedure have added another slow leak to the watertight concepts of the zoning pioneers.

To make zoning more flexible and still maintain a rule of law, the special permit exception or "conditional use" based on an administrative finding that specific standards have been complied with has come into common use. By this method new, otherwise nonconforming uses are permitted to be introduced into any districts where they are deemed to be compatible under suitable standards—for example, private schools, nursing homes or garages in residential areas. A recent development in this area of zoning is the concept of the "designed shopping district" which may be fitted into residential areas.

The fixed guideposts of urban development are tending to be only the major divisions of areas as predominantly residential, commercial or industrial, while the details of community development are increasingly being based on a bundle of performance standards by which compatibility and incompatibility are measured by an administrative agency.

If a new, otherwise nonconforming use can be admitted into a district by special permit, why cannot an existing nonconforming use be permitted to remain, if it can be improved so as to qualify under performance standards?

Thus it has been suggested that a "well located" nonconforming local grocery store in a residence district be allowed to continue indefinitely if its owner brings it up to standards which were similar to those which a community planner might include in the design of a new residential community.

The practical trouble with this procedure today is that it is built upon the shifting sands of the performance standards concept carried to its logical conclusion.

The practical difficulties are obvious. In the first place, performance standards have not as yet been developed to the point where they can be applied objectively to such a situation by an administrative agency or a municipal governing body. Secondly, the Achilles' heel of performance standards is the constant and almost superhuman enforcement problem connected with so many of them. In the third place, the history of the administration of zoning by boards of appeal and municipal governing bodies leads one to the conclusion that the licensing of nonconforming uses would result in a breakdown of zoning in the present state of our objective knowledge of city development and our ability to administer land development regulations.

The logic of licensing nonconforming uses, however, is compelling. Certainly those uses which are today allowed only by special permit could also be permitted to continue under special permit even though nonconforming.

D. EMINENT DOMAIN

There seems little doubt that elimination of incompatible uses is a sufficient public purpose to justify a public taking with just compensation. Zoning by eminent domain, though impractical, was held constitutional in the states in which it was tried. Condemnation of incompatible uses and buildings as a part of a scheme of urban redevelopment now rests upon the firm ground of the recent decision of the Supreme Court of the United States in which the taking of a department store in an area to be redeveloped for residential use was sustained. In this case the property condemned was not itself substandard and under the redevelopment plan it might be sold to other private interests.

Eminent domain is a last resort for the elimination of incompatible uses but one which may be increasingly used in urban redevelopment programs and in "stopblight" situations where the incompatibility of relatively large investments is built-in and permanent and where amortization would take too long. Public opposition to the costs of eminent domain and owner resistance to condemnation will require a clear-cut case to be made for the necessity of removing an incompatible building or use and the public benefits which will flow therefrom. In areas which are not yet substandard but only declining, this will require a more precise knowledge of cause and effect of urban blight than we now have.

Conclusions

From this discussion we may conclude that many incompatible uses may be ordered to be discontinued without compensation.

The term "retroactive zoning" as applied to the elimination of nonconforming uses should be abandoned. All zoning is basically retroactive in nature.

The elimination of incompatible uses of land and buildings can become as normal a part of administration of municipal government as street improvements or urban redevelopment.

Incompatibilities should be classified for administrative purposes into four categories: (1) nonconforming buildings; (2) nonconforming use of buildings; (3) nonconforming use of land; and (4) nonconforming lots.

Every zoning ordinance should prevent the alteration, enlargement, reconstruction after abandonment, discontinuance or destruction of any nonconforming building unless the structure is made conforming or is temporarily continued under the special permit discussed below.

Every municipality should analyze and classify all incompatible and nonconforming uses of land and buildings. Some categories may be dismissed as of insufficient importance or of such a widespread nature as to be ineligible for a program of compulsory conformity. The doctrine of de minimis for example, may rule out minor lot and building measurement nonconformities. While lots nonconforming as to size may be required to be combined with adjoining vacant lots in the same ownership, in general, nonconformities due to up-grading of zoning standards may have to be tolerated until areas are reclaimed by redevelopment from the deadly subdivision and building practice of a generation or more ago.

Analysis of nonconforming uses may lead to their legalization by proper rezoning. In one city in New Jersey, for example, by variance and spot zoning enough heavy commercial automotive uses and buildings were permitted and built since 1946 in a business district so as to change the predominant nature of a whole area. This area is now about to be rezoned for repair garages and similar heavy commercial uses.

In other parts of municipalities, analysis of incompatible and nonconforming uses may lead to the obvious conclusion that nothing short of condemnation or purchase of an entire area under a redevelopment plan will suffice to eliminate the built-in chaos. This is typical of the worst residential, commercial and industrial slum areas of the nation's older cities.

After analysis of incompatible and nonconforming uses, a program of action for large parts of the municipalities can be formulated. All uses of buildings and land which are determined to be of such a nature as to be subject to elimination can be placed under a permit of continuance. Such permits will allow certain structures and uses to continue only for a specified period of months or years. In some classes of uses, performance standards could be required to minimize nuisance factors.

The methods available for the elimination program include: (1) amortization by zoning; (2) injunction as a nuisance; (3) eminent domain; and (4) license by special permit or as a conditional use. Amortization and license could be combined in some categories of uses.

Administration of a general elimination program could properly include a program of municipal acquisition of undeveloped land suitable for certain classes of high nuisance factor uses. This land could be made available to such uses, if they were ordered to discontinue elsewhere. Indeed, without offering nuisance industries a place to go, some municipalities would be open to the charge of "dumping," a charge no longer academic since the Cresskill and Dumont decisions.

Finally, the program of elimination of incompatible and nonconforming uses should take advantage of every type of regulation available to the municipality in addition to zoning. Public health ordinances, police regulations (including traffic regulations), housing laws, and provision of municipal services can all play a part in bringing order into today's chaotic urban scene.

the controls in each of these major parts have been substantially revised.

The New Chicago Zoning Ordinance

Richard F. Babcock

Reprinted by special permission of the Northwestern University Law Review, Vol. 52, No. 2. © 1957, Northwestern University School of Law.

THE BIRTH of the 1957 Comprehensive Amendment to the Chicago Zoning Ordinance was not without pain. The disputes, charges, countercharges, and the headlines and editorial comment by the metropolitan press are a foretaste of the changes this document will bring to control over land use in the city.[1] . . .

The Comprehensive Amendment bristles with experiment. A multitude of troublesome legal questions face even the casual reader of its text. An examination of half a dozen of the most controversial items will indicate the sweep of its departure from customary zoning practice in Illinois.

The classic tripartite division of the municipality into residential, business, and industrial districts has been maintained, but

[1] The charge was made by some segments of the paint industry and the steel industry that the proposed controls over odors, smoke, noise, and also over fire hazards would drive industry away from the city. The Committee changed the provisions to meet most of the demands of the industrial groups. The Committee was also accused of planning to drive 3,000 retail shops out of residential districts by provisions to eliminate, gradually, specified non-conforming uses. The latter provisions were later revised. The greatest furor was raised over the stringent provisions with respect to billboards along boulevards and over the failure of the city to take action against such billboards before the Comprehensive Amendment was adopted.

Residential Districts

The ordinance provides for eight residential districts. Only the first two of these are exclusively single-family districts. The innovation arises from the fact that the six remaining residential districts are not classified according to dwelling type. No longer is there the "Duplex District," "Two-Family District," "Row House District," or the "Apartment House District" so long a familiar pattern of urban zoning. Instead, beginning with the "R-3" General Residence District the ordinance provides in each of the remaining districts that the permitted uses shall include "Dwellings—one-family, two-family, and multiple-family, attached or detached." The controls which are established to set each district apart from the others are not based upon dwelling type but upon bulk and density. Density is regulated by the not uncommon requirement of lot area per dwelling unit, or so-called minimum lot size. These run from 6,250 square feet in the "R-1" Single-Family Residence District to 115 square feet per dwelling unit in the high-rise, "R-8" General Residence District. The Supreme Court of Illinois has recently upheld a minimum lot area requirement of one-fifth of an acre in a suburban village under most extreme circumstances. There can be little doubt that the principle of minimum lot area per dwelling unit is here to stay.

The second method used to control bulk, by which the six General Residence Districts are distinguished, is new and goes under the term "floor area ratio." This is the ratio of the usable floor area of the building to the area of the "zoning lot."[2] Thus, in the "R-1" and "R-2" Single-Family Districts the maximum ratio permitted is 0.5; it is 0.7 in the "R-3" District; 1.2 in "R-4"; and up-

[2] A "zoning lot" is a single tract of land located within a single block, which (at the time of filing for a building permit) is designated by its owner or developer as a tract to be used, developed, or built upon as a unit, under single ownership or control. Therefore a "zoning lot" may or may not coincide with a "lot of record".

ward until the "R-8" General Residence District where it is 10.0. In the last instance, this means that if a builder were permitted to erect a building without setbacks, so that each floor covered the full area of the lot, he could not build more than a ten-story structure. This regulatory device takes the place of any height restrictions, which were a customary part of the old "dwelling-type" system of residential classification. If a builder chooses to set back any of the stories from the vertical extension of the lot lines, he can achieve a corresponding increase in height as he cuts down the floor area.

By these two methods, lot area per dwelling unit and floor area ratio, the ordinance classifies each of the so-called General Residence Districts from "R-3" through "R-8". The result is that any dwelling type can appear in any one of these districts if it can provide sufficient lot area and maintain the required open space. Single-family, duplex and multiple units may be interspersed, for example, as long as the builder provides adequate open space. The planning arguments for this departure from traditional classification are reasonable and, if reasonable, these social and economic arguments are the best legal defense against constitutional attack. It is said, so the defense runs, that the traditional classification by building type in many cases prevents the private redevelopment of rundown areas or the development of vacant parcels, because the builder is unable to achieve an economically feasible unit within the limitations of the particular dwelling-type requirements. Furthermore, emphasis upon standards based upon the amount of open space rather than building type furthers the goal of increased recreational space, as well as more light and air between residential buildings. Thus, in the traditional Duplex or Two-Family District these units, built on separate but adjoining lots, were frequently without adequate open areas. The construction of one multiple-family unit on these same two lots would, under the new standards, be accompanied by more open areas on the lots and greater space between one building and adjoining structures. This argument is accompanied, admittedly with less confidence, by the plea that variations in building type provide an

escape from the sameness of urban living and thus tends to increase property values and help stem the rush to (the sameness of) the suburbs.[3] Finally, the defense concludes with greater confidence, the increased variety of building types does not mean increased pressures on local services such as police, sanitation and fire, provided the controls upon density and bulk are rigorously maintained. It does not follow that under this new system there is any increase in the number of dwelling units per acre of land.

This is not to say that there will be no embarrassment in advancing these arguments before the Supreme Court, as must be done when some irate owner of a single-family home protests the erection of a multiple-dwelling in his block. The rub is that during the past twenty years city and village attorneys have been defending the exclusion of multiple-dwelling units from other residential districts upon traditional grounds of classification by dwelling type. It has been argued, and the argument accepted by the Supreme Court, that the influx of apartment buildings into an area of so-called "higher classification" encourages blight, increases fire, sanitary and traffic hazards, and brings greater noise and destruction of those customary incidents of a neighborhood of home owners. Now it must be alleged that this is not necessarily so because of the new standards by which these "intrusions" are regulated.

Business Districts

The Comprehensive Amendment establishes seven business districts, classified primarily by the uses permitted in the respective districts. A concept, new in Illinois at

---

[3] Aesthetics? The U.S. Supreme Court has advised cities to be less timorous about this old bugaboo: "The concept of the public welfare is broad and inclusive. The values it represents are spiritual as well as physical, aesthetic as well as monetary. It is within the power of the legislature to determine that the community should be beautiful as well as healthy, spacious as well as clean, well-balanced as well as carefully patrolled." *Berman v. Parker*, 348 U.S. 26, 33 (1954).

least, has been introduced to justify the classification of the districts. This concept may best be described by reference to three standards by which any business use shall be judged:

1. The frequency with which the particular business is used by the residential area it serves;
2. The size of the area from which the business use draws its customers; and
3. The extent to which the particular business use tends to interchange customers with other permitted uses in the same zone.

In order to appreciate the practical consequences of these new bench marks, it is necessary to recall the traditional basis for classification of business uses into districts.

Zoning from its inception was looked upon by the courts and municipal officials as a means of protecting residential districts from the degenerative impact of commercial uses. This bias has resulted in an attitude toward commercial and industrial uses which considered them neither as important in themselves nor as necessary adjuncts to efficient and healthy residential development but, instead, as menaces which, while necessary evils, should be segregated and classified on a basis of evil, more evil and most evil. Commercial and industrial zoning has been cast within this framework during the last thirty years. The practical result has been that all commercial uses considered equal in term of their danger to residential districts were grouped together, irrespective of the functions they performed in relation to the residential districts they served. Noise, smell, fire hazard, sanitation: these were and are the standard components of the public welfare which set some business uses apart from others.

The classifications of the business districts in the Comprehensive Amendment to the Chicago Zoning Ordinance make no sense if read in the light of this tradition. In the "B-1" Local Retail District permitted uses include grocery stores, drug stores, barber

shops, beauty parlors, and shoe and hat repair shops. Forbidden in the "B-1" District but permitted in the "B-2" Restricted Retail District are such uses as antique shops, art and school supply stores, book stores and coin stores. By any traditional test these latter uses are no more noxious to neighboring residential districts than those uses permitted in the "B-1" District. Similarly, there is little sense under traditional zoning concepts to the principal distinction between the "B-2" District and the "B-3" General Retail District. In the former no business establishment may exceed 12,500 square feet of gross floor area, while in the latter there is no limitation upon size. The same uses are permitted in both districts.

The pattern of this innovation in business zoning is completed by the "B-4" and "B-5" Service Districts where gas stations, amusement establishments, theaters, travel bureaus, taxidermists and, if you please umbrella repair shops are permitted for the first time. These novel classifications must be substantiated by the three objectives previously noted; frequency of use, area served, and "compatibility" with other permitted uses. The art store is kept out of the "B-1" District (even though arguably it may be less "hazardous" to neighboring residential property than, say, a grocery store), because it does not provide a service "designed solely for the convenience of persons residing in the adjacent residential areas to permit only such uses as are necessary to satisfy more limited basic shopping needs which occur daily or frequently and so require shopping facilities in close proximity to places of residence."

And so with the maximum square foot floor area restriction contained in the "B-1" District (6,200 square feet) and the "B-2" District (12,500 square feet). By any orthodox zoning principle it makes no sense to permit a grocery store of less than 6,200 square feet in area but to forbid a larger grocery store. Yet if one of the objectives is to establish business patterns based upon area served, there is in fact a greater distinction, for example, between two drug stores, one of 6,200 square feet and the other of 12,500 square feet, than there is between a drug store and, say, a frozen food locker. The large store attracts traffic from substantial distances and may create congestion in an area prepared to handle only local shoppers. The unplanned intrusion of the large store into an area of small shops may adversely affect property values of existing stores and may cause major dislocation of public transportation facilities. Limitations based on size alone (rather than use) may appear startling, but such treatment is not uncommon. Certain uses have frequently been permitted in particular districts on condition that they have no more than a specified number of employees, that they sell only at retail or on the premises, that horsepower not exceed a fixed number, or that only a fixed percentage of floor area be devoted to nonretail purposes. Identical uses are separated on the rough but fair assumption that the scope of operation brings different consequences to the locality in which the use is located.

The classification of business uses in the Comprehensive Amendment is no longer the negative concept of relative offensiveness but the affirmative one of the manner in which a particular business use serves the residents to whom it caters.[4] This requires a consideration not just of a particular neighborhood but of the interrelation of all neighborhoods. A particular shopping area cannot be classified as a "once a day" center unless it is known how far the residents in the area must travel to satisfy their "once a week" needs. Any given business area should be classified as an integral part of an entire neighborhood, region, or, indeed, city. The old method ignored this relationship and permitted any business use to come into any business district so long as it smelled no worse or emitted no more noise than other permitted uses.

This old technique undoubtedly kept the dirtiest (commercial) pigs away from the cleanest (residential) parlors. It did not, however, eliminate more subtle evils such as inefficient and dangerous traffic patterns and

[4] All traces of the traditional method of classification have not been eliminated in the Comprehensive Amendment. Taverns remain a parish, placed in "lower" or "heavier" business districts, though on a theory of "area served" or "frequency of use" a tavern might arguably belong in a more restricted business district.

unstable economic conditions within a business district. Viewed in this light it is then arguable that an art supply store has no place in a "B-1" District which typically consists of a few lots at an intersection in a predominantly residential neighborhood.

The "interchangeability" or "economic compatibility" argument is, to this writer, less clear than the objectives of frequency of use and area served. This doctrine advances from the premise that certain uses create "dead spots" in a business district, thereby discouraging customer interchange and disrupting the efficient use of the business property. It is for this reason that theaters are kept out of all business districts from "B-1" to "B-7," except "B-4," and "B-5" and "B-7," which are the so-called Service Districts. Residential apartments, art galleries, clubs and lodges, and laboratories are not permitted on the ground floor in the "B-2" District for the same reason.

The legal defense of these new techniques must start by dismissing traditional arguments. If the corporation counsel's office of the City of Chicago falls into the trap of defending these classifications on the basis of orthodox "fire and pestilence" theories, even with its new look the Supreme Court may take a jaundiced view of the matter. The sound defense of a zoning ordinance is not complex. It requires a clear demonstration of the specific ways in which the challenged techniques benefit the entire community. This requires plausible testimony from qualified individuals that a given program will probably produce a given result. In business zoning this boils down to the preservation of property values (but of business property as well as residential), maintenance of efficient traffic patterns, and the relationship, now and in the foreseeable future, of the particular business district to the residential area it serves. The reason this type of defense, rather than the old argument of damage to residential property, will be essential is because the first lawsuit to challenge this classification will arise when a landowner asks why he cannot put his little, innocuous book store in a "B-1" zone along with those grocery stores, drug stores and beauty parlors, or when a promoter thinks it unreasonable that he is forbidden to erect a 15,000 square foot supermarket in a district that already has two grocery stores, each, however, under 12,500 square feet in size.

Manufacturing Districts

If the sections of the Comprehensive Amendment for Residential and Business Districts introduce new ideas, the provisions for the Manufacturing Districts are revolutionary in Illinois. Gone are the old classifications based upon use. No longer does the heavy industrial district consist of a string of allegedly obnoxious uses beginning with "Abattoir" and ending with "Yeast Plant." Gone is the so-called "Light Industrial District," which concluded with the dubious catchall "and other light manufacturing uses not offensive to neighboring property by reason of the emission of noise, odors and fumes."

In their place the Comprehensive Amendment to the Chicago ordinance proposes three manufacturing districts which are distinguished, with minor exceptions, not on the basis of specified uses but on the basis of standards of performance which, if met, permit almost any industrial use to go into any district. Residences, except for watchmen, are forbidden in all manufacturing districts and only a limited group of business uses are authorized. The performance standards are classified by noise, vibration, smoke and particulate matter, toxic or noxious matter, odorous matter, fire and explosive hazards, and glare or heat. Generally, the standards become more relaxed from the "M-1" through "M-2" to the "M-3" District. One may relish the reaction of the constitutional lawyer when he examines these provisions and ponders such terms as "Octave band, Cycles Per Second," "closed cup flash point," and "noxious odorous matter . . . detectable . . . when diluted in the ratio of one volume of odorous air to four volumes of clean air." The mind

reels with the possibilities on the cross-examination of a zoning enforcement officer before a skeptical judge! The truth is that the lawyer who seeks to offer reasonable comment on the future of this technique finds himself in a field of science where the word of the laboratory technician assumes the overtones of an oracle. Yet a natural yen for a return to an established and well-known pattern in the law of zoning may cloud an admission that the grace of our legal tradition is its ability to embrace and adjust to new methods.

The principle behind performance standards, if not the jargon of the expertise in which they are cast, is not only sound but traditional if we go back beyond the advent of zoning to its ancestor, the law of nuisances. It was zoning law, not the common law, which chose to classify a business enterprise not by its particular impact upon neighboring property but by the general community attitude toward the entire industry of which it was a part. The law of public nuisances had its particular objects of scorn, it is true, but, as far as industry was concerned, the common law judged a factory by the evidence of the harmful effects of the particular use in the particular place.[5] Performance standards resurrect this ancient rule, but superimpose thereon the techniques developed by science which are believed to reduce substantially the guesswork and prejudice which contribute to human error. If a particular factory is willing to install devices which will make it a better neighbor, it shall not be penalized by the indifferent habits of its competitors which customarily relegate them to a zoning district where their usual and offensive noise, smoke or vibrations will least offend. Under the traditional use list that is where the unique one would be placed, whatever its heroic standards.

The patent difficulty with performance standards is not the principle but the ad-

[5] The common law did not generally treat noise, smoke, or vibrations as nuisances per se. It was the impact of the act in the locality in which it took place upon "persons of ordinary sensibilities" that classified it. Zoning law, on the other hand, classified whole industries irrespective of the performance of particular members of that industry.

ministration, an old saw in orthodox zoning but of bitter truth nevertheless. In 1925, Aurora v. Burns[6] upheld the principle of zoning (far more radical than anything embraced in performance standards), but the next thirty years witnessed the loss of one battle after another by municipalities before the Illinois Supreme Court. It is a simple matter for an inspector to determine whether a building houses a paint manufacturer or a machine shop. It requires neither a large budget nor qualified personnel to screen applications for building permits to be sure that a forbidden use does not intrude into a district where the permitted uses are listed by name. Read the list. Vastly more complex is the task of determining whether a proposed machine shop will meet the "M-1" District requirements on noise, vibration or smoke. How does the inspector distinguish from other noises the decibels of sound emitting from a particular plant "on the boundary of a Residence or Business District"? The engineers insist that these are standards which can be substantiated. The time will come soon enough for proof.

Performance standards can find neither hope nor discouragement in court decisions. The Illinois Supreme Court has sniffed at scientific measurement of noise, but not in a setting where it was part of a comprehensive plan. Other cities and counties have introduced the concept, but no appellate cases can be found on point. Zoning ordinances for years have contained smatterings of "performance standards," incidental to the traditional use classification pattern.

Nonconforming Uses

The principle of gradual, uncompensated elimination of nonconforming uses is incorporated in the Comprehensive Amendment. So it was in the 1942 comprehensive amendment to the Chicago zoning ordinance, but the permissible life of a nonconforming use was so geologic that no alderman or enforcement official had to worry that he would be taken seriously. By contrast, in the comprehensive amendment specified nonconforming

business uses must cease operation in eight years, others in fifteen years. If the use is housed in a building "designed or intended for a nonconforming use," the periods are substantially longer.[7] Nonconforming signs in residential districts must be removed in eight years. The nonconforming use of unimproved land must cease in five years. These are periods of time short enough to indicate that the city means business.

This approach to the problem of nonconforming uses is an untested idea in Illinois. The authority is granted by the enabling act, but most cities and villages have preferred to avoid the legal and political risks of telling a property owner that after a given period he must cease using his property for the purpose to which it is now devoted. The 1957 Comprehensive Amendment goes on the theory that the danger spots in zoning are the nonconforming uses. Under the old practice they were frozen, and could not expand; therefore, they were believed to be doomed to elimination. Experience has shown that, to the contrary, nonconforming uses thrive on their monopolistic position or that they serve as comfortable excuses for the intrusion of other nonconforming uses which in turn lead to a breakdown of the entire zoning program. It is believed necessary, therefore, to provide for their elimination without the costly process of condemnation but after a period of grace in which they would enjoy a virtual monopoly and could "amortize" their investment. An analysis of the constitutional arguments, pro and con, is not appropriate to this article. It is sufficient to note that some appellate courts in other jurisdictions have

[7] In such cases the amortization period is based upon the type of construction of the building in which it is located. The Comprehensive Amendment makes a distinction among non-conforming uses which are to be gradually eliminated based upon whether or not they are located in a building which is adaptable to a permitted use. Thus, any nonconforming tavern on the ground floor of an apartment building in a General Residence District must cease operation in eight years. A nonconforming automobile garage or truck terminal, presumably not adaptable to residential use, would be eliminated after a period of time measured by whether the structure was made of brick, concrete, or wood.

[6] 319 Ill. 84, 149 N.E. 784 (1925).

upheld the principle of elimination of non-conforming uses without compensation on the rationale that this was a necessary tool of urban land development and that, as a constitutional matter, it differed in degree, not in kind, from traditional zoning where the use of property was restricted overnight, so to speak, without benefit of a period in which to recover the investment.

Undoubtedly the most eloquent judicial support for this innovation was provided by the California District Court of Appeal in Los Angeles v. Gage. Section 12.23 B and C of the Los Angeles Municipal Code provides that:

> The nonconforming use of a conforming building or structure may be continued, except that in the "R" Zones any nonconforming commercial or industrial use of a residential building or residential accessory building shall be discontinued within five (5) years from June 1, 1946, or five (5) years from the date the use becomes nonconforming, whichever date is later.

In upholding this provision as applied to a wholesale plumbing business conducted in one part of a two-family dwelling in a residence district, the court stated:

> The theory in zoning is that each district is an appropriate area for the location of the uses which the zone plan permits in that area, and that the existence or entrance of other uses will tend to impair the development and stability of the area for the appropriate uses. The public welfare must be considered from the standpoint of the objective of zoning and of all the property within any particular use district. Rehfeld v. City and County of San Francisco, 218 Cal. 83, 85, 21 P.21 419. It was not and is not contemplated that preexisting nonconforming uses are to be perpetual. State ex rel. Miller v. Cain, 40 Wash. 2d 216, 242 P.2d 505. The presence of any nonconforming use endangers the benefits to be derived from a comprehensive zoning plan. Having the undoubted power to establish residential districts, the legislative body has the power to make such classification really effective by adopting such reasonable regulations as would be conducive to the welfare, health, and safety of those desiring to live in such district and enjoy the benefits thereof. There would be no

object in creating a residential district unless there were to be secured to those dwelling therein the advantages which are ordinarily considered the benefits of such residence. It would seem to be the logical and reasonable method of approach to place a time limit upon the continuance of existing nonconforming uses, commensurate with the investment involved and based on the nature of the use; and in cases of nonconforming structures, on their character, age, and other relevant factors.

No doubt there is something about this novel question which arouses the poet in judges.

A multitude of contradictions appear to arise in the application of this major departure from established zoning policy. The amortization provisions in the Chicago ordinance apply to nonconforming business and industrial uses in residential districts, but nonconforming residential uses in business, commercial and industrial districts are untouched. Indeed, only specified nonconforming business uses in residential districts are subject to gradual elimination.[8] Whether these distinctions are justified or represent unequal protection of the law remains to be determined by the Illinois Supreme Court. Decisions in other jurisdictions suggest that it is permissible to pick and choose among those nonconforming uses which shall be subject to elimination.

It is in an adventurous area such as this that the recent and distinct change in attitude of the Illinois Supreme Court toward zoning is significant.

---

[8] The early drafts of the Comprehensive Amendment provided for the gradual elimination of all nonconforming business uses in residential districts. This caused quite a howl from representatives of small grocery stores and delicatessens. The final draft provided, in effect, that all nonconforming uses in residential districts which were listed as permitted uses in the B-1 (local retail) district be allowed to remain. This distinction is justified, if at all, by the belief that the uses permitted in the B-1 districts (e.g., small grocery stores, drug stores, beauty parlors) do not adversely affect residential properties to the extent that "heavier" business uses do. This appears to be a reversion to old notions of classification of business uses (i.e., evil, more evil, most evil) and may be inconsistent with the basic premises underlying the classification of business districts in the Comprehensive Amendment.

The administration of the ordinance is, of course, the heart of the matter. It is an outrageous waste of public monies to prepare a zoning ordinance which will be vitiated by inadequate or inefficient administration. To say, however, that a system prescribed in the text of an ordinance can guarantee that administration will either be competent or sympathetic is to dream. The most that can be asked of the words is that they prescribe methods which if responsibly applied may protect the ordinance from complete deterioration. The provisions of the administrative article suggest that the reformation of the substantive articles of the amendment is not so much rubbish.

A "variation" is the most misunderstood and most abused term in the lexicon of zoning. It can be accurately said that it covers a multitude of sins, most if not all of which are venal! The history of the variation procedure in Illinois is a story of confusion and abuse, best evidenced by the judicial and legislative landmarks beginning with Welton v. Hamilton, running through the various amendments to article 73–4 of the Cities and Villages Act, and stopping (for the moment) with Bright v. Evanston. That history, however, is a separate account which it may be too early to balance. For present purposes it is sufficient to note that no one appears confident that as a legal matter in Illinois there is a clear distinction between a "variation," an "amendment," and that more recent gambit, the "special use". It is to the credit of the Chicago ordinance that the attempt is made to provide a clear delineation between the functions of each of these methods for change of a zoning ordinance.

VARIATIONS

The Comprehensive Amendment has two major departures from customary Illinois practices with respect to variations. Variations in Chicago are the exclusive prerogative of the Board of Appeals. This is mandatory under the state enabling act. The second change is not required by statute and it is the one which has caused substantial dispute in

the public hearings: the scope of the Board's power to grant variations has been narrowed. In effect, a so-called use variation is prohibited by the Comprehensive Amendment. This change is based upon the conviction of the framers that a use variation is, from a planning point of view, a dangerous thing. If a change of use is to be made, then the ordinance should be candidly amended; if this would result in "spot Zoning", then the change should not be made under any circumstances, whether or not it is disguised as a variation. This restrictive objective is accomplished by articles 11.7–3 and 11.7–4 of the amendment. The former article sets out standards to be followed by the Board of Appeals, and the latter enumerates these instances where, if the standards are met, a variation may be granted. The standards are stiff and the authorized variations are few.

The standards set out to govern the Board of Appeals on variations are three, each of which is a mandatory standard imposed by the enabling legislation; the city has no choice with respect to these standards.[9] There is some question whether at least one of the standards makes any sense.[10] The enabling act does, however, authorize the city to implement the standards, and it is here that article 11.7–3 becomes very demanding. Although the consequence may be to outrage property owners who are accustomed to a more relaxed attitude about variations, it is difficult to see where this stiffness is not consistent with a judicial attitude in Illinois which has been suspicious, to say the least, about the administrative standards used by Boards of Appeal in granting variations. Of

[9] The standards are: (1) that the property in question cannot yield a reasonable return if permitted to be used only under the conditions allowed by the regulations in that zone; (2) that the plight of the owner is due to unique circumstances; and (3) that the variation, if granted, will not alter the essential character of the locality.

[10] It is difficult to imagine how the reasonable return standard can be met in cases not involving income-producing property, such as where a homeowner seeks a variation of yard size or lot size, or where a church asks for a variation of the regulations governing off-street parking.

less certain validity is the last provision in article 11.7–3, which gives the Board the power to "impose such conditions and restrictions upon the premises benefitted by a variation as may be necessary to comply with the standards set out in this Section 7–3. . . ." This arguably could represent an improper delegation of legislative authority to the Board but, in view of the fact that the early judicial complaint against such delegation was the failure of the local legislature to establish standards, it would appear reasonable to suppose that this power to attach conditions and restrictions is proper because it is keyed to enumerated standards.

The standards do not permit the granting of variations except in those specific instances set out in article 11.7–4. These variations, of which there are nine, have in common their exclusive application to matters which do not involve changes in use. They deal with relaxation of the regulations with respect to yards, lot size, off-street parking facilities, floor area ratio of non-residential uses in a residence district (e.g., churches), and the area of any sign. The goal is the elimination of use variations. The legal argument underlying this notable change harks back to the early decision in the Welton case, where the court held that the granting of a variation by a Board of Appeals was unlawful. At issue in the Welton case was essentially a change in the use. The Board of Appeals under the old practice, by granting a use variation, could completely change the zoning ordinance which had been passed by the local legislature. By restricting variations to non-use items, such as yard sizes, there is less risk that the Board would be accused of exercising legislative prerogatives. To permit a side yard of three feet instead of the required ten feet, for example, not only is substantially different than permitting a gas station in a residential district, but it also may more clearly be related to a hardship—such as might arise from an oddly-shaped lot. The hardship in the gas station case is hard to disassociate from a pure and simple desire to make more money out of the property, a fact which the Illinois Supreme Court has said is not to be considered in determining the merits of a variation.

AMENDMENTS

The attrition to which earlier ordinances have been subjected has arisen as well from amendments as from variations. The record of so-called "spot-zoning" by the City Council in the past is not encouraging. It is, therefore, unusual and a credit to the Council that the present ordinance makes more difficult the employment of the amendment as a device to accommodate a property owner. The Committee on Buildings and Zoning of the City Council cannot hold a public hearing on a requested amendment until the Committee has received recommendations relative thereto from the Department of Planning and from the Zoning Administrator. The effectiveness of this impartial and expert opinion will, of course, depend not only upon the public spirit of the Committee on Buildings and Zoning, but also upon the independence of the Department of Planning. In any event the requirement is a marked improvement over a procedure where no non-political voice participated in the decisions.

The second unusual provision with respect to amendments appears in article 11.9–8:

When a lot, lots, or parcel of land has less than 100 feet of frontage or less than 10,000 square feet of area, no amendment shall be passed to change the zoning district in which such lot, lots, or parcel of land are located, except where in the event of the passage of such amendment such lot, lots or parcel of land would be in the same zoning district as an adjoining lot, lots, or parcel of land.

The intent of this provision is to eliminate the rezoning of an isolated lot; in other words, to eliminate "spot-zoning." The premise is that there can be no justification to rezone an isolated parcel. If it is in the interest of the community that that parcel be rezoned, then the same reasoning must apply to at least some, if not all, additional parcels in the particular block in which it is located.

Apart from these two innovations the provisions for amendments follow what has become the customary practice in Illinois.

A special use is a device without express statutory authorization but with a history of judicial recognition in Illinois. It is designed to handle the peculiar problems raised primarily by public utilities and public or semi-public uses. The overwhelming proportion of the land area of a municipality is occupied by residences, business uses and industrial uses. Interspersed among them are uses which fall into none of those categories and yet, because of public need, may of necessity belong among any one of the predominant groups. If they are listed as permitted uses in every district, however, it is recognized that the admitted need for the particular "special use" may be accompanied by a serious and adverse impact upon neighboring property. It is for this reason that a more or less homogeneous group of uses is authorized to be located in each of the respective use districts, provided that their location and their design have received prior approval. The Comprehensive Amendment provides that this approval must be by the Board of Appeals without action by the City Council. This delegation of authority to the Board of Appeals is in keeping with prior practice in Chicago but may be open to serious question as to its merits from a planning point of view and its validity. The granting of a special use is not conditioned upon the extremely strict standards established for variations, and the Board of Appeals is granted authority to attach conditions or restrictions upon special uses without the standards which regulate variations by the Board of Appeals. In the one case where the Illinois Supreme Court has had an opportunity to review a special use, it emphasized the fact that, in its opinion, the ordinance did not give the Board of Appeals discretion as to conditions or restrictions. The decision to give to the Board of Appeals this power was apparently based upon the notion that a special use is substantially identical to a variation and that the enabling act makes it mandatory that the Board of Appeals grant variations in Chicago. Of course, a special use is of a different breed than a variation. It is far more similar to a permitted use which is subject to prior approval. To this extent a special use is a legislative matter, the granting of which may affect the entire plan and design of a neighborhood, if not the whole community and, therefore, it should be a function of the Planning Department and the City Council.

Conclusion

These are the most significant innovations in the Comprehensive Amendment. (The regulation of signs and billboards drew the most public attention, but the principles of control have been tried and tested in other jurisdictions.) They are accompanied by dramatic changes in textual form and style which serve to emphasize the departure from the past that the ordinance represents. Any document that is as different and has as many practical and immediate consequences is bound to stir up dissent not only among property owners but among lawyers and professional planners as well. It is, however, this writer's guess that if the administrators will administer and the politicians will not politick, the Illinois Supreme Court will provide a sympathetic forum for many of the innovations in this progressive document.

14

Emerging Legal Issues in Zoning

Charles M. Haar—Part I
Frank E. Horack, Jr.—Part II

This paper appeared originally in Planning 1954, pp. 138–155, published by the American Society of Planning Officials, 1313 East Sixtieth Street, Chicago, Illinois 60637. Reproduced by permission.

Part I

WHEN ONE considers the important factors that many interesting devices of land use control are never tested in the court and, that, even when litigated, the slowness of the judicial machinery may permit a decision only years after the initial challenge, one senses that much of zoning pioneering cannot be perceived by a reading of appellate court decisions alone. Nor can it be adequately analyzed by the law processes in isolation.

With the thought, however, that a cumulative diagram of the zoning decisions as handed down in one year might indicate some interesting relationships, I prepared a chart of the zoning cases decided in the United States last year. There were 248 cases reported; of these, 118 were decided by the highest court of the state. This large number of suits must represent a high proportion of all the cases tried by legal departments of municipalities. In this fact is more support of that fine principle: general propositions do not decide concrete cases—a principle that is no less valid because of the judicial acceptance of zoning that has more or less been the courts' attitude since the landmark *Village of Euclid v. Ambler Realty Company* case. For the facts of the case will often determine the decision; and, of the 248 cases,

a substantial number of decisions rejected the application of the particular zoning provision under attack. The courts clearly recognize no vested right in the continuation of a specific zoning provision; on the other hand, the cases show that amendments are more likely to be thrown out than the original ordinance—perhaps as constituting spot zoning or upon some other ground indicating discriminatory treatment.

Cases involving non-conforming uses and variances are most numerous among the reported decisions. To give numbers more weight than they deserve, 32 cases dealt with non-conforming uses, their establishment, expansion, abandonment, reconstruction, and destruction. Forty-eight cases dealt with variances. One brief observation: while the granting of a variance was sustained in five cases, it was overruled as an abuse of discretion in eight cases. At the same time, while denial of the requested variance was overruled in five cases, a denial was sustained in seven cases. Thus, a somewhat anomalous view of the role of the court in zoning emerges. Instead of being a deterrent to zoning progress as it is too often viewed, the judiciary seems to be strengthening the hands of planners. Variances have long been known to undermine and distort the zoning plan. This fact seems to have been taken into account by the courts. They have tended, more often than not, to support the denial of a variance by a board of appeals; similarly, they have tended, more often than not, to overrule a board of appeals when it has been perhaps too liberal in the granting of such variances.

One interesting feature of this general accumulation of statistics is that the seven states of California, Connecticut, Illinois, Massachusetts, New Jersey, New York and Pennsylvania account for the vast bulk of zoning cases—167 cases in all. More particularly, the three states of New York, New Jersey, and Pennsylvania alone account for some 130 of the 248 zoning cases reported. Surprisingly, the state with the greatest zoning litigation is that harboring the city of brotherly love. To restore proper balance, however, it may be pointed out that this is perhaps attributable to a better reporting of the lower court decisions in Pennsylvania.

110

This explanation may also account for some of the other generalizations we have attempted to draw, and in this connection a discerning statement by Professor Powell may be apt. He described certain institutes of social studies as places where the counters do not think and the thinkers do not count.

One feature of current zoning impresses itself: it is that the most important trend today is what may be characterized as a movement from Euclidian to non-Euclidian zoning.

Euclidian zoning may be described as a system of use control through the demarcation of rigid districts, each with its own set of uses. This older system of zoning, which the reform movement of the early 1900's succeeded in establishing as the framework for the growth of the American city, and which achieved judicial support in the *Euclid* case, is now breaking down. The great demand at the present time for increased flexibility in zoning and planning has led to a gradual withering of Euclidian zoning, not only in the writing of theoreticians in some of the "modern" zoning ordinances themselves, but also in the court opinions. The more flexible type of zoning, in which uses are not wedded to specific districts, shall refer to as non-Euclidian zoning.

The system of zoning enunciated in the *Euclid* case established a compartmentalized city. All the land within the territorial operating unit was divided into districts. In the *Euclid* case, for example, the city was divided into six classes of use districts, three classes of height districts, and four classes of area districts. Use districts classified as to the buildings which could be erected within their respective limits: single family and two-family houses, apartment houses, and finally the bedlam district where all sorts of miscellaneous uses, ranging from sewage disposal and cemeteries to feeble-minded institutions, were to be located. Within each zone, the owner of each lot was free to use it for the use that all the other owners in the district could dedicate their land. An owner —and this is an important legal consequence that flows from this entire theory of zoning— could develop his land as a matter of right, so long as he met the use, height, and area requirements of his district. Indeed, if

refused a building permit by the building inspector, an action for mandamus would automatically succeed.

The achievement of planners and lawyers in erecting this zoning framework for land development is truly remarkable, especially in light of the thinking, political and judicial, of that period. That was an era, you will recall, when American courts were loath to sustain legislative attempts to restrict the free exercise of what were conceived to be the rights of property. Even the fixing of a minimum wage for women was invalidated as an interference with their property right to contract for their services. And, of further interest to us, Mr. Justice Sutherland was the author of the *Euclid* decision. Indeed, it is a stimulating conjecture as to how this Supreme Court justice, the subject of a biography appropriately entitled "A Man Against the State," might validate a new type of drastic land use control. As his opinion candidly declared, land of the plaintiff company in the *Euclid* case was reduced in value from $10,000 to $2,500 an acre. Yet this sharp decrease in property value was not permitted to override the general community interest in land regulation, and the values that the planners had persuaded the court would flow from the zoning of American cities.

The urban scene, dominated by ever-advancing technology and by architectural and engineering ingenuity, is witnessing a multi-sided attack on the older, more rigid type of zoning. Yard requirements have been branded as arbitrary means for achieving certain light and air standards. The old method of bulk control is giving way to floor area ratios. Even more important than changes in standards for individual buildings are those for large scale development. For example, the "patio plan" of Dean Sert and Paul Wiener ignores the street pattern, faces the houses inwards, and makes the traditional lot unit outmoded. The new type of factory, all glass and streamlined, surrounded by shrubbery and playgrounds, presents a different problem of land use mixture than the old type of glue factory. Indeed, there is a basic philosophic change—it may be called "planned irregularity," if one enjoys a play on words—that is coming to dominate the planning profession. Performance standards for all types of activities are emerging.

Perhaps the case that may be singled out as best exemplifying the new trend is *Rodgers v. Churchill*, the famous Tarrytown floating zone case. Here—as the dissenting opinion pointed out rather bitterly—we no longer have even the district, that one stable unit of Euclidian Zoning. The change in the ordinance validated by the New York court made no corresponding change in the map. Instead, owners of plots of ten acres or more were invited to apply for a change in the map and to include in their application, plans for a garden apartment development. Under the traditional Euclidian ordinance the problem would have been met by allowing no apartments at all in one-family and two-family house neighborhoods. Mr. Justice Sutherland, acting on the basing points provided by the planners, assumed that apartments were forever incompatible with residences. The non-Euclidian Tarrytown ordinance states that if 85 per cent of the ten acre tract is left unbuilt, the two uses may be mixed. But where this district may settle is undetermined at the time of the passage of the ordinance; it can be located anywhere within the city limits, so long as the various requirements are satisfied. The zoning map no longer tells all; the applicable district is no longer tagged on to every land parcel.

As a result of increased knowledge and experience—and, no doubt, disappointment with some things that have happened—the search for flexibility in control is accelerating. In fact, some planners have gone to the extent of saying that zoning as heretofore practised may do more harm than good. What this adds up to, it is submitted with trepidation, is a change in orientation from Euclidian zoning toward the British development plan. That system is an outgrowth of the same forces and needs we have been experiencing in the United States. Under the Town and Country Planning Act of 1947, each local authority is authorized to prepare a plan for the development of its territory. This plan is kept flexible by many devices, notably a requirement for a five-year review and a limiting proviso that the plan is not to be bound too much by existing conditions. Unlike our zoning ordinances, this plan does not give rise to automatic rights. Each landowner submits his plan for development for planning approval. This is granted if it is in accordance with the plan and—this is the hub of the matter—if it is in accordance with "any other material considerations" that the planning authority wishes to take into account. Thus, there is no slot-machine approval. Each lot is considered on an *ad hoc* basis. There is no forcing of the planning authority's hand by making it give consent in advance, so to speak; instead, it decides each case only when and if it arises and upon the conditions as they then exist at the time of the proposed construction. The advantages of this for the planner—often for the builder, too, so that he may fit his proposed development into the general community plan—are obvious.

Our present ideas concerning zoning may be even closer to the 1943 English act than to the development plan of 1947 in one sense. This point may be illuminating as a comparison and a contrast. Owing to the war emergency, the British simply slapped a ban on all building. Pending the production and adoption of a town planning scheme by the local authority, no one could build. Permission had to be obtained from the authorities for each proposed construction. Once a scheme was adopted, however, the same effect as under our present Euclidian zoning ordinance would ensue; if the use proposed accorded with the use set down in the scheme, then the person had an automatic right to develop. One consequence flowed most naturally from this arrangement: authorities found it much to their advantage not to pass a planning scheme at all. This gave them an opportunity to review and pass on each proposed development as it came up; for, once the scheme was passed, of course, this greater freedom was gone. In a sense, this perpetual interim development was something that the planners found most advantageous—and it explains the motivating drive behind many of the attacks on the traditional type of zoning in the United States today. The simultaneous search for elasticity in the two countries has developed in response to similar pressures.

In order to achieve standing and to become an accepted part of municipal regulation, any scheme of land-use control must be economically feasible. Some attention should therefore be paid to the underlying economic theory of the traditional Euclidian zoning and that of the new non-Euclidian zoning. A crucial question always for the planner and the lawyer is: are there rational economic considerations as well as health and other social criteria by which the broad powers entrusted to the administrative board can be directed? That is, has the administrative board been given a job to do that can be tested against more or less objective standards? To the extent that the board's decisions make economic sense, they will help to achieve community and, of course, judicial acceptance.

There is one startling contrast between the two systems of zoning in their economic impact on landowners. Traditional zoning saw as the core of the economic problem the attempt of each owner to maximize his own profit in the use of his land. In this pursuit, he will prefer to devote his land to its greatest income-producing use, such as the site for a factory or a department store. While either is a conceivable use of the land, neither is desirable near other particular uses, such as a house. The zoning solution has been to permit each owner to maximize his profit so far as possible but only within the class of uses permitted in the district in which the land is located. At the same time, districts are carved out and uses allocated to them so as to minimize the harm that a new building can do to nearby structures. In a sense, the heavyweight is separated from the flyweight, and then only is a free-for-all fight for values permitted to go on. While not the dominant goal by any means, not perhaps even a conscious one, the result of traditional zoning is to distribute the gain to be had from high income-producing uses, by spreading out the business district through height and bulk limitations.

The economic theory of the non-Euclidian zoning starts off as a reaction. It points out

that landowners under Euclidian zoning scoop off money that builders or developers should have been allowed to spend on buildings. Further, while districting attempts to equalize potential profits, it does so only within a particular district. And since values cannot possibly be distributed in a way to give owners in residence districts a share in the value created by planning in commercial districts, it is not much psychological solace to spread out the commercial values in such a way that an over-large commercial district is created. From his viewpoint, a landowner in a residential district is concerned personally with the fact that potential uses over and above residence are now barred to him. On the other hand, since each landowner has to obtain individual planning approval under the proposed system and presumably will obtain planning permission by proving that his proposed construction is worthwhile, it is all the owners within the entire city—not just the particular landowners within the type of district mentioned above—who compete for their right to enjoy zoning land values.

Under the present system of zoning, values are distributed before they are needed. This often tends to speculative holdings of land encouraged by a zoning plan that has pushed the land into a higher classification than it warrants. In a sense, this contributes to the high land costs that urban redevelopment and urban renewal programs face in attempts to rebuild the core of the city. Indeed, the very act of distributing zoning values at the moment of enacting a zoning ordinance may discourage desirable construction. Under the proposed system of competition for zoning values, where any one of several sites within the corporate territorial limits could serve as a site for a garden apartment but only one site is feasible in view of current market demand for such apartments, the owner or option holder who presents the best plan will be entitled to enjoy the business value. Thus, the new system envisions not only flexible buildings and flexible controls, but also a race between landowners for creating good cities.

Untested and, worse, inarticulated as the case may be for the economic bases of both the Euclidian and non-Euclidian zoning, it does seem true that wherever there is public control of land use, whether of minimum type or of wide scope, the government is going to spread out land values in some manner or other. For by determining the different uses of land, the power to earn varying amounts of income and the ensuing capitalization of values in the market is also decided. Hence, the argument runs that if there must be distribution, let it serve a social purpose. In the Tarrytown case, the social purpose served was the designing of better garden apartment projects. The garden apartment could not be built as a matter of right and there was the entire city instead of just one district from which to choose alternative sites.

Along with this increased flexibility and change in direction of the zoning movement two basic problems may be suggested: standards and monopoly.

Constitutional questions aside, the basic question for the planner is what is administratively wise, which system best insures a democratic and efficient ordering of his controls? Where the districting system is gone, and people no longer have automatic rights to build according to the district in which their land is located, a grave problem of equal protection may arise. If in order to "get" one landowner, it is necessary also to "get" all other people who are similarly situated, strong counteracting pressures against such discriminations will certainly appear. For if to achieve the desired goal of discriminating against landowner A, it becomes necessary to subject all other landowners in the same district to the same economic disadvantages, political pressures and other practical considerations will press in the direction of not taking such action against A. But the fact remains that as the system develops into the flexible type of zoning and each lot is assayed on its own merits, the chances for discrimination loom large. Hence, the need for great detail and specificity in the articulation of applicable

policy become paramount. Methods must be sought to keep the power of the administrative agency within channels that are objectively intelligible to (1) the agency, (2) the reviewing court, and (3) the regulated citizen, so that all three levels may have an intelligent basis for action. The articulation of standards is one field that needs the full cooperation of planners and lawyers.

The second great problem is that of monopoly. While efficient planning considerations may call for one large, concentrated shopping center as opposed to scattered individual stores or a garden apartment project, complex problems emerge when this is joined with the non-Euclidian type of zoning. Thus, the older zoning created a monopoly of use, but, it should be noted, only within the district; the new trends could create this monopoly within one lot. Previously one could not predict where the development value would settle throughout the zoning district. But in the new type of zoning, in a sense, one has selected the very site that will be enriched by the public action of zoning that compulsorily binds all the other property owners within the planning unit. Thus, we may have a greater concentration of monopoly accorded certain selected sites. And, if one parcel is selected as a site, greater is the reward, for the chances of competition from other sites are reduced if it is engineering efficiency that is the ideal (as opposed to the consumer choice efficiency that many small stores render, as is apparent from their continued existence despite their higher prices).

One may safely predict that the fact that a use approval can mean more money will step up pressure from individuals and interest groups. This adverse effect is linked with the previous problem of standards. Where every parcel of land is not to be treated the same as every other parcel of land within the district, it becomes crucial to spell out the criteria by which this differentiation is to be made. It is here that the experience of the planner becomes essential to the lawyer to test the validity and the good sense of a particular regulation, as well as to realize the greatest potential for a more efficient and more livable city.

The new proposals have lent new perspective to zoning activities. They underline what should have become apparent long ago—that an attempt at permanence, whether through an ordinance or in life, is doomed to failure. They also underline another question: is not land-use regulation today, while paying lip-service to the Euclidian concept, really a discretionary system operating primarily through (a) variances, (b) amendments, and (c) exceptions? Have not these safety values, which were originally intended to be only minor features of the zoning system, become the system itself? Studies have been made, especially of Chicago and of some Massachusetts town areas, indicating that most development, certainly large-scale construction, has occurred not according to the zoning map but according to exceptions and variances granted by an administrative agency. Planners have bemoaned the withering away of particular zoning ordinances by the variance and amendment procedures. If, in fact, zoning is largely done today by these devices, would it not be wiser perhaps to openly recognize that fact and then to try to meet and shape land-use controls as they do operate?

The idea of property ownership is so strong in the United States that to say that land no longer carries development rights—as is perhaps implicit in this new arrangement of affairs—is probably doomed to futility. To require, in effect, a declaratory judgment every time a sale is arranged or a particular construction proposed may be far too complicated a system. In essence, the new system would change what is a system of control by board directive, via a system of general regulations, into a licensing arrangement with a franchise necessary for each individual lot. While one may call for new standards and criteria, it is often difficult to elaborate them in any particular situation. One may predict or have a hunch, if you will, that even this type of flexible non-Euclidian system will come under new controls, so that the end will not be a system as here broadly pictured. Just as the present system has moved towards greater discretion and flexibility, by overworking those features of the ordinance that permit considerable changes from the stated standards, so political and administrative realities will compel the formulation of standards and protective devices in any new system.

The problems of freedom and planning—away from the high level abstractions of Hozek and Wooton—call for reconciliation in the emerging zoning controls. Also called for is a unison of the planners' view of things and the lawyers'. Much as the planners and the lawyers in 1916 were able to achieve a type of zoning that, considering the techniques and body of knowledge of the time, was remarkable, so today there is an urgent need for a closer agreement between these two approaches in order to achieve the best possible future development of the land resources of our cities.

Part II

If we review planning and zoning as an operative process of government, again the achievements in our communities are relatively few. In principle, at least, the pioneers of 1914 knew everything that we know today. Generally they sought to accomplish the same objectives that we seek. They had lost faith in the limited objectives of the city beautiful, the erection of great public structures, show places that hid poverty, ignorance, and pestilence. The planning movement of that day was affected greatly by the surge of social conscience among the people. Planning and zoning was no general theory then—it was specifically aimed at the eradication of the slum, the reduction of population density, the elimination of dwelling units detrimental to health, the creation of improved educational, religious, and cultural surroundings as a means of combating adult crime and juvenile delinquency. These pioneers also recognized that street planning, urban transportation, an adequate school system, provision for parks and recreation, and a program for public finance were all essential to land-use planning. ...

The public, however, has not treated their plans and programs kindly in the intervening years. We can scarcely point with pride to the universal success of the planning and zoning movement. Granting that no one can tell how much worse our cities would have been had we not had zoning, redevelopment, conservation, and public housing, it must nevertheless be admitted that we have not eliminated the slum, urban transportation is a greater problem today than it was 40 years ago, we have not achieved adequate schools, park and recreation systems, and we have failed dismally in planning public finance.

In some ways we have lost ground. Where once we talked of human welfare, the elimination of slums, the healthful house, the promotion of social, religious, and cultural advancement, we too frequently emphasize today the preservation of economic values of land, special consideration for business and industry, the protection of the *fine* house, and often we assume that aid for the economic incompetent and for the uneducated is an impossible task. I do not wish to leave the impression that it is the responsibility of planning and zoning to cure all the ills of society, but conversely this fact should not be an excuse for reducing standards of population density, ignoring building codes, or disregarding health and sanitary standards. We should not forget that substandard living conditions under which too large a portion of the population is obliged to exist is frequently not a matter of their own choice, that the structures that they must call their homes are customarily owned or built by others. If it is argued that persons live in these abodes because of their own economic incompetence, then an issue is formed, not for planning and zoning, but for the entire economy. Zoning should not reduce its own standards to accommodate the deficiencies in other areas of the social process.

If what I have said sounds hypercritical, remember that in spite of many obvious failures of zoning it has kept pace with a revolution in urban transportation, with an unprecedented expansion in dwelling units, and with a growth in municipal services that could not have been foreseen 40 years ago. Thus, in spite of its shortcomings, the planning and zoning process must have been measurably successful or it would have been discarded years ago.

A brief inquiry into the causes of zoning inadequacies discloses five principal sources: psychological, popular, legal, administrative, and fiscal. The last four I will discuss at the same time we consider means of improvement in the law. The first should be briefly mentioned now.

Zoning has been weakened in my opinion by the attitude of planners that once a plan is prepared and an ordinance adopted, their job is done and that the plan will be self-executing. In general, they have not assumed responsibility for carrying the plan from the drawing board to the community. This would not have been so serious except for the fact that the lawyer's attitude, when coupled with the engineer's, leaves no one responsible. Lawyers have generally taken the position that they did not participate in the preparation of the plan and therefore have no responsibility to defend its policy when it is attacked. Thus they are willing to let violations go unchallenged or to accept proposals for unwise alteration of the plan by amendment, exception, and variance. Engineers, too, do not take responsibility for giving support.

Many improvements can be made in the legal structure of zoning. Three changes affecting jurisdiction, administration, and enforcement would be of the greatest importance.

In the beginning, zoning approached the problems of land-use negatively. It intended to protect the individual unit of property—the lot or tract. It was considered as auxiliary to and an improvement upon the law of nuisance, which had proven to be too slow and too uncertain to protect the quiet enjoyment of property from all but the most noxious uses. The intensity of land-use increased the probability of injury to adjacent property; so zoning was, and still is, in many quarters considered an urban problem primarily. Zoning thus tied to individual parcels of land was treated as a power to be exercised by the smallest units of government.

Today, we view zoning affirmatively as one of the tools of planning that permits a community to maximize its economic, social, and cultural characteristics in relation to its land. Its objectives are to classify all land so that it will produce the greatest economic value; to insure the highest quality of municipal services at the lowest tax rate; to provide adequate schools and recreation facilities; and to allow efficient management of traffic between residential, business, and industrial areas.

At one time all these objectives were viewed as problems of land management. Today, however, we know that to plan land-use alone is insufficient. Indeed, the most successful planning program of modern time is the Tennessee Valley Authority. In that plan, the social, cultural, and economic life of the region came first—land-use management is but an auxiliary to support the main objectives. The mobility of industry, business, and population both within and without a given community makes property and local government jurisdiction too narrow a focus. Not only the mobility provided by the private automobile, by air transportation, by electric power transmission, and by federal finance makes it possible for the individual, for business, and for industry to migrate freely and rapidly, but also the whole philosophy of our living makes mobility an accepted pattern of our individual and economic lives. Planning and zoning programs founded upon the smallest units of government cannot deal effectively with the adjustments and readjustments that population movements and economic shifts produce continuously.

Furthermore, as population increases and urbanization expands, inter-city problems such as presented in *Cresskill v. Dumont* (28 N.J. Super. 26, 100 A.2d. 182 (1953).) grow beyond the legal power of an individual city and raise issues of policy that a single small unit of government should not be able to determine finally. In that case, two towns had a common boundary line. The property on each side of the boundary was zoned for residential purposes. Then one town changed the classification to business. The court held that the landowners in the other city were entitled to rely on the continuation of the residence classification. There are hundreds of cities in this country with common boundary lines and of course every township and county has them. Thus the problem of the *Dumont* case is certain to increase as land-use controls expand. Under these circumstances, zoning in larger territorial units seems inevitable.

The frictions between urban and rural units of government have similarly prevented intelligent planning and zoning of land beyond the boundary lines of the city, although the urban character of the problem is beyond question. The unfortunate consequence of this hiatus in control is that in the only area where planning and zoning can be effective—that is, where undeveloped land still exists—planning and zoning is weakest or does not exist at all.

At this point, it is important to emphasize that so long as legislatures empower the smallest units of government to exercise the zoning power, those units should not be criticized if they establish use controls that exclude all industry, sharply restrict business, and impede the building of middle- and low-cost homes. I am thinking of such a case as *Fischer v. Bedminster Township* (11 N.J. 194, 93 A.2d. 378 (1952).), where the minimum lot size was fixed at one-half acre and a substantial portion of the land was restricted to five-acre tracts, no industry was permitted, and business was confined to an infinitesimal percentage of the total area. This was the legislative judgment of a majority of the people of the township and was therefore properly supported by the court. So long as the township was the unit for exercising the planning and zoning power its people should have been able to determine the conditions under which they wished to live. The difficulty is that they live in a much larger economic community, and the needs of that community should have a voice in land-management policy of all the smaller segments upon which it depends.

In the same way, even if the establishment of minimum floor size of single-family dwellings has the effect of excluding persons of low income from certain areas, as in *Lionshead Lake, Inc. v. Wayne Township*

(10 N.J. 165, 89 A.2d. 693 (1952) appeal dismissed, 344 U.S. 919 (1953).), so long as the New Jersey legislature gives to the early residents of the township a kind of "squatter's rights" to determine the future character of the community, no theory of representative government or of judicial review of legislative action will justify reversing their decision that they did not want unreasonably small houses in their township.

The gradual absorption of city, town, township, and even county zoning into metropolitan and regional zoning authorities reflects the trend toward larger territorial planning and zoning units. Ultimately, considering the mobile and expanding character of our society, state-wide planning of land-use seems inevitable, although most zoning will no doubt remain within the control of smaller governmental units. Even now on the Atlantic seaboard, statewide zoning and planning are inadequate to meet interstate problems from Maine to Virginia.

The steps by which this transfer of power will be accomplished will inevitably be accompanied by serious governmental and political conflict. The administration of highways, public health, and education has had a similar development. The parallel with school administration is most compelling. The school function originally was the exclusive prerogative of the smallest units of government, but metropolitan districts and county unit systems have steadily increased and the responsibility for education is continuously carried to larger governmental units. Within the past 15 years, the fiscal incapacity of local government has been demonstrated so frequently that the state, through grants-in-aid, has taken over the determination of policy in almost all matters relating to school administration—i.e., school attendance, school terms, curricula, teacher qualifications, compensation, and school building standards.

Unified policy in planning and zoning would be equally desirable, but much more difficult of achievement. The economic competition between cities makes it certain that

no state administration would attempt to plan or zone directly in a manner that might appear to favor one community over another. Thus, I think it can be assumed that state-wide zoning of specific land-uses, either rural or urban, will not occur soon.

But the state is not totally powerless. By statute it could confer upon a state planning authority the power to plan and zone all land that was not planned and zoned locally. This in itself would be a great impetus to a local reappraisal of land-use problems. The state could establish minimum standards of planning and zoning before local attempts were accepted as substitutes for state regulation. By grants-in-aid, the state could encourage the establishment of larger units for planning and zoning and could assist in the recruitment of the professional staffs. Furthermore, the state could establish minimum standards both for zoning and for its administration, which would go far to remove the local pressures and temptations that have done so much to destroy the high purposes for which planning and zoning was established.

The improvement in zoning administration is the second important step in the betterment of zoning legislation. Unfortunately, zoning has suffered too long from the assumption that the only alternative to the autocratic professional European system was the infusion of popular control in all phases of the planning and zoning process. Likewise, zoning administration has suffered from the fact that it antedated the modern development of administrative law. The consequences of these two factors have been to make the administration of zoning ineffective in smaller cities without professional personnel.

Three changes in administration seem desirable: (1) improved standards for land-use and for height, bulk, and area restrictions; (2) the elimination of the use variance; (3) the delegation of power to the professional staffs to determine variances concerning height, bulk, and area requirements.

The assertion that standards are in the interest of public health, safety, and morals has saved many ordinances from adverse judicial decision, but it has failed to produce regulations intelligible to owners, contractors, or administrators. Dennis O'Harrow's proposal for performance standards highlights the inadequacy of our present approach to all zoning regulations. It indicates that the division of land into three major use districts is only a generalization, which may in many instances provide an acceptable land-use management formula but which will in perhaps an equal number of instances provide a limitation on land-use without a defensible basis in terms of the objectives of zoning. The curse of current land-use restrictions is that they impose limitations upon property that a community recognizes, at least in specific instances, as unnecessary and unreasonable and therefore they encourage unjustifiable variances.

The non-conforming use problem illustrates the insufficiency of our present standards. As we all know (although we don't know why), we operate on the assumption that the investment of capital in raw land can be retroactively controlled, but that a similar investment in raw land plus a structure may not be interfered with retroactively. This troubled only a few early planners because they were confident that the non-conforming use would eliminate itself with the passage of time. Experience has proved that this assumption was false. The non-conforming use remains to spawn a host of variances and violations that degrade the surrounding neighborhood and defeat the objectives of zoning. Thus, recent zoning ordinances provide for amortization of the use and structure within a specified period of time. Unfortunately, the normal period for amortization is so long that the real determination is left to succeeding generations unless the owner voluntarily abandons his business. When amortization is fixed for a period of 10 to 20 years, we are not resolving the problem; we are avoiding it. Recognizing the early zoning philosophy that "Rome was not built in a day," I think that it is time that we admit if Rome is to be rebuilt we had better undertake the task immediately.

As an illustration, consider the case of a non-conforming grocery store in a residential zone. We start with the premise that it must be permitted to continue for a reasonable length of time. Furthermore, if the store is well-located its existence may be a benefit as

well as a burden to the residential neighborhood that it serves. Thus, even if it could be eliminated immediately, there would be strong community pressure to continue its existence. If the grocery store is economically desirable it will be just as difficult, if not more difficult, to eliminate it ten years hence.

The application of performance standards to the non-conforming use case seems to provide the ideal solution. The grocery store may continue indefinitely if the owner takes steps necessary to reduce the harm that a retail business imposes on adjacent residential property. If the owner does not choose to eliminate these evils, the operation can be terminated in a shorter time, because the choice is not the arbitrary dictate of the zoning authority but the decision of the owner. In other words, if the vice of a grocery store in a residential district is its increase of traffic, inadequate off-street parking, noise and glare, and perhaps architectural nonconformity, the grocer, if he stands on his right to continue the non-conforming use, could continue operations without structural change for five years. But if he were willing to provide adequate off-street parking, to eliminate advertising signs, to prevent noise and glare, and to make architectural adjustments so that the structure fits into the residential pattern of the community he, having met performance standards, could continue his operations indefinitely.

If compliance of this type is accepted, then there is little justification for the exclusion of other business or industry that can demonstrate that its location will not adversely affect the quiet enjoyment or the economic investment in adjacent property. The difficulty is that we have not developed standards with enough precision to control decisions of this kind. For example, we have not determined the permissible life of a non-conforming use. We have relied primarily on the provision of the Uniform Building Code for the amortization of structures according to the materials used in their construction. But this is a guide for amortizing the structure not the use. This is basically inconsistent because upon the expiration of the amortization period, we do not require the removal of the *structure* but we do insist upon the cessation of the *use*. So far as I know, no attempt has been made to determine the reasonable length of use or whether it would be taking property without due process of law to terminate the use, regardless of the condition of the structure in which the use is conducted.

Although this discussion has centered around the problem of the non-conforming use, it emphasizes the general lack of standards for the administration of zoning ordinances. Until administrative standards are developed with a precision far in advance of what we now have, we can expect a hesitancy upon the part of both planners and lawyers to enforce the law rigorously. Indeed, the present variance practice demonstrates all too convincingly the lack of confidence that zoners have in their own standards.

Variance practice, at least in the smaller communities, is the weakest link in all zoning administration. The two principal legal standards—that the grant is necessary because of the peculiar hardship suffered by the petitioner and that the grant will not adversely affect the community interest—have seldom offered reliable or consistent guides for the courts, the attorneys, or the planners. More importantly, the small number of variance cases that are appealed to the judicial system does not reflect actual practice. It is safe to assert again, at least for the medium-sized city, that the request for a variance is usually granted almost automatically and that the public interest as embodied in the master plan is seldom considered. To reduce the debilitating consequences of this practice, the administrative procedures in zoning ordinances must be revised.

Commendably, a majority of modern ordinances deny to the boards of adjustment or zoning appeals the authority to grant use variances. If the original land-use classification was correct, then a property owner should not be able to do administratively that which he cannot do legislatively—i.e., spot-zone his property. If the original land-

use classification was wrong, or conditions have changed, then not one property owner but all owners similarly situated should benefit by a change in classification. The existence of authority in boards of zoning appeals to change use classifications only subjects the board to local pressures that, regardless of the merits, the board usually finds it is impossible to resist. The time has come for the abandonment of use variances altogether.

Variances also are sought from height, bulk, setback, side yard, and rear yard restrictions. In almost every case, the grant or denial of such a variance will have very little effect upon the over-all plan of the community. Usually such petitions are granted. Many of them should be. Thus the effect of the area-variance procedure is harassment of the property owner. He is delayed in the beginning of construction. He must appear before the board or hire a lawyer to represent him. He must pay a fee and incur other expenses for a result that is almost certain. Appeal under these circumstances lends nothing to the stature of the zoning process. It exists today partially because we lack confidence in zoning standards and partially because of the belief that zoning should be subjected to popular opinion and pressure.

In the adoption of a plan and zoning ordinance, popular notions as to the kind and character of the community should have an important, even controlling, effect; but in the adjudication of the rights and privileges of a particular land owner, the decision might better be left to experts. But one of the difficulties of the limited jurisdiction in which most zoning ordinances operate is that small communities can seldom afford real experts. Therefore, the judgment of three or five citizen members of a board of zoning appeals may be preferred to the decision of an honest but untrained member of the city engineer's office. Where experts are available, however, it would be much more satisfactory if authority were delegated to the enforcement officer to determine height, bulk, and area variances without the necessity of appeal in every case. This would have the advantage of permitting the enforcement officer to make reasonable adjustments that he cannot now make without violating the law and at the same time it would allow him to issue a permit, which he knows will be granted by the board of zoning appeals because of the obvious merit of the case. Psychologically, such a practice would be of inestimable value, for it would reverse the present attitude that encourages people to believe that there is always a way of avoiding compliance with the zoning laws if you are contentious enough or know the right people.

The last but most immediate need for improvement in the zoning process is in the field of enforcement. Fortunately it is also the area that can be most easily improved. It is my thesis that zoning laws are almost universally enforced against the wrong people and in the wrong way. Enforcement is against the land owner by criminal prosecution or by injunction. The result is that enforcement is against a property owner who is usually unaware of the existence of zoning ordinances and most certainly unfamiliar with their provisions. The owner is not considered by the community as a criminal and thus to bring misdemeanor proceedings against him is, in all but the most outrageous cases, hopeless. City attorneys are well aware of this fact and are likewise conscious that strict enforcement by criminal prosecution will have unhappy consequences. It is understandable therefore—at least to lawyers—why zoning laws are not enforced. Even if enforcement is sought by way of injunction, the cost or removal or alteration of a structure in order to comply with the terms of the ordinance appears to the public to be too high a penalty for its apparent benefits. Thus, the law remains unenforced and one violation produces another until ultimately it seems unfair to enforce the ordinance in any case.

City attorneys and the legal profession, however, are not blameless. Most municipal law officers are completely uninformed concerning the principles of planning and zoning and are equally unfamiliar with state zoning statutes and their own ordinances. This is understandable; for law schools, until recently, have not given instruction in this important branch of property law, and so the average practitioner is without knowledge or experience in zoning cases.

At this point, professional planners can aid greatly if they take a more aggressive attitude toward the lawyers. Customarily they accept the lawyer's judgment that enforcement is impractical or that a case will be lost. Contrast the three New Jersey cases mentioned earlier. In each case the planners and lawyers worked in close cooperation in preparing the case for trial. The professional standards by which the basic comprehensive plan was developed were carefully demonstrated to the court. Planners, as expert witnesses, testified specifically as to the effect intended by the regulations and the consequences to the community if the ordinance were not sustained. It was not accidental that in these three difficult and pioneering cases, the planning process was sustained in each instance.

Effective enforcement of zoning ordinances, however, will never be achieved through criminal prosecution. The judicial process is too slow, too expensive, and too uncertain for the day-to-day administration of zoning. The judicial process should be saved for those cases that test new principles or where important private rights are at stake. For cases of admitted violation, the administrative process is quicker, cheaper, and more effective. I am not suggesting that the land owner should be relieved of liability, but I do suggest that the law impose liability on those who are most frequently responsible for violations. Invariably this is the builder or contractor. He should be treated like the real estate promoter who must post a bond to insure compliance with subdivision ordinances. Similarly, building contractors should be licensed. The terms of the license should include authority for its revocation in case of repeated violation and should require the posting of bonds for the faithful compliance with the zoning law. The bond need not be excessively high, for if violations occur the contractor will be unable to procure another and will thereby be excluded from the contracting business. With such provisions incorporated into zoning laws, a city would then have the authority to proceed against those persons who because of their training and business are the very ones that the public expects to know the law and to comply with it. It would prevent the builder or contractor from proceeding without a permit because of his awareness of the city's reluctance to prosecute the land owner. This one addition would go far toward insuring effective enforcement of our zoning laws.

Unfortunately planners do not seem to be concerned with enforcement or the lack of it. This is regrettable, for if we are content with our charts and maps it doesn't matter whether the plans are poor or excellent— unenforced they are dreams, not realities. History should dispel any illusions about criminal enforcement. If planners are really serious about the effectuation of their plans, they must lead the movement to supplement criminal sanctions with effective administrative sanctions.

IT WOULD BE presumptuous for any one man, planner or not, to try to place zoning into perspective in the United States today. The angels of the city growth and development have feared to tread this path, though years of ·experience and ponderous though frequently valuable volumes are used to light the word-obscured way.

Has Zoning Worked?

Step back for a moment and look into the cities which others have built—others than those of us who deal only with regulatory measures and fitful plans. Further, scrutinize our ability to handle the entrepreneurs in land, building, money, water, and air. Are we peers in the power structure with those who negotiate or finance the means for the construction of what planners call "improvements" of these basic commodities? Still looking, then, we must ask ourselves whether zoning, since 1925, has helped to build or rebuild, control or stimulate, good well-planned man-made places for all the things man does in urbanized places? Is there a chance, an off-chance, that we have been captivated by a concept so persuasive and so self-propelling that it seems both a means and an end? Have we allowed ourselves to be lulled into a coma of mass acceptance of words and actions within both reality and mythology? Like the esoteric wiring of a computer, has an idea become so glitteringly enchantingly romanticized that it, as a gadget, has become for some of us as important or more important than the results it was designed to produce?

Perhaps it is the question of "the end" with which we now begin. The end is the American city you have just stepped back to look at. Do you like it? Does it work? Can you identify clearly the results of all the months and years of hard work in drafting ordinances, preparing maps, attending public hearings and Chamber of Commerce meetings, fighting in the courts, pursuing your administrative and legal responsibilities, and attending to limitless detail in the office and field? Have you achieved your ends, except in single-family districts, and are you pleased with results other than these in Class A-R1?

15

Planning Absorbs Zoning

Carl Feiss

Reprinted by permission of the author and the Journal of The American Institute of Planners, Vol. 27, No. 2, May 1961, pp. 121–126.

Dare you search for the place where you eliminated a nonconforming use?

Placing zoning in perspective, judging its accomplishments and lack of accomplishment, we recognize today that the concept of a negative regulatory measure for the control of land use and intensity of development is philosophically opposite from the present-day concept of development and redevelopment with its positive implications. As always the negative and positive are poles apart. We therefore find that where positive programs for development and redevelopment are under way, they frequently come in conflict with the older and more deeply intrenched regulatory measures. Or these older measures are found inadequate to meet the requirements of a positive program, and it becomes necessary to insert rules and regulations which support the design intent. Development and redevelopment imply a design intent which zoning has never served in adequate fashion, other than in broad-brush treatment of existing and expendable uses and attendant height and density controls. The results of what has been done within the powers of zoning and what is being and can be done within the powers of development and redevelopment are hardly comparable. One could cite, of course, successful instances of height control in the District of Columbia or of setback control in New York City as having a direct bearing on development design. However, this is design almost by default, since it averages a concept rather than particularizes it.

Sins of Omission

We cannot hold the original inventors of zoning responsible for a philosophy that did not exist at the time they proposed this ingenious and intricate form of regulation. In fact, it was a fairly simple idea to begin with. Their ideals and their idealisms were irreproachable. Unfortunately, the concept was chiefly legal and administrative; except for its police power, it was not consciously or adequately directed towards the finite elements of community design for better living, working, and playing. We can now regret the apparently uncorrectable errors in the fundamental tenets of zoning, errors which appeared at once but have not yet been fully recognized either by zoning proponents or by the people who go along because they know no better way.

The first and perhaps the most incomprehensible error was that the draftsmen of zoning considered open land or open space to be expendable. This, perhaps more than any other legal concept or lack of legal concept, has abetted the unlimited sprawl which occurs in all urbanizing areas in this country. It should have been recognized at once that to build on land where little or no development existed was to alter its use. To build for residential or nonresidential uses on land which has been used for agricultural or other openland purposes is so clearly and obviously a change in use that it is curious that this omission in the zoning concept was not corrected a long time ago. There are at least ten, maybe twelve, identifiable open-space or open-land uses both public and private. While some zoning ordinances do provide for agricultural uses, these are relatively few and quite weak. The result has been that space, which should have been reserved for both public and private use as part of a general plan and supported by zoning, has not been

so preserved, and nowhere within the concept of zoning is there a basis for the protection of such areas. It should be clear by this time that the term "undeveloped land" must be dropped from our vocabulary and that we must substitute for it a category of open-land use, even when such open land is presently "vacant" or "unoccupied."

Granted this may appear an oversimplification of a very complex problem, but when we consider the accumulation since 1925 of results of this omission of a use category, we must realize that this basic deficiency in the zoning concept is both philosophically and actually indefensible. (I brought this matter before a meeting of zoning and planning experts in New York City nearly four years ago and was met by blank stares and defensive incredulity. It is extraordinary how strongly the adherents of zoning inviolability resent infringements on the rituals.)

The Amateur Hour

The second grave error in the philosophy of zoning is the proposition that it can be adequately and knowledgably administered by politically appointed citizens with neither technical know-how nor a plan to refer to—other than the zoning map. Our law books are now filled with many hundreds of cases, city by city, state by state, year by year, dealing with complex and often contradictory court decisions relating to the actions of local zoning boards of adjustment and the appeals from such actions. Professor Haar, quoted above should have said that, "zoning is the work horse which *drags* the planning movement in this country." As case is added to case, legal confusion, state by state, compounds the difficulties of administering zoning at the local level by even the best-meaning and best-educated citizen zoning body.

In the first instance, the originators, as lawyers of zoning, should have been realistic enough to recognize that technical problems as complex as are those embodied in the framing, modification, and administration of local zoning required more understanding than could reasonably be brought to bear by a voluntary group meeting once or twice a month and deluged with case after case of appeals for variances and amendments. Today, we are dealing with a concept that is incomprehensible to the average person because of its legal and technical complexity. In the zoning of any city, why should we expect a citizen group to vote on the technical changes involved in densities and coverage, in the mathematics of setbacks and floor-area ratios, any more than we would expect a citizen group to pass judgment on the engineering design of a suspension bridge? The design and redesign of cities and their maintenance at the highest possible level of human, economic, and physical value is a task of such magnitude that the validity of uninformed or amateur approaches to it is subject to question. Such approaches are certainly subject to pressure by those special interests with the capacity to enter into, or to employ experts who can enter into, the details of technological complexities.

Myth and Theology

Part of the problem lies in a super-myth structure which has grown out of these legal and administrative complexities. There is also a compelling power of persuasion in enabling legislation and in attendant codes and ordinances which are given the powers of the public purpose through democratic means of adoption. But even more significant is that the regiments of casuists in the interpretation and ritualization of the theology of zoning have now developed the argument that these ceremonies and written dogmas are in the best interests of planning and, ergo, *pro bono publico*.

It is quite clear now that few local public documents rest on a more unstable base than does the local zoning ordinance. This instability is not so much within the law itself as it is a product of the inability of politically appointed and untutored, constantly shifting, boards of appeal or adjustment to hold to the purpose of the ordinance, which is all too frequently better served in the breach than the observance. To this we must add the super-myth of the ability of zoning to remove non-conforming uses. Compounding these are those master plans that illustrate the

zoning dream and hopefully contain those changes which nonconforming use would imply.

The Tool of Planning

Because of the mystical concept that has grown up that zoning "is a tool of planning," we have all hesitated to question those who have the responsibility for the use of this "tool." Regretfully, we are compelled to say that if zoning is considered a tool to attempt to pin down a land- and building-control program, the tool is hardly more than a thumb-tack to be pried loose with one fingernail at the first meeting of the board of adjustment. The tack comes out without skilled craftsmanship and very very little pressure.

What has happened is that zoning is not a tool of planning but that planning has become a tool of zoning. A master plan or general plan which deviates too much from existing zoned uses of land is considered as upsetting the acceptable tax base and real estate values, as well as interfering with the normal speculative process. This is why changes in zoning are so difficult to bring about and, when they are brought about, why so frequently they are only minor modifications of long-accepted ordinances. Few philosophic and administrative concepts have bedded down so securely so quickly. Few need such drastic reform.

The pursuit of the best public interest via the democratic process is never-ending. So also is the constant search for the improvement of human welfare. This means an ever-continuing evaluation of the strengths of the bridges between the people and their government and their law. The quasi-judicial citizen board which exists, in various capacities, in nearly every American city is one of these bridges. In the boards of appeal or boards of adjustment in zoning we find a structure that is inadequate to carry the weight of responsibility for decisions that have far-reaching effect on the nature of man-made environment. It is strongly recommended that research be done by experts in the construction of such bridges, by engineers in the process of good government and good law, to find the methods of either building anew or substituting another structure for the existing one.

It is hoped that the present zoning process can be considered an interim one. Out of consideration for those who are giving so much of their time and effort to administering the zoning process, this would be only fair. And the public, which has perhaps been inadvertently guided into the hope that the zoning processes has safeguarded and can safeguard the best interest of community development, must also come to realize that stronger and more clearly considered positive programs are needed if urban blight and decay are to be permanently eliminated and the deterioration process is to be forever halted.

We know now that zoning has not and cannot provide all the protection it was assumed it could, and that it cannot remove or alter what should not have been done in the first place.

Hen or Egg?

Very early in the development of zoning history in this country, the urgency of the priority in time of planning over zoning was brought forward by both zoning and planning experts. The conclusion of conference after conference was that planning should always precede zoning. The objective was correct but its accomplishment was negligible. The strength of the zoning concept, myth if you will, has been such that over and over again general plans have grown out of the zoning map. Planning considerations for the future of communities have been limited by what would appear to be acceptable within the framework of local zoning practice. The reasons for this are logical and clear. The law gave support to zoning in 1925 but it has never really supported planning. The first break that planning got was in the U.S. Supreme Court decision, Berman vs. Parker, 1954. Herein it was

stated: "The concept of the public welfare is broad and inclusive. The values it represents are spiritual as well as physical, aesthetic as well as monetary. It is within the powers of the Legislature to determine that the community should be beautiful as well as healthy, spacious as well as clean, well balanced as well as carefully patrolled." While this case concerned redevelopment in the District of Columbia, it clearly supported the concept of planning and area design. It gave a new lift to the whole process of urban planned development and in time will stand as an even greater milestone than the Euclid vs. Ambler zoning case of 1925.

We have barely begun to understand what development programming we may now do within the liberalized interpretation of our powers to plan. We do not know that even the Berman-Parker case is adequate for our total purpose. Possibly this is because we are not sure what our total purpose should be. But even so, as planners, those of us who serve the public by working towards the future revitalization of communities and the building of sound new ones take comfort in the fact that such action, at least in part, has been validated as zoning was twenty-nine years earlier. This time lag however has been unfortunate. We cannot yet assess the degree of damage that has been done either by unplanned zoning action or by misguided zeal. We do know that the process has, through its complexity and frequently through its lack of direction, fixed many areas and many uses which by their very nature require reconsideration and redesign. We recognize the positive benefits that have been derived from zoning as a protective device for high-class single-family residential areas. In this application of the zoning process throughout the country we can clearly see the physical results of the "highest type" of restriction. In other areas the protective device has been less successful, and in older areas of cities its application is barely discernible.

The Development Plan

What we must consider now is how to reverse the priorities of planning and zoning in both strength and time. The best tool at our disposal, and also the newest, lies in the strength of urban redevelopment and renewal. Today we must think of urban development potential within the redevelopment or renewal concept as being the more positive and stronger weapon to be used by planners. No more urgent effort can be recommended than the application of these processes to local activity, all sources of financing to be considered but not to be controlling. In the process of planning and replanning and future planning for communities, design requirements for development using renewal powers and action will inevitably modify present zoning patterns. A mechanism has therefore been developed which supersedes the older one, and within the foreseeable future it can place planning in its proper and primary position in local government.

It is true that we are in the very beginning of our understanding of the redevelopment and renewal processes, having had no more than ten years experience with them. Also, there are states which have not yet passed enabling legislation and cities which have not yet adopted the necessary measures to carry out these development processes. And yet, when Baltimore can declare its downtown area blighted and subject to renewal within state law and use its own bond-issue funds to undertake the Charles Center and Civic Center development, beginning without federal assistance—and all within the last five years—we must recognize the great strength that already lies within this new concept. The renewal and revitalization and rebuilding of the Golden Triangle in Pittsburgh was accomplished this same way. This could not have been done through zoning or rezoning or any other existing mechanism of local government other than redevelopment powers. Instances are now multiplying rapidly, with both good and bad plans developing—which is to be expected at this stage of experience. However, we must recognize here a new and very vital element in the total planning of our cities and look at zoning again in relation to this new element.

The Plan Absorbs the Zone

A clear look at the development process

raises the question of whether ultimately the controls of zoning should not be absorbed into planning districts, neighborhood, and citywide development plans and programs, staged, as is suggested in the federal community renewal program, in such a way that their accomplishment can be carried out in sequence or, where feasible, simultaneously. The regulatory measures and covenants which go with the development plan or program on a planning district or area basis would be those which relate specifically to the design of the plan itself and to the uses and purposes to which land and buildings are to be put. A new and more vital role is automatically created for the design planner, whether in public or private service. A valid development plan must relate to a valid community plan within a political subdivision, or within a group of political subdivisions or a region or whatever you may wish. The ultimate scale is still to be established.

Inserted, also, will be required development plans for "undeveloped" land. Orderly development of open land can only take place when it has been planned in advance, as part of a process as valid as that of planning for the replanning and redesign of land cleared by urban redevelopment and urban renewal. There should be no distinction in the planning process between the replanning of old areas and the planning of new and still-to-be-developed lands. The process under consideration is not just that of the change of land use, as mentioned above, but also the creation of an orderly design for a change in land use. This could well mean a development process directed towards the creation of new communities, call them what you will. Such communities must be part of the development process within a political subdivision or of the development process which creates new political subdivisions of an orderly type. Otherwise chaos continues.

While zoning conceivably can be used as a mechanism for setting aside land for orderly development, only in rare instances has this produced desirable results without a development plan. If zoning is applied without such a plan it achieves only a fragment of a plan.

Natural and human resources suffer. Highways, utilities, and services have no anchor. The administrative mechanism, which was not designed for this leadership purpose, has been proved incompetent in this role.

Our thesis therefore appears to be developing that zoning be gradually eliminated as the specific regulatory measure. Substituted for it is the development planning process in selected areas—ultimately to be part of a total community renewal and conservation development process, with zoning, if it is to be retained, constituting a part of the rules, regulations, and covenant system which accompany the development plan and program.

The Design Plan

What do we do with the mountains of zoning rules and regulations, legal decisions, and weighty processes, including the staffs and individuals who have been so intimately involved? In the first place, what is suggested here cannot be accomplished overnight. In spite of all its weaknesses, zoning must be maintained until a substitute has been found which can serve in every part of every community. Much can be chalked up to zoning experience. No matter what we do for a community in the development plan and program, there is invaluable background with zoning regulatory measures which can be transposed to those regulations which must be integral in the design plan for area development. It must be remembered that this design plan does not necessarily involve the clearance of buildings or drastic measures beyond those which would normally be required in the safeguarding or upgrading of an area. Much of what we do will be in the field of protection and conservation. In such areas we may modify the zoning approach by converting it into the performance type of regulation or, even better, making use of the newer concepts of planned development districts and planned development zones.

It can be feared that in the use of a planned development concept we may fall back again on inexperienced and incapable citizens, who make the final determination as to whether the design plan is acceptable. In other words, the equivalent of a board of adjustment may be established, but with many more difficult problems of evaluation before it. There is no gainsaying that the responsibilities of a board of redevelopment and the responsibilities of a planning commission will become increasingly arduous and will require more and more, a high type of citizen participation. The process of training and education for this type of service in itself becomes a major task. Also, there is in this country a serious scarcity of trained design planners and architects qualified to work out the intricate and appropriate schemes for the rebuidling of portions of older cities, the conservation of that which is worth selecting to be conserved, and the planning of new areas. We must devote much of our time and effort to improving our training program to meet these challenges.

It has been interesting to note the examples of success in the rebuilding of bombed-out areas in Europe, particularly in the Netherlands and Great Britain, where design plans and citizens' action appear to have gone hand in hand successfully. It is certainly not beyond our capacity to develop our own abilities along these lines.

It is difficult to answer the question of whether appointed citizens and elected groups can review and administer design plans better than similarly elected boards of adjustment or appeals did for zoning. For the time being, the only valid suggestion seems to be that, where citizens' boards lack this capacity, the locality would be well advised to employ consulting boards of review or panels of trained professionals in these fields. There is one thing that should be remembered. A design plan is a visual interpretation of what should be built, can be built, should be preserved, should be removed. All the facets of a plan are clearly expressed and exposed in drawings, models, diagrams, charts, and specifications. It is not possible to hide a design plan behind the verbiage that so frequently conceals either the intent of zoning or its feasibility.

The public purpose will be expressed in its

choice of design plans, since a locality must approve, through its governing body, the elements of these plans. Whether we are dealing with a small town or a big city, the public's choice will be as varied as the interests of the community itself. This is as it should be if we are ultimately and hopefully to achieve communities which have individuality and character of their own. Obviously, the opposite can occur. An unimaginative outlook may support an unimaginative plan. It certainly has in the limitless FHA subdivisions which presently cover vast areas of our urbanized land.

The history of public taste is a fascinating subject in itself. In these days of easy communication, it is all too easy to soft sell to the national community products with little or no merit. Zoning can do little about this even in those areas where zoning for aesthetics has been an experiment. But today, hopefully and on the basis of many stimulating starts throughout the country, the replanning of old areas and the planning of new indicate that urban pride is returning, that it is becoming more and more the ambition of people in our cities to live, work, and play in attractive and exciting human surroundings, and that they are willing to gamble on experiments as well as to fall back on the safety and safeguards of the banal.

Summary

In summary, then, what is recommended here? Primarily, it is that zoning should be superseded by development planning as part of comprehensive plans as soon as feasible. That every area of a city should be protected and promoted by plans for improvement and development with attendant regulatory measures, which may include zoning, such plans to be given public acceptance in much the same way that zoning ordinances and maps have received public promotion and acceptance in the past. We must step forward with courage into the next stage of environmental design.

We can still make use of the experience we have gained in zoning—particularly in the design of new covenants and rules to support designing development plans. Conceivably, zoning may remain as a generalized supporting legal measure, but it may well become a superfluous procedure. If so, it should be cut out, but not before the development planning design is well established. Otherwise we return to an even more primitive and unprotected situation (which Houston, Texas, likes), not to be recommended here. We are verging on programs for community objectives more readily achievable than in many years of modern planning history. In stepping towards comprehensive community goals through the mechanisms of designed area development plans based on the growing planning powers of renewal, we will be retiring old systems with due honor, but making new history.

Selected References

References to Chapters 1-15

This brief bibliography is intended to provide references to books, monographs, and reports which, in whole or part, place a socioeconomic or political emphasis on zoning. A few journal articles also appear here for which it was not possible to secure publication permission or which could not be included in full for various reasons.

Babcock, Richard F., *The Zoning Game*, The University of Wisconsin Press, 1966.

Bair, Frederick H., Jr., "Is Zoning a Mistake?" *Zoning Digest*, September, 1962.

Fisher, Ernest, "Economic Aspects of Zoning, Blight, and Rehabilitation," *Proceedings* of the American Economic Association, 1942.

Hamilton, Calvin S., "Zoning Administration," *Planning*, Chicago, 1962.

Lovelace, E., and Weismantel, W. L., *Density Zoning*, Urban Land Institute, Technical Bulletin 42, 1961.

National Commission on Urban Problems, *Problems of Zoning and Land-Use Regulations* (prepared by American Society of Planning Officials), Research Report No. 2, Washington, D.C., 1968.

Ranes, Herman, "The ABC's of Zoning," *Planning*, Chicago, 1963.

Reps, John W., "The Future of American Planning: Requiem or Renascence," *Planning*, Chicago, 1967.

Rowlson, John F., "Zoning v. Alternate Value," *The Appraisal Journal*, October, 1963.

Smith, William C., "Municipal Economy and Land Use Restrictions," *Law and Contemporary Problems*, Summer, 1955.

Tough, Rosalind and MacDonald, Gordon D., "The New Zoning and New York City's New Look," *Land Economics*, February, 1965 (Vol. 41), pp. 41–48.

Wolffe, Lenard L., *New Zoning Landmarks in Planned Unit Development*, Urban Land Institute, Technical Bulletin No. 62, Washington, D.C., 1968.

Building and Housing Codes

THE MATERIALS IN Part II are arranged in two groups. The first is devoted to discussions of building codes; the second deals with housing codes.

In some respects the readings on codes fall farthest below the goals set for this book. Until 1968, when the hearings and special research reports sponsored by the National Commission on Urban Problems began to appear, there had been relatively little of an analytic nature in either book or article form on the socioeconomic policy aspects of urban building and housing codes. Most of the socioeconomic writings were descriptive; they were most often prepared by government economist–administrators or by lawyers. Moreover, many of these articles appeared at or soon after the passage of the Housing Acts of 1949 and 1954. The most recent articles, those of the middle and late sixties, are usually associated with some aspect of urban renewal, especially housing, and therefore do not focus on the community as a whole. While recent concern with housing codes is well warranted, it is nonetheless specialized. As indicated in the Introduction, the readings in this Part do not touch upon urban renewal literature *per se*, inasmuch as this area is amply covered in other books of readings. Aside from sporadic conferences on discussions of building code standardization, little has been written on the economic impact and social consequence for *all* land uses of this part of urban public policy in land use control.

The consequences of the conditions I have described are that many of the articles which appear here are old (back to 1949), and many do not have the desired orientation. Nonetheless, they have been included because they represent unusually good description combined with some analysis, and because most of them can be adapted, with a little effort, to a socioeconomic analytic treatment. National Commission studies have not been included in the readings; however, references to many of these studies do appear. It was felt that one of the functions of these readings was to provide additional materials and perspectives that could be combined with the Commission's publications.

There are three articles and a comparative-cost sketch in the first (Building Codes) portion of Part II. The opening article is intended to introduce the reader to codes in general and the building code in particular. Some of the history of codes is reviewed with their legal basis, and standards for judgment and comparison. Another major reading then examines the oft-neglected question of how building codes apply to existing buildings, to repairs, and to demolitions.

The second (Housing Codes) portion of this Part offers six readings. In a selection from a U.S. Housing and Home Finance Agency monograph, Gilbert R. Barnhart makes important distinctions between building and housing codes, shows the principal areas of concern a community should have for its housing stock, and summarizes the old Baltimore Plan of housing code administration, which even today serves as a model of excellence. Warren Lehman's article happily combines housing code concepts with the building code system in a highly effective discussion of housing supply conservation in Chicago. Another major reading in this Part is Joseph Guandolo's article on housing codes and urban renewal. (Despite the general proscription on urban renewal materials, this item was included because of the discussions in it on the zoned housing code, distinctions between building codes and zoning, and the ties between codes and property values.) Two recent articles from the *Journal of Housing* conclude Part II. These articles, while not handling the subject of housing codes directly, do give competent overviews of low-income and low-middle-income family activities and attitudes toward these codes—activities and attitudes expressed in such devices as rent strikes, self-help, and tenant unions.

THE NEED for regulating building construction in the interest of safety and health has been felt in many times and places wherever men have lived under urban conditions. Evidence of this is to be found in the Code of Hammurabi, which dealt with conditions in Babylon about 2100 B.C.; in various Roman laws; in Fitz-Elwyne's Assize of Buildings, which regulated construction in London in 1189; and in a number of early colonial laws in this country. Early legal restrictions were concerned largely with the hazards of fire and collapse, with health conditions appearing at a comparatively late date. In general, the nature of such laws has broadened with the passage of time so that, in addition to safety and health, they now deal also with some aspects of morals and general welfare.

16

Preparation and Revision of Building Codes

George N. Thompson

This paper appeared originally in Building Materials and Structures Report BMS 116, September 1, 1949, *published by the National Bureau of Standards, U.S. Department of Commerce. Selected sections.*

Introduction

Requirements, in the form of building codes, have come to be an accepted feature of modern life in all our large cities and in many small ones. Like most restrictive legislation, they have always been the object of some criticism; but this has been intensified in the period since World War I. In 1921 the Senate Committee on Reconstruction and Production issued a report in which it was pointed out that building-code requirements varied widely and were one source of unnecessarily high construction costs. Since that time various writers and speakers have repeated these charges and have also referred to lack of flexibility in dealing with new materials and new methods of construction. Much of this criticism is justified. However, it frequently fails to take into account the great advances that have taken place in codes in recent years, and it constitutes a negative rather than a constructive approach to the problem. In order to effect further improvement, it is necessary to undertake the tedious and exacting task of analyzing present code deficiencies and working out a pattern of requirements that will assure the primary object of safety while giving heed to legitimate economies and necessary adjustments to changing conditions.

In well over 200 cities and towns each year, work is undertaken on the preparation of a local building code, either as a revision of a former document or as preparation of a completely new series of requirements. Usually this work is entrusted to a group of citizens chosen for their special qualifications or interest. The responsibility placed upon them is a heavy one. Utilizing such materials as they can gather, they must proceed to draw up proposed requirements that, if observed, are to assure the safety of building occupants and of those whose customary activities take them into and about buildings. Yet they must keep an eye on the effect which such requirements will have on building costs, since too rigid requirements may so discourage building activity that not enough new construction will be erected to take care of normal needs. Such local groups usually serve without pay and are called upon to contribute a large amount of time and energy as a matter of public service. They undertake their work conscientiously but are often hampered by lack of information about available material and how to use it.

Students of the subject have pointed out that considerable progress could be made through the adoption of State requirements, leaving local variations at a minimum. Among advantages mentioned are elimination of needless differences in technical requirements and uniform treatment for new materials and new methods of construction. This suggestion has met with some favor, but until it is generally accepted the problem of developing complete local requirements and of keeping them up to date will remain.

For some 30 years the National Bureau of Standards has endeavored to provide helpful information on building codes to a large number of local committees and officials. Investigations carried on at the Bureau in regard to strength, fire resistance, and other characteristics of building materials have produced results of direct usefulness in this field. During the period 1921 to 1934, the Bureau supplied the staff and published the reports of the Department of Commerce Building Code Committee. At present, in addition to continued technical research and contact with public officials on building-code problems, the Bureau is cooperating in the continued development of recommended building-code standards under the procedure of the American Standards Association.

These activities have resulted in the accumulation of much material bearing on building-code problems. It has become apparent through correspondence and other contracts that much the same problems occur in each community and that a discussion of some of their more familiar features would serve a useful purpose. The literature on the subject has been enriched in recent years by the writings of Burton, Miller, Stegner, and others. These have made painstaking investigations of fundamental questions and have recorded their conclusions at some length. The literature is scattered, however, and much of it is not readily available. Frequent reference to it will be made in this discussion.

The method of treatment employed here is in large part that of discussion rather than specific recommendation. Great strides have been made in recent years in bringing divergent opinions about building codes into closer agreement, but the time has apparently not yet arrived when it can be said with assurance that some one method of approach is best for all cases. There is a healthy disagreement on such matters as arrangement

of topics, ideal requirements versus realistic ones, possibilities of simplification, and other matters. Those who have followed such controversies over a period of years are aware that variations in codes are diminishing. Some of the alternatives that remain are, however, so closely equal in merit that it is only fair to describe them in detail pending the time when more conclusive evidence is obtainable.

What the Building Code Is

As already indicated, the building code is a collection of legal requirements whose purpose is to protect the safety, health, morals, and general welfare of those in and about buildings. The code attempts to do this by establishing a series of requirements covering such topics as fire protection, strength of materials, light and ventilation, sanitation, exits, and other matters which have been found to need regulation. It sets forth the least that will be acceptable in each instance. leaving the designer or builder to go beyond this as far as he likes. It creates a system of supervision, making it necessary to obtain a permit to undertake work on a building and providing for inspection of the structure by public officials. It usually carries teeth in the form of fines for violation of the code provisions and gives authority to stop the work if necessary in the public interest.

The usual type of building code covers requirements for construction, alteration, demolition, maintenance and repair, and other activities in connection with buildings and certain other structures. Requirements for interior equipment may or may not be included.

Example—This ordinance provides for all matters concerning the construction, remodeling, alteration, repairing, maintenance, use, moving or removal of buildings and other structures and parts thereof, erected or to be erected in the city; the safety of workers and others during these operations and the safe use of such buildings and structures.

The broad objectives are reflected in the actual requirements. For instance, fire limits are established within which only buildings of certain types of construction may be erected, the object being to restrict the spread of fire in the municipality. Similarly, maximum heights for buildings are given. These are uniform throughout the city for the same type of construction and occupancy, fire protection being again the determining factor. Requirements, concerning alterations touch upon the delicate problem of when old buildings must be brought up to the standards for new ones. The matter of demolition carries with it measures for determining when a building is so unsafe or unsanitary as to justify removal and by what procedure. Provisions for maintenance and repair are bound up with social policies concerned with how far it is expedient to force owners to keep their buildings in conformity with present-day practices. Thus, the contents of the code are something more than a routine statement of technical details. They are, or can be, a dynamic force in shaping the physical character of a community through the standards that are imposed.

Extent of Code Requirements

It is well to think of a proposed local building code not as an isolated document of purely local concern but as a part of a network of requirements that extends over the country. There are some 2,200 local building codes and a number of State codes. Although such codes are developed more or less independently under present conditions, they have a common objective and affect the work of professional men and manufacturing concerns far beyond the borders of the political units concerned. The State building codes usually are limited to certain types of buildings and may or may not apply within the limits of incorporated areas. There are also numerous State laws applying to special occupancies, such as factories and schools. A small number of counties have county building codes.

The pattern of existing requirements is not limited to those forms that have been mentioned but is further extended by zoning ordinances and housing codes. The former, adopted locally in accordance with State enabling acts, regulate the height, use, and

area of buildings in different districts, so that the community can develop in an orderly fashion. The latter, more frequently State measures, are concerned with matters of light, ventilation, sanitation, and safety features applying to residential buildings. When housing codes do not exist, these matters are usually contained in building codes. Finally, there are requirements concerning the equipment of buildings, including the plumbing code, the electrical code, the elevator code, and the boiler code. Custom differs as to whether these form chapters of the building code or are separately published and perhaps separately administered. There are local traditions and differences in municipal organization that account for the varying treatment accorded these subjects. Authorities agree that whether they should be included in the building code or not is largely a matter of local policy. They are closely related to the building code even when not an integral part of it.

It may be stated as a general principle that where a State law is in existence, this takes precedence over a municipal ordinance dealing with the same subject, although the ordinance may be more restrictive if this is desired.

Example of State code provision illustrating relationship to local code—This code shall not limit the power of cities, villages and towns to make, or enforce, additional or more stringent regulations, provided the same do not conflict with this code or with any other order of the Industrial Commission.

Example of local building-code provision in same State—The provisions of this Code shall supplement any laws of the State of Wisconsin relating to buildings. Where requirements of the State Code and the provisions of this Code conflict, the stricter requirements shall govern.

With such a multiplicity of measures to safeguard the public, it is obvious that one of the first things for a local committee to do

Effect on Community

The influence of the building code on city growth is greater than is ordinarily suspected. The requirements, operating over a period of years, affect the physical character of the community to a marked degree. There are other effects which should be realized. If the requirements are so severe as to impose building costs greater than those prevalent in other cities, new industries may be diverted elsewhere, rents may be increased, and other effects produced. If the permissible building heights and types of construction bear no relation to the city water pressure and efficiency of the fire department, insurance rates may be affected. In a standard method for rating cities for fire insurance purposes, the quality of the building code and of its administration is a specific point. If peculiar requirements are made, as is sometimes done, necessitating the use of nonstandard products, manufacturing processes may have to be altered to meet the special requirements of the municipality concerned. Thus, the code can be a beneficient influence guiding the general course of construction in safe channels, or it can be a means of hampering the orderly growth of the community that it is supposed to protect.

is to establish the place of its project in relation to other legal requirements that apply. This can only be done by assembling and comparing the various documents that have been mentioned. The limiting effects of State laws, the extent to which it is advisable to maintain harmony with existing ordinances, or to absorb them, and the advantages of keeping in step with the requirements of other communities in order to avoid unnecessary confusion are all proper subjects for consideration.

Police Power

The building code derives its justification from the police power. This is the inherent power of government to protect the people against harmful acts of individuals insofar as matters of safety, health, morals, or the like are concerned. It is a power forming the basis for State acts and municipal ordinances dealing with these matters and is of indefinite extent, although certain limitations concerning its use are to be found in the Federal and State constitutions and in court decisions. Fundamentally, under our system of government, the power resides in the State and may be transmitted to local authorities through enabling acts authorizing the adoption of building requirements or may be conferred upon municipalities when a charter is granted. Although the use of the power has been more narrowly construed at some times than at others, there is an apparent trend toward broadening its application to include many matters falling under the general head of public welfare.

In order to have a working knowledge of how the code-making power has come into the hands of the local authorities and what restrictions are placed upon it, it is well to consult the State constitution, any pertinent State enabling acts that confer this power on the municipality, and the provisions of the city charter. The corporation counsel, or other person designated to advise municipal officials on matters of law, is in a position to render skilled assistance in this matter.

Tests for Codes

Building codes, being documents which limit and restrain people in their activities, inevitably are targets for criticism. It is important to know whether such criticism is valid or is frivolous and actuated by other than disinterested motives.

There are certain tests that can be applied to an existing local code which will give some indication of whether it is reasonably adequate or is in need of a thorough overhauling. These tests, together with any complaints that have accumulated, constitute the basis for determination of what action, if any, is necessary.

The age of the code is one indication of its quality, for advances in the building art tend to make provisions obsolete. Doubt is cast upon fully 45 per cent of existing codes in this respect, for a recent survey disclosed that

27 per cent of such codes are over 20 years old, while another 18 per cent are from 16 to 20 years. Some further investigation is needed before judgment can be rendered on this score, because frequent amendments and supplementary rulings of officials may have brought the code into closer conformity with current practice than the bare figures would indicate. However, these amendments have a tendency to clutter up the code and make it increasingly difficult to understand. A complete overhauling at intervals of not over 10 years, and preferably at somewhat shorter intervals, is desirable.

Looking into the code itself, the next test is whether the contents are reasonably clear and explicit and can be readily located. This applies not only to the wording of individual sections but to the way in which sections are put together so that they form a logical series of interrelated requirements. Experience with ambiguous provisions has led commentators to emphasize this point. Certainly, if a designer or builder is expected to observe the law, he should be given a fair chance to ascertain what is required. It is equally true that the administrative official should have the backing of a document that leaves little or no room for argument. Ease of reference implies a complete index and adequate cross-referencing wherever necessary.

What might be termed the underlying philosophy of the code as evident in its requirements is also important. If it has been thought necessary to write into the code a great amount of minute directions and specifications, one of two things may have happened: Changes in the art of construction may have forced frequent amendments or may be responsible for complaints that the particular things specified in the code no longer apply. In either case a lack of flexibility of adjustment to new conditions is indicated. On the other hand, if the code is expressed in terms of what is required in the way of strength, fire resistance, and so on, leaving the determination of what will do the job to appropriate tests, a better chance for keeping requirements abreast of changing conditions will have been afforded.

A third way of appraising the code is to examine it for the extent to which national standards have been used. These standards for quality of materials, for methods of testing, and in some cases for methods of construction, have been widely accepted and furnish a definite basis for accepting or rejecting proposed elements of construction. When advantage is not taken of these useful devices, a doubt is cast on whether full use has been made of all available methods for keeping the code up to date. One thing that should be watched especially in this connection, however, is the date of the standard used, if this is given. The pages of codes are strewn with dead standards which have long since been superseded by more modern requirements.

Evidence of careless draftsmanship is another cause for holding a code to be in need of revision. Examples of actual errors in codes are the use of the term "feet" for "inches"; two different requirements for the same thing; transposed column headings in stress tables; and the use of the term "maximum" where "minimum" is meant, or vice versa. Such errors may be patent because of their very absurdity and thus cause little harm, but they cast doubt on the soundness of other provisions and tend to create disrespect for the code as a whole.

If the examination of these general features of the code has resulted in an unfavorable reaction, examination may proceed to details. It will be found that the code contains certain assumptions and estimates which may or may not assure safety. Included will be requirements about live and dead loads, live-load reduction factors, permissible working stresses, thicknesses of walls, and thicknesses of fire-protective coverings. The less these partake of the character of estimates the more will they satisfy the purpose for which they are intended. To appraise them, it is necessary to compare them with values suggested by outstanding authorities in the building-code field, references to which are available.

The attitude of the code toward acceptance of new materials and new methods of construction is important. Innovations are multiplying today and are demanding equal treatment with older materials which have proved their worth. If clear and explicit requirements are lacking in regard to the procedure to be employed, the code is deficient in meeting one of the most pressing problems of building regulation today.

Examination of the features mentioned should give a good idea of whether a few well-selected amendments will accomplish all that is needed or whether the task of preparing a new code should be undertaken.

Performance Basis

There are several ways of wording requirements. One is to state the exact materials that must be used for a given purpose, and frequently the exact sizes and other details. If these are used, it is assumed that the desired results will be obtained.

Example—All cast-iron, wrought-iron, or rolled-steel columns, including the lugs, and brackets on same, used for vertical supports in the interior of any fireproof building, or used to support any fireproof floor, shall be entirely protected with not less than 4 inches of hardburned brickwork, terra cotta, concrete, or other fireproof material, without any air space next to the metal, securely applied. . . .

Another way is to state the desired results and leave the details out except as they may be cited for illustrative purposes.

Example—Iron or steel columns shall be protected by material or assemblies having a fire-resistive rating of 4 hours for Class 1, fireproof structures, and of 3 hours for Class 2, fire-protected structures, except that interior columns in Class 2, fire-protected structures, for residence purposes need have only 2-hour protection.

The first way is clear and definite, but it makes no allowance for varying resistance of protective materials. The second is clear and definite so far as it goes, but throws no light on what materials and thicknesses are acceptable. If it is accompanied by examples or by information in an appendix to the code

listing what materials have passed the test, a complete picture is obtained. The particular virtue of this method is that new materials become available for use as soon as they have demonstrated their value under test. With the first method an amendment to the code may be necessary to accomplish this purpose. There is a well-founded principle that it is not reasonable to specify both the required result and the manner in which it should be accomplished. If the latter is given, the result must be assumed while if the former is given, freedom should be left to adopt any legitimate way of achieving it. Building-code requirements are in a transitional stage today in which more and more emphasis is being placed on performance as demonstrated under standard test. The general principle has been widely endorsed and is finding its way into many recent codes. It is not feasible to word all requirements this way, for no standard test may have been developed in some cases or the subject matter may not lend itself readily to this treatment. Increasing attention to principles of performance may be expected to suggest further developments in this field. It will be found profitable to subject each proposed requirement to analysis to see whether it can be so worded that the end is emphasized and the means to the end offers as great a choice of methods as possible.

Acceptance of New Materials and Methods

The rapid introduction of new materials and methods of construction represents problems to every municipal building department. To a considerable extent these problems will be anticipated through the use of the performance basis already mentioned. It is necessary to supplement this, however, by some provision which will make it possible to pass upon the new development without unnecessary delay. Various methods are in use, such as approval by the building official, approval by a local board, or submittal of an amendment to the code.

Example—The Inspector of Buildings shall have full authority to approve or disapprove any device, material or construction proposed to be used in building construction in the city of Minneapolis, not specifically provided for in this ordinance, and may base such approval or disapproval upon the results of satisfactory evidence of competent and impartial tests or investigations conducted by others, or upon the results of satisfactory tests made under his direction.

Example—For the purpose of securing for the public the benefits of new developments in the building industry with respect to construction, materials, processes and methods and appliances to insure public safety, the Board may make or cause to be made at the expense of the promoter or submitter, investigations of new materials or modes of construction intended for use in the construction of buildings or structures in the city of Wilmington which are not provided for in this ordinance and not prohibited thereby and shall adopt and promulgate rules of practice and regulations setting forth the conditions under which such materials or modes of construction may be used. It shall have the power to make similar investigations at the expense of the promoter or submittor in cases where a recommendation to Council for amendment of this ordinance is contemplated.

The problem has been considered by the Sectional Committee on Administrative Requirements for Building Codes A55 of the American Standards Association which has recommended the following treatment, which gives recognition to the use of prefabricated assemblies:

4-8. *Alternate materials and constructions:*
(a) The provisions of this Code are not intended to prevent the use of any material or construction not specifically authorized by this Code provided any such alternate has been approved.
(b) The building official shall require sufficient evidence to substantiate any claims that may be made regarding the use of such material or construction and shall approve them, provided he finds that for the purpose intended the proposed design and the material, method or system meets the requirements of this Code for safety and health. . . .
Note—In jurisdictions in which acceptance of alternate materials or constructions is vested in a board or in the local legislative body, appropriate changes in

the wording of this Section should be made.
(c) Materials and constructions which have been approved shall be used and installed in accordance with the terms of approval. All such approvals, and the conditions under which they are issued shall be reported and kept on file, open to public inspection.
(d) Where the component parts of prefabricated assemblies are not readily accessible to inspection at the site, the building official may accept certification that the assembly as installed at the site is identical with specimens upon which approval was based. If mechanical and electrical equipment is so installed as not to be readily accessible to inspection at the site, certification may be required that such equipment complies with applicable laws and ordinances.

This provision is supplemented by others relating to tests which provide complete machinery for dealing with the matter. In larger cities where it is possible to organize a board, this provides a broader base for judgment than the opinion of the building official. In either case difficulties will be encountered in passing upon radically new types of construction unless standard methods of tests have been developed and facilities are available for having tests made. Fortunately, attention is being given to further development of standard test methods for assemblies by a committee of the American Society for Testing Materials which has already produced several tentative standards.

One of the responsibilities of the local official or board will be to select approved laboratories where tests may be conducted at the expense of the manufacturer and whose reports may be accepted as disinterested and conclusive. The method of acceptance by amendment to the code is a much slower process and may be subject to as much, if not more, danger of political or other influence, than the method of acceptance by an official or board.

This matter of giving adequate attention to new developments in the construction field has been emphasized repeatedly in comments on building codes. It is one matter deserving of special attention by a local committee.

17

Powers
and Procedures
for Ordering Repair
and Demolition
of Existing Buildings

Gilbert R. Barnhart

This article appeared originally in A Report on Administrative Procedures for Enforcement of Building Regulations, April 1959 *published by Housing and Home Finance Agency, Washington, D.C. Selected sections.*

THIS CHAPTER deals generally with the problem of enforcing the maintenance of standards in existing buildings. It is limited to discussion of the procedures used by building departments. Also, the discussion applies generally to maintenance in dwellings, as well as in other types of buildings and occupancies.

One fact of the greatest importance has to be recognized. That is, that a program of enforcing the maintenance of certain standards in existing buildings over an indefinite period of time involves a local policy decision to place emphasis on such a function. Such a decision does not necessarily mean that the regulation of new construction will receive less attention, but it does indicate that the building department is concerned about what happens to buildings after construction.

The process by which the building department regulates conditions in existing buildings is quite different in approach from that which is used when an application for new construction is submitted and the department issued a building permit. By signing for a permit to build, the applicant has indicated his intent to build his structure in an approved manner and if he does not do so he has violated the permit.

In the process used to correct deficiencies or substandard conditions in existing buildings, the building department is still exercising police power, but the department no longer has its clientele approaching and submitting itself to the laws. Rather, the initiative is now placed upon the department to discover violators of the laws it administers and proceed against them in a manner that will insure compliance with such laws.

In one sense, the use of certificates of occupancy represents an attempt to carry the licensing or permit process over to existing buildings to establish a continuing relationship between the building department and owners and tenants. In such cases, the owner is "licensed" to occupy and use his own property subject to approval by the building department. The acceptance and effectiveness of licensing or permitting individuals to occupy and use their own property is questionable in the opinion of some building officials.

The ordering process used to raise the standards of existing buildings usually operates as the result of a complaint, and occasionally from routine periodic inspections.

When substandard conditions in existing buildings are discovered, the building official must issue some kind of corrective order on the basis of criteria set forth in the code. In most cities, what may be called a "deterioration standard" is used as a basis for ordering correction, while some cities attempt to define substandard conditions as nuisances and authorize the building official to order such nuisances abated. In the latter case, the enforcing official has to see that the nuisance as existing meets the definition of the code while, in the former, he must be certain that the building has deteriorated to the degree at which the code provision authorizes him to act. If the deterioration can be measured so that it can be proved, the official may then proceed to order the building repaired, vacated, or torn down.

Demolition of a building, except where dangerous conditions exist, is usually the last resort in the process of controlling existing buildings. However, it has occasionally been attempted to extend the deterioration concept to permit demolition if the building has deteriorated beyond a point, usually stated in percentage of its original value, where it would be too costly to repair.

Inspection of Existing Buildings

Building codes invariably authorize the building official to inspect existing buildings to see that they are kept in a proper state of repair and maintenance and continue to meet code standards.

One of the more comprehensive clauses for the inspection of existing buildings is found in the Detroit building code which states:

> The commissioner shall cause to be inspected from time to time and as nearly as possible, once a year, all buildings of public assembly, school buildings, halls, armories, theaters, buildings used for manufacturing and commercial purposes, hotels, hospitals, apartment houses, tenement houses, and all other buildings occupied or used by large numbers of persons; and fences, billboards, signs and other structures, for the purpose of ascertaining the safety thereof.

Because of a heavy workload on new construction, the Detroit department does not make periodic inspections of multiple residences, but it does receive information from the health and fire department inspectors who are continually inspecting such buildings. The building department will inspect all complaints filed, either signed or anonymous. The routine inspections made on theaters, hotels, and large commercial buildings are subject to a fee ranging from $2 to $30 as established by the board of rules.

Unless the code creates a dramatic duty to enforce maintenance standards, building departments seldom make systematic periodic inspections.

Cleveland is an exception to this rule, probably because the building department is charged with the enforcement of the housing code as well as the construction code. The Cleveland building department separates housing inspection from inspection of new construction, and different personnel are used for each function. In theory, the Cleve-

land housing inspectors are divided into districts within which they are supposed to make inspections of all buildings. But at the present time the heavy work load required of these inspectors in conducting surveys of certain blighted areas has forced the staff to inspect only upon complaint from their districts.

In carrying out their respective functions, several municipal agencies other than the building department enter buildings and make various inspections. In the course of these activities, a number of violations and conditions which fall within the building department's jurisdiction are discovered. If procedures are established for reporting such violations and conditions to the building department, that department will be greatly strengthened and aided in enforcing the codes and ordinances under its control.

Certificate of Occupancy

As mentioned above, an attempt to establish continuing control of buildings after the building department has passed upon the original construction has been tried in many places by the issuance of a certificate of occupancy. Such certificate has conditions attached to it so that the building department may reinspect the premises from time to time. Such certificates are usually confined to buildings which are used for commercial purposes such as rooming houses and business buildings.

Milwaukee extends the certificate of occupancy to private dwellings and has the most comprehensive provisions covering the issuance of certificates of occupancy of any of the cities studied. Milwaukee divides its occupancy classifications into groups running from A to H.[1]

[1] Group A occupancies are factories, offices, and mercantile buildings; Group B are theaters, assembly halls, and churches; Group C are schools and places of instruction; Group D are hotels, apartment houses over four families, asylums, convents, row houses, and hospitals;

The code states that no building may be occupied without a certificate of occupancy and that "a separate certificate of occupancy shall be procured for each occupancy and use."

The code provision then puts the burden of obtaining a certificate on the owner. It states:

> The inspector of buildings shall issue such certificate of occupancy, or the renewal of an existing certificate of occupancy, after an application therefore has been filed in his office by the owner, or his agent, if after inspection it is found that such building, structure, or premises, or part thereof, complies with all of the regulations of this code and all other requirements of law or ordinance applicable to the proposed occupancy. Such certificate of occupancy shall indicate the use of the building, structure, or premises, or part thereof. The certificate of occupancy shall be posted in a conspicuous place in the building *** and shall not be removed except by permission from the inspector of buildings.

The Milwaukee code makes provision for temporary certificates of occupancy which may be issued before a building is completed. Buildings abandoned will not be permitted to be reoccupied until a new certificate has been issued and if any change is proposed from one class of occupancy to another, the owner must obtain a new certificate, and his building will be inspected to assure that it will safely contain the new use. The building official in Milwaukee also makes use of the certificate of occupancy as a device for periodic reinspection of buildings of certain classes. The threat of revocation of the occupancy permit is also an effective means of securing compliance with any orders which may have been issued for maintenance and repair of buildings covered by the certificate. The certificate of occupancy is used quite extensively for this purpose.

Group E are high-hazard occupancies; Group F are dwellings, duplexes, and all row dwellings and apartment housing not more than four families; Group G are accessory buildings, sheds, and lumber storage buildings; and Group H are stadia, bleachers, and circus tents.

Interestingly enough, however, it has been found that many cities look upon the certificate of occupancy as nothing more than a statement of final approval which they will issue only upon request of the owner so that he will be able to display such a certificate to insurance companies and prospective buyers of his property.

Criteria and Procedures Used for Ordering Repair and Demolition

As pointed out above, the criterion for regulating substandard and dangerous conditions can be either some degree of deterioration from a recognized code standard, or maintenance of a nuisance. However, if reliance is to be placed on the nuisance concept, this concept has to be defined if it is to serve as a guide for an administrative program.

After the building official has determined that there exists a condition which he may order repaired or abated, he must proceed carefully under established procedure. One of the most elaborate and complex of procedures is found in the Kansas City, Mo., building code. Briefly, it provides that if the building commissioner finds a nuisance to exist, he "shall cause a notice in writing to be served upon the owner or owners, upon the tenant and occupant thereof, if any, and upon the holder or holders of any encumbrances or general tax lien thereof, if any, ordering and directing said building or structure to be put in a safe or sanitary condition or be removed or demolished."

If the order, which gives the owner 5 days to begin correction of the condition, is not obeyed, the building commissioner then files a complaint or information against the owners in the municipal court of Kansas City. Upon verifying the report by the commissioner that his order was not obeyed and a nuisance exists, the court may order the condition abated within a reasonable time. The court now retains jurisdiction while the abatement order is being carried out and the building department inspects periodically to see what progress is being made and reports this to the court.

If the court order is ignored, the commissioner may "in his discretion" request the director of public works to let a contract for the demolition of the building. The contract may provide that materials salvaged may be sold to defray expenses incurred by the city.

The Cleveland code also outlines in some detail the procedure for action against violations of the code in existing buildings. The code provides for declaring buildings unsafe after a certain procedure has been followed. The code states:

> All buildings or structures which are structurally unsafe, insanitary or not provided with adequate safe egress, or which constitute a fire hazard, or are otherwise dangerous to human life, or which in relation to existing use constitute a hazard to safety or health by reason of inadequate maintenance, dilapidation, obsolescence, or abandonment are, severally, for the purposes of this title, declared to be unsafe structures. All such unsafe structures are hereby declared to be illegal and shall be abated by repair and rehabiliation or by demolition in accordance with the following procedure.

The procedure requires the building official to find the owner of the building and serve him with a written notice of violation, served according to the procedure for the service of legal notices. The building department is required to make "a diligent search" for the owner after which the department may mail a notice by registered mail to the last known address of the owner with a copy of the notice "conspicuously posted" on the property concerned. The code states that "such mailing and posting shall be deemed legal service of such notice." The notice must state which code provision is being violated and shall order either repair or vacation of the building.

The procedure requires the department, if the repairs are not made, to order the building vacated by posting a notice stating:

THIS STRUCTURE
IS IN A DANGEROUS CONDITION
AND HAS BEEN CONDEMNED
AND ITS USE
HAS BEEN PROHIBITED
BY THE COMMISSIONER
OF BUILDING AND HOUSING

Such notice remains on the premises until

the repairs or demolition is accomplished and it is unlawful for anyone to remove the sign or enter the structure, other than for purposes of making repairs, until the order of the commissioner has been obeyed.

The corporation counsel who handles building department cases in Cleveland has emphasized how important it is that the department of building and housing follow the ordering procedure to the letter as stated in the code. If it is not followed, the case collapses, for the courts consider the procedural steps set forth in the code as administrative due process to which defendant parties are entitled.

On the other hand, the building commissioner in Cleveland has pointed out that this procedure sometimes takes 2 or 3 years to complete. He believes the procedure could be simplified without denying due process to anyone.

Code provisions which authorize the building official to measure the extent of dilapidation of a building would seem to give him an adequate basis for correcting substandard conditions.

Such a provision gives the building official a degree of discretion to act as an expert in determining the extent to which a building has deteriorated. Milwaukee provides for a discretionary evaluation of deterioration in its code which states that "the amount and extent of deterioration of any existing building, structure, or equipment * * * shall be determined by the inspector of buildings."

The Milwaukee building code has one of the most precise statements on the limitation of alterations which may be made to buildings which, because of zoning and fire limit laws passed since the building was built, are in violation of these regulations. The code states that such buildings may not be altered more than 50 per cent of the assessed value during their lifetime. If they have been altered to this extent, the building department will issue no further permits to the owner for any additional alterations unless the building is made to conform to the fire limit or zoning laws.

This is an attempt to solve the thorny problem of retroactive legislation which plagues building departments when they attempt to attack old buildings under the provisions of a new code. The expense of bringing an old building up to the standards of new zoning and fire limit laws would in many cases be so great that the owner would prefer to remove the building rather than repair it.

The Milwaukee code makes a distinction between deterioration of buildings which otherwise conform to the code and those buildings which do not. Nonconforming buildings, which are usually those built before the code was enacted, may be declared illegal and ordered removed if they have deteriorated to 50 per cent of their assessed value; while conforming buildings may not be declared illegal and ordered removed until they have deteriorated 60 per cent of their value. Buildings whose structural supports and beams have deteriorated 25 per cent may be ordered vacated until the necessary repairs are made. The building official in Milwaukee determines the extent of deterioration by inspecting all of the essential features of the entire building, adding up the percentages of deterioration of all its parts deemed essential to safety. If his inspections satisfy him that the building is unsafe and if particular percentages add up to the required total which allows him to proceed, he orders the building vacated or destroyed, depending on the extent of dilapidation.

The owner of a building condemned under this procedure took the case to court where it was decided that the building official had to offer the owner an opportunity to repair the building before he had it removed. The court, however, allowed the building official to state the conditions by which the building could be made safe for use. As a result, the economic burden created by the definition of safety was so great that the owner decided to demolish the structure.

Nuisance Abatement

The nuisance provision in the Cambridge,

Mass., code states:

> A building or structure which is erected or maintained in violation of any provision of this Code shall be deemed a common nuisance without other proof thereof than proof of the unlawful construction or maintenance, and the Superintendent may abate and remove it in the same manner in which boards of health may remove nuisances.

The plumbing code of Detroit defines a little more precisely which conditions constitute a nuisance. The code provision reads:

> *Nuisance.* The word nuisance shall be held to embrace public nuisance as known at common law or in equity jurisprudence; and whatever is dangerous to human life or detrimental to health; whatever building structure or premises is not sufficiently ventilated, sewered, drained, cleaned or lighted, in reference to its intended or actual use; and whatever renders the air or human food or drink or water supply unwholesome, are also severally, in contemplation of this article, nuisances; and all such nuisances are hereby declared illegal.

Other code provisions do not attempt to define a nuisance but rather give the official, as in Charlotte, N. C., the right to "define and declare nuisances and to cause their removal by or abatement by summary proceedings or otherwise."

The nuisance abatement provisions of various building codes are seldom used by building officials except as a last resort against extremely recalcitrant violators. Injunctive relief is also seldom used, according to information received from building officials. A member of the Cleveland prosecutor's office pointed out that a suspended sentence under the misdemeanor provisions of the building code acts very much like an injunction in that the contempt power of the court may be used to punish the violator if he does not obey the mandate of the court.

Emergency Condemnation

All of the codes analyzed in this study include emergency clauses which authorize the building official to order a building torn down in cases of emergency when by so doing he would be protecting the public safety. A typical emergency provision is found in the White Plains code which states:

The decision of the commissioner shall be final in cases of emergency which, in his opinion, involve imminent danger to human life or health, and not subject to appeal. He shall promptly cause such building, structure, or portion thereof to be made safe, vacated, or removed. For this purpose he may at once enter such abutting land or structure, with such assistance and such cost as he may deem necessary. He may vacate adjacent structures and protect the public by an appropriate fence or such other means as may be necessary, and for this purpose he may close a public or private way.

Cost incurred shall be paid out of the city treasury on certificate of the commissioner. Such costs shall be charged to the owner of the premises involved and shall be collected in the manner provided by law.

Costs for emergency repair or condemnation are usually paid out of the municipal treasury, and the municipality later takes action against the owner to recover the costs.

No clear pattern of action as to the use of the emergency power has been obtained from either questionnaires or interviews, except that the power is rarely used.

It is doubtful whether any building official would rely upon the emergency clause to remove the general run of substandard housing.

18

Certificates of Occupancy

New York State Department of Commerce

This article appeared originally in Zoning in New York State, *published in 1949 by the Department of Commerce, State of New York.*

BOTH THE building code and zoning ordinance generally contain sections relative to certificates of occupancy. However, the purpose for requiring such a certificate is not identical under the two ordinances.

The certificate issued under the building code certifies that the structural conditions have been fulfilled, specifies the class of occupancy permitted, the maximum live loads that may be applied to the floors, and the number of people that each floor may accomodate. Upon a change in use, a new certificate must be obtained. It is required that the certificate be posted.

The types of uses specified in the building code, are of a different character than those included in the district regulations of the zoning ordinance. In a building code, the buildings are generally classified, with respect to use and occupancy, as public, institutional, residence, business, industrial and storage buildings. The type of construction as to fire resistance ratings for these occupancies is specified. Under the zoning ordinance we are concerned with the proper use of land or buildings with respect to the district in which they are located, the height to which structures are erected and the open spaces about them. The technical considerations of construction are not involved.

Under both the building code and zoning ordinance the occupancy certificate protects the owner or occupant, serving as proof that the building complied with the regulations in effect at the time of construction or alteration, or that the use is a lawful nonconforming use.

Whenever it is possible to do so, a statement should be included in the building code that no certificate of occupancy shall be issued for any building that does not comply with the provisions of the zoning ordinance. This simplifies the regulation that pertains to the certificate in the zoning ordinance. An additional convenience is to incorporate the occupancy permits under the two ordinances into one document. The section pertaining to compliance with the zoning ordinance is made a separate paragraph.

The necessary section may read as follows:

Certificate of Occupancy. No land shall be used or occupied and no building hereafter erected, altered or extended shall be used or changed in use until a certificate of occupancy shall have been issued by the Superintendent of Buildings in accordance with the provisions of the building code.

If the requirement in the zoning ordinance must be more inclusive, this section may be modified as illustrated below:

Certificate of Occupancy
1. No land shall be occupied or used and no building hereafter erected, altered or extended shall be used or changed in use until a certificate of occupancy shall have been issued by the Superintendent of Buildings, stating that the building or proposed use thereof complies with the provisions of this ordinance.
2. No nonconforming use shall be maintained, renewed, changed, or extended without a certificate of occupancy having first been issued by the Superintendent of Buildings therefor.
3. All certificates of occupancy shall be applied for coincident with the application for a building permit. Said certificate shall be issued within 10 days after the erection or alteration shall have been approved as complying with the provisions of this ordinance.
4. The Superintendent of Buildings shall maintain a record of all certificates and copies shall be furnished, upon request, to any person having a proprietary or tenancy interest in the building affected.
5. No permit for excavation for, or the erection

or alteration of or repairs to any building shall be issued until an application has been made for a certificate of occupancy.

In some instances provision is also made for temporary certificates for a limited period. Under such circumstances an additional paragraph may be included. Such a provision is illustrated below:

Under such rules and regulations as may be established by the zoning Board of Appeals and filed with the Town Clerk, a temporary certificate of occupancy for not more than thirty days for a part of a building may be issued by him.

Some municipalities do not require certificates of occupancy for new construction, but for a change in use only. Under certain conditions, such as in rural agricultural areas, certificates may not be desirable for farm buildings or uses, or they may be dispensed with completely. If this is done the ordinance will state under the section heading "none required," so as to allay any fears on the part of farmers who would be affected.

There is no question, however, that the proper enforcement of zoning regulations is aided by requiring certificates of occupancy. It is the most effective means of assuring that the work done under a building permit has been done in accordance with the provisions of the building code and zoning ordinance.

19

How Code-Enforced Waste Can Make a $1,500 Difference in the Sales Price of Two Identical Houses

Reprinted by special permission from the December, 1963 Issue of House and Home. Copyright © by the McGraw-Hill Publishing Co., Inc.

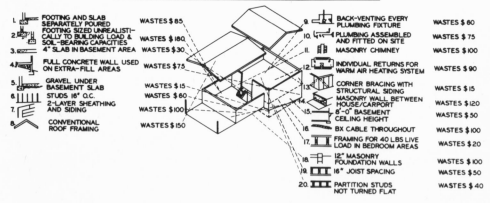

HOW CODE-ENFORCED WASTE CAN MAKE A $1500 DIFFERENCE

1. FOOTING AND SLAB SEPARATELY POURED — WASTES $85
2. FOOTING SIZED UNREALISTI- CALLY TO BUILDING LOAD & SOIL-BEARING CAPACITIES — WASTES $180
3. 4" SLAB IN BASEMENT AREA — WASTES $30
4. FULL CONCRETE WALL USED ON EXTRA-FILL AREAS — WASTES $75
5. GRAVEL UNDER BASEMENT SLAB — WASTES $15
6. STUDS 16" O.C. — WASTES $60
7. 2-LAYER SHEATHING AND SIDING — WASTES $100
8. CONVENTIONAL ROOF FRAMING — WASTES $150

9. BACK-VENTING EVERY PLUMBING FIXTURE — WASTES $60
10. PLUMBING ASSEMBLED AND FITTED ON SITE — WASTES $75
11. MASONRY CHIMNEY — WASTES $100
12. INDIVIDUAL RETURNS FOR WARM AIR HEATING SYSTEM — WASTES $90
13. CORNER BRACING WITH STRUCTURAL SIDING — WASTES $15
14. MASONRY WALL BETWEEN HOUSE/CARPORT — WASTES $120
15. 8'-0" BASEMENT CEILING HEIGHT — WASTES $50
16. BX CABLE THROUGHOUT — WASTES $100
17. FRAMING FOR 40 LBS LIVE LOAD IN BEDROOM AREAS — WASTES $20
18. 12" MASONRY FOUNDATION WALLS — WASTES $100
19. 16" JOIST SPACING — WASTES $50
20. PARTITION STUDS NOT TURNED FLAT — WASTES $40

Figure 1: A $16,500 house plagued by typical code troubles. Practically no builder would be confounded by *all* $1,500 of the code-waste shown in the composite horror above. But practically every builder is confronted with enough of these items (plus many not illustrated) to be forced to add about $1,000 per house to his sales price. The house shown is a 1,200 sq. ft. split-level for a hillside. It has six rooms, including three bedrooms and two baths. Its size is close to today's typical merchant-built model. Adapted from *House and Home* art.

IN THE SALES PRICE OF TWO IDENTICAL HOUSES

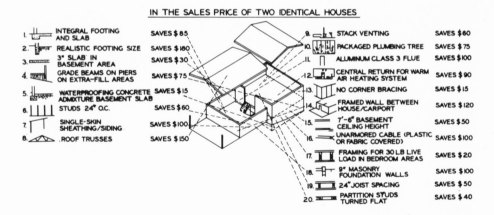

1.	INTEGRAL FOOTING AND SLAB	SAVES $85
2.	REALISTIC FOOTING SIZE	SAVES $180
3.	3" SLAB IN BASEMENT AREA	SAVES $30
4.	GRADE BEAMS ON PIERS ON EXTRA-FILL AREAS	SAVES $75
5.	WATERPROOFING CONCRETE ADMIXTURE BASEMENT SLAB	SAVES $15
6.	STUDS 24" O.C.	SAVES $60
7.	SINGLE-SKIN SHEATHING/SIDING	SAVES $100
8.	ROOF TRUSSES	SAVES $150
9.	STACK VENTING	SAVES $60
10.	PACKAGED PLUMBING TREE	SAVES $75
11.	ALUMINUM CLASS 3 FLUE	SAVES $100
12.	CENTRAL RETURN FOR WARM AIR HEATING SYSTEM	SAVES $90
13.	NO CORNER BRACING	SAVES $15
14.	FRAMED WALL BETWEEN HOUSE/CARPORT	SAVES $120
15.	7'-6" BASEMENT CEILING HEIGHT	SAVES $50
16.	UNARMORED CABLE (PLASTIC OR FABRIC COVERED)	SAVES $100
17.	FRAMING FOR 30 LB LIVE LOAD IN BEDROOM AREAS	SAVES $20
18.	9" MASONRY FOUNDATION WALLS	SAVES $100
19.	24" JOIST SPACING	SAVES $50
20.	PARTITION STUDS TURNED FLAT	SAVES $40

Figure 2: The same house for $15,000. It takes advantage of the advances in today's new housing technology. Unfortunately for homebuilders and homebuyers, much of that new technology is not permitted by most of today's archaic code restrictions. The original drawings for the examples shown here were prepared for *House and Home* by architect Arnold Kronstadt, long an apostle of code reform. Kronstadt is noted for his 1959 analysis of the conflicting requirements of model building codes for one- and two-family houses. Adapted from *House and Home* art.

20

Local Development and Enforcement of Housing Codes

Gilbert R. Barnhart

This article appeared originally in Local Development and Enforcement of Housing Codes, *published in 1953 by the Housing and Home Finance Agency, Washington, D.C. Selected sections.*

THE FUNCTIONS and machinery of local government have been created from time to time as responses to recognized problems and to furnish needed services. The regulation of building construction under building codes grew from the need for protection against fire and structural failure. When it became apparent that the unplanned growth of communities led to certain undesirable results, zoning and the function of city planning were introduced and have been widely adopted.

Housing Quality and Community Development

Many cities are now recognizing that the quality of housing is a factor which has an enormous influence upon the individual and the community. Cities are realizing that the quality of housing involves more than safety from fire and structural failure. It involves, at a minimum, the state of repair of the dwelling structure, the kind and state of repair of equipment and facilities, the space provided per occupant, adequate light and air, and the neighborhood environment, which in itself is a complex thing.

Consequently, many cities are seeking ways to assure that their housing will meet minimum standards for some or all of these criteria. At present, housing quality (as defined in this way) is not covered by the purposes, technical requirements, or administration of most building and other construction codes, or by zoning ordinances.

Building codes normally require buildings to be constructed in such a way as to sustain safely the loads expected from the type of occupancy and to be reasonably safe for such occupancy against fire hazards. These codes usually contain a general requirement that buildings be properly maintained, but this requirement is usually not strongly enforced. Plumbing and electrical codes state how plumbing and electrical systems and facilities shall be constructed and installed, if there is to be any installation, but usually they do not require that houses have particular kinds of sanitary or electric equipment. Zoning ordinances are, of course, specifically designed to aid in creating and preserving desirable environment of residential and other areas. But their normal provisions do not reach some of the most important factors in the housing environment.

There are four major elements which have to be treated in attaining and maintaining a given minimum level of housing quality. *First*, there is the presence, particularly in older cities, of dwelling structures and dwelling units which lack basic sanitary and other equipment and facilities and which are in various states of disrepair. Many of these places were built before the evolution of modern standards of dwelling design and before the adoption of existing building and zoning regulations.

Second, there are conditions in the environments surrounding existing dwelling structures, such as utilities, streets, transportation systems, etc., which constitute or contribute to poor housing quality. Some of these conditions, as in the case of bad dwelling structures and lack of facilities and equipment, developed during a past period when there was no effective plan for growth or zoning control. These environmental conditions contribute independently to housing quality, in the sense that they can markedly reduce the total quality of housing in sections where the dwelling structures and units are otherwise fairly good.

Third, there is the general tendency of dwelling structures and their provided facilities and aging equipment, and of environments, to deteriorate over a period of time. Even well-designed modern construction will deteriorate unless repaired and maintained; and as long as cities grow and change, residential environments will be subject to decline in quality.

Fourth, in some cities there may be a small percentage of newly created dwelling units which are being built without one or more of the items considered necessary for minimum housing. These deficient new units may be created by conversion of old structures or even by new construction.

The older substandard dwellings and the worst of the bad environments are inheritances from an urban past when standards were lower or different, or in the case of bad land use, when there may have been no locally applicable standard or guide. In contrast, the tendency of buildings and equipment to wear out arises from normal uses and is always present. The decline of a good environment can arise from the high mobility of residential population and the changing character and location of business and industry. Finally, the assurance of minimum quality in the new housing supply requires continuous attention.

The old historical conditions can be eliminated in particular structures and locations, but the normal forces of deteriorating change and the tendency toward expedient lowering of standards are dynamic factors which have to be dealt with currently by the community through a variety of continuous activities.

A number of cities which have established public programs to improve and stabilize the quality of housing base their programs upon the enactments and enforcement of a local housing code. This is a local ordinance which requires dwelling structures and units to have minimum facilities and equipment, limits the density of occupancy, and requires that the structure, facilities, and equipment be maintained in good condition. The ordinance also may require that the dwelling unit and its immediate surroundings be kept clean. Most housing codes apply retroactively to existing dwellings because they are aimed at correcting a backlog of existing defects.

Purpose and Method of This Report

This report is a brief explanation of the contents and administration of the housing code, considered as one of the means by which localities identify and apply minimum standards for housing.

Two major topics need to be explored. One concerns the standards employed in these codes. The other concerns the pattern of cooperative policies and administrative procedures that have been developed among certain local governmental and private agencies and groups to promote compliance with the code standards.

In the United States there are 484 cities of 25,000 population or more and 232 cities of 50,000 population or more. *The* 1950 *United States Census of Housing* has reported on the physical condition of dwelling structures and on certain items of their equipment in the 209 cities which had a population of 50,000 or more in the 1940 decennial census, or in any later census taken before 1950. From these nationwide reports and from miscellaneous sources, it appears that a large number of cities in many parts of the country will have an active interest in considering minimum housing standards and, if they adopt housing codes, in devising methods for their administration.

To offer minimum standards for structural condition, equipment and facilities, maintenance, density of occupancy, and environment, which would be acceptable and enforceable by local authorities in many different places would call for an enormous amount of study. It would also require a detailed investigation of the operation of a large number of local government systems in order to determine that any one administrative plan is demonstrably better than another.

It has not yet been possible to examine standards and administration on such a large scale. Therefore, this report uses examples of standards and administrative methods, rather than generalizations based on comprehensive information. However, the examples are chosen for the most part from actual codes and from operating administrative systems.

The Standards and Technical Requirements of Housing Codes

Cities in the United States are just beginning to accept the establishment and application of minimum public standards of housing quality as a continuing public function. Such programs may be said to be in an experimental stage. In fact, the country is just beginning to measure housing quality on a comprehensive basis, as is evidenced by the growing use of local housing surveys and by the United States Censuses of Housing of 1940 and 1950. It is also important to keep in mind that at present the selection of minimum standards may be made under pressure to find a quick remedy for conditions which have been accumulating for many years. Understandably, there is great emphasis on and need for retroactive remedies.

THE PROBLEM OF FUTURE STANDARDS

However, even at this early date, long before current deficiencies have been corrected to any extent, it is most important that cities give equal attention to the future effect of any housing standards that may be adopted. The correction of existing substandard conditions is the portion of the task that should diminish, while the application of adequate standards to new housing is the portion which will grow in size and importance. Fifty years hence the greater part of the then existing housing supply may consist of units that will have been built since the present time. Therefore, the kind of standards which will have been incorporated into these units will largely govern the general quality of housing at that future date.

The development of minimum standards for new housing for the purpose of assuring long-term stability of housing quality is much more complicated than writing standards to apply to existing conditions. The later type of standards can be developed to correct specific conditions which can be observed and even measured to a certain extent. But public standards which are meant to apply to future construction must take account of factors which will change with time. The future will probably bring technical improvements in housing structures and equipment and also changes in economic factors which may affect the feasibility of applying different levels of technically possible standards.

This report does not deal with the nature of any standards which would be adequate on a long-term basis for new housing. That is a separate subject. It must be pointed out, however, that minimum housing standards are at present in a trial and error stage of development. Standards in present housing codes which are enforceable on old dwellings probably will not at the same time be advanced enough to serve as minimum requirements for the new house of 10, 15, or 25 years hence.

In the long run, the ability to afford relatively high standards of housing depends upon the ability of the general economy to produce and consume at increasingly higher levels. Also, the ability of a large percentage of the population to afford good housing standards depends upon such other economic factors as the pattern of income distribution and the cost of housing construction and maintenance compared with the cost of other common necessities.

If the general efficiency of the economy continues to increase, and if production efficiency in house-building rises in the future by more than the increase in efficiency in other industries, the relative cost of housing may fall. If this takes place to a sufficient degree, noticeably higher standards of housing structure and equipment may become economically feasible. This will move the attainable standards for new housing to a higher level, and will increase the gap between them and what are now considered feasible requirements. Then, in order to obtain housing which incorporates the

higher standards, consumers may become
willing to spend relatively more of their
income for housing than they would if the

higher standards, consumers may become
willing to spend relatively more of their
income for housing than they would if the
the inducement of improved housing were
not available. Thus, an effective demand may
be created for the higher standards.

The possibility of such a result raises the
question whether higher future standards for
new construction, which communities may
consider necessary for their well-being, can
continue to rest upon police power concepts
and the enforcement of codes by public
authorities. Historically, the power to enforce
public standards has been limited to what is
necessary for minimum health, safety, and
welfare. However, legislatures enacting future
housing codes and administrative authorities
and courts enforcing them may follow the
lead of the housing industry and the public
and hold that the future minimum includes a
measure of comfort and utility.

The possible inadequacy of the police
power as a basis for future minimum
standards suggests that such standards may
be best developed and applied by private
means operating within the construction
industry and within individual communities.
This would leave to the publicly enforced
standards of the housing code the job of
providing a lower limit on conditions in
older buildings and neighborhoods.

THE EFFECTIVE PURPOSES OF PRESENT
HOUSING CODES

At present there is probably no single
collection of information covering a wide
enough variety of local housing conditions,
needs, and local abilities to permit a definition of the exact function of the housing code
as it may be used in all cities. However, the
probable function of existing housing codes
can be inferred by inspecting the provisions
of some of these codes and noting their
possibilities and their limits.

Some examples of housing code content—
There are three main subjects which are
covered in most existing housing codes. The
first covers minimum facilities and equipment which are required in each dwelling
unit; the second covers the maintenance of
the dwelling unit and of facilities and equip-

ment; and the third covers the conditions of
occupancy of the dwelling unit.

A comprehensive coverage of provisions
on required facilities and equipment will
include: lighting (general, toilet); ventilation
(general, toilet); garbage and waste disposal;
heating; water supply; sewerage disposal;
sink; bath; toilet; and egress.

A comprehensive coverage of maintenance
provisions will include: general sanitary
condition of dwelling unit; sanitary equipment; heating equipment; chimney and flues;
other fire hazards (electric wiring, inflammable liquids, etc.); pest infestation; internal
structural repair; external structural repair;
and dampness.

A comprehensive coverage of conditions of
occupancy will include: general room crowding (persons per room, persons per sleeping
room); area crowding (sleeping area, non-
sleeping area); doubling of families; separation of sexes; living units with businesses
(prohibited under certain conditions).

It is noticeable that the requirements for
the repair and maintenance of structural
elements of dwellings tend to rely on general
words and phrases such as "good repair,"
"safe condition," and "sound, useable condition." In a few codes, for certain conditions, there are quantitative standards. For
example, the Charlotte, N.C., code defines
as being among conditions which make a
building dangerous or unfit for human habitation "interior walls or other vertical structural members which list, lean, or buckle to
such an extent that a plumb line passing
through the center of gravity falls outside the
middle third of its base;" and "supporting
member or members which show 33 per cent
or more of damage or deterioration or non-
supporting enclosing or outside walls or
covering which show 50 per cent or more of
damage or deterioration."

Of all the codes studied, the Durham,
N.C., code relates standards for repair and
maintenance most directly to the standards
for new construction. The Durham code
provides: "The public officer may determine
that a dwelling is unfit for human habitation . . . if he finds that such dwelling does not

conform to the following minimum standards . . . (c) all portions of the enclosure of such dwellings, including roof, flashings, exterior walls, basement walls, floors resting on ground, and all windows and doors exposed to the weather, shall be of such materials and so constructed and protected as to comply strictly with the standards set up and included in the building code of the city of Durham, being chapters 28 and 29, code of the city of Durham, 1947, as amended."

In general, however, a study of housing codes gives the impression that there is a distinct gap between the structural requirements of the housing codes and the relevant requirements of building codes applicable to new construction.

All 14 codes studied contain standards for general light and ventilation of habitable rooms by means of windows. The Durham, N.C., code requires at least one window in each room. The other codes specify minimum areas of windows and window openings for ventilation. . . .

Richmond and Roanoke permit approved mechanical light and ventilation, and Milwaukee permits approved mechanical ventilation as alternatives to the requirements. . . .

Eleven of the fourteen codes contain standards for the size of rooms used for sleeping. Richmond, Baltimore, Chester, and Roanoke require each room used for sleeping to contain 400 cubic feet of air space and 50 square feet of floor space for each person 12 years or over, 200 cubic feet of air space and 30 square feet of floor space for each person under 12 years, and at least 60 square feet of total floor space in any room used for sleeping. The Norfolk standard is the same, except for the last requirement, which is 50 square feet. Portland, Ore., requires 400 cubic feet of air space for each person over 14 years old, 300 cubic feet for each person over 6 but not over 14 years, and 200 cubic feet for each person 6 years or under. Kansas City, Mo., requires 400 cubic feet of air space for each person over 6 years, with no sleeping room having less than 60 square feet of floor space or a ceiling less than 7 feet high.

Milwaukee requires 50 square feet of floor space for each person 12 years or older, and 25 square feet for each person under 12. St. Louis requires 40 square feet of floor space for each person. Greensboro requires 100 square feet of floor space in each sleeping room; and Charlotte requires 100 square feet in the first bedroom and 70 square feet in each additional bedroom.

Apparent limits of the housing code's function —With the exception of the Portland, Ore., code, the codes consist mainly of provisions to improve or eliminate some of the undesirable conditions in existing dwellings. In order to improve existing conditions, these provisions are made retroactive.

Most codes apparently have not been written in contemplation of the higher standards generally observed by current construction or of the probable future rise in housing standards, although all the codes apply to new construction as well as old. As they apply to new housing, they do insure, at least, that new units will meet the requirements made upon existing units.

It should be noted that most present housing codes limit their provisions to the physical elements, equipment and facilities, and occupancy of the dwelling structure or dwelling unit. A few require that yards be kept clean, but most do not attempt to control elements in the housing environment.

The reason for this is plain. Conditions contributing to housing environment include: the amount and distribution of open space on the lot around the structure, the relative amount and character of non-residential land uses, the volume and character of street traffic, the availability and condition of public water and sewer systems, the availability and quality of public sanitation services, the availability and quality of public school and recreational facilities. The housing code or the building code or the zoning ordinance may set limits on lot coverage, but the major control of land use is a zoning matter, and the other factors are either properly the subjects of other ordinances or are not susceptible to direct control.

There are some exceptions to the limited function of the housing code, as indicated in the foregoing paragraphs. Los Angeles and Portland, Ore., have adopted housing codes which may be said to be oriented toward the control of new construction rather than toward existing substandard conditions, although each code provides for correction of existing deficiencies. The Portland code clearly distinguishes minimum requirements for maintenance, equipment and facilities applicable to existing dwellings, from similar requirements applicable to new construction. The latter are in greater detail and are higher than those for existing dwellings. The Los Angeles code contains extensive requirements for new dwelling construction, plus detailed definitions of "substandard residential building" and "dangerous building". The procedural part of the code then provides for inspection and repair, vacation, or demolition of such substandard and dangerous buildings.

One more aspect of the function or scope of the codes should be noticed. This is the decision whether or not the minimum standards shall apply to apartment houses, hotels, and rooming and boarding houses, as well as to 1- and 2-family dwellings. Many housing codes cover all dwelling units without distinction between private dwellings and other types of residential occupancies, and apply the same standards to all dwelling units. This seems to be particularly true of codes in the smaller cities. Again, the Portland and Los Angeles codes are exceptions. In these codes there are some differences between the standards applying to 1- and 2-family dwellings and those applying to apartment houses, hotels, and other residential occupancies.

To summarize the effective scope of typical housing code standards:

1. They are generally limited to the quality of the dwelling structure, to the nature and use of its equipment and facilities, and to the density of occupancy.

2. They do not affect land use or other important factors which create the general environment.

3. They are more often written to serve as minimum requirements for old dwellings than as optimum criteria for new construction.

THE DEVELOPMENT OF WORKABLE STANDARDS AND REQUIREMENTS FOR LOCAL HOUSING CODES

A suggested method for standards-making—
There are two ways of approaching the solution of problems involved in the development of cities. One is the identification and study of all the factors of growth and change which shape the city. This is the method of the city planner who is seeking an overall perspective. The results of this method are the city plan and broad programs for improvements of general features of the city.

The other approach is to the specific and detailed conditions of some one feature of the city for the purpose of changing some of these detailed conditions in a specific manner. This is the method followed by codes and regulations of the local government, although regulation is not necessarily or always involved in carrying out this method.

Both approaches are useful. The general city plan identifies types of problems and the detailed method provides some of the means for solving some of the problems.

A knowledge of existing problems and a knowledge of the capabilities of specific remedies play an equal part in the task of developing any particular program for civic improvement. This principle applies especially to the development of any remedial program which uses regulatory powers, such as a housing code.

There are two reasons why this is true. One depends upon the traditional assumption that the powers of government will be used only to the minimum extent necessary to obtain a result in the general interest. Such assumption has the effect of limiting regulation to situations where there is a relatively precise and clearly defined need for public action. It is traditionally assumed that the number of such situations will remain small. Consequently, the proper use of regulation is viewed as a response to a circumscribed and definite need.

The second reason depends upon the traditional attempt to discover precise causes for problems and to develop precise remedies for such causes. This method, when successfully used, results in the identification of definite, and therefore limited, causes of definite and limited problem conditions.

The combined effect is that programs using code regulation should be designed and administered as a set of definite remedies for a corresponding set of definite defects.

The main causes of poor housing quality have been pointed out. These are deterioration of structures, absence of basic sanitary and other equipment and facilities in structures and dwelling units, overcrowding of land and dwelling units, and bad physical environment. In most cities which have the problem, such conditions exist in various degrees.

There will be individual dwelling structures and units in various numbers, and environments of various extent which have just begun to decline. A relatively small effort will probably suffice to restore good conditions and prevent further decline.

There will be other individual dwellings and environments, in various numbers, and of various extent, which have declined further or were originally of lower standard. More extensive repairs to structures, installation of equipment and facilities not originally provided, and perhaps rather extensive measures to correct incompatible land uses and provide better community facilities may be called for.

Then there will be still other structures and environments, in various numbers and of various extent, which are beyond redemption except by extensive rebuilding of structures and/or replanning of land uses, community facilities, etc.

These different types and degrees of conditions may exist separately in well-marked areas, or they may be mixed and scattered over most or all of the city.

It is important to note that there are two logically distinct steps in the selection of local housing standards. The first step is the discovery and recording, by a systematic inspection or survey, of the actual conditions of structures and environmental surround-ings in the city. This is a fact-finding process. This process will show which types and degrees of conditions exist. The second step is concerned with establishing the minimum housing standards which are practicable and enforceable for the particular city.

The essential part of this second step is the making of a judgment as to which of the specific conditions disclosed by the inspection or survey can be removed successfully by the enforcement of a housing code. Such conditions can then be covered by specific standards or requirements in the local housing code. All housing conditions of the types covered by the code will then fall into two classes: conditions equal to or better than the code provisions, which are considered to be in compliance with the code; conditions lower than the code provisions, which are considered to be substandard and therefore subject to application of the code through enforcement processes.

The decision as to which local conditions can be corrected by a housing code consists essentially of balancing several considerations. These considerations are of the following types.

There are the objective data on the physical condition of local housing which presumably have been collected and analyzed as the result of continuing inspection and record-keeping of municipal agencies or by a special housing survey.

There are other data reflecting local economic capacity to pay for some given level of housing quality. These data include: (1) income of owner-occupants and income and rents of rental-occupants of housing which is likely to come within the scope of any housing code which might be adopted; (2) the costs of making the typical repairs and installations which would be required by any code which might be adopted, both in existing and new housing; (3) cost of correcting certain environmental conditions which contribute to poor housing quality by making public improvements; and (4) the present and proposed administrative capacity of the city to apply and enforce any housing code.

This last element is itself complex and needs some explanation. It involves the enforcement load—the number of substandard units which will have to be inspected to apply the code uniformly, the number of inspectors needed to handle the enforcement load, the budget needed for such an inspectional staff and associated supervisory personnel. It also involves the degree of support and assistance the code-enforcing agency can expect from other local government agencies in enforcement of the housing code.

These various types of information can then be put together, in somewhat the following fashion, to arrive at the final selection of workable minimum standards. Starting with the picture of existing kinds and degrees of housing deficiency, the essential question is: Which of these deficiencies can be corrected to a degree which will not impose unreasonable costs, which will be supportable as necessary for health, safety, and welfare, and which can be enforced with the personnel and local government organization which will be provided?

An example, adaptable to any city, which illustrates the theory is the procedure followed currently (February 1953) by the staff of the Philadelphia Housing Association, which is drafting a revised housing code for Philadelphia. A representative code-drafting committee makes the choice of standards after considering a series of working papers prepared by the staff of the Housing Association. For each proposed standard or requirement, the working papers present and analyze data on each of the following topics: (1) nature of proposed standard or requirement; (2) nature of standard or requirement in existing housing code; (3) reasons supporting proposed standard or requirement; (4) analysis of relevant present housing conditions in *Philadelphia Real Property Survey of 1934, Philadelphia Housing Survey of 1951, and 1940* and *1950 U.S. Census of Housing*; and (5) probable results of enforcement.

Perhaps a further explanation is necessary to put the foregoing discussion of standard-making into a proper perspective. The foregoing method is suggested as a thorough, careful method for developing practicable local standards which can meet the tests of adequacy as well as practicality. However, no such elaborate method will be needed to determine what needs to be done to improve the worst of the conditions which exist in the worst of the slums.

Such conditions probably would never have occurred in their worst forms if existing requirements and powers in building codes, health ordinances and regulations, and zoning ordinances had been enforced at an effective level. The worst conditions are the simple product of simple neglect by the property owners, legislative and executive officials of the local government, and by the general public.

Therefore, commonsense judgments will be adequate to determine the simple remedies and standards needed for immediate improvement of the rockbottom slums. The more elaborate process of fact-finding and measurement through surveys and study of census data and balancing of various factors is for the development of a long-term minimum standards program for the entire city.

The Baltimore Plan: A Case Study

This brief summary of the program of enforcing minimum housing standards in Baltimore is not intended to suggest this program as a model which would work in all cities. It is included in this study as a "case," to show the elements of a fairly complete program in one city. The officials who are responsible for the creation and operation of the Baltimore Plan are themselves diligent to emphasize, on the one hand, that the program has been designed to fit Baltimore's particular housing situation, and on the other, that their program and any other like it cannot be simple and easy and free of perplexing difficulties.

The significance of the "Baltimore Plan" for slum rehabilitation lies not in the mistaken idea that it is a quick "cure-all" for all the problems of urban blight, nor in the misconception that it is a limited effort designed to alleviate the physical conditions of the worst slums. The Baltimore Plan is significant

*The Structure of the Housing-Law
Enforcement Program*

in that it directs major efforts at discovering and eliminating the basic causes of blight as well as at eliminating the accumulated symptoms.

The officials, staff personnel, and interested citizens who have devoted great effort in this long-range experiment believe that blight would not exist if it were not permitted to exist. Slums don't "just happen," and it is upon this assumption that the Baltimore forces for good housing and living conditions have moved forward. Slums are seen to be a result of neglect by the city government, landlords, tenants, and the community.

In Baltimore, the first step was to provide vigilant and continuing enforcement by the city government of its various existing housing laws. From this first step, the persons responsible for the Baltimore Plan sought to reach into education, recreation, social welfare, and other public and private services to bring them all to bear on the blighted areas.

At the outset of this program Baltimore found itself in the position of many other municipalities which have let their oldest sections arrive at conditions which are serious threats to the physical and mental well-being of the inhabitants.

The persons living in these distressed areas for the most part came from the lowest income groups and possessed little education. As a result, this group in general was less aware of its own needs in terms of services the city could supply than any other group in the city. The services of the city, which were limited to begin with, naturally were directed into the areas where they were demanded by well-organized and vocal neighborhood improvement associations.

The areas which needed the services of the city the most were those which had received the least attention, and they had become more neglected as the slum conditions increased. One of the key elements in the Baltimore Plan is to reverse this trend and to recognize the responsibility of the city government for directing proportionate services to the neediest elements of the population.

The overall program for improvement of living conditions includes not only a program for enforcing housing laws, but also a program of urban redevelopment and low-cost housing. While the low-cost housing and urban redevelopment programs are aspects of the total long-range program for better housing in Baltimore, this chapter describes only the structure and operations of the housing-law enforcement part of the total program.

The machinery through which the city attempts to bring about an ever more vigorous program of housing-law enforcement includes: (1) the existing building, zoning, fire, and housing laws, (2) a Housing Bureau in the Health Department; (3) a Citizens' Advisory Council, appointed by the mayor to advise the Housing Bureau; (4) a Division of Rodent Control in the Health Department; (5) a Sanitary Detail in the Police Department; and (6) a specialized Housing Court to which all cases involving violations of all housing laws, with the exception of the zoning ordinance, are brought.

The basic laws which provide the legal groundwork for the operation of the Baltimore Plan are the building code, the fire prevention code, the electric code, the zoning law, and an Ordinance on the Hygiene of Housing. ["Appendix A" is cited here.] The Bureau of Building Inspection and the Fire Department have the primary responsibility for the enforcement of the first four of these laws, and the Health Department and the Sanitary Detail of the Police Department both conduct enforcement activities based on the Ordinance on the Hygiene of Housing.

The Ordinance on the Hygiene of Housing authorizes the City Health Commissioner to adopt rules and regulations deemed necessary "for the protection of the health of the city". Unlike many other housing ordinances or codes, the Baltimore ordinance does not rest upon a special grant of power in the State statutes to regulate the minimum conditions of housing such as found in the States of Michigan, California, and North Carolina, but simply on the power of the health department to abate nuisances.

The Housing Bureau of the Baltimore City Health Department was established early in 1951. The Bureau is headed by a director who is appointed by the Mayor and is responsible to the Commissioner of Health. The main function of the Bureau is to provide a central coordinating agency for all housing-law enforcement activity in the city. The aim of the Bureau is to provide uniform and coordinated procedural and policy attacks on the basic problem of substandard housing by all city departments.

The Bureau handles all complaints under the housing ordinances and regulations; enforces those ordinances and regulations on an area and block-by-block basis; initiates procedures to prevent the development of additional areas of substandard housing and blight; and develops enforcement standards, policies, and procedures which, when approved by the Commissioners of Health, are binding on all other bureaus and sections of the Baltimore City Health Department.

In addition to these internal methods of attacking the problem of blight, the Housing Bureau is assigned the responsibility of promoting the overall objective of the Baltimore Plan by stimulating interest of individual citizens and citizens' groups, and by developing educational programs aimed at gaining the continuing cooperation of owners and occupants of substandard housing in blighted areas.

The Director of the Housing Bureau is assisted by an Advisory Council appointed by the Mayor. The Council actively participates in bringing a broad educational program to individual citizens and organized groups, in educating owners and occupants of substandard dwellings, and in the general program planning of the work of the Housing Bureau.

The Housing Court is probably the most effective single device worked out in the overall housing-law enforcement program in Baltimore. This court is established to deal only with housing and sanitation violations. It was developed out of one of the magistrates courts under a special arrangement worked out by the Mayor of Baltimore and the Governor of Maryland. Cases are brought before the court by inspectors from the Bureau of Building Inspection, the Fire

Prevention Bureau, the Health Department's Housing Bureau, Division of Rodent Control, Plumbing Bureau, and Division of Community Sanitation, as well as by the special squad of police sanitarians.

The only types of housing violation which this court does not hear are zoning violations, which are heard in the magistrates court of the districts in which the zoning violations occur.

The Housing Court meets twice a week to hear cases. The record of its decisions and the precedents which it has established constitute the basis for a higher standard of uniformity in applying the municipal housing laws than would probably be found if the Court did not exist to provide a central review. In addition, publicizing the Housing Court's enforcement decisions by press and radio has had the educational effect of substantially reducing the number of cases requiring legal action.

Another important feature in the enforcement program which directly relates to the effectiveness of the Housing Court and the overall success with enforcement actions is the thorough preparation of the record of administrative actions and facts by the inspectors of the Housing Bureau before cases are presented to the Court. The Legal Action Report and the Procedure for Use of the Legal Action Report ["Appendix A"] used by the Housing Bureau provide an exemplary standard of careful preparation of the record of administrative enforcement actions and substantive facts surrounding each case. The inspector is provided with detailed instructions for preparing the case for summons, steps after issuance of summons, and the use of the legal action record during and after appearance in Court.

Another important feature in the enforcement program which directly relates to the effectiveness of the Housing Court and the overall success with enforcement actions is the thorough actions and facts by the inspectors of the Housing Bureau before cases are presented to the Court. The Legal Action Report and the Procedure for Use of the Legal Action Report used by the Housing Bureau provide an exemplary standard of

careful preparation of the record of administrative enforcement actions and substantive
facts surrounding each case. The inspector is
provided with detailed instructions for preparing the case for summons, steps after
issuance of summons, and the use of the legal
action record during and after appearance in
Court.

The program of the Housing Bureau
includes enforcement on a block-by-block
basis in selected areas of the City, as well as
action on complaints on a city-wide basis.
The areas for the block-by-block enforcement efforts have been selected in cooperation with the Department of Planning, the
Housing Authority of Baltimore City, and
the Redevelopment Commission.

Each house in a selected block is inspected
and the owners and tenants are notified of
violations of the Hygiene of Housing Ordinance. Specific instructions are given for the
correction of the violations within a specified
period, and reports of violations of other
housing laws are transmitted to the appropriate city departments.

The owners of a dwelling unit are generally
responsible for:

1. Maintenance of every dwelling and every
   part thereof in good repair and fit for
   human habitation.
2. Elimination of overcrowding of dwelling
   units within structures and of people within
   dwelling units.
3. Elimination of all fire and safety hazards,
   correction of all structural inadequacies, and
   maintenance of heating equipment and
   electrical wiring in good repair.
4. Removal of rotted, rat-infested wooden
   fences and frame additions.
5. Elimination of blind or inadequately lighted
   and ventilated rooms.
6. Replacement of illegal outside toilets with
   adequate, serviceable inside toilets.
7. Installation of adequate water supplies in
   kitchens.
8. Maintenance of all sanitary fixtures in
   proper repair.
9. Provision of adequate drainage of premises.
10. Elimination and prevention of rodent and
    vermin infestation.

Occupants are required to:

1. Keep in a clean condition that portion of the

property which they occupy or over which
they have exclusive control.
2. Provide conforming containers for the
   disposal of garbage and trash.
3. Remove all accumulations of garbage, trash
   and debris.
4. Store all furniture, firewood, and other
   materials so as to eliminate rat harborages.
5. Eliminate all vermin infestation.

In addition to this two-pronged attack by
placing responsibility on both the owner and
the occupant, the Housing Bureau has
attempted to bring into action municipal and
private agencies to aid in the following:
repair of defects in alleys, streets, and foot-
ways; general abatement of community-wide
nuisances; reestablishment of efficient city
services where necessary; neighborhood
school programs designed to teach the fundamentals of community sanitation in relocation of families through the Housing
Authority of Baltimore City and various
social agencies; provision of municipal
recreation facilities; use of vacant land by
neighborhood groups for recreational facilities; and other civic and interdepartmental
programs aimed at rehabilitating the entire
life of the blighted areas.

The social agencies have assisted in the
relocation of families, and one of the important phases of the Housing Bureau's program
has been to make the residents of the pilot
area (described below) aware of the existence
of the social agencies and their functions.

As stated at the beginning of this section
on the Baltimore Plan, the emphasis of the
plan is not in terms of stop-gap efforts, but
rather in terms of educating the entire
neighborhood in a new way of living. Basic
ideas of the financial and health value of
continued maintenance and repair are
brought home to both the property owner
and the occupant. When administrative enforcement devices fail and the violator is
brought into court, the experience is utilized
not only to gain compliance with the specific
regulations, but also as an opportunity to
instruct the violator in the overall purposes
of the program.

THE PILOT PROGRAM

What is known as the pilot program within
the Baltimore Plan was established in 1950

after several years of enforcement of housing laws on a block-by-block basis. The pilot program is a method of concentrating all relevant public and private powers and resources to improve substandard housing in an entire neighborhood. In March 1950, the Chairman of the Citizens Advisory Council wrote the Mayor of Baltimore that:

> The efforts which comprise the Baltimore Plan have, until now, been based on law enforcement and have been directed at improving the physical condition of slum dwellings. But it is not only board fences, outside hoppers, physical decay and rats which make an area a slum. It is also the spirit and attitude of the people who live and own property there. The city not only has at its command facilities for requiring people to clean up their dwellings to acceptable minimum standards but also facilities for enlarging their opportunities and aspirations for decent living. It has tools to work with their spirit as well as their houses. Education and recreation are perhaps the two most obvious but there are others in and out of city government. . . .
>
> Your Advisory Council recommends therefore that a pilot program be conducted to determine the potential available to the City under a program which would bring to bear on an entire neighborhood the full combination of forces available to the City—law enforcement, education, recreation with the fullest possible participation by the people in the neighborhood and by interested educational, religious and civic groups throughout the community.
>
> Only upon completion of such a program will it be possible to define and appraise the Baltimore Plan, program its operations, and establish its proper place in a master plan for attacking Baltimore's slums.

As a result, the pilot program was started, and with the help of the Department of Planning, the Housing Authority, and the Redevelopment Commission, an area consisting of some 27 blocks was marked out to receive intensive treatment under this program.

This area included 3 blocks rated by the Housing Authority as "rockbottom" slums; 8 blocks were rated as "bad." The rest of the area was blighted in varying degrees.

An elaborate arrangement of committees was organized to administer and evaluate the operation of the pilot program.

The Law Enforcement Committee was organized of representatives from all areas of government concerned with the administration of municipal services, improvements, regulatory control, and enforcement. On a pattern laid down by this committee, there was established a method for providing coordinated inspections, administration, and enforcement of various housing regulations.

Baltimore, like many cities, has overlapping and duplicating ordinances. In each case where a violation was covered by two or more ordinances the strongest was invoked.

A team of five inspectors representing the four government departments which had responsibility for housing and building law enforcement—fire, building, electrical, health, and police—worked out a joint inspectional technique and a Joint Violation Notice Form. This team jointly inspected most of the houses in the 27 blocks and noted violations on a form which outlined to the occupant and owner all violations of the zoning ordinance, electrical code, building code, Housing Hygiene Ordinance, fire prevention code, and Ordinance on the Abatement of Nuisances and the Prevention of Disease. Thus, the violator was presented with a composite listing of all housing and building law violations in one document at one time. The Housing Bureau has the responsibility of issuing this Joint Violation Notice.

At first, the homes were reinspected by the interdepartmental team after the lapse of the 30-day period provided for initiation of corrective action by the violator. After some experience, the joint reinspection was abandoned and the reinspection was done by the inspector of the bureau responsible for the original violation notice.

If the requirement listed in the Joint Violation Notice had not been met, a 10-day extension of time was granted if the work seemed to have progressed satisfactorily. If no work was in progress, legal action was initiated. Where special circumstances seemed to arise, the case was brought before a special interdepartmental hearing board established for the pilot program. This board had the power to grant further extensions of time before instituting legal action.

The Neighborhood Committee was an

essential part of the pilot program and was composed of leaders and residents in the area. Under this committee there operated two other committees; the first was a committee to determine the broad needs of the neighborhood, and the second was a block committee consisting of residents from each block whose responsibility it was to inform all other persons living in the block of the general purpose and progress of the program.

The Education Committee was appointed by the Superintendent of Public Instruction in order to develop a comprehensive educational program in the schools and for adults in the area. As a result of the work of this Committee, two public schools in the area initiated intensive programs of housing and community sanitation.

The Social Service Committee was appointed by the Local Council of Social Agencies. This Committee was divided into groups to study the provisions for medical care, family and child care, and group work and recreation. During the summer months of the first year, a recreational program was established for various age groups in one of the large churches in the neighborhood, and the staff was provided by the Brethren Volunteer Service Unit. The Department of Recreation allocated funds to lease two small adjoining lots and equip them as a playground for small children.

The Project Analysis Committee was established to guide the various studies made of the pilot program and to analyze data accumulated by various agencies. This Committee was also assigned the work of determining the overall costs of the entire program.

Community Consultants were used during the initial stage of the program to provide expert advice in the fields of medicine, public health, education, and recreation. These men served the entire program in an advisory capacity. Later, the services of this Committee were discontinued.

The Steering Committee was provided to coordinate and schedule the entire activities of the program. A member from each of the above committees sat on the Steering Committee, as well as representatives from related organizations and interest areas.

Several specialized committees and groups were established as the actual operation of the pilot program began to evolve. These included:

The Paint Manufacturers Committee which donated paint for general beautification and decoration purposes.

Fight Blight, Inc., was established as a nonprofit corporation to procure additional funds to match the funds, allocated by the Encyclopaedia Britannica Films, to produce a sound film of the entire program.

Fight Blight Fund, Inc., was formed, as a private nonprofit corporation, to make loans to owner-occupants who were faced with violation orders for extensive repairs, but did not have the financial resources to pay for the total cost. A statement from the preamble of the Bylaws of the Fight Blight Fund, Inc., sets forth the purpose of this unique organization:

As this program (Housing Law Enforcement) has advanced, the owners of dwellings within the areas from time to time selected by the Housing Bureau of Baltimore City for special attention have been required to make extensive improvements. A great majority of the owners who are occupants of these premises are people whose financial resources are extremely limited to the extent that there is little or nothing left for repair and alteration after the debt requirements are met. The city's enforcement program subjects these people to penalties and financial outlay that they are unable to meet under any circumstances. There is in many instances no remaining equity for financing by way of mortgage.

This organization is formed to meet the situation thus developed. It proposes to finance worthy owner-occupants in these specially selected areas through loans, the proceeds of which will be dedicated to the making of the necessary improvements and repairs. The funds necessary to the financing of these loans will be contributed by public spirited citizens, firms, and organizations as outright gifts for this public purpose. No person, firm or corporation will receive any profits from these operations and the contributions will be an irrevocable gift for charitable purposes.

The Brotherhood Service, Inc., was also organized as a nonprofit organization and was composed of members of the Church of the Brethren and others. This organization obtained funds for the purchase of a dwelling in the heart of the slum area, and with funds supplied by the Maryland Home Builders Association, the house was rehabilitated to serve as an example of what physical improvements could be made to provide a clean and comfortable home out of a converted substandard dwelling. Members of the Brethren Volunteer Service were trained to staff the house which was used as a community information and referral service to provide information to citizens of the neighborhood who came with problems which could best be handled by various public and private agencies in the city. Members of the Brethren Volunteer Service also assisted resident owners with home repairs and conducted recreational activities for younger children.

The organizational and enforcement structure of the Baltimore Plan is in many ways peculiar to the problems and organization of the City of Baltimore and could not be expected to be duplicated in any exact sense in other communities. It is the spirit and the overall approach with which the blighted areas have been attacked which is Baltimore's important contribution. It is the feeling which pervades the top official structure operating the Baltimore Plan that the people are the important element, not the houses, not the recreational facilities, not the streets, not the elimination of trash and garbage, but the people who must be brought to see a new future which they can build for themselves—a future which it is hoped will last long after the last inspection team has left the neighborhoods.

21

Building Codes, Housing Codes and the Conservation of Chicago's Housing Supply

Warren W. Lehman

This article appeared originally in the University of Chicago Law Review, Vol. 31 :1, Autumn 1963, 180–203. Reproduced by permission.

VARIOUS MEANS, increasingly sophisticated, have been employed by governments in an attempt to control the maturation, aging, death and resurrection of our city neighborhoods. From simple fire and health regulations, government activity has extended to zoning, comprehensive building and housing codes, electrical and plumbing codes, to public housing, slum clearance and finally to programs designed to encourage the conservation and rehabilitation of existing buildings. Each of these programs has failed as a panacea. Today, as these devices cumulate about us, the hope is that a proper combination of all will do what no one could by itself: provide "a decent home and a suitable living environment for every American family."[1]

Of these programs, the one attracting the greatest interest today is the rehabilitation of existing housing. It is recognized that the nation's housing stock represents our largest national asset, and that "if we are to meet today's housing needs, we cannot depend on new housing alone." Simply put, we cannot

[1] *Housing Act of 1949*, sec. 2; 63 Stat. 413; (1949); 42 U.S.C. 1441 (1958).

as a nation afford to tear down and replace all of the dwelling units we consider substandard. If we want better housing, we must learn to maintain and improve what we already have. This, at least, is the official reason. Other factors are important. One is growing recognition that large scale clearance is expensive and has not worked very well. While it has a salutary effect on the immediate neighborhood, it is commonly believed that new slums develop faster than they are cleared.[2] There has also been increasing community resistance. Residents who are to be cleared oppose the dislocation of community life. Critics charge that the end-product is a mass of planning blunders expressed in sterile architecture. Opposition is common from whites who identify urban renewal with the expansion of the Negro ghetto and from churches, especially the Catholic Church, which do not like to see parish life disrupted, nor to expend spirit, energy and money for rebuilding.[3]

[2] This opinion, while frequently expressed, is difficult either to support or to disprove. One would expect that the United States Census would provide adequate data, but the Bureau of the Census changed its definitions of housing quality between 1950 and 1960, so that it is impossible to make direct comparisons over the years. And, even if the definitions were comparable, other problems would make comparison difficult. During the fifties there was considerable clearance, which probably resulted in the elimination of a great proportion of the housing that could be described as slum or blighted because of dilapidation or the absence of plumbing facilities. It is possible to have housing facilities that are quite bad, even though there is adequate plumbing and no fear that the housing is about to collapse. Buildings may be so overcrowded and filthy that they can properly be described as blighted, though they lack those characteristics with respect to structural soundness and adequacy of plumbing which the census uses to distinguish housing quality. Census standards have become too crude to provide an adequate measure.

[3] This last is not a criticism of the churches; if anything, it is a criticism of urban renewal. The Catholic Church, at least in Chicago, has become strongly community oriented in its approach to urban problems. The Church's desire for neighborhood self-control and stable communities is related to a frank concern for the problems of the parish in a changing neighborhood, in view of the fact that Catholic congregations have shrunk rapidly when a neighborhood

But rehabilitation as conceived today is not a unitary program. Even in conservation areas there is clearance, both because structures have decayed beyond economic rehabilitation and because space may be required to provide additional community facilities, change traffic patterns and provide tracts of appropriate size and shape for resale to private developers. There is common agreement that the existence and enforcement of codes[4] designed to set standards for human habitation and building construction are prerequisites to a successful rehabilitation program. The purpose of this comment is to consider how Chicago's building and housing codes are affecting the city's rehabilitation program.[5] There is strong evidence to suggest that the city's

has shifted from black to white in a short period of time. A preference for rehabilitation over large-scale clearance is a reasonable corollary of the approach suggested by the above. If community organization is viewed as the principal means of solving such problems as racial segregation and as a tool for achieving neighborhood conservation and development, it follows that large-scale clearance, which destroys one community and puts great burdens of absorbtion on adjoining communities, would be looked on with disfavor.

[4] Housing and building codes are the two basic types. A building code sets standards for new construction, and includes detailed structural requirements. A housing code is a minimum code for human occupancy applicable to all buildings; it has effect on the structure itself only by implication. The housing code sets such standards as plumbing facilities required per person, family, or dwelling unit, without setting the standards for the equipment itself or its installation. Similarly, the housing code requires such things as garbage cans, screens, and temperature to be maintained where the landlord supplies heat. There is a certain amount of overlapping, as where the housing code sets exit requirements, room and window sizes which have an obvious connection with the structure and its design. Basically, however, the building code can be considered a new-construction code, and the housing code a standard for existing buildings.

[5] It must be borne in mind that the two programs are administratively divided, rehabilitation being largely within the province of the city's Department of Urban Renewal, while code enforcement is largely the responsibility of the city's Department of Buildings, with help in some areas from the Fire Department and the Board of Health. The separation presents problems of administrative coordination.

vast rehabilitation program—50,000 of Chicago's housing units are in areas designated for conservation—is more likely to be frustrated than aided by present building regulations. If this analysis is valid, it may be possible to generalize from it, for the troublesome characteristics of the Chicago codes are common to many larger cities.

I

Though terminology has changed under the influence of the study of human ecology, today's problem of urban blight is essentially America's perennial housing problem. Building and housing codes, designed originally to set a floor under the safety and health standards of habitable structures, provide a guide to the dimensions of that problem. Housing codes as we know them today are probably the direct result of the tenement building, "introduced in New York as a means of producing congestion, raising the ground-rents and satisfying in the worst possible way the need of the new immigrant for housing."[6]

Prior to 1902 in Chicago, there were two separate lines of building restriction—fire safety and health. Health restrictions, largely aimed at conditions outside the home and directed at the control of epidemics, were enforced by Health Department officials at their discretion—an unsatisfactory arrangement. Fire safety restrictions (from which our

[6] Mumford, Sticks and Stones, 1924, p. 109. Allison Dunham of the University of Chicago Law School disagrees with the idea of insidious intent implied by Mumford. Dunham argues that the dumbbell tenements (so named because vertical airshafts designed to bring light and air to center rooms in long, narrow buildings gave the floor plan the appearance of a dumbbell) were built according to the standards of the time —standards that we have since rejected. It is possible that the truth is some amalgam—that the standards of the time were colored by avarice and prejudice. It should be noted that no private low-income building has been undertaken since controls on tenements were applied; the only new housing built since the turn of the century for such people has been subsidized.

present building codes developed) existed in Chicago as early as 1849; the Department of Buildings, however, was not created until 1875 and then only to administer a code designed to assure structural safety. In 1898 the Department was given a revised code and new powers for dealing with violations.[7]

A movement directing public attention to the inadequacies of housing for working class people originated in England during the last quarter of the nineteenth century. The movement spread rapidly to New York, where Jacob Riis was its principal spokesman. The same concerns in Chicago led to the organization of the Chicago City Homes Association, a welfare group centered around Hull House that surveyed tenement conditions in three of the city's worst neighborhoods. Its report, published in 1901 and signed by Jane Addams as well as two women from the socially and economically prominent McCormick family, vividly depicted the foul conditions of tenement living. Within the following year, Chicago adopted a tenement code that can aptly be described as the city's first modern housing code. In the problem areas pointed out by the survey the new code went far beyond earlier health or building regulations. Land coverage was restricted so as to leave some open space between buildings; occupancy standards and minimum room sizes were set; minimum window areas were determined; running water and interior toilets were required.

Despite the tenement code and the continually more detailed building codes it was possible to say in 1935 that efforts to date "have not yet brought about slum clearance, nor provided, on anything but a pitifully small scale, good homes that workingmen and workingwomen with low wages can afford to rent." And almost twenty years later, in 1954, the Citizen's Committee to Fight Slums stated that Chicago had

[7] Neither the health nor safety requirements dealt adequately with the tenements where the sources of difficulty were excessive land coverage, inadequate light and air, unsanitary interiors, inadequate plumbing facilities, and overcrowding.

"twenty-three square miles of blighted areas and . . . fifty-six square miles of threatened middle-aged residential neighborhoods. . . ." Just yesterday, so to speak, it was pointed out that the city has 50,000 units in areas slated for conservation.

It is clear that the housing problem is still with us. In assessing the effects of the 1902 tenement code, Edith Abbott said,

> For approximately thirty-five years the sanitary authorities have been trying to enforce [it] . . . and they have found it impossible to require expensive structural changes or to evict the unfortunate tenants for whom no better homes are available at rents they can probably afford. . . . No one of the sanitary officials has known what to tell these poor tenants to do. The people cannot pay the rents that are asked for better and larger homes. Household congestion . . . is a condition that comes from scarcity of decent apartments at rents that are low enough to be within the purchasing range of the great mass of earners, and other low-income family groups. Bad housing and slums, therefore, remain together as one of the consequences of low wages, and it is difficult to see how, even if slums are abolished, they can be kept from reappearing unless people have adequate earnings to pay adequate rents. A permanent housing subsidy is probably the only alternative. Bad housing goes back to the same cause as poor and insufficient food. But bad housing is more obvious, a reproach to city pride, while underfed people can be more easily kept out of sight.[8]

II

Edith Abbott's summary raises most of the problems facing us today as the successors of the old tenement laws and structural safety laws are called upon to aid in the newest effort to solve the housing problem—rehabilitation. It is worth stressing again one notion in Miss Abbott's remarks: "For approximately thirty-five years the sanitary authorities . . . have found it impossible to require expensive structural changes. . . ." That is, it was impossible to bring existing structures into conformity with the tenement code because of the costs imposed by the Code. Before a building owner will invest in rehabilitation (or new construction) he must

[8] Abbott, *The Tenements of Chicago, 1908–1935*, 1936, pp. 59–61.

be able to foresee a market in which the housing can be disposed of at a price that will compensate him for his investment. It is obvious that no one would invest as much in rehabilitation in the Maxwell Street area as one would in the Old Town Triangle. Maxwell Street is the city's open-air market: Old Town has become a prestige area for artists, intellcetuals and those who wish they were. In a free market situation, money will flow for rehabilitation to those areas where the added investment is justified.

The first principle for the design of codes, both building and housing, is that they must bear a reasonable relation to existing conditions. If standards set are too low—if the economy can afford and the market generally demands higher standards—there is little point in having a code cluttering up the books.[9] On the other hand, "exceptionally high standards will result in a program with costs which no reasonable community can hope to undertake." The effect will be either circumvention or a general raising of prices that will encourage overcrowding. This is obvious with examples that are sufficiently exaggerated such as the Maxwell Street—Old Town comparison. But in matching a code to a real-life situation, it is necessary to be more subtle. An additional cost of a few hundred dollars can make the difference when the decision is whether or not to rehabilitate. But such relatively small differences are hardly noticed by the courts which in fact impose on owners improvements costing thousands of dollars per building. In order to see the effect of such rulings, bear in mind that a cost to tenants of ten dollars per month for each thousand dollars invested

[9] Professor Dunham indicated in a private conversation that the City of Chicago had made an error in its Building Code which left, for several years, a loop-hole that would allow a developer to build without providing hot water. It is quite clear that no new buildings were constructed during this period that actually lacked hot water. Why, then, impose the requirement. In fact, so long as other restrictions are imposed, generally putting new housing in a certain price range, no one specific restriction is necessary, for consumers in that price range will expect that such things as hot water would be provided. If there were no restrictions at all, much cheaper new housing would be built, probably including some lacking hot water.

by a landlord is considered quite reasonable. And this cost will normally be borne by the housing consumer.[10] The point is emphasized by looking at the problem on a city-wide basis. If we assume that the 50,000 units in conservation areas in Chicago are rehabilitated as desired and that it costs $2,000 per unit to do so,[11] the new investment in buildings would amount to $100,000,000. At the rate of $10 per month per $1,000, additional rents would be $1,000,000 per month. If this were paid, the 50,000 families involved would not be able to spend that $20 per month elsewhere. Or, if they responded by doubling up, the owners would be left with their investment standing idle.

The costs to a community of codes with excessively high standards are not to be measured in dollars alone. Such codes will be used as weapons. They may be used by prospective purchasers to soften sellers.[12] They can be used by building contractors and suppliers as a means of drumming up business.[13] They can be used as weapons to

[10] Perhaps the difficulty in the courts is the questionable public image of the gouging slum landlord, from whose pocket it is assumed that the price of code conformance or rehabilitation can be easily and justly extracted.

[11] In fact, much old housing requires investment much greater than $2,000 to bring it into a condition appropriate for its area.

[12] It was suggested to the author that one method of improving your bargaining position when negotiating a house purchase is to report the building to the Department of Buildings, so that the owner will be put under the threat of court action if he fails either to sell or improve.

[13] A businessman whom I interviewed had been ordered at one time to tuckpoint his building; he believed this to have occurred because a local tuckpointing contractor was in need of work. The same requirement was imposed at the same time on a neighboring building. The businessman was asked by the judge supervising compliance whether he had been referred to a particular contractor by the inspector. He had not been, but the fact that the judge should inquire suggests the gambit has been tried. It should be noted that there is general agreement that there is now much less graft in the Department of Buildings in Chicago than there was a few years ago.

assure party regularity. And they can be used simply for graft.[14] Louis Brownlow summarized this point admirably:

> Politically, the benefits will be considerable if cities make their codes conform to economic and technological reality, even if they do not go beyond the removal of what many builders consider the necessity of corrupting inspection forces to buy revision of public laws imposing antiquated and unnecessary restrictions. . . .[15]

The purchase of code revision through payments to building inspectors is only one of several ways in which the codes are avoided. Codes are modified by the Building Department[16] and the Municipal Court[17] through

discretionary enforcement. Finally, they are modified by the acceptance of fines by owners.[18]

In 1962, approximately $385,000 in fines were imposed by the Municipal Court for code violations. Using again as a rough means of comparison the $100,000,000 cost for rehabilitating the 50,000 units in conservation areas, the disproportion of building fines can be seen. It would take over 250 years before the fines imposed by the city equalled the cost of rehabilitating these areas. Under these circumstances, it is no wonder that a fine may be accepted in preference to bringing a building into conformance. Fines imposed, it has been said, are so small in relation to the cost of rehabilitation that they amount to licensing fees for code violations.[19] Nor is equitable relief the answer. In 1962 equitable orders issued out of the Cook

---

[14] The businessman interviewee suggested that the small businessman accepts building inspector grafts as a normal expense. He estimated that he had paid inspectors $200 over the past ten years and would probably have paid more had he been less persistent and resourceful. In one of his bouts with the department he patiently installed a safety relief valve on a hot water tank in three different positions, each time exactly as the inspector directed. On another occasion he was ordered by the Fire Department to remove the lath and plaster from the walls of his shop, leaving the bare brick exposed. Subsequently, a building inspector tried to get him to reinstall it. The interviewee stated that when he first entered business for himself he did not recognize the inspector's approach. While some were quite frank, others would come in and "hem and haw around" until an offer was made. Generally, he said, inspectors want only small sums—$5 to $20 —so that the owner will not be pressed to appeal to higher authority. It is ironic that the interviewee remembers with particularity one Fire Department inspector who *refused* an offer of $10 and went about his business with fairness and dispatch after the offer.

[15] Brownlow, "The Proposed Temporary Illinois State Housing Commission," *Report of the President's Conference on Home Building and Home Ownership, Slums, Large-Scale Housing, and Decentralization,* Gries and Ford, ed., 1932, p. 117.

[16] Sidney Smith, Acting Commissioner, Chicago Department of Buildings, stated in a public appearance on April 30, 1963, that anyone having difficulty complying with the city's new electrical code (which requires electrical outlets every 12 feet and electric lights in all closets over five square feet) should come in to see him, and that he would be reasonable in enforcing the require-

ments with anyone reasonable enough to discuss the matter. He said also that he thought the code might not be enforceable retroactively, as it apparently purported to be, and that he did not want to be in the position of being "bound" by a code that is unenforceable.

[17] Calvin Sawyier, member of the Board of Directors of the Metropolitan Housing and Planning Council, an attorney, and one of the principal drafters of the Chicago Housing Code of 1956, expressed the opinion that the Building Department should not over-use the equitable remedies obtained in the Circuit Court of Cook County (vacate orders, receivership) for fear the Circuit Court would become as inured to housing violations as has the Municipal Court (which operates, in effect, as a compliance board).

[18] It has been suggested that some slum owners have tried to charge off building fines as normal business expenses for income tax purposes.

[19] There are at least two interrelated reasons for the low fines. One is that the Municipal Court judges have been reluctant to make use of the procedure that allows them to impose the maximum fine for each day that the violation is known to have existed. Sawyier expressed the opinion that one reason for this reluctance was that the inspector who made the initial inspection often did not make the final inspection or was not the one who appeared in court, so that there could be no testimony regarding the length of time the violation had existed. The second reason is that the building court views itself, apparently, as a compliance board, although there is compliance machinery within the agency, and the court is supposed to be the last resort of the Building Department for dealing with cases of complete recalcitrance.

County Circuit Court with respect to 567 buildings. If this procedure were counted upon (and figuring an average of two units per building), it would take over forty years to deal with these same 50,000 units.

Codes that are not enforceable because they are too rigorous lead to corruption and wholesale avoidance. They lead to disrespect of the law; they lead architects, even officials when it suits their purposes, to encourage avoidance.[20]

Another result of overly rigorous codes is unequal enforcement. After noting that a highly exacting housing code is unsuitable for existing low rent areas, William Nash, writing for A.C.T.I.O.N., says, "local code officials find a stiff code has great utility in their neighborhood-conservation areas." The temptation is certainly there to enforce a stringent code in limited areas in order to achieve urban renewal policies that are not directly related to the basic health and safety standards that a housing or building code is intended to achieve.[21] And, for better or worse, such unequal enforcement is widely recommended by urban renewal experts.

Question can certainly be raised about the limits of the police power by persons subjected to agency initiated, uniform inspection of limited areas, whether that selective enforcement is initiated as an integral part of a federally supported urban renewal project, or simply at the discretion of the local building department. The argument that the enforcement is necessary to health

and safety is considerably weakened by failure to carry out similar enforcement in other, often worse, areas. Question can also be raised by the persons subjected to rigid Housing Code enforcement in areas where the building inspection does not occur at the initiative of the Department. In order to maintain the appearance of uniformity it is necessary to prosecute such offenders as rigorously as offenders in conservation areas. What this means, however, is that the individual owner singled out for attention because of the testiness of his neighbors or tenants or because a local contractor needs business, or because of the unacceptability of his politics, is likely to be crucified on a cross of equal enforcement.

The need for relating codes to economic conditions has been recognized by others than Miss Abbott. Harry Osgood, Director, Urban Renewal Division, Sears Roebuck, writing with A. H. Zwerner of the H.H.F.A. legal staff, states:

> Effective enforcement of codes embodying raised standards presupposes, wherever a truly substantial segment of the population is affected . . . that the people can afford the higher standards.[22]

Economists Davis and Whinston say:

> If the existence of slums per se violates one's ethical standards, then, as economists, we can only point out that for elimination of slums the main economic concern must be with the distribution of income, and urban renewal is not sufficient to solve that problem.[23]

The point that ideal housing and building codes should conform to economic reality is also shown by the suggestion of these economists that a zoned housing code might be developed on a voluntary basis, the zoning

---

[20] This is an impression that would be difficult to substantiate, but it is my opinion that the staff of the Rehabilitation Section of the Department of Urban Renewal will wink at minor violations when dealing with a person who is attempting a kind of rehabilitation that will make them look good; that is, where the code and the possibility of successful rehabilitation conflict, they will choose—sensibly enough—the latter.

[21] This was done in St. Louis. It is also being done in Chicago, though Acting Commissioner of Buildings, Sidney Smith, has denied that there is any inequity in code enforcement by district. Whether or not this pattern is being followed in Chicago is a factual question. The door-to-door inspections being carried on in Hyde Park are certainly not used throughout the city as a means of determining whether violations exist. All in all, the assertion that enforcement is uniform throughout the city seems highly doubtful.

[22] Osgood and Zwerner, "Rehabilitation and Conservation," 25 *Law and Contemporary Problems*, 1960, pp. 705, 721.

[23] Davis and Whinston, "The Economics of Urban Renewal," 26 *Law and Contemporary Problems*, 1961, pp. 105, 112.

III

being based not on whether there is a conservation program, but upon the character of the housing in the area. It is assumed that if the planner responsible develops an appropriate code he will obtain the assent of the community. If his proposal is inappropriate—If it fails to gain assent—the planner goes back and tries again, until he produces a code that is acceptable. It is assumed that owners will invest the maximum that is economically reasonable where they have assurance that other owners will do likewise. Where, without knowledge of the intentions of other owners, one owner considers whether or not to invest in rehabilitation, he is faced with a "prisoner's dilemma," the logical solution of which is to do nothing.[24]

Much the same point was made by Brownlow in 1932 in respect to building codes:

> The whole matter of *governmental regulation* in the housing field occupied by the private capitalist should be studied with a view to relieving the real estate operator of conditions that impede him in his work and that are not necessary for the public safety, health and welfare. . . . The study also should . . . include an inquiry into the problem of how public laws for the regulation of buildings erected by private capital may be amended, in the light of the best modern usage, so as to still further protect the public safety, public health and public welfare; and at the same time further to assist and not impede the work of the real estate operator.[25]

Some evidence has been adduced indicating that the City of Chicago has excessively stringent codes, codes that overregulate and that are not uniformly enforceable:

1. The Code is differentially enforced by geographic area, indicating a recognition that the Code could not be uniformly enforced throughout the whole city. (Some differential enforcement may be occasioned by federal requirements for approval of urban renewal programs.)

2. The municipal courts are quite lenient in enforcement, which, while it may in part suggest ignorance or corruption, almost certainly demonstrates that there is a strong feeling on the bench that the Code is too harsh.

3. The Department of Buildings is willing to deal "reasonably," at least on some specific matters, with building owners.

4. Threat of Code enforcement is apparently a very effective form of blackmail, which would not be the case if Code conformance were economically reasonable.

5. Housing codes can be used, at least since *Kaukas v. City of Chicago*,[26] to require an unknown but undoubtedly large number of building owners to invest thousands of dollars per building.[27]

Another indication that Chicago's Housing Code is overregulatory is the common belief that a building inspector can go into any existing building and find violations. An interviewee told the story of a friend who had built a new plant according to plans approved by the Department of Buildings. When the inspector showed up, he was told not to bother putting his hand out because the new building complied fully with the code. The inspector asked the owner whether he would like to tear down a wall after showing him the Code requirement that the wall violated. The owner continued to pay. It is difficult to

---

[24] As long as the owner considering remodeling does not know what other owners intend to do, the most satisfactory decision on his part is not to invest; if others do not as well, conditions will go along as they are; if others do, the first owner will reap unearned benefit from the others' improvement of neighborhood standards. However, a mutual decision to invest is likely to work to the profit of all.

[25] Brownlow, *supra* note 15. Despite substantial agreement, confusion arises because in some areas, especially small cities and towns, there is a real problem with inadequate regulation. The frequent calls for stronger and better codes almost certainly apply to those numerous towns with no codes at all, or with thoroughly inadequate ones. It is unfortunate that concern with inadequate codes obscures the difficulties created by overly adequate ones.

[26] 27 Ill. 2d 197, 188 N.E.2d 700 (1963).

[27] The discovery in the Denver, Colorado area that local codes could add as much as $554 to the cost of a house led to the adoption, in all but two communities of that area, of a minimum uniform code.

judge the accuracy of such stories, but if it is true that minor violations can be found in most buildings, the code is not consonant with economic and technological reality.

When the city is entering upon a large scale program of rehabilitation, it is particularly important that such conformity be achieved. If the Building Codes demand more than can be afforded, potential renovators will decide against investment, rather than put themselves in a position where they will be forced to do more than seems economically justified to them. William Spooner, a Chicago architect who specializes in rehabilitation, was asked whether in his experience building and housing code requirements interfered with rehabilitation. Spooner emphatically stated that they did and listed several problems that he had encountered.

1. Exit requirements. When the number of units in a building is changed, a rehabilitator is normally required to conform with the Building Code. Frequently one result is to require the addition of a second internal stairway. This, Spooner feels, is unnecessary (considering the cost) in buildings with a small number of units, not over three or four stories high, twenty-five feet in width, and fifty to sixty feet in length. One internal stairwell in these circumstances, perhaps with the addition of an external stair or ladder, should be sufficient. The requirement of two stairwells, he feels, is reasonable in a high-rise building occupied by two or three hundred families. But dividing the cost of a

$1,000 improvement cost, the table below shows how the cost of the improvement would affect rents.

Moreover, the necessity of increasing rent levels is not the only problem. There is the prior question: considering this added cost, will renovation be undertaken at all?

In 1932, the requirement of a second internal stairwell was considered one that could be eliminated without any reduction in safety. The requirement is by no means universal today. The FHA does not require more than one egress per apartment in three story buildings when the number of units between fire walls is nine or less. Philadelphia, whose building code is successfully enforced, also permits a single internal stairwell in small multi-story, multi-unit buildings. The Board of Fire Underwriters' *National Building Code* requires at least two exitways from all multi-story, multi-unit buildings, but they may be either internal or external. Finally, it should be borne in mind that the majority of deaths due to fire are not the result of burning, but of smoke inhalation. This suggests that ventilation requirements are more important for personal safety in fires than are exit requirements.

2. Noncombustible wall requirements. The requirement that stairwell walls in four story buildings be made with noncombustible framing—not simply that they be given noncombustible surfacing—makes it impossible in most renovations of such buildings to use existing framing. The new framing must be of lightweight steel or concrete block. The needless work and material involved in providing noncombustible framing, Spooner feels, should more properly go into amenities.

Taking due regard for the amount that can be wisely invested in an existing building, it is almost always true that a builder will be better off investing in modernization of kitchens and bathrooms, adequate wiring and built in storage facilities, than he would be investing in steel framing within stairwell walls. When substantial sums are expended on structural improvements, even more must be spent to provide the amenities that will

*INCREASE IN MONTHLY RENT
DUE TO IMPROVEMENTS*

If the building contained:	If the improvement costs:	
	$5,000	$10,000
3 units	$16.67	$33.33
4 units	$12.50	$25.00
6 units	$8.33	$16.67

second stairwell between the tenants of buildings of three to six flats places upon them an excessive burden.

The *Kaukas* case indicates that a second stairwell may range in cost from $5,000 to $10,000. Using the $10 per month per attract those who can afford to pay for the structural improvements.

Once again, it must be remembered that we are dealing with small buildings with relatively few units. There are two reasons for requiring fireproof stairwell frames. One is to protect the building; the other is to protect the residents by assuring adequate means of egress. The latter will be satisfied if the residents can move down a stairway and through a passage during the time that the passage will resist fire. How long it takes people to get out is a question of the number of the people and the width of the passage. By the formula of the *National Fire Underwriters' Code*, a normal stair width of thirty-four inches is adequate for a population of forty-five persons per floor. The buildings we are speaking of are almost certain to have thirty-four inch wide stairways, but have populations considerably less than forty-five persons per floor. That means that there is a wide margin of safety and that rapid passage through such a stairway should be possible without congestion. The incombustible wall requirement is excessive; it adds an extra margin of safety, where safety is already high, at considerable cost.

If a building is left as it is, the incombustible wall requirement is not applied; if the building is remodeled, but the number of units not changed, only two-hour surfacing is required. The requirement for non-combustible framing applies, then, only when there is remodeling that results in a conversion.[28]

3. Noncombustible external structures.

---

[28] There are a lot of bad words in the housing field, of which *conversion* is certainly one. In fact, proper conversion may be the only way to make economic use of large, old buildings. Conversion, therefore, can be socially useful, as the only practical means of preserving our national housing resources; and that, after all, is the goal of community conservation. After all, conversion means a change of use; when conversion results in lowering density, the public sympathy for stringent control of the increase of density should favor conversion. It may, but the Building and Zoning Departments often do not see things that way.

It is not permitted to build frame structures, except fences, within six feet of a lot line in the greater part of the city. In the older sections of the city especially (most of which are within the fire zone), lots tend to be very narrow—sixteen, twenty and twenty-five feet. Twenty feet is a very common width for row-house lots. Thus on a twenty foot lot, any frame structure must be built within an eight foot wide strip down the center of the lot.

This restriction raises problems in two different situations—where extensive remodeling is being done and such frame structures are desired for reasons of aesthetics and convenience and where, probably most often in poorer areas, the code would otherwise accept an external frame stairway to satisfy exit requirements. Among people who are inclined to do extensive remodeling of old buildings, open decks, covered patios and other yard structures are very popular; small yards are arranged for serving and entertainment in line with contemporary design ideas of blending exterior and interior decor. Standard practice in these situations is to show on the permit application that a structure such as that desired already exists and that it is to be repaired. Even where eight feet are sufficient to build the desired structure, competing aesthetic values and especially the value of maximum use of limited space may argue for lot-line building. Comparable costs quoted by Mr. Spooner indicate that the required noncombustible construction will run about three times the price of frame construction (he cites $350 as the cost for a frame open-deck and $1,000 as the cost for one in noncombustible materials). Where adjoining buildings are of noncombustible shell construction, the price of code conformity seems far too high.

The second trouble situation is where regulation requires the addition of an external stairway. Again, this situation is most likely to arise in dense, inner-city areas, where the reasonable, and perhaps the only possible, location is in, on or near the lot line. Because the stairway must be non-combustible the owner is faced with an insoluble cost dilemma.

Applying Building rather than Housing Code standards when there is to be a change in use or an extensive remodeling may force a person planning improvements to do more than he can afford. As long as nothing is done conditions considered objectionable by new building standards will continue. As soon as renovation is undertaken, the Building Code is invoked; the renovator, before he can consider adding amenities, must absorb the cost of bringing the building into conformance with a code enacted after the building was constructed. The cost of doing so may well be prohibitive. The result is to discourage rather than encourage renovation.

That Chicago codes are excessive and detrimental to rehabilitation was confirmed by a Government housing official, who prefers to remain anonymous. With the exception of some projects of special public interest almost all applications to the Chicago FHA office for federal guarantees of remodeling loans are rejected. They are rejected because of problems raised by architectural standards. One large group is turned down because the remodelers are restricting their programs to minimal face-lifting: The reason, according to the official, is that the remodelers do not want to undertake major rehabilitation, requiring a Chicago building permit. They want to avoid the added expense that would result from being required to comply with the Building Code. Others are rejected because they fail to comply with FHA structural requirements. Recognizing the problem resulting from its own standards, the FHA is, at this writing, preparing to publish a new minimum standard regulation specifically designed for community conservation areas. The new standards are less stringent, so that the FHA can make loan guarantees on a greater proportion of the buildings in conservation areas. The government housing official interviewed believes that these changes will not help in Chicago. The reason is simple: The FHA is lowering its standards in recognition of the special problems of rehabilitation; the City of Chicago is not doing the same. Although it may be possible to get FHA approval, it will still in some cases be impossible to get a permit from the Department of Buildings. Chicago's present code stands squarely athwart the path to a successful rehabilitation program.

IV

It is apparent that a successful program of rehabilitation in Chicago will require that the city go through the same process as has the FHA—an overhauling of codes with a view toward the special problems of rehabilitation. The Building Code was intended to apply to new structures. The Housing Code was intended to apply to existing structures. When rehabilitation was unimportant to the community's housing supply, application of the Building Code to the remodeling of houses was expedient. But this mechanical application is not desirable when rehabilitation becomes important. In drafting a code applicable to existing buildings that are to be renovated, the following points should be kept in mind.

1. The rehabilitator should be encouraged, rather than penalized, for undertaking a rehabilitation program. Initiation of a program of rehabilitation should not invoke standards that make costs prohibitive.

2. Fire safety requirements should be judged in terms of total cost measured by the number of units that would have to be brought into compliance. This cost should be weighed against the known injuries to persons and property attributed by actuaries to the absence of the safety feature in question. It is idle to talk of perfect safety; we go through the same balancing process in not requiring buildings to be tornado-proof, in not uniformly requiring cars to be equipped with safety belts, and in not requiring restaurants to be bomb-proof. Each of the decisions necessarily represents an assessment of the cost and the risk.

3. No requirements should be imposed that cannot be justified as necessary to maintain minimum conditions of health and safety consonant with the ability of the city to absorb the cost.

4. Standards should be set only after a careful examination of the structures located within present and potential conservation

areas and a reasoned evaluation of the economic possibilities. Architects experienced in rehabilitation should be consulted.

5. It should be borne in mind at all times that a rehabilitation program will not succeed if the only rehabilitation actually carried out is "caprice rehabing"—rehabilitation regardless of costs to satisfy the sophisticated tastes of the well-to-do. Rehabilitation will be successful only if it does not raise overall housing costs so much as to produce marked dislocation. The vast majority of owner-occupants of small buildings should be able to rehabilitate sufficiently to meet code standards without pricing themselves out of their own buildings. Apartment building owners should be able to comply without pricing out their tenants.

Stringent building codes were promulgated at a time when renewal was not at the center of public attention. But contemporary experts in the housing field often continue to favor stringent codes as a means of obtaining renewal objectives. Such a use of the codes creates a dilemma. The higher the code standards, the more effective their use to further renewal programs. But the higher the standards the more difficult they are to enforce where the poor live. It is conceivable that a point will be reached—it may have already been reached in Chicago—where enforcement of the stringent code in the poorer areas is worse than no code at all.[29] High standard building codes may also discourage rehabilitation by all except the well-to-do.

When, as now, rehabilitation can be

[29] An argument similar in effect to this is made by Banfield and Grodzins, *Government and Housing in Metropolitan Areas* (1958), though in somewhat different circumstances. They suggest, in discussing building codes in suburban areas, that excessively restrictive county codes may encourage incorporation of developments where state legislation allows incorporated areas to escape building and zoning laws. They conclude that "regulations of the larger unit should be established at minimum levels." Within a large city, the code cannot be legally avoided by certain areas, but it can be *de facto* avoided by selective enforcement.

compelled by housing codes requiring the initiation of remodeling and a building code setting high standards for its completion, community rehabilitation can only be achieved at the expense of a change in the socio-economic character of the neighborhood.

A minimal standard code will protect the poor and encourage rehabilitation. This solution requires either (1) that housing and building codes be looked at and rewritten with a view to requiring only those safety and health measures that the society can afford for all its members and with a view to the specific problem of rehabilitating existing structures, or (2) that a separate code be designed specifically for rehabilitation.

A third suggestion has been offered—zoned housing and building codes. Though most legal observers believe zoned codes would be unconstitutional, many urban renewal people favor them and they are not without their legal supporters. The zoned code resolves the dilemma posed by the attempt (using a single code) to set minimal health and safety standards for the protection of the poor while at the same time setting high standards for urban renewal areas. The resolution is to have different codes for different areas. I do not intend to enter the constitutional debate more than to say that the opponents of zoned codes are concerned with the classification problem (the standard of classification ultimately is whether the housing is intended for the rich or the poor) while the supporters point out that zoning by use, type and size of structure is not inherently different than zoning according to the characteristics of structures covered by housing and building codes. (Obviously, zoned codes are not a solution to all the problems that I have discussed, unless the zoned codes themselves conform to those standards in respect to the areas they cover.)

But more than constitutional problems are raised by zoned codes. Zoned codes are commonly tied to a timetable for rehabilitation or replacement of all substandard housing in the community. According to Krumbiegel's original suggestion, residential areas would be classified according to whether they are to be demolished, rehabilitated, or protected; others [complicate] this arrangement by dividing areas for demolition according to the timetable for their destruction. Areas designated for demolition from, say, five to twenty years hence would be assigned codes of a severity increasing with the projected life span. The most obvious problem with this notion is that urban renewal planning and financing are now on a relatively short run basis. There is presently no mechanism for financing the staged redevelopment of the entire housing supply. To enact zoned codes without a corresponding commitment on the part of state and federal governments would be to accept a cart without a horse.

A more fundamental problem is that there is no reason to assume that five years from now it will be more economically feasible than it is now to house all Americans according to, say, the standards of the FHA, or the Board of Fire Underwriters, or the Housing and Building Codes of the City of Chicago. We face today the problem of dealing with rapidly increasing unemployment due to automation, increasing resistance on the part of state and local governments to the continuing burden of public aid and increasing disillusionment with the public housing program. It is well to be reminded here of the economists' words quoted above.

> If the existence of slums per se violates one's ethical standards, then, as economists, we can only point out that for elimination of slums the main economic concern must be with the distribution of income, and urban renewal is not sufficient to solve that problem.[30]

One cannot dispose of the problem of income distribution by arguing that we will reach our urban renewal goal in planned stages rather than all at once. The situation is rather like that of a child offering five pennies for a ten cent ice cream cone after seeing another boy's nickel rejected as inadequate. One can say that without a solution to the problems of automation and income distribution within the next twenty years, we will be wracked by revolution, and thus we might as well, in our housing planning, assume that those problems will be solved. There is some force to this argument, but it would be help-

30 Davis and Whinston, *supra* note 23.

ful if someone were to give us rough guidelines as to approximately where we will be, approximately what we can afford or even how much it would cost to reach the goals we have already set for ourselves in our codes. And who will pay—how will the income distribution problem be resolved? Not only is the horse not there to pull the cart, but there is no clear idea where the cart might be pulled, were a horse available.

If we do not make the assumption that zoned codes are a step toward staged repair and replacement of all substandard housing, but assume, rather, that they are a static definition of neighborhoods by economic class, another set of problems arises. First, there is the huge political hurdle of designating an area as low standard. I doubt that the political fortitude exists to do so. The poor would be resentful of the institutionalization of their condition; the middle and upper classes, always embarrassed by the poor, would be resentful at having their consciences troubled. In making these designations, one must say either that the poor will stay in the areas they now inhabit (and they will not be able readily to escape those areas because of the higher costs imposed by the zoned code in other areas), or that the poor will live in some areas where they do not now live. This latter arrangement, doubly aggravating, is the one most likely to be necessary. The poor always live in the worst areas, those that will be slated for demolition. The hope is that their lot will be improved by their removal to nearby areas now occupied by those one step up the social ladder. If the low income area to be cleared is occupied by Negroes or Puerto Ricans, the political dynamite needs no spelling out.

The difficulties in zoned codes raise serious question as to why the well off should not be left to fend for themselves. The answer, of course, is that urban renewal is not intended to protect the well off, who could fend for themselves by moving to the suburbs, but to lure them away from leaving the city. But the costs and the problems of either uniformly high or zoned codes are too great. It is clear that codes sufficiently high to discourage rehabilitation are no use at all. It is not clear, if high standards are necessary to successful urban renewal (to solve the problem of the "prisoner's dilemma"[31]) that other means cannot be found.[32]

[31] That is, one possible justification for a high code may be to overcome the inertia in rehabilitation caused by the "prisoner's dilemma." This inertia is likely to be most pervasive in areas of large apartment buildings that are absentee-owned. This inertia might be overcome by appealing to the pride and aesthetic sensibilities of owners—confronting them with architectural renderings of how their buildings might look after rehabilitation, and following through with presentation of a reasonable plan for financing. The process is, however, a slow one, and some officials favor more coercive power. There is, however, no clear evidence as to how strict a code must be to set off a program of rehabilitation. The most successful rehabilitation would be one in which people were moved to improve and maintain their buildings in ways that no existing or contemplated code could enforce, ways that reflect either pride and confidence in the community or effective market demand for good housing. This suggests that one way of overcoming the "prisoner's dilemma" for the real estate investor is full employment and a reasonable vacancy rate.

[32] In addition to the means suggested in the preceding note, there are others that might be tried. One is property standards for an urban renewal area set by covenant. Thus, the requirements must be economically reasonable, or it will be impossible to dispose of the property. (Or, I would assume, using eminent domain, the municipality would have to absorb at least some of the loss resulting from the imposition of standards not economically justified by the pre-

While the principal purpose of this comment is to point up the problems in conversation areas produced by application of a code designed for new housing, it is worth mentioning that if the principles suggested for a rehabilitation code were applied to codes generally, they would eliminate many of the collateral ill effects produced by overregulation. Opportunities for blackmail would be reduced; respect for the law would be increased; codes could be enforced with good conscience and an even hand; evasion would not be more profitable than conformance.

The role of a housing code in rehabilitation should not be misunderstood. It should not impose the highest standards that it is hoped conservation programs will achieve. It is a common experience that the owner asked to comply with minimal codes decides then, while he is about it, to invest much more. Basically, improvements will be made if they can be afforded, in the largest sense of that word. Code enforcement may be necessary to prick people into action, but it cannot successfully tell them exactly where to go, once they have begun.

renewal community.) Another, which might be achieved either by covenant or legislative action, would be a sort of subinfeudation, the development of smaller, limited, governmental units within the city. Conceivably, a city could set a minimal code, and such sub-governmental units could set even higher standards should they choose to do so. Leaving the problem of standards beyond the minimum in the hands of the residents of a small area is entirely different from having either uniform or varied standards imposed by the city government.

Most cities have in force local laws of various types to control the construction of housing, including building codes, fire and safety measures, sanitation and health ordinances, zoning ordinances and other police power measures.[1] *But the housing code which covers occupancy and maintenance as well as other aspects of dwellings is foremost in terms of practical effectiveness.* It is believed that only about 65 cities have housing codes of a comprehensive nature which encompass in one ordinance the regulatory measures covering housing, including many requirements normally found scattered in several different codes and ordinances.

Current Housing Codes

The importance of housing codes has been recognized under Federal law. The Housing Act of 1949, as amended, provides that no contract shall be entered into for any loan or capital grant for urban renewal, no mortgage shall be insured under section 220 or section 221 of the National Housing Act, as amended, and no annual contribution or capital grant contract for low-rent public housing under the United States Housing Act of 1937, as amended shall be entered into unless there is presented to the Administrator by the locality a *workable program* of the community for utilizing appropriate private and public resources to eliminate and prevent the development or spread of slums and urban blight, so as to encourage needed

22

Housing Codes in Urban Renewal

Joseph Guandolo

This article appeared originally in The George Washington Law Review, Vol. 25:1, October 1956, 9–44. *Reproduced by permission.*

urban rehabilitation and to provide for the redevelopment of blighted, deteriorated or slum areas.

The workable program, according to a requirement of the Housing and Home Finance Agency, must include as an essential element a plan for the enactment and enforcement of adequate codes and ordinances prescribing minimum occupancy standards for dwellings. This H.H.F.A. requirement, in part at least, is based upon Federal statutory provisions requiring that consideration be given, in the granting of Federal aid for urban renewal, to the enactment and enforcement of adequate housing codes.

In general, a housing code establishes minimum requirements respecting the condition, the maintenance and the occupancy of dwellings and the condition and maintenance of utilities and facilities in dwellings to the extent deemed necessary to achieve safety, health and general welfare objectives. Housing codes prescribe regulatory measures for the maintenance, occupancy and supplied facilities of structures and are concerned primarily with health, safety and sanitation requirements of buildings after they have been constructed.[2] But certain housing code

[1] In England, under the Housing Act, 1936, a local authority may order the vacation and prohibit the use of any house occupied by persons of working classes and determined to be unfit for human habitation if the owner declines to carry out the necessary restoration work. The standard applied in determining unfitness for human habitation is that of "an ordinary, reasonable man." The Housing Repairs and Rents Act, 1954, confers powers on local authorities to regulate houses in clearance areas and to purchase houses for reconditioning, and enables landlords to make an increase called a "repairs increase" in rent as an incentive to improve the condition of the premises. The Public Health Act, 1936, placed on local authorities the duty of inspecting houses and other buildings with a view to their maintenance in a proper condition.

[2] Housing codes must be differentiated from building codes and zoning ordinances which essenitaly are applied prospectively, although housing codes may by reference or otherwise include provisions of building, plumbing, electrical, and other codes. Building codes are con-

requirements may indirectly influence the design and construction of new buildings as well.

The housing law must be broad enough to cover all dwellings, irrespective of the date and type of construction, the nature of the occupancy, the character of the ownership or the location. Housing conditions and the physical aspects of housing vary materially in different geographical regions within the United States, in different communities and in different sections of the same community. The housing code must be predicated upon an objective study and analysis of the particular conditions prevailing in the respective community and must be tailored to fit such conditions.

The two main functions of a housing code are to prescribe minimum standards[3] of housing quality and to provide procedures and sanctions for their enforcement. The housing code contains (a) requirements respecting facilities and equipment in dwellings, including lighting, ventilation, garbage and waste disposal, heating, water supply, sewage disposal, sink, bath, toilet and means of egress; (b) maintenance requirements covering general sanitary conditions and equipment, heating equipment, chimneys and flues, fire hazards, electric wiring, inflammable liquids, pest infestation, internal structural repair, external structural repair, and dampness; and (c) limitations on occupancy,

including general room crowding, persons per room, persons per sleeping room, area crowding, sleeping area, non-sleeping area, and other factors leading to over-crowding. The procedures and sanctions are covered by provisions (a) indicating what dwellings and structures are within the purview of the code, (b) defining what the respective responsibilities of the owner, the tenant and the lessee are, (c) prescribing penalties and other sanctions for violations and (d) providing for the administration and enforcement of the code.

A recent publication, Provisions of Housing Codes in Various American Cities, tabulates the results of a review of the major provisions of the housing codes of 56 cities[4] and the model housing code of the American Public Health Association entitled "Proposed Housing Ordinance". Most of the existing housing codes are included in the study. The population of the 56 communities ranges from less than 10,000 to over 2,000,000. The codes included were enacted between 1930 and 1955 by such cities as Denver, Buffalo, Baltimore, Cincinnati, Los Angeles, Pittsburgh, Portland, Oregon, and Washington, D.C.

In such tabulation the major provisions in the 57 housing codes have been catalogued under twelve tables, the titles of which outline the general contents of the codes, viz, I—Administrative Powers and Procedures, II—Definitions, III—Space and Occupancy Standards, IV—Light and Ventilation, V—Sanitation Facilities, VI—Standards and Requirements for Structural Elements, VII—Provisions for Covering Substandard Conditions of Structural Elements, VIII—Heating Requirements, IX—Electrical Requirements, X—General Criteria Defining Substandard Conditions, XI—Separate or Special Substandard Conditions Which Are the Basis for Special Remedial Action and XII—Separate or Special Provisions Specifically Relating to Hotels, Rooming Houses, or Lodging Houses.

---

cerned primarily with the physical aspects of new construction, including structural safety, fire protection, building materials, and building processes. Zoning ordinances regulate density of land coverage, height, size and other features of structures, location of buildings on lots, types of use, and other aspects of land uses. New York in 1916 was the first city to adopt a comprehensive zoning ordinance, the impelling immediate objective being the protection of Fifth Avenue against the encroachment of manufacturing establishments. Today more than 1,200 communities have zoning ordinances, Houston being the only exception among cities of over 250,000 population. Every state has enabling legislation for zoning.

[3] The term "standards" is used in this article to mean the minimum requirements imposed under a particular code or ordinance.

[4] Chicago is not included in the study. After a year of preparatory work, the city enacted a housing code in 1956 to go into effect in January, 1957.

The lawyer may be particularly interested in those portions of the study relating to the enforcement techniques authorized and showing the difference in powers vested and procedures prescribed for the enforcement of requirements. These differences extend to the form and manner of giving notices of violation; the holding of hearings; jurisdiction of the hearing officer appeals; orders to repair, vacate or demolish structures; remedies upon violation of orders; vacation of premises, placarding building as unfit; making repairs with public funds; demolition of building by public officers, power to prescribe rules and regulations; power to act in emergencies; and other aspects of enforcement.

The effectiveness of a housing code depends upon its contents and its enforcement. A housing code with adequate standards must be implemented with firm and vigorous enforcement to insure proper results. In many cities, the enforcement of housing codes has been inadequate and fraught with difficulties. Typical of the enforcement problems are the lack of sufficient staff and funds; the dispersion of inspection and enforcement responsibilities among several departments or bureaus; the handling of inspections solely upon a complaint basis, not upon an area basis; the ineffectiveness of court actions; the lack of relocation housing for the people displaced through enforcement activities,[5] and the inability of the home owner to pay the cost of repairing and altering a deteriorated house or of the tenant to pay the higher rents resulting from the additional capital expenditures which a landlord would have to make. Practical economic, legal, political and social problems confront public officials enforcing housing codes. These factors and other local conditions will govern the type of requirements incorporated in a housing code and the scope and intensity of the enforcement program.

Enforcement techniques to compel compliance with housing codes generally follow a pattern and include such measures as

orders to make repairs; orders to make repairs if the cost thereof is reasonable in relation to the value of the structure, e.g., where the cost is not more than 50% of the value; orders to demolish if the cost of repairs exceeds the prescribed percentage of value; orders to vacate; direct demolition by the enforcing official; placarding buildings as unfit for human habitation or dangerous; making of repairs by the enforcing official; imposing of lien for cost of repairs made by the enforcing official; and withholding necessary permits, licenses or certificates.

Enforcement requires the full cooperation of public officials and support of the general public. It cannot be successfully carried out in an atmosphere of indifference, favoritism or venality which tends to encourage the unscrupulous to exploit both tenants and properties and disillusions the public. Enforcement may be materially encouraged if the courts play their role with a clear understanding of the problems involved and importance of the program to the welfare of the community. Local courts, it has been found, have been ineffective in many cities in disposing of housing cases. Such cases are characterized by delays, dismissals and inadequate punishments. The establishment of a special housing court (or in smaller communities the assignment of a special judge) to hear housing cases and code violations may facilitate materially the enforcement program. It is no less essential than a traffic court for traffic violations. A special housing court, by becoming familiar with the enforcement program, its problems and its importance, may provide prompt and effective judicial administration of housing cases and mete impartial and firm justice, with punishments severe enough to deter.

RETROACTIVE MEASURES

Buildings in existence when a housing code is enacted are subject to the regulatory measures therein. The application of modern housing code requirements to old buildings may appear to be unreasonable or arbitrary; it may seem inequitable to insist that old structures be reconstructed to conform to

---

[5] It has been reported that the enforcement of building and fire ordinances in one city would mean that 100,000 people would be tossed into the street.

secure the general comfort and health of the public.

new codes.[6] However, the retroactive application of housing legislation to require the repair and alteration of buildings is a recognized proper exercise of the police power. The Supreme Court has asserted that "in no case does the owner of property acquire immunity against exercise of the police power because he constructed it in full compliance with the existing law." To hold otherwise would in effect preclude the taking of appropriate steps to end slums in the future. The Washington court expressed this view in these forceful words:

> There is no such thing as an inherent or vested right to imperil the health or impair the safety of the community. But, to be protected against such impairment or imperilment, is the universally recognized right of the community in all civilized governments; a protection which the government not only has a right to vouchsafe to the citizens, but which is its duty to extend in the exercise of its police power. . . . It would be sad commentary on the law, if municipalities were powerless to compel the adoption of the best methods for protecting life in such cases simply because the confessedly faulty method in use was the method provided by law at the time of its construction.

The New York court has held that the retroactive application of a tenement law to require the replacement of school sinks with water closets in tenements in cities of the first class is a proper exercise of the police power for the protection of the public health and is not violative of the Fourteenth Amendment. In a later case the owner of an apartment building built prior to 1901 in accordance with the building code of that time claimed that a new statute providing new requirements and higher standards for the protection of health and safety was arbitrary and unreasonable and deprived him of his property without due process of law. The court upheld the validity of the statute and stated that the enactment involved an exercise of the police power to

Minimum Standards in Current Codes

Housing codes should be cast in the legal framework of the police power and the foregoing legal limitations, namely, equal protection of the laws, due process of law, deprivation of property without just compensation, unlawful searches, impairment of obligations of contracts, and unlawful delegation of authority. The police power doctrine and such legal limitations largely govern, from a legal point of view, the type of requirements and the procedural and enforcement provisions that may be incorporated in housing codes.

Housing codes in prescribing minimum requirements for dwellings fix the minimum level of housing quality in the community. These minimum requirements and the more detailed requirements prescribed by other related codes, such as building, plumbing, sanitation, fire and electrical codes, in combination comprise the set of standards for dwellings in the community. The end product of the continued, effective enforcement of an adequate housing code (if coupled with other urban renewal activities) will be better housing in better, more attractive surroundings.

Minimum standards in housing codes vary with conditions in different communities. They are based upon the operative housing facts in the community. The establishment of such standards cannot be based upon precise and definite physiological, economic, and social factors. A wide range of acceptable minima, depend upon varied conditions and judgments, is possible. It is important, however, to establish the level of minimum standards as high as possible within the justifiable range.

Low minimum standards may merely perpetuate substandard housing. Minimal standards, it has been asserted, produce only minimal housing and do not change materially the basic character of the area. Housing codes containing low minimum standards of nuisance theory and geared solely to the

---

[6] A recent housing code of a large city was practically emasculated by a provision making it applicable only to dwellings where, upon change of tenancy, permits for remodeling or alterations or certificates of occupancy were requested.

elimination of housing quality, attuned too literally to the housing unfit for human habitation may result in some improvement of dwellings and undoubtedly may readily escape successful challenge in court. However, these low standards ordinances cannot inject into the deteriorated neighborhood the vitality and healthy glow of a decent environment and cannot fundamentally change the character of a blighted area.

Many housing codes presently in force are designed to attain public welfare as well as health and safety objectives and contain requirements establishing a level of minimum standards sufficiently high to produce satisfactory urban renewal results, provided the codes are effectively enforced. Through the intensive enforcement of such codes and through other urban renewal activities, a community may be enabled to carry out a sound program for the elimination and prevention of urban blight. Realistically, so much needs to be accomplished in so many cities respecting the enactment and the enforcement of housing codes with even low minimum standards that a general raising of minimum standards in the ordinary housing codes of city-wide application, to promote broadly the general welfare and to exceed requirements generally based upon the protection of health and safety, may not be practicable for the immediate future.

Higher Standards; Aesthetics

At this stage in the development of the housing code, a substantial contribution to the solution of the urban blight problem may be made by the enactment and enforcement of housing codes containing requirements and provisions, in line with the needs of and conditions in the community, which are generally comparable to those included in modern housing codes presently in force, such as those of the City of Los Angeles, Philadelphia and others.

The incorporation in a housing code of requirements providing for standards of housing quality which are too high for the economic status of the owners of the property or too high for general acceptance in the community may cause a general breakdown

of the enforcement program. How far a community should go in raising standards upon a city-wide basis under its housing code is a matter of judicious balancing of the need for sound neighborhoods on the one hand and legal and practical impediments on the other. The proper level of standards is what can be made acceptable in the community under an effective enforcement program.

However, the proper upgrading and renewal of certain neighborhoods in a community may require for such neighborhoods minimum standards of housing and environmental quality which are higher than those generally applicable throughout the city under the housing code. For example, standards higher than those imposed under the housing code may occasionally be necessary to enable property owners to obtain necessary financing for home improvements in an urban renewal area. Lenders and investors too frequently have been reluctant to finance improvements in a neighborhood that lacks or is not expected to have the attractiveness and amenities necessary to protect private investments therein.

Higher minimum standards of housing quality for such purpose may conceivably extend into the field of so-called "aesthetics", a chameleon-hued term calculated to inspire misunderstandings and fears of exaggerated extensions of its application. The concept of aesthetics is herein confined to physical attractiveness of dwellings and environment to the degree necessary to encourage private capital to finance home improvements in the area. Thus, requirements for exterior painting of dwellings[7] and the cleaning up and proper maintenance of yards and grounds, and other construction and maintenance activities respecting dwellings which are imposed for the purpose of improving the

---

[7] The whitewashing of interior walls and ceilings was required under housing laws in force in New York City as early as 1867. As early as 1914, nine city ordinances and seven state laws imposed requirements for the whitewashing of walls of dwellings. The promotion of public health was undoubtedly the legal basis for such measures.

appearance of the dwelling and its environment and upgrading a neighborhood may be deemed aesthetic in nature. Some of this "aesthetic" type of upgrading may be accomplished through the effective enforcement of existing, modern housing codes. The removal of broken-down fences, shacks and other structures, the elimination of accumulations of debris and the proper maintenance of yards may be accomplished under such codes. Voluntary supplementary action by property owners and tenants may assist in the attainment of the desired objectives.

The enforcement of requirements to meet minimum standards of attractiveness, cleanliness and orderliness of dwellings and surroundings may protect and enhance property values. The neighborhood becomes a more desirable place in which to live; property tax receipts are increased and better public services and better public facilities can be provided to promote the public health, the public safety and the public welfare. Aesthetic considerations recognized under the law come under the exercise of the police power for the general welfare. Minimum standards designed to assure environmental cleanliness, orderliness, neatness and attractiveness are not separable from considerations of the general welfare.

Although some form of aesthetics is involved in many recognized municipal activities, such as parks, parkways, streets, smoke abatement and numerous other public improvements and services, some courts have not accepted the introduction of aesthetic considerations as one of the purposes of municipal regulations of property. The Texas court has bluntly declared that ". . . it is not the law of this land that a man may be deprived of the lawful use of his property because his tastes are not in accord with those of his neighbors." The Pennsylvania court has been equally forceful in its denunciation, declaring in a zoning case that:

> . . . neither aesthetic reasons nor the conservation of property values or the stabilization of economic values in a township are, singly or combined, sufficient to promote the health or the morals or the safety or the general welfare of the township or its inhabitants or property owners, within the meaning of the enabling Act of 1931, as amended, or under the Constitution of Pennsylvania.

In his *Commentaries on the Law of Municipal Corporations* (1911) Judge Dillon almost half a century ago recognized that the law on the question of aesthetics was undergoing development. This development, insofar, at least, as questions under the Fifth and Fourteenth Amendments are concerned, has now matured to the point of clear acceptance by some courts of aesthetic considerations alone as sufficient legal justification for police power regulations of property. Mr. Justice Douglas has declared that the concept of public welfare is broad and inclusive and that:

> The values it represents are spiritual as well as physical, aesthetic as well as monetary. It is within the power of the legislature to determine that the community should be beautiful as well as healthy, spacious as well as clean, well-balanced as well as carefully patrolled. The unanimous opinion in *Berman v. Parker* marks a clean break with earlier judicial precedents. It is a landmark case which will set the pace for a general judicial acceptance of aesthetic considerations alone as adequate for police power regulation of property and bring about the fulfillment of the plea that:

> If "public welfare" has not done so already, it is high time it took on a meaning for the courts which it has done for the rest of the world.

In the final analysis the matter is not one of taste, as the Texas court in the Spann case suggested. Rather it is a matter of economics and the protection of community values. That which is attractive adds and maintains value; that which mars depreciates value. To the question invariably raised as to the standards or guides which are to be controlling, the only answer that can be made is that the standard is that which is applicable in so many other fields of the law, namely, what an ordinary reasonable person would regard as appropriate. Apprehensions regarding possible abuses of the exercise of the power do not justify a denial of the power.

The legitimate use of governmental power is not prohibited because of the possibility that the power may be abused.

Perhaps the principal justification for imposing higher standards of housing quality, including so-called aesthetic requirements, may be the protection of community values. In addition to facilitating the flow of private capital to renew substandard areas, higher minimum standards, effectively enforced tend to protect properties from depreciation in value caused by the menace of deterioration of neighboring properties and surroundings and thereby stabilize, and even enhance, property values and protect sources of municipal revenues. In the case of *State ex rel. Saveland Park Holding Corporation v. Wieland*, a zoning ordinance required the building board of a village to make a finding before the issuance of a building permit that the "exterior architectural appeal and functional plan" of the proposed structure will not be so at variance with those of other structures in the immediate neighborhood or the character of the zoning district as to cause a substantial depreciation of property values in the neighborhood. The court said:

> We have no difficulty in arriving at the conclusion that the protection of property values is an objective which falls within the exercise of the police power to promote the "general welfare," and that it is immaterial whether the zoning ordinance is grounded solely upon such objectives or that such purpose is but one of several legitimate objectives. Anything that tends to destroy property values of the inhabitant of the village necessarily adversely affects the prosperity, and therefore the general welfare of the entire village. Just because in the particular case now before us, property values in a limited area only of the village are at stake does not mean that such threatened depreciation of the property values does not affect the general welfare of the village as a whole. If relator is permitted to erect a dwelling house on its land of such nature as to substantially depreciate the value of surrounding property, there is danger that this same thing may be repeated elsewhere within the village, thus threatening property values throughout the village.

If the preservation of property values may constitute a legitimate objective of zoning ordinances, it would appear that the preservation of property values would also constitute a legitimate objective of other

urban renewal regulatory measures. A dwelling in poor condition and out of character with other dwellings in the area may result in the deterioration of nearby dwellings and eventually the entire neighborhood. Once a neighborhood starts on a downward trend, it continues its downward trend at an accelerating pace unless preventive measures are invoked. Property values decline, property owners suffer economic losses, and the municipality experiences a diminishing tax base and losses of tax revenues, the more prosperous residents move to the suburbs and an in-migration of lower income people results.

The Supreme Court in the *Berman* case indicated that the concept of the public welfare represents values which are "aesthetic as well as monetary." The regulation of private land use in the interest of conserving natural resources has been repeatedly sustained as a proper exercise of the police power. Statutes prohibiting the waste of natural gas and crude oil, the protection of agricultural and industrial enterprises, the preservation of fish and wildlife, the securing of adequate drainage to protect land, and other regulations of land have been sustained as a proper exercise of the police power.[8]

The Zoned Housing Code

As early as 1927 the suggestion was made that the principle of variable standards, varying to meet local conditions, which had been applied so successfully in zoning, be incorporated in a housing law so that different code requirements would be imposed in different districts. More recently, the Com-

[8] A case involving the protection of one type of property through the exercise of the police power in the uncompensated destruction of another type of property is *Miller v. Schoene*, 276 U.S. 272 (1928). In this case cedar trees were destroyed without compensation under a Virginia statute because they were infected with cedar rust, were within two miles of apple orchards, and endangered the apple orchard's investment. The statute was held a valid exercise of the police power.

missioner of Health of the City of Milwaukee, Dr. E. R. Krumbiegel, proposed the enactment of state enabling legislation to authorize the City of Milwaukee to enact a so-called "zoning housing code." The zoned housing code, as proposed by Dr. Krumbiegel, would supplant the ordinary housing code, and would prescribe variable standards in the community by providing for the establishment of different districts or areas for which a different set of standards would be made applicable.

Varying degrees and conditions of blight may prevail in different portions of an area and in the different dwellings and other structures in the area. Although standards may be devised to upgrade a neighborhood area to a given level of housing quality, the application of such standards may entail differing degrees of intensity of improvements in the various portions of the area and as among the different dwellings and structures involved. Under the Krumbiegel proposal, areas for demolition, for rehabilitation, and for protection would be created and different minimum standards applicable to each of such areas would be prescribed, the standards being graduated upward in the respective areas in conformity with the quality of the housing existing in the area in question. In addition to classification on the basis of housing quality, a classification by housing types would be included by which a graded set of standards would also be established for private dwellings, two-family dwellings, multiple-family class A dwellings, and multiple-family class B dwellings respectively. There would also be a separate set of minimum standards for each of the four dwelling types in rehabilitation areas and in protection areas, but in demolition areas there would be no variation in standards by dwelling type. The maintenance of buildings and structures, including garages, barns, outbuildings, stores, factories, warehouses, fences and any other structures or buildings located on land is to be in accordance with appropriate maintenance standards or kept in a state of repair comparable to the general level of the state of maintenance and repair of similar structures in the same neighborhood.

The zoned housing code offers interesting possibilities for comprehensive urban blight programs. Although serious legal questions based on the Fourteenth Amendment can certainly be propounded, a legally sustainable zoned housing code can probably be enacted. The necessary classifications under the code to treat with the varying conditions in a city would have to be supported with convincing evidence, and the delineation of the different types of areas under the code would have to be based upon differences in characteristics and conditions reasonably justifying the application thereto of the different standards prescribed in the code. Drawing the line of demarcation among the various areas for imposition of the specified controls may be difficult. But difficulties in the delineation of such areas need not necessarily invalidate the classification involved.

Several factors favorable to judicial acceptance of zoned housing codes may be cited, including the presumption of validity of ordinances, recognition by some courts of the objective of conservation of property values, the protection and enhancement of property values and assessments for taxation purposes, the judicial deference to legislative determinations of reasonableness of the standards prescribed, the expansiveness of the concept of the public welfare for police power purposes, the judicial acceptance of the establishment of somewhat comparable zoned districts under zoning ordinances[9] and the likelihood of judicial recognition of the legislative attempt to cope realistically with existing conditions by prescribing different remedies for different conditions.

The development within the framework of the law of a zoned housing code as an effective instrument for blight elimination and prevention presents a challenge to public officials, particularly city attorneys, to make a valuable contribution to legal techniques essential for the preservation of the vitality of our cities.

[9] A zoning ordinance establishing an entire village as one residential district, under home rule powers, has been upheld in *Valley View Village v. Proffett*, 221 F.2d 412 (6th Cir., 1955).

T HE POLICE POWER is the power of the state to protect and promote the health, safety, and welfare of its inhabitants. Housing codes are enacted by local governing bodies under a grant of this power. Lawful exercise of the police power undoubtedly limits the way in which a property owner may use or maintain his property. But it is justified on the ground that it is reasonably necessary to protect the public health and advance the interest of the community.

The Police Power as the Legal Basis of Housing Codes

Building codes, zoning regulations, and housing codes are all based upon the police power of the state. Building codes prevent the construction or maintenance of structurally unsound buildings. Zoning regulations restrict the use of land. Housing codes usually specify minimum requirements for the provision of facilities and the maintenance of dwellings.

Most housing codes, for example, contain specifications for the following:

facilities: bathrooms, toilets, sinks, etc.
maintenance of dwelling unit and equipment: owner and occupant responsibility, cleanliness, etc.
occupancy: number of persons per unit of area, sleeping quarters, etc.

The enforcement of housing codes is, by definition, the enforcement of such minimum requirements or standards.

The basic provisions of housing codes in different cities are similar. Nevertheless, minimum standards vary considerably. These variations may be dictated by "legal" factors as to how far the courts in the jurisdiction will uphold housing code standards as reasonable exercises of the police power. Or they may be influenced by "community" factors like climatic conditions, local customers, public acceptability, or previous codes and regulations in force.

GRANT OF THE POLICE POWER TO
MUNICIPALITIES

As a creature of the state, a municipality

23

Municipal Housing Codes in the Courts

Robert M. Oster

This article appeared originally in Report from A.C.T.I.O.N., No. 11, *New York, N.Y., September 1956.*

may use the police power only if such power is delegated to it. Delegation may be general under a constitutional home-rule charter or a municipal charter. The city of Baltimore, for example, is granted the right to enact police measures under its charter from the state of Maryland. Or the delegation may be *specific* in the form of designated powers (like the specific power to enact a housing code) granted by the state through the municipal charter or special legislation. Within the scope of the delegation, the police power may be exercised locally by taking any reasonable measures to protect the health, safety, and welfare of the citizens.

In order to bring its enactment and enforcement within the scope of the police power, a housing code usually begins with a statement that its purpose is to protect the health, safety, and welfare of the municipality's inhabitants. Under such a code an owner is required to improve or even to demolish a structure, since he holds his property subject to regulations imposed under the police power. Elimination of unsafe and dilapidated structures falls under the power to protect the public health, safety, and welfare, and therefore is within the police power of the city.

Today, "municipal power to declare, prohibit under penalty and abate nuisances exists, it has been held under the general or police power." But as indicated in a leading

185

text on municipal government law, the common law doctrine of nuisance does not mark the limit of the legitimate control of private land use. The exercise of the police power is notably broader than the scope of the nuisance doctrine. Thus a housing code, promulgated under the police power, solves one of the chief problems of legal engineering. It "substitutes positive standards of fitness for the ancient nuisance doctrines and establishes administrative practices which make these standards effective."

EMINENT DOMAIN AND POLICE POWER

At this point we should note the difference between a taking under the power of eminent domain and regulations enacted under the police power. The Fifth Amendment to the Constitution of the United States and similar provisions in state constitutions prohibit the taking of private property for public use under eminent domain without just compensation. But the owner whose property is regulated under a valid exercise of the police power is not entitled to compensation. "Damages in such cases are considered *damnum absque injuria*, and the law presumes that the party damnified is compensated by sharing in advantages arising from such beneficial regulations." Consequently, a city can require alterations of existing dwellings without paying compensation when the alterations are reasonably necessary to insure the public health. Since the housing code is based upon the police power, the owner is not entitled to compensation for action validly taken under the code.

THE POLICE POWER: A CHANGING CONCEPT

The concept of the police power tends to change with time. What is called an improper exercise of a state's police power today may be designated a reasonable and valid exercise tomorrow. The dynamic nature of the police power is illustrated by use in the field of zoning. As a general rule, a municipality cannot "zone for aesthetic objectives" under the police power. But aesthetic objectives

may be taken into consideration in a case where the zoning regulation may be sustained as a proper exercise of the police power for reasons of public health, safety, or morals. Thus a case-by-case exception to the general rule has built up. And a trend toward upholding zoning for aesthetic objectives as valid exercises of the police power *seems* evident in many jurisdictions.

The case of *Berman v. Parker*, decided by the United States Supreme Court in 1954, may well be an indication of the general expansion of concepts in the field of governmental control over private property. In upholding an exercise of the power of eminent domain under the redevelopment law of Washington, D.C., the court stated that legislation can be enacted to make the Capital "beautiful as well as sanitary." On this subject, William L. Slayton has noted that "it would appear now, however, that our traditional concepts of property rights would have to give way somewhat in order to meet and solve the problems of our deteriorating older areas."

Limitations upon the Police Power

The police power on which the promulgation of housing codes rests is not unlimited. The health, safety, and welfare of the community must be protected, but so must the lawful rights of the property owner to the use of his land.

What are the limits to this exercise of the police power and upon what are they based? The United States Supreme Court has said that "the police power is one of the least limitable of government powers, and in its operations often cuts down property rights." Nevertheless, legislation under the police power may only impose restraints on the freedom of property ownership which are reasonable and not arbitrary, and which bear a reasonable relation to the objective sought by the restraints.

A property owner's rights are protected by the Fourteenth Amendment to the Constitution and similar provisions of state constitutions. A state may not deprive a person of property without due process of law. Due process requires a notice and a hearing and

ultimate judicial review. It also demands a
general respect for the ownership of property.
In other words, any restraint must be
"reasonable" and necessary to protect the
public health, safety, and welfare.

Nor may a state deny a person equal
protection of the laws. Where legislation
aims arbitrarily at one class and no rational
distinction exists for the difference in
classification, a property owner is denied
equal protection of the laws. But legislation
does not necessarily violate the equal protection clause if various cities within the
state are affected differently by housing
regulations, or if legislation applies only to
certain dwellings and excepts others.

Since the courts ultimately determine what
is reasonable and hence not an arbitrary or
discriminatory exercise of the police power,
two cases in the housing code field may be
compared.

The two cases are *Givner v. Comm. of
Health* and *Brennan v. City of Milwaukee*.
Any one involved in the drafting of a housing
code should read both cases and the respective provisions of the ordinance with which
they deal.

The *Givner* case upheld the Baltimore
regulation requiring that every dwelling unit
have a bathroom, but permitting the bathroom to be shared when there are no more
than two dwelling units in one structure.
The explanation accepted by the court for
this exception was that in two-dwelling unit
structures there are usually two family groups
and therefore a common interest in keeping
the shared bath clean.

In the *Brennan* case the Wisconsin court
struck down a section of the Milwaukee code
which permitted one bathtub for each two
apartments having no more than three rooms
each. In other sections, the ordinance
specified the number of roomers per bath in
a rooming house. This seemed to the court
to indicate that the ordinance was concerned
with the number of persons who share a bath.
Therefore the court held that the index based
on number of rooms, as it appeared in the
exception, was not "rational."

Milwaukee has since amended its housing
code, specifying the number of *persons*
permitted to share a bath, so as to meet the
objection of the court that the ordinance did

not bear reasonable relation to the objective
sought by the legislation.

In the recent case of *Richards v. City of
Columbia*, the South Carolina Supreme
Court upheld the Columbia, South Carolina,
Housing Code over the objections of the
property owner that the ordinance permitted
the taking of property without due process
and denied equal protection of the law. The
court stated that "the courts will not interfere
with the enforcement of such regulations
unless they are determined to be unreasonable, which conclusion we cannot reach with
respect to the definite requirements of the
ordinance."

Limitations placed upon the police necessarily change as the concept of the police
power changes. Thus an "unreasonable"
standard today may be "reasonable" in the
near future. But how far will the courts go in
allowing the police power to be used to
establish above-minimum standards on the
ground that these conditions will be desirable
in the near future? "Historically the power
to enforce public standards has been limited
to what is necessary for the minimum health,
safety, and welfare. However legislatures
enacting future housing codes and administrative authorities and courts enforcing
them may follow the lead of the housing
industry and the public and hold that the
future minimum includes a measure of
comfort and utility."

It is not easy for the owner of a dwelling
to have a housing code provision declared
unconstitutional. In the *Givner* case, the
court indicated a reason for this difficulty:
"But if the matter is fairly debatable, the
court will not substitute their judgment for
that of the board or official charged with the
duty of promulgation or enforcement."

The owner will also be met with the concept of presumption of constitutionality of
statutes and ordinances, including those
promulgated by the municipality. In
McQuillin on *Municipal* Corporations, it is
noted:

Courts are reluctant to pronounce a police
measure too unreasonable and invalid or un-

constitutional, and they are governed by the fundamental rule that the legislative branch is entitled to broad discretion in the exercise of the police power, as to the object thereof, the subject regulated and the mode of regulation adopted; but courts must and will interfere, when called upon in a proper case, and pronounce void an abuse or excess of legislative power under the guise of an exercise of the police power.

Administrative Procedure Used To Enforce Housing Codes

The enforcement of housing codes raises questions about the validity of administrative procedure involving inspection, notice, hearings, appeal, and delegation of authority. Inspection provisions, for instance, raise constitutional questions under the Fourth Amendment to the Constitution and similar state provisions regarding searches and seizures. Similarly, administrative procedure for notice and hearings raises questions of due process of law. On the due process question, the Florida Court has stated: "We recognize the fact that the police power is a very broad one and that its exercise is necessary for the welfare of the community, but the right to exercise the police power does not carry with it the unqualified right to destroy private property without due process."

INSPECTION

A housing code would be ineffectual without the power to inspect dwellings. Inspection by the health officer seeking to enforce the housing code may involve the constitutional right of persons to be secure in their home against "unreasonable searches and seizures." Some courts might hold that this right would be invaded by a health department inspection without a search warrant.

The question as to constitutionality of the housing inspector's right of entry has not been decided. Although few people refuse to allow an officer admittance to inspect a dwelling, one case of such a refusal has come

before the United States Supreme Court, *District of Columbia v. Little.* The Supreme Court, as is its usual practice, refused however to deal with the constitutional issue since the decision could be based upon another ground. This question of constitutionality may very well be litigated again in the near future.

The Proposed Housing Ordinance of the American Public Health Association authorizes inspection at reasonable times. The 1954 Housing Code of Philadelphia, Pennsylvania, specifies the hours within which inspection can be made. In most cases, entry is not a problem, if advance notice is given and the inspection is made at a reasonable time.

NOTICE AND HEARING ON VIOLATIONS

Before a local agency can take action to enforce a housing code against a property owner, notice and hearings on alleged violations must be given. "Notice is required both to give the person affected an opportunity to be heard and to apprize him of the defects to be remedied so that he has an opportunity to remedy them." Most housing codes carefully provide for the owner to be notified of alleged violations of the code.

Most housing codes also explicitly give the interested property owner an opportunity to be heard during the process of administrative determination. The Housing Code of Morristown, New Jersey, provides for a hearing and gives the owner the right to "file an answer to the complaint and to appear in person, by counsel, or otherwise, and give testimony at the time and place fixed in the complaint."

APPEAL

Most housing codes provide for a court appeal according to the procedure used in the jurisdiction. An owner whose property is affected has the right to have a court determine whether the interference or taking is lawful. Thus the Proposed Housing Ordinance of the American Public Health Association permits any person aggrieved by the decision of the health officer to "seek relief therefrom in any court of competent jurisdiction, as provided by the laws of this state."

Under housing codes, questions may arise whether the delegation of power to an administrator is proper and has been exercised within required boundaries. The problem is met specifically in cases where an administrator exercises powers which are largely discretionary in promulgating regulations or ordinances. Generally the delegation of power is improper if the administrator is given arbitrary discretion without definite standards to guide him. The previously mentioned *Givner* case dealt with the question of adequacy of standards in a delegation of the Commissioner of Health of the city of Baltimore. The delegation was upheld over objections that the city had improperly delegated its police power to the Commissioner of Health.

In the case of *Richards v. City of Columbia*, also mentioned earlier, the courts declared unconstitutional certain delegations of legislative authority in the Columbia Housing Code on the ground that their provisions did not "contain a sufficiently definite standard or yardstick." But this decision does not mean that the entire ordinance was voided. In accordance with the usual separability provisions in ordinances, only the offending provisions are stricken.

An Order To Repair or Alter Dwellings

Because a housing code is designed to bring local dwellings up to minimum standards set by the code, provision for the issuance of an order to repair or alter an existing structure is basic. The period of time specified in various codes for making the required repairs or alterations varies. The Morristown, New Jersey, Housing Code allows a maximum of ninety days. The Greenville, South Carolina, Housing Code states that repairs are to be done "within the time specified by the order." Some codes provide that the order shall give an owner a detailed account of the specified sections of which there is an alleged violation.

An order to repair or alter structures represents a valid exercise of the police power.

The Massachusetts Court, for example, upheld a Boston ordinance requiring alteration of buildings to provide water closets. The court stated that the statute in question was undoubtedly within the powers of the legislature as a police regulation. The required maintenance of particular facilities and conditions is also a valid exercise of the police power. Thus a municipality may legally require that a minimum degree of heat be maintained.

CHALLENGERS TO AN ORDER TO
REPAIR OR ALTER

Besides challenging an order to repair or alter on the ground that his rights have been violated under constitutional provisions discussed above, an owner may challenge the order on the ground that he complied earlier with regulations and ordinances previously in existence. Moreover, the owner may claim that the housing code cannot operate retroactively on his property. Or he may argue that compliance with the order to meet the minimum standards will cost too much money and result in hardship to him.

Most courts will probably answer the contention that the property owner complied with previous regulations by following the decision of the United States Supreme Court in the case of *Queenside Hills Realty Co. v. Saxl*. There the Supreme Court said that "in no case does the owner of property acquire immunity against the exercise of the police power because he constructed it [the dwelling] in full compliance with existing laws." In an earlier case, the Supreme Court reached the same conclusion in stating that the claim of vested interest cannot be asserted against a valid exercise of the police power since it would hinder "progress." A decision of the New York Court of Appeals is in agreement: "Because a state has tolerated slums in the past it is not precluded from taking appropriate steps to end them in the future."

Are these decisions unfair in the case of an owner who builds a structure in compliance with a 1955 regulation or code and finds later that it does not meet the requirements of a 1956 code? It may be answered by stating that the owner holds his property subject to the valid exercise of the police power. He must realize that he will suffer if his property endangers the health, safety, or welfare of the community.

Even if hardship is great and an owner is forced to vacate and close rather than repair, court decisions do not sympathize with the owner of substandard dwellings. When the courts balance a property owner's interests against conditions considered to imperil the health or impair the safety of the community, the community interest overcomes claims of previous compliance. It would be "a sad commentary on the law if the municipality were powerless to compel the adoption of the best methods simply because the confessedly faulty method in use was the method provided by the law at the time of its construction."

Important financial considerations are raised when an owner is required to repair a building that complied with previously existing codes and regulations. A building valued at $25,000, for instance, might need an expenditure of almost that amount of money to bring it up to minimum standards. Installation of new bathrooms or minimum ventilation can be costly. Is there any limit to the municipality's power to make the owner repair or alter his building?

In the case of *Adamec v. Post*, a property owner challenged the alteration requirements for old-law tenements on the ground that the cost of conformance would be unreasonable. The New York Court of Appeals held that the legislature could impose the requirements even though they might result in hardship to the owner. Moreover, the court stated that the proportion of alteration expense to assessed value or market value of the old-law tenement could not be a criterion of whether the legislature acted reasonably in requiring the alteration.

But if the expenditures will be very large, that fact may be material in deciding whether the method or means adopted was an unreasonable demand upon the individual for

the benefit of the public. The expenditure must not be "an unreasonable exaction either with reference to its nature or its costs."

An Illinois court in 1907 discussed the problem involved in requiring large sums of money to be expended for alterations. In the case of *Masonic Fraternity Temple Association v. Chicago*, the court concluded that the cost of the alterations ($200,000), the loss per year ($50,000), and the loss of property ($18,000) was too much to ask. "Men do not hold their property by any such insecure and dangerous tenure." The court warned that "if this municipal legislation ... can be enforced under these circumstances, so can any other like regulation which might be made as to buildings only recently completed in which millions of dollars have been invested."

These cases suggest that the limit of a municipality's power to require expensive repairs or alterations is not always readily determined. Some housing codes, however, set certain limits. They provide that the proper authority shall order the repairs if they can be made at a cost not in excess of a specified percentage of the value of the building. The Morristown, New Jersey, Housing Code, for example, specifies a fifty percent limit. The Greenville, South Carolina, Housing Code sets a maximum of seventy-five percent.

These and other codes state that the owner at his option may "vacate and close the said dwellings." But if the cost of repairs or alterations exceeds the stated percentage limit the proper authorities may order the dwelling to be demolished. Some housing codes permit standards to be relaxed if the expense of required alterations would result in extreme hardship. The Columbus, Georgia, Housing Code provides that the time in which repairs must be completed may be extended up to 36 months. The Norfolk, Virginia, Housing Code specifies that in case of undue hardship, less than full compliance may be permitted.

The problems raised by financial considerations in an order to repair or alter and the limits set by housing codes deserve further study in relation to their fairness to the owner and their treatment by courts of different jurisdictions.

The case of changing a building from one conforming use to another sometimes arises in the enforcement of housing codes. Suppose an owner who receives an order to repair his property decides that the required repairs will be too costly. He feels that the expense of installing new bathrooms, windows, or ventilating systems will not be reflected sufficiently in increased rental income. But if he thinks that the property would earn more income as a warehouse or loft, he may wish to spend his money in changing the use of the property. He has a right to do this if the change complies with the zoning ordinance.

The right to change from one conforming use to another has generally been upheld by the courts. In the case of *New York Health Department v. Dassori*, for example, the court ruled that even though buildings cannot be made fit for human habitation, they need not be destroyed if they can be made usable for other purposes. The courts in this and other cases on changes of use refer to nuisances; housing codes with compulsory repair or demolition provisions were not involved.

When structural safety is involved as well as unfitness for human habitation, the fact that the building is not used as a dwelling is not controlling. Every use of the building is prohibited. But if the building is otherwise "safe," a court may permit a property owner to change the use of a dwelling which is *unfit for human habitation* even though he has a repair or a demolition order under a housing code.

An Order To Demolish Dwellings

When a building reaches a specified state of disrepair, some housing codes provide for demolition of the structure. As in the case of an order to repair, the owner is given a reasonable or specified amount of time to accomplish the demolition. This power to cause property endangering the public health, safety, and welfare to be destroyed rests upon the police power and the power to abate nuisances. Housing codes which call for

repair of a dwelling if the cost of repair does not exceed a stated percentage of the dwelling's value contain a companion section providing for demolition if repairs amount to more than the stated percentage of the value. A provision of this kind was upheld in 1953 by the North Dakota Court in the case of *Soderfelt v. Drayton.*

Cases may arise in which an owner is ordered to demolish his dwelling because it falls within the percentage requirements, but he prefers to repair instead. The owner in the *Soderfelt* case, for instance, wanted to repair his building after receiving a demolition order under a city ordinance providing that if a building requires repairs equal to more than 50 percent of the building's value, the building may be demolished. The court concluded that since the municipality could have the power to condemn and did not exercise it unreasonably, the building must be demolished.

Some case law, however, indicates that the owner should be given a right to repair. A court said in one case that the need for total destruction of the building must clearly appear: "Destruction is the last resort."

Questions raised by the right to repair and its application under housing codes seem to be of basic importance. Should an owner be denied the right or privilege to make repairs if he is willing to invest his time and money in order to bring a building up to the requirements of the housing code? Or can the municipality within its police power declare that any building requiring alterations costing more than a specified or unreasonable amount must be demolished regardless of the owner's willingness to repair?

In some cases considerations of the entire neighborhood and surrounding area may enter into the question. A building requiring extensive repairs for instance, may be a blight upon the area even though it meets minimum standards. The problem seems to be recognized by Slayton. It should be remembered though that a housing code is intended merely to raise all structures to *minimum* standards. It is not supposed to cause structures to be demolished because they do not match the quality of neighboring dwellings whose facilities are higher than the minimum. Slayton suggests that a more promising method of obtaining the removal of buildings which meet minimum standards and yet fall below neighborhood standards is to use the power of eminent domain (and compensate the owner) under the municipality's redevelopment powers. He proposes that area-wide redevelopment legislation be amended to permit the acquisition of scattered parcels in a neighborhood conservation program.

A suggestion has been made that a city should be zoned for housing standards. Utilizing the police power the legislation would be drafted to provide for a gradation of standards in the different areas within the city. For example, the standards in an area to be cleared for redevelopment would be less stringent than those for an area planned for conservation. Undoubtedly constitutional questions would arise from such a zoned housing code, but further study of this type of legislation might prove valuable.

Failure To Comply with an Order To Repair or Demolish

In the absence of effective penalties, some owners of substandard property would not voluntarily bring their dwellings up to the standards set by a housing code. For this reason, devices must exist to compel owners to repair or demolish, or permit the municipality to do so. These devices may include fine and/or imprisonment, placarding and vacation, and liens for the cost of public repair or demolition. Some codes, such as the Greenville, South Carolina, Housing Code, contain all these devices. Other codes limit themselves to the imposition of fines and prison sentences along with the placarding and vacation of dwellings.

FINE AND/OR IMPRISONMENT

The proposed Housing Ordinance of the American Public Health Association specifies a fine and/or imprisonment for failure to comply with orders issued under the code. A similar section is found in most housing codes. Some like the Cambridge, Massachusetts, Housing Code, call only for the imposition of a fine. There is a wide range of fines imposed by the different housing codes. Most codes also provide that each day's continued violation is a separate offense and a fine may be levied for each day a violation continues.

Threat of fine and possible imprisonment may appear sufficient to force an unwilling owner to bring his property up to the standards set by a housing code. But often the owner of the substandard property will treat a small fine as a cost of doing business. Up to now, the enforcement of housing regulations has been lax and the possibility that a prison sentence will be imposed is very slight.

PLACARDING AND VACATION

Besides providing for fine and/or imprisonment, housing codes usually contain a provision giving the power to placard and order the vacation of a dwelling whose owner has not complied with the order to repair or demolish. The placard may read: "This building is unfit for human habitation: the use or occupation of this building for human habitation is prohibited and unlawful." It is a valid exercise of the police power, and not a violation of the Fourteenth Amendment to the Constitution, to prohibit the use of a building until an order to repair has been complied with satisfactorily.

Placarding and an order to vacate add to the forces compelling an unwilling owner to bring his property up to standard. No rental income flows from property which has been placarded and vacated. A fine cannot be paid out of rent receipts and treated as a cost of doing business, for there is no longer any business.

But a placarded and vacant dwelling serves no useful purpose. The owner receives no income nor does he have a dwelling to live in. The closed unit decreases the supply of available dwelling units. Any families vacated from the structure must find quarters elsewhere. Although problems of relocation are not within the scope of this report, some housing codes provide for consideration of the matter.

LIENS FOR THE COST OF REPAIR OR DEMOLITION BY THE MUNICIPALITY

Besides being useless, a vacated and placarded building may contribute to neighborhood blight. A house with broken windows and a placarded front door may deter owners of adjacent property from repairing their dwellings. The presence of the empty building undoubtedly would hinder a neighborhood conservation program.

To deal with a reluctant owner in this case, many housing codes specify that "if the owner fails to comply with an order to repair, alter, or improve . . . a dwelling, the Building Commissioner may cause such dwelling to be repaired, altered or improved . . ." Noncompliance with a demolition order may result in demolition by the Building Commissioner. Similar provisions are included in the Housing Codes of Morristown, New Jersey; Sarasota, Florida; and Plainfield, New Jersey; to name a few.

Under these provisions, the municipality pays for the cost of repairs, alteration, or demolition. But "the amount of the cost of repairs, alterations, or improvements, or vacating and closing, or removal or demolition by the Building Commissioner shall be a lien against the real property upon which such cost was incurred . . ." The St. Louis, Missouri, Code provides for the submission of repair bills to the owner. If he fails to pay them, a lien results. The placing of such liens is generally accepted as a valid exercise of the police power. But policy considerations and legal questions arise as to their application.

The lien may put a burden on the property owner and may result in the forced sale of his property. A suggestion has been made that the repair or demolition expense should be collectible only at the time the property is transferred, or that the municipality furnish loans for further improvement. While these measures would lighten the property owner's burden, they would tie up municipal funds for an indefinite period of time. On balance, their use possibly may be considered desirable.

The imposition of a lien raises the question of priority. Can liens for the cost of repairs or demolition carried out by the municipality under a housing code be made superior to liens or mortgages existing at the time the repair or demolition was accomplished? Authority exists to the effect that prior mortgages may be subordinated to claims of laborers and to claims for improvement expenditures—because, as the court said, the mortgagee benefits by the greater value of the property on account of the labor and material; improvements should not be prevented by the fact that mortgages already exist on the property.

But in the case of *Central Savings Bank v. City of New York*, the New York Court of Appeals stated:

> It is no answer to this suggestion that the property has been improved to the extent of the expenditures. They may or may not add anything to the land value, and on foreclosure the sale may not bring one penny more to the mortgagee. . . . The improvements may or may not enhance the value of the mortgagee's security. . . . We may fairly assume that the lien given to the city for the improvements very materially affects the mortgage security, the property of the mortgagee, and abrogates the contract he has made with the mortgagor.

Here the New York Court held that the legislature has no power to impair the obligations of existing mortgages by enacting a statute which gives liens for labor and supplies priority over mortgage in force before the statute was enacted. In this case, the provisions impaired the obligations of contract in violation of the federal constitution and also violated the due process clause of the state constitution.

Some housing codes provide explicitly for priority of a lien for the cost of repairs or demolition. The Greenville, South Carolina, Housing Code states that the "lien shall be superior to all liens, thereon, except those for taxes and paving assessments, and which may, if necessary, be enforced through the Circuit or County Courts." But no general statement can be made about the validity of these liens in holding priority over existing liens in all jurisdictions. Competent legal advice as to how local courts have treated lien laws is essential in determining what a housing code can accomplish.

Lien provisions in a housing code seem desirable for a number of reasons. The building is repaired or demolished and the work is done. The dwelling does not add to blight in the area. The owner cannot complain, because his property has only been brought up to minimum standards set under the housing code. Actually, the threat that the city may repair or demolish and impose a lien may induce an owner to take action himself rather than let the city do the work.

The priority of these housing code liens, however, might tend to inhibit investments in mortgages, since the municipality could get a prior lien on any property in this manner. But such a threat is not considered to be substantial; the advantages of the lien law appear to outweigh the disadvantages.

Criticisms about Housing Codes

The recent trend toward housing codes has been accompanied by two major criticisms. One is that housing codes set up no more than minimum standards. The other is that they are inadequately enforced.

The criticism that codes specify standards which are too low is reflected in the 1954 hearings in Washington, D.C., on the proposed housing code. But census reports and other studies indicate that the conditions of much of our existing housing is *below* code standards.

The adequacy of code enforcement was recently criticized in the foreword to an issue of *Law and Contemporary Problems* (1955) on "Urban Housing and Planning." It was stated that the enforcement of housing and building legislation to date has been "most unsatisfactory." This also seems to be the viewpoint of The President's Advisory Committee on Government Housing Policies and Programs.

Yet "housing law enforcement" is an essential part of any program for urban renewal today. Enforcement, in fact, may "trigger a chain reaction" which might raise standards even higher than the minimum required.

Some codes, such as the Housing Code of Kansas City, Missouri make special provisions for area enforcement. Cities like Baltimore have found the "pilot program" (area-wide enforcement) most successful. Other cities continue to use the "individual structure throughout the city" (complaint) method.

Besides determining the type of enforcement approach to use, a municipality must also decide whether to enforce the code by utilizing branches of the city government or by creating new branches. Some codes provide for the creation of new hearing boards, departments of the city government, coordinating committees, and so on. The San Antonio, Texas, Housing Code (1955), creates a Citizens Housing Council and a Board of Housing Appeals. In June, 1947, Baltimore established the first Housing Court in the United States.

However, organized, an enforcement program must be vigorous. Otherwise even a good housing code will fail in its ultimate purpose.

24

Mᴏʀᴇ ᴛʜᴀɴ 7 million low-income Americans subsist on some form of public assistance, including some 1.1 million families with dependent children. As Alvin L. Schorr pointed out in a study, *Slums and Social Insecurity,* "Though less directly than public housing, to be sure, public assistance is the largest national program concerned with the housing needs of the poor."

What kind of housing does public assistance purchase? Less than 20 per cent of all public assistance families are believed to be in public housing. Aside from those in public housing, the vast majority of welfare families appear to be confined to the poorest housing available. In 1966, for example, 89 per cent of the families on welfare in Chicago and 85 per cent in Oakland, California, lived in so-called target areas as defined by the Office of Economic Opportunity. In New York City, an estimated one-quarter of married mothers and one-half the unmarried mothers receiving Aid for Families with Dependent Children live in "rooming houses considered undesirable for family living," according to a recent survey. In Maine, where many AFDC families live in rural areas, four out of five assisted families in 1960 lacked central heating in their homes; more than half lacked all three of the "essential" plumbing facilities: running water, bath, and exclusive use of a toilet.

Although national figures are lacking, the kind of random surveys cited above paint a bleak picture of how most welfare families live. They confirm what many public officials have long known: namely, that public funds have been subsidizing a substantial portion of the nation's slum housing.

This fact was dramatized in hearings last year by a Senate subcommittee examining the federal role in urban affairs. Subcommittee chairman Senator Abraham Ribicoff (D), Connecticut, said that the federal government—through its share in local public assistance programs—spends an estimated 2 billion to 4 billion dollars a year on slum housing. Even the lesser figure is considerably more than the federal government spends on all of its programs designed to provide *standard* housing for the poor.

The Ribicoff subcommittee heard many persons, in and out of government, testify

Rent Withholding, Rent Strikes, Tenant Unions, Mandatory Statewide Housing Standards

Reprinted from the Journal of Housing, *published by the National Association of Housing and Redevelopment Officials.* Vol. 24, June 1967, pp. 256–261.

on what could be done to improve housing conditions for the poor, especially the welfare poor. An obvious solution would be to increase the supply of public housing and to make such housing more accessible to welfare families, who presently make up 28 per cent of public housing tenants. Such a solution would probably be acceptable only if a scattered site approach were used. Present thinking by housing and welfare officials seems to indicate that the housing needs of the welfare poor can be met only through a combination of public housing and some yet-to-be found alternatives.

This article attempts to round up some of the ideas and techniques being tested out to help welfare families acquire standard housing. And, because the housing problems of welfare families are very often identical with the problems of all families affected by the current antipoverty struggle, the article also makes special reference to the emphasis on legal rights of the poor as they relate to tenant-landlord relationships, including cases where the landlord may be a local housing authority.

Shelter Allowances

In accordance with provisions of the Social Security Act, assistance in federal-state welfare programs must be given to recipients without stipulation as to how the money they receive is to be spent. Nonetheless, the assistance grant is based on the cost in the recipient's area of purchasing various essentials, including shelter. The "shelter allowance," theoretically, should enable him to purchase standard housing of sufficient size to accommodate his family in at least modest comfort.

In 29 states and the District of Columbia, however, the shelter allowance is based not on the actual cost of securing adequate housing but on what the recipient is actually paying for his quarters—*but only up to a set maximum*. A survey last year in the District of Columbia, where the shelter maximum has not been raised since 1953, found that 51 per cent of all families receiving Aid for Families with Dependent Children (AFDC) were paying more than the maximum for housing, not all of which was up to standard. In Texas, among Old Age Assistance recipients, the amount budgeted for shelter, fuel, and utilities was less than $30 per month in 97 per cent of the cases.

In order to purchase decent housing, then, many welfare families have had to skimp on food, clothing, and other necessities. Where racial bias keeps them locked in already overcrowded ghettos, they may even have to pay above the maximum for substandard housing, as the report from the District of Columbia shows.

While calling for increased maximum shelter allowances, welfare officials have generally been reluctant to exert pressure on landlords to fix up buildings occupied by welfare clients. In some cases, welfare departments have sought to move clients out of buildings owned by landlords who refuse to make needed repairs. Last April, welfare officials in Cleveland removed 12 families receiving AFDC from a complex of three tenement buildings that had been the subject of stories in the local press. But moving families out of dilapidated buildings, Cleveland officials found, was no assurance that the families would find any better housing elsewhere.

As Mr. Schorr noted in his report, most welfare agencies, even those which provide counselling in finding adequate quarters, regard housing "as not fundamentally their business." Social workers, they argue, are not trained to look for code violations nor do they have the authority to make landlords correct violations.

The tendency has been to cite the housing code enforcement agencies, where they exist, as responsible for seeing that welfare clients live in safe and sanitary surroundings. But a strong code enforcement program, by itself, can hurt the welfare tenant as much as it helps him by forcing an increase in rents as landlords bring their properties up to standard.

Rent Withholding

A technique that combines the efforts of code enforcement agencies and welfare departments is being tried in several states to help welfare families improve their housing conditions. Known as rent withholding, it enables welfare departments to hold back shelter allowances of occupants of dwellings with numerous and serious code violations. The Cook County (Chicago) department of public aid adopted such a policy without statutory authority in 1961 (a 1965 Illinois statute "legalized" the procedure) and New York codified the practice in 1962 in what is known as the Spiegel law. Rent withholding has also been tried or contemplated in a number of other states, including Pennsylvania, Ohio, and California.

In most cases, the shelter allowance is restored when the landlord brings his property up to standard, provided the welfare tenant is still in residence. In some cases, for example Pennsylvania, the money withheld is placed in an escrow account and returned to the landlord after necessary repairs are made. During the time rent is withheld, the tenant is protected against eviction for nonpayment. He is not protected, though, from eviction for other reasons.

Under the New York rent withholding law, the state is authorized to make direct payment of rent to the landlord in behalf of the welfare tenant. The law authorizes withholding of this money where the building or dwelling is found to be unsafe, unsanitary, or otherwise in violation of the housing code until these conditions are corrected. New York law further protects the tenant by preventing his eviction during the withholding action.

A major difficulty in administering rent withholding is the lack of coordination between various city agencies responsible for seeing that tenants are housed in safe and sanitary quarters. For example, the withholding of rents by the welfare department is contingent upon the code enforcement agencies' declaring buildings unfit. But code enforcement agencies in most cities are not staffed or funded to notify welfare officials when buildings in which their clients are living have been declared unfit.

In some cases in New York and Chicago, the withholding of rents, especially in buildings with a large proportion of welfare tenants, has forced properties into receivership. As pointed out by Philip Schorr in "Only as Much as the Rents Will Bear," the receiver is then denied the very rent monies he needs to bring the building up to standard because welfare departments have tended to treat receivers in the same manner that they have treated recalcitrant landlords.

Perhaps the biggest drawback to rent withholding is that it does not insure that the welfare tenant will be able to find decent housing within the maximum shelter allowance. It is essentially a negative step aimed at penalizing a landlord for failure to keep his property in adequate repair; it does not find adequate substitute housing for the tenant. In cities where adequate housing within a low-to-moderate price range is in short supply, the welfare tenant probably will be unable to find substitute housing.

According to the Bureau of Family Services of the Department of Health, Education and Welfare, rent withholding "is only workable when the state applies no maximum limit on the welfare grant and in communities that have protective housing codes well administered. . . . There must also be a reasonable vacancy rate in moderate rental housing so that the recipient is able to move elsewhere if the slum landlord fails to respond."

Despite pessimism about the effects of rent withholding, welfare officials in some cities have found it to be, if not an optimum weapon, at least partially effective in bringing recalcitrant landlords into line. Used in conjunction with concentrated neighborhood code enforcement and receivership programs, rent withholding may achieve the goal of bringing housing for welfare recipients up to minimum standards, at least.

In Chicago, for example, evidence turned up by city code inspectors in selected neighborhoods is turned over to the department of welfare. Under state law, the Cook County director of public aid can then notify landlords with numerous code violations that they have 10 days to clear up discrepancies before the welfare department begins withholding rent. Since July 1965, rents have been withheld under this program from owners of 219 buildings housing 1045 welfare families. More important, owners of more than 65 structures have brought their buildings up to standard after rents were withheld. Undoubtedly, many more landlords brought buildings up to standard to avoid the possibility of withholding.

Since the Spiegel law in New York took effect in 1962 allowing welfare departments to withhold rents under certain conditions, the New York City welfare department has withheld rents in more than 13,000 cases. In about half these cases, landlords brought eviction proceedings and were successful in winning judgments only about 40 per cent of the time. It might also be noted that attorneys furnished by the welfare department have appeared in nearly all cases on behalf of the tenant. The welfare department claims that in most cases where landlords did not take legal action, needed repairs were made and rent monies restored.

A number of urban areas in upstate New York have also reported successful use of the rent withholding device. Erie County (Buffalo) withheld rents in some 508 cases over an 18-month period, resulting in necessary repairs in about half the cases. Monroe County (Rochester) held back rents on 148 properties over a recent seven-month period with about the same degree of success. Although most reports indicate that rent withholding is more successful in cities with housing codes and inspectors than in rural areas, it is encouraging to note that, even in sparsely populated counties of New York, landlords have responded to warnings by welfare departments by making needed repairs.

Housing Standards

Despite its growing acceptance as a means of ensuring that welfare families have safe and sanitary housing, rent withholding is still not widespread. A major difficulty is the lack of state standards for what constitutes safe and sanitary housing. This was brought out in the Ribicoff hearings.

In order to remedy this situation, Senator Ribicoff has introduced a bill (S.589) that would amend the Social Security Act to "provide for the establishment or designation of a State authority or authorities which shall be responsible for establishing and maintaining standards of health and safety for the quarters or other premises in which recipients of aid to the aged, blind, disabled, and dependent children reside and which are secured on a rental basis. . . ." A similar bill was introduced last year in the House by Representative William B. Widnall, the ranking Republican on the housing subcommittee of the Committee on Banking and Currency. The Widnall bill was not acted upon, however.

By encouraging the establishment of minimum standards for housing occupied by welfare recipients, Senator Ribicoff presumably would be giving welfare agencies more leverage to cut off rents to owners of substandard buildings.

Rent Strikes

Sometimes confused with rent withholding is the rent strike. The two actions both seek the same objective by the same technique, i.e., denying the landlord his rents until he corrects serious deficiencies in his buildings.

The important difference, however, is that rent withholding, *per se*, is carried out by an official government agency—the welfare department—whereas a rent strike is initiated by the tenants themselves. In the case of a rent strike, the tenants cease paying rent to the landlord and instead pay the money into an escrow account. Barring any legal action, the landlord does not recover the money in the escrow account until he satisfies tenants' grievances over the condition and operation of the building.

The rent strike can be used in a greater variety of ways than rent withholding by a welfare agency. For one thing, it can be used more effectively against substandard buildings in which only a few tenants might be welfare recipients. Thus, it can deprive a recalcitrant landlord of all rents, not merely those paid through the welfare department. Further, a rent strike may be directed against any type of landlord—a local housing authority as well as a private property. Rent strikes or threatened strikes have been used to dramatize tenant grievances in public housing projects in St. Louis and San Francisco, among other places.

Finally, not all grievances of welfare tenants have to do with substandard physical conditions. Rent strikes against housing authorities, for example, have also been threatened to protest such grievances as lack of privacy, arbitrary rules, and inadequate police protection.

Since a rent strike does not operate as an official, legalized process, it must rely on a great deal of organization and cohesiveness among the tenants of a building. It also requires certain skills and resources that are often beyond the reach of low-income tenants. In Chicago, for example, it took the resources of Dr. Martin Luther King's Southern Christian Leadership Conference and organizers from the Industrial Union Department of the AFL-CIO to organize the city's first massive rent strikes, the results of which have been described as inconclusive. As Nicholas von Hoffman of the *Washington Post* has noted, tenant organizations have a tendency to "fall apart after the first excitement is over and the dullness of . . . slum life re-impresses itself." Moreover, because of the "outside the law" character of the rent strike, tenants often find themselves in jail as well as out on the street.

New York amended its Spiegel law in 1965 to permit rent strikes under certain situations. The city of New York has since listed 57 separate grounds, the existence of any one of which in a building would permit tenants to withhold rent without being subject to eviction or prosecution for nonpayment. Charles G. Moerdler, the city's building commissioner, estimates that 11.5 million dollars in rents could have been withheld by tenants last year if full advantage had been taken of the law. The city is currently engaged in a pilot project in the Bronx to develop a three-part inspection form to help landlords and tenants determine which violations in their buildings are rent-impairing. In many buildings, according to Mr. Moerdler, it is only a matter of one or two violations that could be cleared up quickly and inexpensively.

Under the new law, tenants can stop paying rent only if the violation or violations were not caused by their own actions. Furthermore, the landlord has to have been officially notified of the violation or violations by the city and given six months in which to correct them. After the tenant begins withholding rent, the landlord may still institute court action to evict the tenant. In such a case, the tenant must deposit with the court the amount of rent involved. Should the landlord win the case, the rent money is restored to him; should he lose, the money is refunded to the tenant, who is not required to pay any further rent until correction of all rent-impairing violations.

The Pennsylvania law that allows the welfare department to withhold shelter allowances also permits non-welfare tenants to withhold rent after a building or dwelling is declared unfit for human habitation. The tenant, however, must place the money he would normally pay in rent into an escrow account. When the landlord corrects the conditions that caused the building to be declared unfit, the escrow money is turned over to him. If, within a year, the building is not certified as fit for human occupancy, the escrow money is refunded to the tenant, who pays no further rent until the building is certified for occupancy.

Where some legal sanction exists, the rent strike is a potentially powerful weapon for forcing recalcitrant landlords to bring their buildings up to standard. It requires, however, strong tenant organizations that can provide not only legal services to help tenants assert their rights but also incentive for the tenants to stick it out in a building until the cause of the strike is adjudicated. One of the major problems associated with any rent withholding action is getting the tenant to stay put, for, once he chooses to leave a building, the case against the landlord evaporates.

Tenant Unions

Recognizing the need for strengthening tenant organizations in low-income neighborhoods, civil rights and anti-poverty groups, with an assist from organized labor, have developed an unusual hybrid—the tenant union. Combining labor union with community action tactics, the new tenant unions have sought to bargain collectively with owners or managers of groups of buildings over the terms of occupancy. Where successful, the unions have negotiated "contracts" covering such items as rent levels, maintenance, and grievance procedures.

The tenant union movement started last summer during Chicago's rent strikes. Its chief sponsors have been Dr. Martin Luther King's Southern Christian Leadership Conference and the Industrial Union Department of the AFL-CIO, which, through the United Auto Workers, supplied experienced organizers and financial backing.

From the formation of the first union in April, the tenant union movement seemed to gain rapidly, notably among tenants of buildings in so-called fringe areas (on the verge of becoming slums). By July, there were seven tenants unions in the city ranging in size from 300 to 2000 members. Rather than concentrating on single buildings, the unions sought membership among residents of several buildings under common owner-ship or management. By the end of the sum-mer, the unions had managed to negotiate six major contracts, prompting one real estate broker to foresee the "beginning of a very serious revolution."

In one instance, a union representing 1000 tenants negotiated with a landlord a proce-dure for handling grievances that would give the tenants the right to withhold rents while their complaint was being processed. An-other union won the right to have any impasse in future negotiations subjected to binding arbitration by a neutral party.

Most real estate operators seem to take a view toward tenant unions that has perhaps been summed up best by Jay J. Strauss, a Chicago realtor. Writing in the May-June issue of the *Journal of Property Management*, he said, "I feel strongly that the tenant union movement is probably the most im-portant single threat to the rental housing industry existing today."

Not all property managers, however, feel this way. John Condor, a partner in the Chicago firm of Condor and Costalis, said after his firm had signed a contract covering some 2000 tenants in 25 buildings owned by the company and another 20 managed by it: "I am more or less happy about it . . . this neighborhood is in danger of rapidly deteri-orating and I feel the best possible way to save it is through community organization."

While private real estate operators have been either unalterably opposed to tenant unions or more or less resigned to them, an important non-profit housing sponsor sees a lot of good coming out of these fledgling organizations. Speaking at the Building Re-search Institute seminar in Washington in May, Victor R. de Grazia, executive vice-president of the Kate Maremont Foundation, said that, in his opinion, there is nothing better than a tenants union to lay down the law to other tenants. In other words, a tenants union can work to the benefit of landlord, whether he be a public housing authority or a private operator, by making tenants observe the maintenance provisions of a contract that they, themselves, had a part in drawing up.

What Will Work?

Whether rent withholding, rent strikes, tenant unions, state standards—or all of them together—will make a significant im-provement in the housing conditions of wel-fare recipients and other low-income families is problematical. For the time being, these techniques can only be seen as random tactics in a grand strategy that has yet to be formulated for ridding the nation of sub-standard housing and providing low-income families with enough money to live in the standard shelter that should replace the slums. What is apparent currently is that this evolving strategy includes government inter-vention in traditional tenant-landlord re-lations and an active role on the part of tenants in deciding how they are to be housed.

WORKING IN CLOSE cooperation with a neighborhood anti-poverty group, as well as other city agencies, the Division of Housing Improvement of the city of New Orleans is engaged in what has been called a total neighborhood participation approach to stemming blight in one of the city's most important working class districts. The approach is unusual, if not unique, in many respects: it requires that tenants, as well as landlords, assume responsibility for keeping their homes safe and sanitary; it sets short-term goals for achieving decent living conditions that even the lowest-income family can reach without hardship; and it depends more on neighborhood pride than on official coercion to achieve compliance with the city's housing code and other relevant ordinances.

The experiment is being carried out in the Irish Channel district, a strip of land along the Mississippi River containing some 5000 dwellings. In close proximity to the commercial heart of New Orleans, the Irish Channel was, until not long ago, a modest but stable workingman's neighborhood. There was a great deal of pride in living in the "Channel" and a high incidence of homeownership. There are still some important advantages to living there: in addition to its proximity to downtown and other jobs, it is well served by the city's excellent public transit system (which has preserved the 10-cent fare); it has an ample supply of decent and moderately priced housing, with rentals ranging from $60 to $90 per month.

Nevertheless, in recent years, the Irish Channel has been declining. Many of the longtime residents have gone, bringing in families of relatively lower incomes and job skills. The neighborhood is racially integrated and, although the different racial groups appear to be getting along as neighbors, there is a danger that the Channel could become a ghetto. Where there was once a great deal of homeownership, there is now mostly rental properties. The neighborhood, indeed, is one of seven target areas for the poverty program in New Orleans.

Since May 1, 1968, the housing improvement division has had a housing inspector working full-time in the Irish Channel and recently added a second inspector. In addition to coordinating his work with other city

25

Tenant Responsibility, Short-term Goals, Self-help, Neighborhood Pride

Christopher J. Bellone

Reprinted from the Journal of Housing, published by the National Association of Housing and Redevelopment Officials. Vol. 25, October 1968, pp. 522–526.

agencies, the inspector works closely with the Irish Channel Action Foundation (ICAF), a group supported by private funds as well as by the Office of Economic Opportunity. The inspector is also in close contact with residents of the neighborhood; when he is not out conducting inspections or assisting tenants and landlords in other ways, he is on call at a centrally located neighborhood center.

The experiment in total neighborhood participation in housing improvement has concentrated, initially, on a 53-block area containing about one-fourth of all dwellings in the Irish Channel. Plans call for expanding the program to the remaining area of the neighborhood, once all phases have been tested in the smaller area.

Survey of Conditions

The first phase of the experimental program consisted of a survey of housing conditions in the 53-block area to determine the relative deterioration of property in the neighborhood. The survey was carried on simultaneously with a drive to clear the area of abandoned automobiles and accumulations of trash and to identify vacant lots that could be turned over to the community for recreation and other social purposes.

The structures in the 53-block area are generally detached or duplex frame houses, with some four-plexes and multiple dwellings housing up to 20 families. As noted above, rentals are mostly in the $60 to $90 per month range. The survey covered 985 dwellings, of which 336 were rated "good", 526 "fair" (needed some repairs), and the remaining 123 "bad" (needed major repairs). The ratings were based on a thorough exterior check of the houses. Assisting in making the survey were ICAF community organizers, who had received instruction from the city housing inspector.

Following the survey, which took about six weeks, the housing inspector started a series of regular inspections. In this phase, he has notified tenants of violations for which they are responsible and either he or one of the community organizers has offered advice or assistance on how the tenants could make their homes more livable.

Building Owners Notified

Once the tenants have corrected their violations, the building owner is contacted. He is given a definite time period in which to bring his property up to code standards or face the possibility of being brought into court.

In the Irish Channel program, no violation against a property owner is filed with city hall until each tenant has made an effort to improve his living conditions. As a result, instead of being viewed as an attack on property owners, code enforcement becomes a cooperative effort by the city, tenants, and property owners to improve the neighborhood. The results of this approach have been encouraging.

For example, in addition to making inspections on the 123 "bad" structures in the area, the housing inspector has been asked to perform 47 inspections or reinspections on units rated good or fair. These came at the request of tenants and owners. Any tenant or owner, in fact, may call upon the housing inspector for specific instructions on improvements he can make, regardless of the condition of his home or property. The idea is to have as many people as possible become actively engaged in improving their own block.

Reinspections at the end of the second six-week period showed work was in progress on 143 housing units, including 96 units in 34 buildings rated bad in the survey. An additional 18 of the bad houses had been vacated and one had been demolished. In some cases, tenants had been encouraged and assisted in moving out because the landlord refused to repair the building. It has since been estimated that about three-fourths of the worst houses are on the way to becoming more livable and in only one instance has a landlord had to be hauled into court.

The Irish Channel program actually tries to avoid bringing tenants or landlords into court. Nevertheless, if the landlord is not persuaded by the efforts of his tenants to make some repairs of his own, he is notified that his property will be reinspected in 30 to 60 days. If the needed repairs are not substantially under way by then, the inspector will contact the owner by telephone or in person to find out why. Sometimes the inspector finds a genuine case of financial hardship and will try to counsel the landlord on how to get the necessary financing. Often, however, the job of repairing the building seems so vast that the property owner simply doesn't know where to begin. The inspector will perhaps encourage him to get started on one relatively small item, such as replacing rotted weatherboards. Once the owner does get started, he usually moves on to making the major repairs.

Abandoned Cars

In addition to checking the condition of housing in the Irish Channel, an important part of the block-by-block survey was the identification of abandoned cars and trash accumulations. The survey spotted 169 derelict vehicles in the neighborhood. A police officer assigned to the housing improvement division during the survey period placed stickers on each of the cars giving the registered owner three days in which to have it removed. By the end of the six weeks, all but three of the cars had disappeared from the neighborhood. Through the cooperation of the people in the neighborhood, the three remaining derelict autos were traced to an owner in a public housing project in another neighborhood. He was then given a specific time to remove them.

Cooperation between the people in the neighborhood and the housing inspector has caught on so well that the sticker campaign has since been dropped. Now when a car is abandoned in the neighborhood, the housing inspector can count on someone from the neighborhood calling up and reporting the owner. The owner is then notified to have his car removed.

During the block-by-block survey, accumulations of trash and garbage around houses was also noted. Residents of these houses were informed that they were responsible for removing these refuse piles within five to 10 days. Since many of the residents could not afford to hire a truck to haul the refuse away, the city sanitation department scheduled "crash trash pickups" on each block. Because of the city's shortage of funds, special prison crews were assigned to the trucks.

On the special pick-up days, residents were asked to put all of their refuse on the street. Anyone failing to put his refuse out on the day the sanitation truck sweeps through his block is required to pay for its removal. The crash program has been so successful that a private contractor has offered to make extra trash pick-ups on certain blocks for a minimal fee per family.

Recreation Space

Getting rid of the abandoned cars and trash helped with another part of the program, making more space available for recreation purposes. During the six-week survey, 14 vacant lots were located, most of them littered with old cars and refuse. Two of these have since been cleared, graded, and surveyed for a fence. One of the two lots belonged to a private owner who was per-

suaded to make his lot available for a summer recreation program for neighborhood children after residents, through their block council, agreed to clear the lot and obtain liability insurance on its use.

In another case, the housing inspector discovered that one of the vacant lots had been given to the city several years ago but that a junk dealer had been using it all along. The dealer was asked to vacate the premises or face a court order.

All of this happened within about a 12-week period in a neighborhood that had been trying for over two years to acquire some play space for its children. Although recreation space remains critically short, a start has finally been made through the self-help efforts of the community and with the cooperation of the city's housing division. A generalized fear that their neighborhood was in danger of becoming a full-blown slum encouraged Irish Channel residents to organize around a program that they viewed as crucial.

Working with ICAF Staff

What has also helped make the experiment in neighborhood improvement successful has been the weaving in of code enforcement with the overall program of the Irish Channel Action Foundation. The ICAF staff not only has become familiar with the city housing code but has also helped educate tenants about the code. In addition, the housing improvement program has been widely publicized by ICAF community organizers and by the housing inspector.

Education begins with the community organizer's visit notifying the tenant of violations uncovered by the survey that he is responsible for correcting; or it may start at a "bull session" at a block council meeting, with the housing inspector leading the discussion. The emphasis on the tenant's responsibilities under the existing housing code is seen as giving the tenant the necessary leverage or bargaining power when it comes to having the landlord carry out his obligations.

There is still another reason for educating the tenant on his own responsibilities under the code. The New Orleans Property Owners Association has organized a city-wide tenant referral system. A tenant who has a history of abusing property soon finds himself blacklisted when it comes to seeking decent housing.

Concurrent with the educational program has been a public relations campaign to give the widest possible exposure to the Irish Channel experiment in neighborhood improvement. In the neighborhood, itself, the May, June, and July issues of the *St. Thomas Newsletter*, a mimeographed paper that reaches some 1900 households, have featured the housing inspector's presence and activities and listed the types of conditions tenants would be responsible for correcting.

The special projects department of Channel 4, one of the local television stations, prepared a documentary on housing conditions in New Orleans that highlighted activities in the Irish Channel. Walter Randall, the housing inspector in the area, was featured. The *New Orleans States-Item* ran a feature series on the Irish Channel target area that included a description of how Mr. Randall locates and obtains permission to clear vacant lots for vest pocket park and recreation development and an interview with a family that he referred to the neighborhood center's family counseling unit. *Dixie-Roto*, a Sunday supplement, has collected feature material on how a group of residents cleared a vacant lot for a playground.

The publicity not only has helped sell the code enforcement program but has made it much easier for the ICAF community organizers to reach residents in the community. When an organizer contacts residents about conditions that need correcting, he is also able to tell them about the various programs of the local anti-poverty agency. Many families reached for the first time as a result of the code enforcement program have been referred to other agencies at the neighborhood center for assistance with problems not directly related to housing conditions. Others have been encouraged to join block councils where they can work with their neighbors on constructive solutions to neighborhood problems.

Inspector in the Neighborhood

What has undoubtedly contributed to the good reception code enforcement is receiving in the Irish Channel is the location of the housing inspector in the neighborhood. Mr. Randall is available at least sometime during the day at the neighborhood center to receive calls from tenants whose homes he has inspected, from landlords who have destructive tenants, from tenants and landlords who request inspections, and from others who seek his assistance on a variety of problems.

Mr. Randall's presence at the center has also enabled him to work closely with other social service and neighborhood agencies headquartered there. For example, when he found one woman who was about to be evicted from her home because of bad housekeeping habits, he was able to refer her to the family counseling service, which helped her improve her housekeeping skills. As a result, the eviction notice was rescinded.

In addition to working with the agencies at the center, Mr. Randall serves as an effective liaison between the neighborhood and the city government. He was at least in part responsible for having a police officer assigned to putting stickers on abandoned cars and for having special sanitation crews assigned to clearing the neighborhood of accumulated refuse. He is credited with persuading the city recreation department to deliver river sand and to promise equipment and supervision for the vest pocket playgrounds that were created by clearing vacant lots of trash and abandoned cars.

One of the more interesting episodes demonstrating the good communications that have been established between the residents and the housing inspector concerns a condemned house that was being used as a base of operations for a dope pusher and fence for shoplifters. Once this information was passed on to Mr. Randall, he saw to it that the house was immediately boarded up.

He has also devoted a good deal of time to giving instruction and personal assistance in home maintenance skills. When the Irish Channel program started. Mr. Randall was told to "do whatever you can." This has meant showing residents how to paint walls, put down linoleum flooring, fix screen doors, install cut-off valves, etc. He also provides information on how to finance major home improvements or buy property. In some cases, where the tenant happens to be a "little old lady" or otherwise unable to make his own repairs, the inspector has picked up a hammer and done the job himself. The aim, though, is to get residents to do their own repairs and maintenance.

Getting Results

The core of the experiment in a total neighborhood approach to improved living conditions has been the use of short-term code enforcement. The term means the setting of early-date deadlines that will elicit fast action by tenants and landlords; periodic checks are made to see that they are meeting these deadlines. Within reasonable limits, it is the tenant or the landlord who sets his own time schedule for improvements. Failure to meet these deadlines can result in a fine.

In addition to the threat of fines, the city has sought compliance with the housing code by offering awards to tenants and landlords who show outstanding voluntary compliance. A recent candidate for one of the housing division's certificates of merit has been a landlord with a long case record of complaints filed against his properties. Since the program began, he has completely rehabilitated six of his worst units.

Also helping to make the program successful has been the setting of realistic goals for tenants to reach. Repairs expected of a tenant are seldom costly unless he has torn holes in the walls or been responsible for other major property abuses. Generally, the tenant is expected to (a) remove trash, garbage, or other debris from the premises;

(b) maintain the interior of the building in a clean and sanitary condition; (c) obtain proper receptacles for disposing of garbage and trash; (d) provide shut-off valves for gas fixtures such as heaters and stoves; (e) restore any equipment or part of the dwelling that has been willfully destroyed. Tenants are also encouraged to repair broken windows and screens, paint walls or floors, install proper floor covering, and make their homes as attractive as possible.

The landlord is held responsible for the general condition of his building. This includes replacing rotten weather boards; providing sufficient plumbing, heating, and electrical facilities; and repairing or replacing interior and exterior walls, rotten plaster, leaking roofs, etc.

The results of the program, thus far, show that voluntary compliance in the neighborhood is exceeding anything obtained from past code enforcement efforts, which mainly involved bringing recalcitrant landlords into court. In the past, rather than make necessary repairs, landlords tended to blame tenants for damage and seek, with a great deal of success, to get continuances of their cases in the courts. Tenants, in turn, resented the fact that landlords seldom made repairs. They showed this resentment by their own lack of interest in maintaining their surroundings. One woman, in fact, had allowed some 800 pounds of trash to accumulate in her apartment and had made no effort to clean it out until Mr. Randall, the housing inspector, appeared on the scene.

The results of this experiment have shown the effectiveness of encouraging landlords and tenants to work together. It has also proved what can be done when city agencies and neighborhood organizations cooperate. The division of housing improvement is now drawing up plans to offer the same cooperative services to the other six target areas in New Orleans.

Selected References

References to Chapters 16–25

Advisory Council on Intergovernmental Relations, *Building Codes*, Washington, D.C., 1966.

American Society of Planning Officials, *Regulatory Devices*, Chicago, 1969.

Colling, Hal, "Who's to Blame for the Building Code Mess?" *House and Home*, January, April, June, 1964.

Journal of Housing, The, "Multi-unit Licensing, A Slum Control Device," April, 1958.

Journal of Housing, The, "Rent Withholding as an Aid to Housing Code Enforcement," May 1968.

National Commission on Urban Problems,

1. *Building the American City*, Part III, Codes and Standards, Washington, D.C., 1968.
2. *Costs and Other Effects on Owners and Tenants of Repairs Required Under Housing Code Enforcement Programs*, Washington, D.C., 1968.
3. Frank P. Grad, *Legal Remedies for Housing Code Violations*, Research Report No. 14, Washington, D.C., 1968.
4. Robert Hale and Aliceann Fritschler, *Present State of Housing Code Enforcement*, Research report prepared by National Association of Housing and Redevelopment Officials, Washington, D.C., 1968.
5. *Hearings Before the National Commission on Urban Problems*, Vol. 2, Los Angeles; June-July 1967, San Francisco. U.S. Government Printing Office, Washington, D.C., 1968. (See also Volumes 3 and 5.)
6. Allen D. Manvel, *Local Land and Building Regulation*, Research Report No. 6, Washington, D.C., 1968.
7. Eric Mood, Barnet Lieberman, and Oscar Sutermeister, *Housing Code Standards; Models for Housing Code Administration*. Research Report No. 19, Washington, D.C., 1969.
8. Joseph S. Slavet, *Costs and Other Effects of Removing Housing Code Violations*, Research Report, Washington, D.C., 1969.
9. Joseph S. Slavet and Melvin R. Levin, *New Approaches to Housing Code Administration*, Research Report No. 17, Washington D.C., 1969.

Taxation

MANIPULATION OF URBAN land use and development by tax policy is of recent origin in the United States. To date, the most dramatic forms of real-property-related tax policy have appeared in the Internal Revenue Code and in administrative interpretations by the federal Internal Revenue Service. Most of these federal policies are familiar; they include the capital gains tax as applied to real property, accelerated depreciation, and deductions for property taxes and mortgage interest. The policy behind these devices is rarely explicit but clearly appears to bear on the supply, cost, and welfare of real estate in general and housing in particular. The significance of these devices for particular land use aggregations (or cities) over time has never been thoroughly investigated nor understood. Similarly, the effects of these policies are largely unknown. Many of the thirty-eight states with income taxes parallel some of the federal real-property policies and thus add to the impact of upper-level government policy on urban land use.

It is at the local, municipal, and metropolitan levels that tax policy related to land use is still very much in flux. Within the past decade there has been substantial evidence that much more serious thought is being devoted to the relation between taxation and urban development than ever before. This increase in concern is separate from, although related to, the development of the urban economy and of the low-to-middle-income housing supply by fairly long-established devices such as outright subsidy and property-tax exemption or abatement. Most of the recent municipal-level thinking about property tax and land use is of a mild reform nature, focusing on improvement in the assessment procedure, on questions of how improvements to structures—particularly old residential structures—should be assessed, on the assessment of subdivision lots still in the hands of the subdivider, on the treatment of tax-exempt property by exemption removal or *in lieu* payments, and on use of the special assessment procedure. Under pressure from large-scale private builders a drastic version of tax reform, described as a land tax or site-value tax, is under serious consideration, although not yet at the operational level. This tax, once referred to as the "single tax" of Henry George, is in use in other countries, including Western

Canada, South Africa, Australia, and New Zealand. In the United States, a modified form of the land tax, establishing different tax rates for land and buildings, has been in operation in Pittsburgh since 1913.

Aside from the perennial property tax problems of uniformity and equity, the policy objectives of municipal-level tax manipulation seem to be threefold. First, concern has been with slum prevention and deterioration control. Closely allied to this problem has been the maintenance and preservation of the central city's core, with particular emphasis on the central business district. Third, but rising in importance, have been the linked metropolitan development difficulties of land speculation and sprawl.

The readings in this Part deal with the tax forms and problems mentioned in the preceding paragraphs. It will appear that there are serious omissions on the subject of taxation and metropolitan area land use. These omissions are calculated and are covered, in large part, in the next section of the book, which deals with metropolitan development.

Although the literature in the field of land use and taxation was scant for many years, that deficiency is gradually being rectified. The list of selected references, nearly all recent, will attest to this trend. The readings themselves, combined with the reference materials, should give the researcher, public official, and student a good grasp of this part of the field of urbanism and urban land economics.

Despite the fact that there are only nine articles in Part III, they have been separated into two groups. This division sets off to better advantage the readings which concentrate on the controversial site-value tax in the second group. While there is some discussion of this tax in the readings of the first group, such discussion is mixed in with other tax policy proposals. In general, the first group tries to give some of the best recent thought on the total gamut of tax policies that are thought suitable to a land use control function. In all of the readings on taxation the thinking of the traditional economist is more evident than in other Parts of this book. As in the other Parts, the thought of lawyers and planners is woven in with that of the economists.

26

THE SUBJECT of land use control normally evokes notions of zoning, subdivision control, or some similar application of the police power. Some persons recognize that a wider range of powers exists capable of affecting land use, such as the power of eminent domain, governmental proprietary power, the power of governmental spending, and the persuasive ability of the executive. Unfortunately, however, the power to tax is rarely recognized as an available land use control device;[1] and rarer still are examples and programs which use the taxing power to achieve desired land use objectives.

The Taxing Power as a Land Use Control Device

Orlando E. Delogu

This article appeared originally in Vol. 45, No. 2, of the Denver Law Journal. *Copyright 1968 by the* Denver Law Journal, *University of Denver (Colorado Seminary), College of Law. Reproduced by permission.*

The Failure To Recognize the Power To Tax as a Land Use Control Device

The extent of the failure to recognize the relationship between the power to tax and land use objectives is best evidenced by the almost total lack of coordination in municipal government between property tax assessment policy and land use planning policy. Local tax assessors, acutely aware of revenue needs, tend to value lands not at their present use value but at their potential market value if used in some problematical highest and best capacity. For example, agricultural or open land in the path of future subdivision development will often be valued as land capable of being subdivided many years before the area is actually needed or desired for that purpose. This practice raises the tax burden substantially and often forces subdivision, simply to pay the tax when both the owner of the land and the local planning agency may have desired to retain the area in its open or agricultural state. The past and present disappearance of many rich agricultural areas and scenic open-space or wooded areas near growing urban and suburban complexes can be attributed in part to these assessment practices. The

irony of the situation is made complete when we recognize that the community may (now or in the future) be spending a portion of its tax revenue to acquire land for park and open-space purposes, which the land use planner has recommended. In this situation there is not only a failure to use the power to tax positively to achieve land use control objectives but taxing policy is actually at cross purposes with and serves to defeat land use objectives.

Another aspect of local government tax policy which has a negative effect on local land use objectives is the practice of immediately raising the assessed value and thus raising the property tax on properties which have recently completed improvements. These improvements may have been made as a matter of personal or civic pride, in response to the enforcement of a building or housing code, or as part of a neighborhood rehabilitation program. Whatever the motivation, the fact is that a desired land use objective, *viz.*, the care, maintenance, and improvement of real property, is less likely to occur because an immediate and direct penalty attaches. The greater the extent to which the land use objective is sought to be advanced (the higher the value of the improvement), the greater is the penalty.

1 This paper makes no attempt to lay out or justify the historical and changing relationship between taxation as a revenue-gathering device and taxation as a regulatory device. Instead it assumes what to almost all authorities in the field of taxation is self-evident, i.e., that both of these goals are explicit or implicit parts of every form of taxation historically used or in use today.

These examples clearly evidence a failure either to perceive the relationship between taxing power and land use objectives or to reconcile tax policy with these objectives. Theoretically, tax policies having negative effects on land use objectives are capable of being corrected, and, perhaps of greater importance, a range of positive uses of the taxing power can be developed which will encourage acceptance and achievement of land use objectives. Both devices which eliminate (or minimize) existing conflicts between taxing and land use policy and positive programs capable of using the power to tax to achieve land use objectives can be designed. Whether or not these devices and programs, as simple as some of them may be, will be used is another question—a question of political will.

Correcting Conflicts between Tax and Land Use Policies

In many instances the conflict between local tax assessors and land use planners could be remedied by legislation which required that the market value of comprehensively zoned land, and thus its assessment value, reflect only those alternative uses permitted under the applicable zoning ordinance instead of those land uses which necessarily presuppose a zoning change. California has enacted legislation specifically aimed at achieving this end:

> In the assessment of land, the assessor shall consider the effect upon value of any enforceable restrictions to which the use of the land may be subjected. Restrictions shall include but are not necessarily limited to zoning restrictions limiting the use of land and any recorded contractual provisions limiting the use of lands entered into with a governmental agency pursuant to state laws or applicable local ordinances. There shall be a rebuttable presumption that restrictions will not be removed or substantially modified in the predictable future and that they will substantially equate the value of the land to the value attributable to the legally permissible use or uses.

A similar Florida statute directs that "[a]ll lands being used for agricultural purposes shall be assessed as agricultural lands . . . regardless of the fact that any or all of said lands are embraced in a plat of a subdivision or other real estate development." These statutes do not conflict with constitutional or statutory requirements of tax uniformity if these requirements are interpreted (as they usually are) to mean that taxes must be uniform only within reasonably differentiated classes and categories of property. The process of zoning establishes such classes and categories of property. Consequently, the highest and best land use permitted in one zoning district (and thus the property tax burden imposed) may be substantially different from that of another district without breaching the concept of uniformity. Uniformity will only demand that all land similarly zoned be similarly taxed.

The conflict between local tax policy and land use objectives caused by the immediate upward reassessment of properties which are improved seems capable of being remedied by establishing a period of years during which the assessed valuation on improved or repaired properties would not be raised. This time period would allow repair and improvement costs to be assimilated into the fair market value of the whole property before a reassessment takes place; and in the case of commercial and industrial properties a major portion of these costs could be recovered under existing depreciation, improvement write-off, and maintenance and repair expense provisions of federal and state tax codes. Thus, tax policy would become an incentive rather than a deterrent to achieving land use objectives. Existing Wisconsin tax legislation, which includes a lengthy justification of the substantive tax provision and a statement of the desired land use objectives, takes this approach exactly:

a. Any city, town or village may establish a conservation area (hereafter in this subsection referred to as "area") by resolution of its governing board. Such resolution shall state:

1. The boundaries of the area;
2. The substandard, outworn or outmoded condition of the industrial, commercial or residential buildings in the area;

3. That such conditions impair the economic value of the area;
4. That the continuation of such conditions depreciates values, impairs investments and reduces the capacity to pay taxes;
5. That it is necessary to create, with proper safeguards, inducements and opportunities for the employment of private investment and equity capital in the replanning, rehabilitation and conservation of the area;
6. That through rehabilitation, conservation or replanning the area may improve the general welfare of the city, town or village and protect its tax base:
7. That by virtue of additions, betterments, or alterations made to the structures in the area, the health, safety, morals, welfare and reasonable comfort of the citizens will be protected and enhanced.

b. Any improvement made by an owner commenced after the adoption of a local ordinance or resolution, through private investment to any existing completed structure in the area shall be deemed to be made for the purposes and objectives of the area and shall be excluded by the assessor for such locality in arriving at the assessment of the real estate, but not to exceed the maximum amount established by the municipality in the exemption period specified in par. (c), provided that the actual cost of such additions, betterments or alterations to the owner of the property is $200 or greater.

c. The assessment exemption granted by this subsection may continue for five assessment years and shall not be extended beyond that time. The maximum value of any assessment exclusion for said five-year period shall be either $1,000 or 10 per cent of the value of the improved property.

The approach which this statute embodies also does not appear to conflict with tax uniformity requirements. A reasonable classification of property is established (improvements to existing structures) to which a different assessment or tax policy may legitimately be applied. Furthermore, uniformity requirements have never been interpreted to mean that the legislature is deprived of its power completely to exempt certain classes of property from taxation.

Positive Programs Which Use the Taxing Power To Achieve Land Use Goals

In addition to eliminating tax policies having a deleterious effect on land use, tax programs can be devised to facilitate the achievement of planning goals. Some of these programs appear quite innocuous in scope while others are more far-reaching. Most will require legislative action to bring them into being. However, some may require nothing more than appropriate action by the Internal Revenue Service or by state departments of taxation. A commercial or industrial taxpayer, for example, could be allowed to have the benefit of an accelerated depreciation schedule under federal and state income tax codes for expenditures which serve stated land use objectives. This approach was taken by the federal government to spur investment spending during the early and mid-1960's. It seems particularly well-suited to situations where repairs or improvements as part of an area rehabilitation program are desired or where installation of costly air or water pollution control equipment is desired. Wisconsin has enacted legislation limited to stimulating construction of waste treatment plants and purchase of pollution abatement equipment. The legislation provides for a complete write-off in the year of cash disbursement of the full cost of such equipment or construction. Similar federal or state legislation could be broadened to benefit a much wider range of land use objectives. Furthermore, this approach could be extended to individual income taxpayers who repair or improve their properties in accordance with a publicly declared land use objective by allowing them to deduct all or part of the cost of these repairs or improvements on their individual federal and state income tax returns.

Another opportunity to using the taxing system to achieve land use objectives arises when the public's interest in a given piece of land can be fully satisfied by acquiring less than the "fee" interest in that piece of land, i.e., purchasing an easement. Easement purchase is widely advocated by planners today, and an increasing number of governments (local, state, and federal) have used this device to gain access to or over certain lands, to preserve scenic areas, or to conserve marsh, woodland, and open-space areas.

Permitting private landowners to treat payments received for relinquished property rights as a capital gain instead of ordinary income would tend to encourage the sale of easements to agencies of government. There is some indication that such treatment would be allowed for the sale of a perpetual affirmative easement;[2] but, if the easement purchase device is to become a useful tool in the hands of governmental agencies, every conceivable type of easement (positive, negative, perpetual, and those for a term of years) should be accorded capital gains treatment.

A more far-reaching tax program which seeks to achieve land use objectives is one which frankly recognizes that uniformity may not be desirable in all situations. For example, Wisconsin's taxation of forest crop lands largely frees these lands from general property taxes but subjects the lumber crop to taxation at the time of severance (or harvest). Forest crop land is statutorily defined and represents a category of real property into which any landowner may place his lands. The purpose of the program is to

> encourage a policy of preserving from destruction or premature cutting the remaining forest growth in this state, and of reproducing and growing for the future adequate crops of forest products on lands not more useful for other purposes, so that such lands shall continue to furnish recurring forest crops for commercial use. . . .

By removing the burden of general property taxation based on some present market value which looks to a more or less future speculative or potential highest and best use, the taxing system induces landowners to use their land for forest crop purposes.

Recently, New Jersey took a similar

---

[2] However, even as to this type of easement, the suggested tax treatment is not completely assured, but turns on a limited number of Internal Revenue Rulings and possibly on the quantum of rights relinquished by the landowner.

approach to meet a desired land use objective. The state constitution was amended to allow agricultural and horticultural lands to be taxed at non-uniform rates, thus allowing their continued existence in close proximity to rapidly urbanizing areas. Like the Wisconsin forest crop tax, the New Jersey approach recognizes a land use objective and then seeks to adjust the taxing system to allow the achievement of that objective. Both states frankly recognize that there are some public goals which justify non-uniform property taxation.

Completely eliminating uniformity requirements in property taxation might also be considered. Some will think this suggestion radical—a complete departure from concepts of equal protection and fairness. However, when one recognizes that there is really very little uniformity in the property tax system today because of variations in local assessment, the early failure to insist upon state-wide uniformity (uniformity is demanded only within individual municipal units), and a failure to demand uniformity among all types and classes of property (uniformity is demanded only within individual classes of property), the suggestion hardly appears more than a candid recognition of present reality. Non-uniform property taxation could incorporate any number of safeguards and would as a matter of course be expected to deal equally with property taxpayers who in fact were similarly situated. The rationale for such an approach to property taxation is that there are so many combinations of land type and land use in existence that are not uniform that a system of property taxation which recognizes this non-uniformity is fully justified.

The legislature could establish a hierarchy of land use objectives to be accorded appropriate tax treatment. For example, dumps and junk yards adjacent to major highways, scenic lakes, or coastal areas could have a high property tax. Similar activities situated more discretely could have a lower property tax. Slum tenements, old warehouses, abandoned or damaged buildings, and unusable dockyard facilities could be taxed heavily while low-income housing, subdivisions which cluster house units in order to retain an open or natural area, and rehabilitation projects could be induced by favorably low property tax treatment.[3] Property taxes aimed at discouraging certain land use activities can be increased (made more onerous) in a step process over a series of years until the objective is achieved.[4] Highly favorable property tax treatment designed to induce a desired type of land utilization could be ended after a given number of years or could also employ a step process which eventually levels out at the average rate of taxation for such activities and which thus serves to concentrate the tax incentive in the early years of the undertaking. The point is that such an approach is a direct harnessing of the property tax system to land use goals: The system can act as a deterrent to remove or relocate undesirable land uses or as an incentive to induce desirable uses.

An even more dramatic departure from present methods of tax collection which might serve land use objectives in our society is complete abandonment of property taxation as a means of revenue collection. Many critics feel that the property tax is inherently inequitable because it raises general revenues by taxing only some property owners or types of property within the community. It is alleged that if the property tax is not inherently inequitable it nonetheless produces inequitable results because of the limitations we have placed on the concept of uniformity and because of the difficulties of administering the tax. Many feel that it stifles investment and that the historical nature of statutory and case law in existence with respect to this tax renders it relatively inflexible—incapable of adapting to meet other community goals such as land use objectives. In short, persuasive arguments can be made for raising needed govern-

mental revenues by some alternative means— a method free from all of the defects listed above and one which would leave local governments free to determine land use goals and objectives without the necessity of working within or around the present property tax system. A trend in the direction of reducing state and local governments' reliance on the property tax as a source of revenue is already evident. In 1929, over 60 per cent of all state and local receipts were derived from property taxes. In 1966, only 28 per cent of such receipts were derived from the property tax.

The proposal to abandon the property tax at this time is consistent with recent proposals by Walter Heller and Joseph Pechman which advocate an increased reliance upon the income tax revenue gathering capacity of the federal government. They argue that the progressive income tax is more equitable, that the administrative machinery for collection is established, efficient, relatively inexpensive to maintain, and could easily be expanded if necessary. Their proposals call for a sharing back to the states of a portion of the total revenues collected, and one can easily imagine a second stage of sharing by states to local governments.[5] The advantage that such an arrangement would have with respect to land use objectives is that incentives aimed at corporations and individuals could be made part of a taxing system which would uniformly cover the entire nation and which would thus give uniform national impetus to these objectives. Furthermore, the formula for sharing back the collected revenues from the federal government to the states and from the states to local units of government could take into account the degree to which these state and local units of government adhere to legislatively adopted land use objectives. For example, states

---

[3] The proposal being made is that once the concept of preferential property tax treatment to achieve land use objectives is accepted, the legislature, after viewing the complete spectrum of such objectives, can and should establish a hierarchy or set of preferences between those objectives so as to accord to each appropriate property tax treatment.

[4] This proposal is loosely analogous to a number of other concepts in the law which utilize essentially coercive devices to achieve desired ends or to deter undesirable types of action, e.g., punitive damages, triple damages, penalty taxes.

[5] The second stage of sharing will pose few difficulties. Most states, to some extent, already share general state tax revenues with local units of government either on an unrestricted basis, to augment local tax revenues, or on an earmarked basis, for particular local expenditures of statewide concern (most frequently education).

which make an effort to deal effectively with air and water pollution would be entitled to relatively more money than states which neglected these problems. Cities which make a vigorous attempt to ameliorate problems of ghetto schools and housing, waste disposal and treatment, and urban transportation would be entitled to relatively greater sums than cities which neglect their responsibilities in these areas.

To some extent these incentive devices already exist in federal and state tax sharing and aid programs,[6] but they would have greater weight if incorporated as part of a national system of income taxation and revenue sharing which at the same time contemplated the abandonment of the property tax and which consequently would be the principal source of revenue for all levels of government.

The abandonment of the property tax does not depend on expanding the federal income tax mechanism to fill the void and produce needed revenue. Individual states, many of which already have an income tax and collection machinery, could perform the function quite satisfactorily. They could program into their respective income tax structures incentives designed to achieve land use objectives, and they also could share the taxes collected with local governmental units in a manner which induces compliance with land use goals.

It would not be impossible to extend the principle inherent in federal and state tax-sharing programs (or grant-in-aid programs) to individuals and corporations. That is, individuals and corporations that undertake to carry out at their own expense legislatively endorsed federal, state, or local land use objectives would qualify for a subsidy or grant-in-aid which would cover a portion of

the total costs incurred.[7] Tax revenues expended in this manner induce private funds to be spent on essentially public land use objectives. The partnership of public and private funds is healthy, and the fact that private as well as public benefits may accrue should not deter an exploration of this approach.

Milton Friedman and others have advocated a "negative income tax" as a means of assisting (making payments to) individuals whose income falls below some minimum level. A variation of this approach might be applied, for example, to housing improvement. Individuals whose residences did not measure up to building code standards would qualify for a money payment which could be used only to make those necessary improvements which would bring the house up to code standards. The farther below the code standards (that is the more run-down the structure was initially) the larger would be the payment. If the substandard housing unit is a rental or an apartment house and the owner is indifferent to its condition, the payment could be made to the tenant, to a tenants' union, or to a local court to insure that the sums paid were in fact allocated to the improvement of the housing unit. The owners of such structures should not object to their improvement by these means, and to prevent the possibility that owners with newly refurbished structures would either raise the rent or evict the present tenants, lease arrangements could be entered into at the outset of the repair and improvement program.

Another taxing approach which would further land use objectives is one which relies on a combination of special assessment concepts and the concept of effluent charges. Special assessment tax theory holds that a

---

[6] A familiar example is state school aid formulas which favor consolidated districts over independent or unconsolidated districts. Federal aid programs which condition assistance on the existence of coordinated and comprehensive planning efforts similarly create a strong incentive to act in the desired manner.

[7] The federal income tax system, in the form of personal deductions and exemptions and in the manner it allows corporations to define and handle business expenses and depreciation, already gives incentive and impetus to a wide range of goals which Congress has deemed socially or otherwise desireable. These include dental and medical care, consumer purchases of housing, automobiles, and other durable goods, religious and charitable contributions, capital goods investment spending, and soil conservation expenditures.

levy on property for special benefits conferred upon such property by a governmental act or improvement may be collected. The concept of effluent charges maintains that an economic entity that disposes of its waste products in the waters of a state may be required to make a payment to the state for that privilege. It is in the nature of an excise tax. The revenues collected by such a charge either could be paid over to those individuals injured by the water pollution or could be expended to erect water pollution control and treatment facilities. The present proposal is simply to subject every undesirable or offensive land use situation to a system of taxation based on one or the other or both of these two theories. The size of the tax would be measured by the costs incurred by the public to remove or correct the undesirable or offensive situation. For example, public improvement of a slum tenement would confer a special benefit on the owner of the building justifying a tax in the nature of a special assessment. The tax could cover all or only a part of the total costs incurred.[8] The costs to the public of planting and maintaining a screening to block from view a dump or junk yard would be the measure of a tax more akin to the effluent charge. The privilege of carrying on this activity in an undesirable and indiscriminate manner may be allowed to continue, but the cost of ameliorating the undesirable effect upon the rest of the community will be forced back on the owner of the dump or junk yard facility. Should the community desire to create by purchase and then to maintain a park or open-space area in a particular neighborhood, a portion of the costs of such an endeavor might well be passed on to those landowners whose property values are enhanced by the creation of such a facility. To the extent that the creation and continued maintenance of such a facility in the neighborhood is more nearly a privilege than a right and clearly confers a special benefit on

neighborhood residents, a tax measured by the costs of initial acquisition and upkeep does not seem unreasonable.[9]

Once again, a hierarchy of undesirable land use situations and countervailing public actions could be constructed by the legislature and appropriate tax rates imposed designed not only to discourage the private continuation of these undesirable situations but also to produce a fund which would enable public repairs or improvements to be made. In some instances the public action will confer a direct benefit on a private landowner, and in other instances the public action will simply provide for an adequate buffer or shield so that adverse effects of the undesirable situation will not be felt by an entire community. In either case the essential fairness of such an approach is clearly evident, for the direct beneficiary of a public improvement is called upon to bear part of the cost of such governmental action and the creator of an unsightly or otherwise adverse land use condition bears the cost of amelioration.

Conclusions

Present systems of taxation in this country neither provide for accomplishing land use objectives nor do they remain neutral. In far too many instances taxing systems contradict and serve to defeat land use objectives. However, contradictions can be corrected, and tax programs which facilitate the attainment of land use objectives can be developed. A range of such programs in outline form only has been presented in this paper. Each is capable of being expanded, tailored to meet individual objectives, and developed in the course of actual application—but the promise is there.

The extent to which oil and gas depletion allowances in the federal income tax system have spurred extractive and land exploiting

---

[8] A tax which covered only part of the total costs incurred would simply recognize, as many special assessment situations actually do, that there is some degree of general benefit in almost every public improvement, even those which ostensibly and most directly benefit only a few individuals.

[9] It is very analogous to the concept of waste-load surcharges, employed by municipalities to defray sewage disposal costs, and to user charges generally.

activities is ample proof that a similar harnessing of the taxing power to the attainment of a wide range of land use objectives would also be successful. It is hard to imagine that a tax-incentive program which even approached present oil and gas depletion allowances would not be capable of producing clean air over cities most in need of air pollution control activities or clean water in lakes, rivers, and streams most in need of attention. It also seems hard to believe that many other undesirable and offensive land use conditions which today exist in our society could not be induced to change for the better by taxing systems which provide adequate tax incentives or penalties.

However, tax reform has never been an easy process in our society. Advocates of conservation, the wise use of resources, and environmental improvements have no strong lobby in Congress or state legislatures. Our society is only now awakening to the dimensions of the problem in these areas and is rather belatedly discussing and developing tools capable of achieving land use objectives. The power to tax is such a tool and should be thoroughly examined and effectively used. The principle of the carrot and the stick is an old one. It has been made to work before—it can be reasonably and fairly applied and made to work again.

THREE OVERLAPPING problems of great complexity confront us in this topic. In addition to being individually difficult, these problems act and react upon each other so that we are confronted with a very labyrinth of causes and effects. These problems are: patterns of governmental structure, land use patterns, and fiscal policies. The last should include public expenditure and debt, as well as tax, policies.

Since it is obviously impossible to deal adequately, or even superficially, with these labyrinthine passages in one paper, or even in a single volume, it is necessary to pinpoint my discussion to tax considerations and to only a few of them. I shall exclude federal and state tax impacts and local nonproperty taxes. This leaves the large and important field of property taxes, and even this is too much to be adequately covered.

27

Taxation and Development

Mabel Walker

This article appeared originally in Planning 1962, pp. 102–107, published by the American Society of Planning Officials, 1313 East Sixtieth Street, Chicago, Illinois 60637. Reproduced by permission.

Some Preliminary Considerations

In this concentration on a few points, however, it is desirable to remain aware of the related subject matter. Moreover, before anything meaningful can be said, even in this limited field, we do need to take a few seconds for some preliminary orientation.

Consideration of land development and taxation has been, and is, largely a matter of blind fumbling because we do not yet know what we are trying to achieve. The various professional groups involved in this complex subject have not done their homework sufficiently well to enable us to handle this topic competently. The tax economists have largely ignored the study of taxation impacts on land use. The political scientists have a long way to go in evolving a satisfactory pattern of local governmental units. Moreover, from my limited point of view, I have not been able to discover that planners have devised any ideal patterns of land use distribution for various categories of populated places. Even the land use data that have been compiled are far from satisfactory so we are attempting to evaluate the effectiveness of various taxing devices in fostering an *unknown* ideal pattern of land use for *nonexistent* logical patterns of local governmental units.

What Are Our Objectives?

At the outset we need to give some thought to our objectives in considering tax reform and land development. Three questions are paramount:

1. What type of land development are we talking about?
2. Do we seek equity and incentive for all taxpayers, or only for the urban redeveloper?
3. What is the planner's goal: a healthy economy or a more productive real estate tax?

WHAT TYPE OF DEVELOPMENT?

What type of land use are we attempting to bring about through tax policies? Are we trying for industrial plants, office buildings, large commercial establishments, high-rise apartments, single-family homes, rehabilitation of existing structures, open spaces, public buildings, transportation routes, or what? Effective methods to be used will vary for different types of development. Preferably, we should be seeking a balanced pattern of development of all these uses, but the ratios of land use that would be appropriate for Atlantic City and for New York City would be quite different, and neither

217

would be suitable for Washington, since the desirable distribution of land uses varies by the size and other characteristics of a city.

It would seem to be desirable to establish goals in land use planning before we try to achieve those goals by tampering with the taxation system. Before goals can be set, however, we need a great deal more statistical information on existing patterns of urban land use and we need this information broken down by various categories of cities. Moreover, before even this can be done satisfactorily, it is necessary that some group evolve a more satisfactory classification of land uses and secure the adoption of such a classification by planners who make land use surveys.[1] It is presently not very enlightening for a public official or a lay citizen who is trying to evaluate land use policies to discover, for example, that one city lumps railroad acreage with industries, while another includes it under utilities, and others show it separately. There are many other discrepancies in current classification of land uses.

We hear considerably more about shaping our tax policies to encourage industrial development than we do even about tax policies to foster urban renewal. Quite different incentives and deterrents are considered in the two connections. Local personal property taxes on machinery and intangibles and state taxes on corporate income are the prime tax targets in industrial development programs, whereas local real

[1] There are three major needs with respect to urban land use data: (1) A model scheme of land use classification adopted by an authoritative body and generally followed in making land use surveys. (2) A central clearing agency for correlating the data available as a result of individual city surveys. (3) A suitable classification of cities for use in analyzing the data. It is not particularly helpful to combine suburban, resort, and more well-rounded cities in one coverage. Moreover, cities showing highly erratic patterns of land use should be excluded from the statistical analysis unless the sample is large enough to prevent such examples from distorting the statistical results and giving a false idea of the normal pattern of land use.

property and federal income taxes are most frequently mentioned in connection with urban renewal. Sales taxes, chain store taxes, gross receipts taxes, and others also have a bearing on certain types of development.

Tax revenues must be obtained. The possible sources of productive revenue are limited. We are, therefore, confronted with a choice of evils. Moreover, the proper tax pattern for one community is not necessarily the one that would be appropriate elsewhere.

EQUITY AND INCENTIVES FOR WHOM?

The second objective to be clarified is whether we are trying to get equity and incentives for all taxpayers or only for the promoters of a few selected projects. The majority of tax proposals designed to affect land use relate to deterrents or incentives for specific groups. But if the tax system is so restrictive that taxes must be abated in order to get specific projects advanced, then the question arises whether the tax system may not be stifling development generally, regardless of whether that development consists of a major enterprise or merely mending the porch on a private home. A city is not going to achieve economic health by means of fostering a few specific enterprises, or even selected categories of enterprise. What will it profit a city to have a few urban renewal showplaces if all the little property holders find that the tax system penalizes them for maintaining their properties in good condition?

If the tax system of a city so inhibits private developers that certain projects can be accomplished only by special tax favors, then the city had better give its tax system a rigorous overhauling. Justice for all seems a more worthy objective than special favors for the few.

A HEALTHY ECONOMY VERSUS A MORE
PRODUCTIVE REAL ESTATE TAX.

Now for clarification of our third objective: In advocating land development programs, is our goal a healthy economy or more revenue from the real estate tax? Sometimes I wonder if we are not placing taxes on too high a pedestal. There are things that are more important to a community than the tax yield.

With an economically and socially healthy environment, an alert community that is granted sufficient leeway by the state should be able to provide the necessary revenues but a downgrade community will have a difficult time taxwise, whatever it does. If we put the major emphasis on tax productivity, rather than on the community well-being, we may find that we have lost both.

I do not intend to underrate the importance of adequate tax revenue, but I would like to see the emphasis on adjusting the tax system to the economy and not the economy to the tax system. The tax system both can, and at times should, be adjusted to a changing economy. To try to adjust the economy to a static tax system may seriously impair the viability of the economy. This will in turn affect the productivity of the tax system itself.

Goals in Property Tax Reform

Against the background of these hurried preliminary observations, let us consider briefly the matter of property tax reform. There are a few broad primary goals of real estate tax reform that would probably be accepted by most students of taxation. They are: a more logical pattern of taxing units, improvement of administrative procedures, checking erosion of the property tax base, and broadening of the local tax base in large cities through use of nonproperty taxes.

MORE LOGICAL TAXING UNITS

At the very crux of our problem is the fragmentation of the local taxing units and the inequality of tax resources among them. This situation will probably become steadily worse as a result of current residential, industrial plant, and shopping center trends.

Such homogeneity as small taxing units formerly enjoyed becomes less and less as large industrial plants move to a small governmental unit, thereby greatly enriching its tax sources, while the plant workers frequently locate in other small units, thereby burdening them with the education of their children. Comparable situations exist with respect to shopping centers and some other large-scale developments.

Not only are revenue difficulties arising because the taxable resources and the governmental burdens in these units are highly unequal and are becoming more so all the time, but also because many of the units are too small to employ full-time assessors and to afford and utilize some of the technical aids essential to equitable assessment. This fragmentation affects the central cities as well as the suburban and rural areas. In some cities we have as a taxing unit only a truncated core which is cut off and surrounded by the suburban satellites.

Revenue inadequacies, friction, and dissatisfaction with the property tax will markedly increase if we continue to try to muddle along under the present jurisdictional setup. This problem of fragmentation of taxing units should be first on the reform agendum.

IMPROVEMENT OF ADMINISTRATIVE PROCEDURE

Improvement of administrative procedure is another primary goal. To a large extent, this is conditional upon securing a larger taxing unit.

The property tax is not easy to administer. Trained personnel are needed for the equitable assessment of even relatively modest homes. As properties increase in value, the difficulties become greater. The task of assessing large industrial complexes is far beyond the capacity of most assessors, yet some of these establishments are found in small rural areas having untrained assessors.

Not only is revenue lost, but substantial injustice is done to some taxpayers, who may be paying far more than they should while others escape their fair share of the tax burden. Research studies in state after state have documented instances of inequitable assessment. In a recent study in Ohio, it was shown that variations in the assessment of individual properties within the same city ranged from 12 per cent to 108 per cent of sales values.

Automatic data processing is being developed in federal tax administration. We can probably anticipate the time within the near future when it will also be widely used in state and local tax administration. This may perhaps offer the hope that we may finally be able to approach scientific assessment of property.

But computers are geared to large enterprises. They are beyond the reach of the small unit. When ADP comes to be used in property assessment, we shall face some revolutionary changes. It may be that small units will contract with larger ones for the assessment of their properties; it may be that several units will cooperate on a regional basis; or it may be that we shall have much larger local units.

CHECKING EROSION OF THE PROPERTY
TAX BASE

One of the most serious threats to local finance is the persistent and increasing erosion of the real property tax base.

It seems to be part of our national psychological heritage to consider property tax exemption as an ideal means of promoting worthwhile enterprises, dispensing charitable aid, furthering social reforms, or showing esteem and gratitude. There is little or no recognition of the fact that many of these objectives could be more effectively, more economically, and more equitably achieved through a direct and visible subsidy. Instead, we prefer the devious, never-count-the-cost method of chiseling away at our property tax base, in true devil-take-the-hindmost fashion.

Not only are we granting the time-honored exemptions to governmental, educational, and philanthropic agencies and enterprises, but we extend partial or complete exemption to public housing, homesteads, veterans, the blind, aged citizens, impoverished widows, and the president and professors of Brown University. This process of granting exemptions feeds upon itself. As more and more exemptions are granted, the tax burden becomes higher upon the persons left to carry the load, so a clamor begins to be heard for even more exemptions.

To the state legislator, the granting of property tax exemptions seems an easy, painless way of currying favor with a pressure group. There is no conspicuous price tag, certainly not at the state level. But as the property tax base is more and more eroded, pressure from the cities for increased state aid is intensified. There is no painless way of meeting social obligations. Checking the erosion of the real property tax base is a primary reform goal.

BROADENING THE TAX BASE IN
LARGE CITIES

The fourth primary reform is broadening the tax base in the large cities by using nonproperty taxes. Discussion of possible alternatives is too large a subject to treat here. The two most productive sources are local income and retail sales taxes.

One caveat should be entered at this point. The fact that a large city, or a populous county, may need and is justified in seeking additional tax sources does not imply any justification for bolstering up uneconomically small units by allowing them additional taxing sources.

Other Reforms

The above goals are something like the Ten Commandments. They are standard precepts that are honored in the breach. Something new and different would be much more appealing.

A far-reaching tax reform that has had considerable advocacy is that improvements be exempted from taxation, or taxed at a much lower rate than land. It is argued that the part of the tax that falls upon land tends to stimulate development and to bring about more effective utilization of the land, both because it tends to make the holding of unimproved land burdensome and also because it tends to depress the price of land because of the capitalization process, thereby making land easier to acquire. The part of the tax that falls upon buildings tends to retard improvements, as it increases the cost of operating existing structures and also represents an added cost which the builder must consider in new construction.

The present tax setup is such that old rundown properties frequently yield higher profits than high-grade properties. The heavy burden of the property tax on improvements in some communities makes it impossible for developers to construct desirable projects.

The financial stringency of the American cities is so great, however, that it seems unlikely that the tax on improvements can be dropped or even substantially lowered—at least in the foreseeable future.

Instead of differentiating tax rates on land and improvements, another type of reform that has been suggested is to have the capital value tax apply only to land and to impose in addition a special tax on earnings from both land and improvements. A further suggestion which could be used in addition to the one just mentioned is to apply a special increment tax to any gain in land values to be

imposed at the time the property was transferred.

A land tax based on capital value, plus a special tax on the income from real estate, plus an increment tax on land at the time it was sold would not impair the revenue and would also probably be politically somewhat less unpalatable than a heavy land tax. It would, however, be strongly opposed by speculators. It would also be opposed on the grounds of administrative difficulty. It does not appear, however, that the problems would be more insuperable than some involved in the present system.

Basic reforms of the kind discussed here would tend to bring about greater equity among taxpayers generally and would avoid the onus of benefiting only a minor segment of the taxpayers. Moreover, they would strengthen, rather than undermine, the local tax base.

28

Opportunities
in Taxation
for Achieving
Planning Purposes

Charles Abrams

This article appeared originally in Zoning Digest, Vol. 18, No. 6, June–July 1966, pp. 193–199, *published by the American Society of Planning Officials, 1313 East 60th Street, Chicago, Illinois 60637. Reproduced by permission.* © 1966 *by the American Society of Planning Officials.*

OF THE THREE powers in the government power plant, the one least explored for its impact on urban development is the tax power. Its potentials and applications include its employment (a) as an encouragement to better planning and housing, (b) as a deterrent to bad planning or poor housing, and (c) as a compulsory device to enforce essential land development.

The United States is unique in the development of its tax power on real estate. As an *ad valorem* tax that levies on property irrespective of whether it is income-yielding or not, it differs from the British and similar tax systems. Its merits, such as they are, are that it is old and established; as a tax *in rem*, it is easy to collect, impossible to avoid by leaving the jurisdiction, and impossible to conceal. It originated when the ownership of real property was the surest test of the ability to pay and when the amount of property owned was a rough measure of income and hence of the just proportion of the tax burden. It has survived in a period when intangible property has moved ahead to become the most important form of wealth in the economy and a more accurate index of the capacity to pay.

The imperfections of the real estate tax loom larger as social and racial problems have become intensified in the central cities. Both the tax rate and assessed valuations have steadily increased so that the central city has had to resort more and more to levies on less stabilized sources including intangible property. This in turn contributes to the general flight of wealth and industry from the cities, accentuating the burdens of the growing social commitments enforced upon these cities. Thus while the cities' social problems and their educational needs, pensions, and payrolls are rising, their springs of revenue are drying up. A generation ago, municipalities were collecting more taxes than the national and state governments combined, but their take, which had been 52 per cent of total in 1932, had dropped to 7.3 per cent 30 years later. In 1902, the combined net revenues of federal, state, and local governments were less than $1.4 billion, but by 1964 they exceeded $158 billion, of which the federal share was now more than two-thirds.

Thus while the federal government has replaced the local tax collector as the principal recipient of tax revenues in the nation, it has not as yet assumed a corresponding responsibility for the social and educational burdens that have fallen on the cities. Unable to tax for its needs, the central city has borrowed so that local debt between 1946 and 1964 rose from $13.6 billion to $68.4 billion. In the same period, federal debt increased only from $269 billion to $312 billion. On a per capita basis, local debt just about quadrupled while federal dept per capita actually decreased.

The increased tax burden, the attractiveness of suburbia for industrial and residential settlement, and the social and racial problems in the central cities have forced some ambitious localities to offer special tax inducements to industrial and residential development, which in turn has been sapping the older cities of some of their sources of revenue. To retain its middleclass families, New York City grants tax exemptions of various kinds for slum clearance undertakings such as Stuyvesant Town and for Mitchell-Lama projects for moderate-income groups in cooperative and limited dividend projects. It also offers special tax exemptions for rehabilitation by private enterprise. Boston has given tax subventions to commercial and residential property under its limited dividend and urban renewal program, while public housing generally benefits from tax exemption wherever projects are built.

Tax exemption to induce industrial settlement is a growing device. This has taken form in exemptions of industrial real estate and in the use of tax exempt bonds to finance the settlement of industrial corporations which include the operations of such corporations as Armour, Allied Paper, Olin Mathieson Chemical, American Machine and Foundry, Borg-Warner, Georgia Pacific, and United States Rubber. The first bonds for such purposes were issued in 1959 for only $5 million, but from 1959 to 1963, there were 16 additional issues, and in the four years up to 1963, more than three times the amount of industrial bonds were issued as in the preceding 20 years. The use of these tax exempt bonds is heading toward a bizarre stage, with one city of only 610 people marketing tax exempt bonds totalling almost $50 million. Another with 300 residents recently issued $25 million in bonds. A Holiday Inn has been financed with such bonds, and real estate operators are now moving into the opportunity by organizing special districts which have been able to float large tax exempt issues to help them develop their utilities. Thus, one real estate development firm issued more than $55 million in tax exempt bonds to build Foster City, and speculative developers in California have issued about $9 million in general obligation bonds of their new community. In one California case, a bond issue was unanimously approved by the only two voters in a tract of land, both of whom were officials of the land-owning company; $178 million of tax exempt bonds were floated to reclaim and develop a parcel of land assessed for tax purposes at about $354,000. Similar bonds have financed cableways for skiers and similar adventures. A number of California urban renewal agencies have issued such tax exempt bonds secured by the potential tax revenues, and in California alone these bonds total more

than $64 million. The fact that the buyers of such bonds pay no income tax is one of the important inducements to investors.

Simultaneously, vast amounts of tax exempt bonds are being issued by public authorities either for established public purposes or under the public benefit theory now covering a wide range of public purposes which were formerly private. Many of the private purposes are now "incidental" to public purposes, as in the case of the $550 million of tax exempt bonds to be issued by the Port of New York Authority, which is constructing two 110-story buildings in downtown New York to be rented largely to commercial tenants. The rents collected from the private tenants will be more than sufficient to pay off the bond issue. This is but one illustration of the uses of the tax exemption privilege as a means either of attracting industry, increasing real estate revenues, or meeting para-social needs.

The federal depreciation factor is another inducement to development in cities and elsewhere. With the tax system taking 48 per cent of corporate profit and as much as 70 per cent of individual profit, developers have sought to take advantage of the highest depreciation a given building permits.

The more costly the building, the greater the deductible depreciation; the larger the mortgage, the smaller the actual investment and the greater the proportion of depreciation to actual stake. This is where FHA rental and urban renewal operations work to the investor's advantage. The 90 per cent mortgage enables him to buy a building with a big depreciation factor while committing very little cash. If the annual rate of allowable depreciation is greater than the annual cash profit, the owner can pocket the profit while taking a loss for income tax purposes. He will not only pay no tax on the cash profit earned, but he may charge his book loss against any other profits he may have made.

If handled deftly, for example, an investment of $487,000 for a taxpayer in the 70 per cent bracket would actually net a profit of 10 per cent annually while the book loss would range annually from $60,000 to $250,000. The investor should have recouped his whole investment through the tax shelter in the first three years and thereafter have additional deductions until the end of the depreciation period.

These are figures for an investor to conjure with. If he is in the 50 per cent tax bracket, the tax he avoids paying should, in a proper transaction, more than equal his cash investment in the first few years even if there is no cash profit. One of the troubles with the play is the bureaucracy involved with renewal transactions and, while the game may be attractive on paper, many an investor has wound up behind the eight ball, which turned out to be a huge unplayable ball of red tape.

It is wrong, moreover, to single out urban renewal investment as the only or even the main form of tax dodge. Its tax benefits exist in all big building operations and are a pittance compared to oil depletion allowances, tax exempt bonds, and other escapes. Depreciation, moreover, is taken by all business enterprise. If it did not exist, the returns expected on FHA and urban renewal investment would have to be much greater to attract investors and builders.

I should also mention the impact of depreciation and capital gains on city development as well as on the sterilization of city development—an important aspect of the tax process on which I have seen nothing written. The central cities are composed mostly of old buildings, many of which have been held by the same owners and are now fully depreciated. When a building is fully depreciated and an owner desires to sell it, he receives at best only 75 per cent of the proceeds. Rather than sell it and keep only 75 per cent, he inclines toward mortgaging it for 60 to 75 per cent and thereby pockets about the same amount as if he sold the property; he can simultaneously reap the net profit left above the mortgage and carrying charges. The sales proceeds left over to the owner are even less if he happens to have mortgaged the property

earlier and pocketed the mortgage proceeds. If he then decides to sell the property, what he pocketed from the mortgage is taxable so that he may pay as much as 50 per cent or more of the sales proceeds to the federal tax collector. Under either circumstance, the owner will be disinclined to sell. The result is that considerable property in the older cities, much of it in the central areas, can no longer be voluntarily sold and assembled for much-needed new developments. This is responsible for a growing catalogue of old buildings that persist in the central cities and retard neighborhood regeneration. Resort to the condemnation power in cases of urban renewal and other public uses is awaited by the owner since when the property is condemned, the realized capital gain need not be paid if the proceeds are invested in other real estate within a year.

If voluntary renewal of central areas is to be stimulated, it would only make sense to offer the same benefits to the voluntary seller of property as is offered to him when his property is condemned or when he is a home owner. I should like to see this aspect of urban development explored more thoroughly, for I believe that it is becoming one of the principal deterrents to urban development and is contributing to holdouts in much-needed strategic central improvement.

Still another example of the lack of constructive thinking on the tax power in urban development is the case of Puerto Rico. Puerto Rican officials have proposed legislation designed to curb speculation by levying a 75 per cent tax on capital gains made from land sales. Not only will this encourage leasing rather than home ownership but, for a commonwealth dependent on private investment, the proposed legislation is bound to be construed by industry as a prelude to unsound tax policy in other areas of investment.

Tax policy is sometimes used as a means of preserving open space, golf courses, and other desirable uses by offering a low tax rate as long as the preferred use is maintained and forcing a payment of the accrued taxes should the land be sold for speculative development. This might well be adapted as a means of preserving historic sites. A tax exemption could be given to the building owner, provided he agrees to maintain his building as a historic site and grants a first refusal to the city to purchase. The accrued taxes could be credited to the city on its purchase price.

Another interesting use of the tax power is the enforcement of idle land development. This was first used in the Henry Hudson stockade when settlers refused to develop land and a tax was imposed as a means of enforcing such development. The device has not been used again in the United States as far as I know, but it was recommended by a United Nations mission, of which I was a member, in Pakistan and in the Philippines. In these countries, land ripe for development was being held out of use. Since the land was free of taxes while population was simultaneously surging and the introduction of public facilities was adding to land value, it paid the landowner to continue holding the land unimproved and benefitting from the increase in value. In Pakistan, a law was enacted on the recommendation of the mission to designate "use areas" which were defined as areas ripe for development and which remained undeveloped. If within a prescribed period the land was not developed, a 3 per cent tax would automatically be imposed upon the property. This could be usefully employed in the United States where developable land is held out of use. The tax could be higher than the regular tax. But it should not be levied except as part of a master plan which designates the taxed land for development according to a time schedule and a proper zoning plan. By combining the tax measure with master and zoning plans and a time schedule, the land would tend to be developed for its most appropriate use.

Drastic tax measures have been advocated in California where land prices have risen sharply in recent years. In less than eight years, typical lot sizes in Alameda and Contra Costa counties increased by 15 to 20 per cent, but prices doubled. In Marin and Santa Clara counties, lot sizes were about 15 to 20 per cent more, but the lot costs rose by over 150 per cent. Los Angeles' lots gained about 25 per cent in size but rose almost 250 per cent in price. In the Bay Area, if the lot had

remained constant, the price would have doubled.

These sharp rises in the price of raw land have revived ethical controversies on the right to speculate in land and have refreshed dormant nineteenth century theories for taxing land increment and curbing land speculation. Continued speculation and price rises, it is said, impede housing production and rocket consumers' costs.

Despite the dramatic price rises in land, however, only half the price rise is attributable to the increase in the price of the raw land. Another 29 per cent of the total cost increase has been due to changes in development quality and standards while about 21 per cent came from changes in lot size.

Rises in land costs must also be matched against rises in income and rises in house cost generally. The average price of sites nearly doubled in the last 12 years, but more than half of this increase can be attributed to higher income in terms of current dollars. An indeterminable amount of the price rise also results from the tendency for investors to spend more for land. About one-third of the increased cost of sites can be explained by the fact that land prices rose faster than income.

A big question still to be resolved, however, is whether land cost has presently reached the point where more drastic political processes should be employed and interfere with normal market processes. Although rising land costs are prejudicial to the average wage earner, it is only one of the high components in an aggregation of high housing costs. The increase in land cost, for example, is still less of a factor in monthly shelter cost than interest rates—interest and amortization in fact account for more than half the monthly cost of housing. Moreover, price rises are not all profit, and one putting cash into speculative land loses the interest on the money invested (or pays interest if the site is mortgaged) as well as land taxes. Land prices, therefore, must go up at least 7 per cent annually or the speculator is bound to lose in the longer run. His hope is that land prices will rise faster than the sum of his taxes and his loss of interest. In this respect, speculation in land is a risk much like the freezing of cash into goods. Loss as well as gain may result from the gamble—in an unanticipated rigid zoning law, in the arrival of a housing surplus, and other hazards.

This does not mean that no new public land policies are needed. It is often, in fact, existing policy that contributes to high land cost—zoning laws that limit use or that enforce excessive lot sizes. Local assessed valuations do not keep pace with rising land values and should. In Contra Costa County, for example, land was so underassessed that the county was forced by the State Board of Equalization to raise its assessment ratios on developed and undeveloped land.

Some landowners are being unjustly enriched by public improvements for which no recoupment is made through assessments-for-benefit. But enrichment is not unjust when a legitimate speculation brings a profit. It becomes unjust when an improvement, the cost of which is charged to all the tax-payers, apportions its dividends only to a few. The betterment accruing to the owner due to roads, streets, water, and other public improvements should be at least partly recaptured by the public incurring the expense.

In sum, the planner and planning official have placed entirely too much emphasis on the restrictive applications of planning and on the use of eminent domain powers and have under-emphasized the impact of tax policy—both as a spur to proper development and as a limitation on land abuse. The three powers in the government power plant need to be related, and the tax power, both in its inducing and restrictive aspects, should be reexamined for its impact on development and sterilization of development.

As long as private enterprise is the main instrument in American growth and environmental development, tax levies and tax incentives will be among the dominant factors governing the emergence of the American scene. Major studies of federal, state, and local tax policies as they affect land development are urgently needed, and I hope they will receive the attention of the city planning schools and the public agencies.

THE EMPHASIS of this article will be more on land development issues, with tax implications playing less of a primary role. In these terms then, "Land Development and Tax Implications as One of the Determinants" might be more accurate. Although this is partially quibbling, it does identify the emphasis slightly more meaningfully.

Some aspects of land should be mentioned which involve the pace of development and its decision-makers. Only upon analysis of why certain decisions are made will we be led, perhaps, to tax matters. As such, another qualification is that the arena here will be one of newly developing areas, although there is some reference to renewing areas. Urban renewal areas, for example, are not skipped as a matter of lesser importance or priority, but simply for convenience, and to get a little more depth into one facet of the subject, admitting, perhaps, it is at the expense of breadth.

Too, forewarned is forearmed. This paper takes advantage of personally familiar grounds, and it's always wise to be in the right part of the confidence spectrum. Although there is reference to other documents, much of the thoughts here come out of a research study that was completed several months ago at the University of Washington called, "Locational Factors: Suburban Land Development." This was a research program, extending for over a year and financed by a private enterprise, which attempted to analyze the land change picture in suburbia and consider the factors which contributed to the change. It is understandable, then, that the focus of this paper will concern the dynamics of suburbanization and land development issues and, furthermore, the appraisal of taxation as one of these issues.

Changing Land Uses

The Institute of Research in Social Sciences at the University of North Carolina, while making some investigations of land development patterns in the Piedmont area, suggests that there has not been much investigation of the behavorial determinants of land development. They point out that land development is first motivated by "priming

29

Taxation and Development

Myer R. Wolfe

This article appeared originally in Planning 1962, pp. 107–117, published by the American Society of Planning Officials, 1313 East Sixtieth Street, Chicago, Illinois 60637. Reproduced by permission.

action" such as highway location decisions or other ones of public policy, in addition to private decisions such as industrial locations. They hypothesize that only then do a series of "secondary actions" occur, taken by such people as the real estate developers and builders, who are in turn followed by the individual families, institutions, etc. Here is a broad and initial clue to the settlement patterns that have occurred and are occurring over the suburban landscape. As part of the so-called priming action, then, the Washington study was concerned with accessibility as an initial feature of what gets built where, and obviously we were compelled to go into other factors as well. For example, questions of the nature of the accessible land, its topography, its soil, its proximity to public utilities and water, all reflecting on costs, arose. These are features having some effect on the process of not only what gets built and where, but also when. Then, too, we were forced to look at intangibles, such as the influences of amenity —a view over a body of water, the reputation of the school system, etc.—which also entered the comprehensive picture.

The assumption was made that these factors were in effect amalgamated in the decisions made by various individuals and agencies, so the consumer (home owner or renter) presumably at least has some of these considerations in mind while making

227

his locational choice, and he represents the market. The builder-developer and his aides in assessing that market exercise decisions involving many of the forces cited in the foregoing in choosing one tract over the other and one period of time against the other. Mortgage lending and insuring institutions also, deliberately or otherwise, consider the factors which reflect on locational choice in their loan and investment policies. In ameliorating issues involving public benefit and private profit, local levels of government undergo a rationale in determining location by utilizing zoning and planning powers and so on, which influence the way the land is used. That there are tax issues involved in some of these decisions is obvious, and the broadest clue thus appears.

In studying the process of suburban development, we assumed that the location of new housing, both the large tract developer's detached house and the rental multifamily residence is an indicator of a number of intertwined elements which are involved in that process. Such elements were represented by:

1. *Natural and man-made determinants.* The physical conditions of the site (cost and amenity items), proximity and accessibility features (cost and convenience items), and other amenity items and social considerations represent forces influencing the draw or pull of various locations, one over the other.

2. *The decision-makers of suburban development.* Various cost vs. benefits of these determinants, among others, are weighted by the consumer in selecting a residence, by the builder-developer of that residence, by the agencies involved in the mortgage, and by local government in its efforts to acquire rational community-wide use of the land.

3. *Growth conditions reflective of development dynamics in general.* Item 1 above represented the selective pull or attraction of a location, and 2 represented actual development steps commencing with the site decisions. Furthermore, recorded data documented changes by holding up the

feature of geographic relationship of central city to suburb against: (1) the general changes in land ownership, reflecting the assembly or disassembly of large tracts; (2) historical platting patterns; and (3) the indications of land cost differences over time. This, coupled with growth and land availability projections, suggested overall potential land use changes in various locations at various times.

After a turn of isolating these actions and recorded material, they were brought to one focus to obtain a realistic picture of the ferment in suburbia. While this was relatively successful, one thing, however, was omitted. We did not dig into the tax issue separately since, presumably, it was wrapped up in the decision makers' rationale. It was not ignored as such, yet it was not initially appraised as a strong determining variable. However, as the study progressed, more and more we found that one mysterious point kept creeping into the various decisions as such. Taxes.

It is not the premise, although it may seem that way, to describe our study and its findings and conclusions, reported in a tome of some 600 pages. It is, however, opportune to use it as a background and, moreover, to emphasize that the one issue that we had ignored continually came up before us. The turnover in land, for example, seemed to be directly connected with speculative activity which we surmised had to do with investment money influenced by tax opportunities. On the other hand, real estate taxes seemed to be no deterrent whatsoever in selecting one location for initial development over another. It's ironical, admittedly, that an inquiry on land development factors which did not include the tax issue initially, is now being debated by the person who admits leaving it out. However, it is plain that land development involves other things, but it also brings in aspects of taxation, assessment practices, land speculation, income tax, surplus money, and the like.

The Land Game

It is clear that any consideration of land,

the word used in a broad sense, must start off with some institutionalized premises. The whole history of nations and their governments is wrapped up in land reform and land tenure patterns, which in turn are influential in shaping the urban form. Therefore, we must start with the point that it is simply Americana to speculate in land; the unearned increment is a God-given right and land is a commodity. This is somewhat of a generalization, yet it can be documented. In perusing one of the numerous popular journals on "How to Make $700,000,000 on Real Estate Profits" (not the correct title but one descriptive of a number), it can be found that speculative property is ranked pseudo-objectively by the average yield of profit, safety of capital, management effort required, the down payment, tax shelters, etc. The best areas in the country are examined for this and, of course, the gain in selling prices is emphasized. Warnings are given in the best of these journals, but somehow they are ultimately overcome by the statistics such as the lots which are bought for $1000 in 1950 that sell for $5000 in 1954, and that result, by 1958, in a sale price of $8000! The fact that tax matters are a force in this is axiomatic.

Everyone is familiar with "a land office business." Everyone knows of the swings and the fluctuations in land prices, the highs of 1890, 1907, 1925, and the 1960's, and the lows of 1894, 1908 and 1933. The basic premise of the *House and Home* magazine issue on land (August 1960), was that the current gyrations in land speculation were inhibiting the whole housing picture. In other words, inflated land costs could move good housing out of the market, and shortages of land that were occurring were not actual but artificial. The emphasis, however, was that as artificial as that shortage was, it was real in the sense that undeveloped land existed, but it was unavailable due to high land costs which were inflationary and the result of speculation. We have already suggested that this is not new. We further suggest that this is explained by "highest and best use" concepts or dicta of some real estate experts. This highest and best use outlook which, of course, is economic only, is basic to the free market process of the

traditional speculator and entrepreneur. This point strikes home when it is crystalized into our governmental actions where the assessor is bound, sometimes by law, to appraise properties based on a market value which often contemplates a use not permitted by the zoning ordinances emanating from the same unit of government.

Laura Kingsbury, in *The Economics of Housing*, pointed out the disagreement between classical economists in their views of the values of land. Moreover, she also evaluates the so-called practical people, including the appraisers. Among the latter, the nature and identification of the investment are the criteria for such appraisal, and the most common determination of value for unimproved property is simply one of sales comparison. Thus, to repeat, whereas on the one hand one public office presumably attempts to assure a rational land use disposition (the planning commission or department), the other (the appraiser) is rating the so-called value of properties by measurements which almost universally hover around the latest sales prices of property in the vicinity. This is emphasized because it simply reflects some of the institutional outlooks on land and its appraisal, sales, etc., and yet it indicates the conflicts which come about because of them.

As we draw into issues which bring up taxation as relevant to land development, it becomes apparent that several kinds of taxes must be considered. As we have already intimated, the property or real estate tax has some impact on such development by way of assessment practices. In the publication, *Guiding Metropolitan Growth*, the Committee for Economic Development pointed out that the principal source of revenue at local levels has been the property tax, even though this dominance has decreased. However, by 1957 approximately 50 per cent of the general revenues of local governments were still produced by this tax, and, therefore, assessments were still very much significant. Indeed, the very idea of a tax on land as being meaningful is and has been a controversial one. Henry George and the Single Tax, tax on land and/or vs. improvements, progressive taxes, and differing taxes on differing land use types are part of the sound and fury that has been gone over in considerations of this basic tax. We all know that the original concepts of such a tax were that it was reflective of wealth and presumably the ability to pay. It also contained dimensions of ease of application where properties were tangible and seizable, even though now it is questioned in terms of being reflective of that ability because of the dimension of the benefit received, and because it has been called a tax on improvement.

It has its effect on land development by encouraging or discouraging industrial locations, seeking "cheap land," for example, or encouraging lower or higher densities in redevelopment areas, and the like. To put this in a regional or metropolitan light, one has only to reflect on the fact that various communities, enclaves, districts, each with their own taxing powers, encourage, let's say, industrial location, or discourage it because of tax issues alone. This hardly lends itself to a rational pattern of land uses in city planning terms Dick Netzer found it "grotesque," in a paper presented at the Regional Science Association meeting this year on "Alternates to Property Taxes in Urban Development," that we are supporting the idea that each taxing jurisdiction in a city region should be a "... 'balanced' community with its own industrial district, commercial area, and zones of higher, upper middle, and upper income housing." On the other hand, there are those who would not quarrel with the philosophical basis of the real property tax and take a stab at the way it is applied, and this brings us back to the assessors again. Whatever the patterns may be in the East, on the West Coast the assertion is made over and over again that the assessor is doing the planning in that as more intensive land uses come closer, farm properties, for example, pick up the "values" of the nearby property and are simply taxed out of their current usage, since the farm becomes an uneconomic unit.

For the purposes of this paper, a quick check was made as to whether there was any meaning whatsoever to the fact that the assessment practices were really militating against the use of good farm land. In a rapidly growing suburban district of Seattle, one area of some 150 acres was studied, which consisted of 14 lots varying from $1\frac{1}{2}$ to 39 acres. It was situated on good agricultural soil and being farmed as such, yet was adjacent to a new large development of tract houses. The increase in assessed values over a five-year period was some 138 per cent up to the present time. To check whether this was meaningful, another similar area, consisting of approximately 103 acres which included 10 lots varying from $\frac{1}{2}$ to 39 acres, was evaluated. However, it was *not* adjacent to a tract development, but was in a good soil area in the general vicinity and also used for farming. In examining this control example, the percentage increase of assessments was some 129 per cent for a similar period of time. In observing these two percentages, one could say that the difference is not enough to interpret that a more intensive land use has affected the property nearby. However, what is more interesting is the fact that while both areas rose about the same in percentages, the primary study area "value" jumped some $2\frac{1}{2}$ times per acre several years after the nearby housing development took place. We hasten to point out that this is a limited study using a very small unit of measurement. The pattern goes like this: (1) speculative turnover (resales) of land goes on comparatively slowly in far-out areas; (2) the assessor's office takes note and begins to assess the properties as if ripe for development; (3) applications for rezones commence; and (4) comparable development (adjacent) takes place and the fire really starts.

Also, the very ability of the appraisers to judge market values is questioned in itself. As pointed out, latest sales figures seem to be the most popular method. More esoteric gestures hover around "close, but not too close" measurements. [I.e.], the land or facility might be close to a school or park, but not too close; close to existing developments, but not too close; close to sewage disposal facilities, but not too close; etc.

These are the criteria of the lending and mortgage issuing institutions in their appraisal techniques, although a good deal of lip service is given to the more scientific methods. Still others question the administrative practices of assessment, to bring in more qualification. Examples of lack of training for such appraisals, the lack of time to keep up on the appraisals that might be involved in a dynamic and growing area, and the lack of personnel to keep up with this growth, all militate against the optimum application of assessments even if basic tax ideas are not questioned at all. The important thing here, though, is that land use configurations and timing of development are influenced.

Where the property tax has been under consideration thus far, any discussion of land development cannot go on without considering the income tax. This cannot be documented without gaining access to the files of the Collector of Internal Revenue, which is not easy, to put it mildly. However, it is safe to say that the capital gains gimmick makes the investment in land for the amateur a favorable and traditional way to take care of his surplus or not-so-surplus money. Since profits from capital assets which are held over six months are taxable as long term capital gains, this means that such a tax will be on 50 per cent of the profits at half one's regular income tax rate, or a maximum of 25 per cent, whichever is less. In addition, all carrying charges such as interest and taxes and the like can be deducted while holding speculative property as well. In any case, for a comparatively small outlay of funds, large properties can be tied up until they are sold, and when sold at a profit, a long term capital gains is procured. Operating losses from other income property which can be applied against profits in other years, and additional advantages such as these, are not gone into here. The point is that because of the advantages in the make-up of the Federal income tax, a tremendous amount of investment and speculation goes on in land, and certainly in the peripheral areas. This results in fragmentation of the land tracts. It also results in rising prices where land changes ownership comparatively quickly with each party purchasing not for development purposes but for investment purposes, similar to buying shares on the stock exchange as a speculative gesture.

A statement by Edward Eichler before the Assembly Interim Committee on Governmental Efficiency and Economy of the California Legislature, September 28, 1960, pointed out that his organization, which has built some 8,000 homes in the post war years, has found that ten years of speculation in California land has all but determined its ultimate use. He described tracts which are now too expensive for low- or even middle-income housing as the result of helter-skelter private manipulation resulting in a sprawl surrounding the large cities. He suggests a provision to tax agricultural land to encourage it to remain agricultural and so reflect that use instead of presuming to add higher tax rates which reflect speculative values only.

That same issue of *House and Home* mentioned previously indicates that land prices for home buildings since 1950 have gone up from 100 to 3,760 per cent, and brings in the fact that this is a result not only of private individual investment but that of syndicates as well. Once more a dichotomy arises in that aids and grants through planning, urban renewal, etc., come down from the Federal government to assist in orderly urban development, yet a tax policy exists which encourages directions often opposed to those posed first. While there is recognition of the values of planning and implementation of careful land use plans on one hand, the same units of government foster private-endeavor speculation on the other so as to make difficult that which they encourage in the first place. Business and occupation and other taxes which may influence industry and commercial uses to locate where they may avoid paying for their general and social overhead costs are further examples of similar issues.

Categories of Remedial Proposals or Actions

There are a number of actions or discussions occurring which hover around remedies for the problems of taxation which impinge on aspects of land development. While these are not inclusive, the following represent some general categories that the present doings fall under:

1. EFFORTS TO ALTER THE PROPERTY TAX

Here one take-off from the Single Tax school of thought proposes the taxation of land values only, and thus to untax improvements, or the taxation of land at higher rates than building improvements. The experience in Australia and New Zealand on site value taxation presumably works by reducing taxes where improvement values are high, thereby benefiting such properties while exerting a constant pressure on owners of land alone to put it into production. These countries have had actions such as this since the turn of the century, and are continually held up as being examples of the successful application of the land tax. Mary Rawson, in the publication *Property Taxation and Urban Development*, published by the Urban Land Institute, suggested that land value tax tends to lower asking prices for land, thus making more available while at the same time discouraging speculation and holding.

In 1961, California's legislature studied a constitutional amendment to make possible a site value tax when considering proposals to set a locality's tax on land at higher rates than improvements. While no action was taken, a number of interesting comments were made by tax groups, tax reform academicians, etc., the Australia and New Zealand examples being cited, as well as that of Pennsylvania which is supposedly the only state that already has a graded property tax. There, "... it has discouraged the holding of vacant land for speculation and provided incentive for building improvements. And the distribution of the tax burden is particularly beneficial for the home owners. There is no doubt in my mind that the graded tax law has been a good thing for Pittsburgh."

(Pennsylvania Governor David L. Lawrence, *House and Home*, June 1961.) Netzer also seems in favor of a land value tax, and supports this premise by mentioning Ralph Turvey, who, in *The Economics of Real Property*, suggests this as well.

Another modification is one by Professor Lorned Cook of the Department of Economics at Pomona College, who in a memo last year suggested consideration of local communities and districts taxing residential properties only. The premise here is that commercial and industrial property would be taxed on a metropolitan basis, with the proceeds redistributed or reallocated to the local jurisdiction. In this manner, an intercity competitiveness would be discouraged and greater equity would be provided by "pulling tax receipts from the kind of properties which are necessarily unevenly distributed in a metropolitan area." This would tend to discourage the competition between communities so as to reduce the reliance of the local communities on the property tax. In addition, the principle of benefit comes in again in that the services which are related to property, namely streets, paving, lights, etc., are tangible as they are charged against, let us say, residential land use. On the other hand, education, Professor Cook makes the point, does not have such a singularly apparent relationship between the base on which one is taxed and this particular thing that he is paying for.

These are some thoughts which are trying to get at urban locational implications, in that the tax policy should not be a motive in the location of industry, the prime traditional taxpayer, for example, in matters concerning optimum metropolitan land use patterns. This is also applicable to land which is overzoned for commercial usage because the entrepreneur wants to gamble, and potentially higher tax incomes from these more intensive uses would supposedly bring greater revenues to the coffers of the city. This has to do with the never-never land outlooks that industry and commerce pay more than their way, residential does not, etc. In any case, there has been much in the literature concerned with these matters that treats the effects of taxation on land as something different from that on "capital," and suggests that land value taxes be applied to land as site value alone, for locational reasons as well as for purposes of alleviating consequent false shortages. These variations bring in dimensions of the new metropolitan areas and the urbanized patterns of regions, particularly in the mass produced suburbs. Even the tract builder has forsaken his old comrade, the developer-subdivider, because the latter has created a shortage of large land tracts which the large-scale builder certainly must have in order to keep his business going. This means land costs must be available that are not so prohibitive that he cannot pass them on to the consumer, and thus keep the price of the product under the barrier of resistance.

That same issue of *House and Home* stated that current taxes penalize land development, land improvement and home building by "multiplying the local taxes the owner must pay as soon as the new house is built on his land or existing buildings are improved." In switching from property taxes to income taxes, they also make the point that today's taxes are "taxing away most of the profit from land development and house building at ordinary income tax rates," while they "subsidize land speculation by undertaxing the land as long as it is left idle or under-used and taxing the profits of land speculation less than half as heavily as the profit of land development and home building are taxed." This leads to the next element of change that is being proposed.

2. MODIFY THE INCOME TAX

Efforts were considered to change the tax laws covering real estate sales last year, and further action seems to be going on this year in Congress. As of about the first of this year, Representative Keogh of New York suggested another approach to get at the speculative activity in real estate, which probably will reach the Congress and will be given serious consideration. The major provisions of this plan are that the relationship between being taxed at ordinary income and capital gains rates would vary and only property which is held for seven years or more would benefit by having all its gain become taxable at capital gains rates.

3. CHANGE ASSESSMENT PRACTICES

In the past, underassessment made it possible for land to be held cheaply for years and thus aid speculative endeavor. The breach widened and there was a marked difference between sale prices and the true and fair value as assigned by the assessor's office. More recently, with the surge of reassessment studies, particularly in the new suburban areas of the Western cities, tax rates have gone up considerably to finance the new schools and public improvements which are being built, and the old saw of going out in the country to escape high taxation of the cities is reversed completely. Comparable houses in suburban communities are often paying double or more in yearly property taxes and, as pointed out previously, even the "vacant" agricultural lands are absorbing much higher taxes. Thus, the other paradox arises that these comparatively extensively used properties are being taxed as a reflection of the intensive uses nearby.

Action in the latter case has taken place in the State of Maryland, for example, which enacted a law in 1960 (House Bill 87) which provided that ". . . land actively devoted to farm or agricultural use shall be assessed on the basis of such use and shall not be assessed as if subdivided. . . ." In a letter sent to this reporter, Mr. James O'Donnell, Director of the State Planning Department, points out that the population of Montgomery County, an agricultural area adjoining Washington, D.C., grew from 164,000 in 1950 to 340,920 in 1960. In becoming urbanized, it was obvious that the pressures on land were tremendous, and he reports that average agricultural land values increased from $300 in 1954 to $680 in 1959. These prices brought on wording such as the following, extracted from the legislation: ". . . that the assessment of farm land shall be maintained at levels compatible with the continued use of such land performing and shall not be adversely affected by neighboring land uses of a more intensive nature . . . to prevent the forced conversion of such open space to the more intensive uses as the result of economic pressures caused by the assessment of land . . ."

The State of Hawaii enacted new legislation in June, 1961 which concerned itself with the basis for assessing lands according to their value in certain uses. A State Land Use Commission was created and the state is classified and districted into three major classes of uses: urban, agriculture, and conservation. Among other things, the adoption of land use regulations for these districts is encouraged, and adjustments of assessing practices are studied and filed with the Department of Taxation with consideration to the uses going on as well as the uses which might ultimately go on.

The interesting thing, other than the fact that this is the state exercising the zoning function at that level in addition to allowing it to be used at the local level, is the section which they call "dedicated lands." Here, within an agricultural or conservation district, a property owner may dedicate his land for specific purposes and have his land assessed at that use value. At the initial petition for consideration, a study is made as to the suitability of the land for the intended use in terms of productivity of land, etc., and possible conflict with the overall development plan for the state. If these conditions are satisfied, then ". . . the petition to dedicate shall constitute a forfeiture on the part of the owner of any right to change the use of the land for a minimum period of ten years. . . ." There are a number of other details, but another significant implication here is that there is, of course, a special tax assessment privilege, and if the land owner does not observe the restrictions on uses of his land, ". . . all differences in the amount of taxes that were paid and those that would have been due from assessment of higher use shall be payable with a 5% per annum penalty from the respective dates these payments would have been due."

The Maryland law has been furthered to the point where a state-wide zoning action takes place in broad categories of land use.

Where logical and extensive land uses are desirable as part of the planning and development program, assessment practices are modified so as not to direct economic sanctions against the land owners who may also wish to keep it that way.

The Role of Public Policy

In suggesting the main streams of change, it should be noted that more dramatic proposals have been and probably will continue to be made. Land nationalization schemes, premises which limit public or private ownership, progressive taxes on land (originally suggested by Jefferson by the size of various tracts), the Single Tax as such, in which all taxes would be supported by the tax on the unearned increment of land, and other modifications such as the English Town and Country Planning Act of 1947, which was a tax on betterment or development rights, etc., are examples. Some broad conclusions that taxation policies and, moreover, their application are partially deterministic of land development patterns are unquestionable. There seems to be some agreement that some taxes are at best archaic for contemporary urbanization patterns.

There are some interesting dichotomies inherent in government policies at all levels which presumably foster sensible growth patterns on one hand, and encourage land shortages and sporadic irregular development consequences on the other. As an analogy, we note here the bifurcated policy of general welfare, which manipulates interest rates in terms of general economic conditions, while at the same time affecting the number of housing starts and types. Very often the first is done at the expense of the second. More germane, to repeat, the government makes expenditures for land planning and development purposes while at the same time encouraging speculation, scatter, and shortages by the income tax device. A second bifurcated policy at the local level of government is one which compels the assessor to arrive at some true or fair value of land without considering the zoning for this land, and even being forced to ignore it. In both cases, the planning and development issue is strongly involved.

Two general courses of action lie before us. We might resolve some of the philosophical, political, and institutionalized manifestations that exist (it happens, but happens slowly), and then it might be comparatively easy to make decisions as to the economic and *social* cost vs. benefit aspects of taxation that influence land. The taxation picture is one part of a complex picture which affects: (1) the *timing* of development, and which land is so used first; (2) the *pattern* of development reflected in scatter and skipped-over undeveloped areas; (3) the *character* of develop-

ment, ranging from various density implications to land use changes on the regional and metropolitan level; and (4) *planning* of areas, which gets into the facets of assessment vs. zoning, appraisal theory (highest and best use, close but not too close), etc. While planning, for example, often seems to be trying to force private property owners to make decisions contrary to those which they think will be profitable, the community itself could clean house in matters that affect land development and taxation by letting the right hand know what the left hand is up to.

30

Effects of Property Taxation on Slums and Renewal: A Study of Land-Improvement Assessment Ratios

A. H. Schaaf

This article appeared originally in Land Economics, Vol. 45, No. 1, © 1969, pp. 111–116, published by the Regents of the University of Wisconsin.

This study was given assistance by the Center for Real Estate and Urban Economics, University of California, Berkeley. The author gratefully acknowledges the assistance of Jay Maxwell and Leonard Nathanson.

THIS ARTICLE reports the results of an empirical study of two familiar propositions concerning the effects of property taxation on urban slums and renewal: (1) that tax assessment policies tend to foster and perpetuate slums and (2) that the placing of a greater emphasis on land as opposed to improvements as the property tax base constitutes a desirable method of stimulating slum renewal. We will analyze first the argument that property taxes encourage slums, discussing the nature of the argument and the empirical evidence developed in this study concerning it. We will then examine some possible effects of shifting from a tax based on land and improvements to one based on land only.

Tax Policies as Causes of Slums

The argument that property taxation acts to foster and perpetuate slums constitutes, in its most logical and correct form, an attack upon tax assessment policies. If slum properties are assessed at lower ratios of their current market values than are other properties, particularly properties that have just been renewed, it is clear that property taxes will deter renewal. Slum uses would be taxed at a lower percentage of their asset value than non-slum uses and any rational property owner will, *ceteris paribus*, hold his asset in the use with the lowest tax rate.

Methodology of the Study

At first glance it might appear that the most direct way to test the validity of the "undertaxed slums" argument would be to compile independent appraisals of "slum and non-slum" properties and then to compare these appraisals with the tax assessor's valuations. However, real property appraising is not an exact science and such a study would amount to little more than an exercise in "second-guessing" the assessor. The methodology employed here relies entirely upon data compiled by the assessor. These data consist of assessed valuations of land and improvements, and the ratios between these valuations.

Land-improvement ratios have been used in other studies as evidence that slums are "undertaxed." In both New York City and Dayton, Ohio, investigation indicated that land-improvement ratios did not vary according to conditions that the investigators considered indicative of slum conditions. In New York the comparison was between land-improvement ratios in the city as a whole and those in a number of designated slum clearance areas. In Dayton the comparison was between areas with different degrees of "blight" as determined by the study group.

The similarity of the ratios was taken as evidence by both of these study groups that the tax assessors were undertaxing slums by underassessing the land. As stated in the New York City study: "In the light of the general assumption that slum properties consist of miserable buildings on highly valuable land, it is startling to find that these land-use ratios are almost exactly those of the entire borough. Further, the New York study states: "These figures suggest that, at the present time, land in slum areas is not assessed in terms of market value, but is written down to reflect the inadequacy of the existing improvements and the deterioration of the immediate neighborhood." Reviewing both its findings and those of the New York study, the Dayton study similarly concludes that "there seems little doubt that the two studies provide formidable evidence that building/land ratios do not reflect blight."

The present study compares land-improvement ratios of properties in 79 areas of northern Alameda County, California. The total area of the study consists of the cities of Oakland, Berkeley, Alameda, Emeryville, Albany and Piedmont, a highly urbanized region in which virtually all types of urban land uses are represented. The 79 sub-areas are fortuitous groupings of contiguous properties. The County Assessor records his data in several books, each corresponding to a contiguous geographical district. We will call each of these a Map Book Area (hereinafter referred to as MBA). The assessed values of the land and the improvements are separately and individually totaled for each MBA by the assessor.

These MBAs form the units of our empirical analysis. The ratios between the land and improvement value totals were computed for all MBAs. Land use, zoning and census data were then consulted in order to determine to the fullest extent possible the land use and demographic characteristics of each area. A tabulation summarizing all of the data may be obtained from the author. We shall list here only the median and two extreme values of each category of data. The land-improvement ratios—i.e., land values as a percent of improvement values—varied from 92.9 per cent to 29.0 per cent with a median of 50.0 per cent. Thus, in the median MBA, the total assessed value of the improvements was twice that of the land.

INDICES OF SLUM CONDITIONS

In order to follow the methodology of comparing land-improvement ratios in slum and non-slum areas, it is necessary to develop some measures of slum conditions. The term slum is most commonly used to denote an

Effects of Property Taxation on 237
Slums and Renewal: A Study of
Land-Improvement Assessment Ratios

area of bad housing or, more broadly, a bad residential environment. It follows, however, that the delineation of a slum depends upon the standard used to measure housing conditions. Probably the most complete standard that has ever developed is that of the American Public Health Association. The Association rates an urban area on the basis of the facilities of the dwelling units, structural deficiencies, conditions of occupancy and environmental conditions. However, the Association has never established a precise number of penalty points that would serve to mark a dwelling as substandard or an area as a slum.

We are also interested in the effects of taxes on blight. The term blight is often used interchangeably with slum, the implied distinction sometimes being that a blighted area is not quite as bad as a slum. In a more precise usage, however, blight may be employed to denote urban areas that are not in optimum use due to some inhibiting or retarding factor. Of particular interest to us is the argument that a low tax rate is one such factor.[1] If property taxes were to increase more than property values following renewal and the post-renewal use were considered to be a more efficient and desirable use of the site than the pre-renewal use, tax policy would be a cause of blight.

Three indices of slums and/or blight (under-utilization) are employed in this study: (1) *Median Income* was estimated for each MBA on the basis of the Census Tract data reported in the 1960 Housing Census. Income has long been recognized as closely associated with housing quality. A conspicuous feature of virtually any urban slum is the relatively low income of its resident population. The median MBA incomes range from $3,200 to $16,300; the median of all 79 MBAs is $6,400.[2]

[1] Other blighting factors that have been cited include area-wide disamenities that are beyond the power of any individual property owner to correct and also unrealistically high asking prices for pre-renewal properties.

[2] The median household income assigned to

(2) *Age of Improvements* is measured by the percentage of all residential structures built before 1919. Old structures are another common feature of urban slums since they permit a reduction in shelter amenities and resulting shelter outlays. They are of particular interest to us, however, because the predominance of old buildings in built-up urban areas should result in relatively high land-improvement ratios if tax assessing is being done correctly. This follows virtually by definition since the old improvements will be substantially depreciated due to obsolescence and deterioration, while the land value is unaffected by these forces of time. Thus, regardless of whether old buildings denote slum conditions per se, the relationship between land improvement ratios and the presence of old buildings provides a check on assessment practices.

The basic data for the measure employed here are Census Tract counts of the number and percentages of all residential structures built before 1919. The same procedures were used to derive these MBA percentages as those employed in determining median MBA incomes. The incidence of old structures in the MBA's range from a low of 0.0 per cent to a high of 85.2 per cent; the median of all the MBA percentages is 34.8

(3) *Under-Utilization Index* represents an attempt to measure the degree to which the land in a given MBA is not in its most productive long-term use. This is not necessarily a slum condition index although many slums, typified by old buildings on highly accessible land, are undoubtedly approaching a point of profitable reutilization. However, it is often tacitly and incorrectly assumed that all slums fit this situation. This assumption is an important part of the "undertaxed-slums" argument in that it is

each MBA is a weighted average of the incomes reported for the various census tracts or portions thereof, that lie in the specific MBA, with weights assigned according to the percentage of the total MBA land area that is occupied by each tract.

alleged that slum assessments do not reflect fully the potential reuse value of slum land.

Our interest in this study is to search for evidence that would help determine whether or not tax assessments are reflecting reuse values. Accordingly, under-utilization should be associated with high land-improvement ratios regardless of whether or not the particular area is a slum. Some slums may have a high potential reuse value while others may simply be areas of poor housing populated by low-income households attempting to reduce their shelter outlays.

The index employed here was computed by subtracting the percent of total MBA land zoned for low-density, residential use from the percent of total MBA land actually being so used.[3] The only data in the present study that might shed some light on possible under-utilization were those on land use and zoning. It appears plausible to expect that under-utilization is more likely to exist when the zoning of a parcel permits a higher valued use than the parcel's current use. The index employed here is based on the idea that low-density residential use in areas zoned for commercial, industrial or high-density residential use is the most certain and outstanding case of possible under-utilization. The under-utilization indices of the MBAs vary from 10 per cent to 91 per cent; the median of all 79 indices is 35 per cent.

ARE ALAMEDA COUNTY SLUMS UNDERTAXED?

Table I contains rank correlation coefficients of land-improvement ratios and the three independent variables discussed above for the 79 MBAs, as well as the rank correlation coefficients among the independent variables themselves. As might be expected, the three independent variables are generally rather highly correlated—often more so than they are with land-improvement ratios. This situation limits the usefulness of multiple regression techniques, and rank correlation coefficients were used as the means of analyzing the data. It should be noted that all of the coefficients in Table I have the expected or

[3] If no land was either zoned for, or used for, low-density residential use, high-density residential zoning and uses form the basis for comparative measurement.

Effects of Property Taxation on   **239**
Slums and Renewal: A Study of
Land-Improvement Assessment Ratios

"right" signs and that the levels of significance indicated are for one-sided tests.

Accepting our earlier argument that correct assessment policies obtain when market value-assessed value ratios are constant, the data in Table I are certainly not unfavorable with regard to property assessments in Alameda County. Of the three independent variables examined, the incidence of old buildings has the highest correlation with land-improvement ratios. This is as it should be since old buildings have by definition depreciated in value and should be associated, *ceteris paribus*, with high land-improvement ratios. One could hardly argue that in Alameda County land values are "written down to reflect the inadequacies of the existing improvements" as was concluded in the New York City study discussed previously.

Low income has a significant but lower correlation with high land-improvement ratios. Again it may be argued that this is as it should be. Low income does not necessarily denote under-improved real estate, although it generally does denote areas with low residential amenities, i.e., "slums." The tendency for such areas to be located on close-in, accessible land and improved with old, well-depreciated buildings often causes their land-improvement ratios to be relatively high. However, "shantytowns" and modest-income residential areas improved with small, inexpensive houses might not be located on particularly valuable land. In this case, low income would not be associated with either high land-improvement ratios or old buildings.

There are, in fact, two examples of the latter situation in this study. The MBAs in parts of Albany and East Oakland show relatively low land-improvement ratios, low incomes and few old structures. Visual inspection reveals that these are areas occupied by modest single-family homes. They lack appeal for higher-income residential uses and in general have little appeal for non-residential uses. Thus, although populated by households with below-average incomes, they are not underdeveloped and are correctly assessed when exhibiting average land-improvement ratios. They also represent areas occupied dominantly by lower-middle income residents but with few buildings constructed prior to 1920.

The under-utilization index developed here is very weakly related to land-improvement ratios. Thus, there is little evidence in this study that the assessor has considered alternative and potentially more valuable uses when considering land values, as he should if assessing on the basis of market value regardless of the current use of the property. However, it is entirely possible that the lack of such evidence in the present study is due simply to the absence of any good measure of under-utilization. Perhaps the chief flaw in the present case is the reliance on zoning classifications to represent a realistic estimate of a parcel's most profitable use, particularly in the near future.

Effects of a Shift to Site-Value Taxation

The use of land value as the sole base of the property tax has long been recommended by various social critics, journalists, economists and diverse professionals involved in the study and development of urban real estate. In essence, they argue that a land

Table 1—Cross-classification of rank correlation coefficients

	Land-Improvement Ratios	Median Income	Age of Structure	Under-Utilization Index
Land Improvement Ratios	—	—0.19*	0.40**	0.09
Median Income	—0.19*	—	—0.73**	—0.41**
Age of Structure	0.40**	—0.73**	—	0.21*
Under-Utilization Index	0.09	—0.41**	0.21*	—

* Significant at .05 level.
** Significant at .01 level.

tax cannot be shifted because taxation has no supply-reducing effects on a non-reproducible commodity such as land. Thus, a shift to site-value taxation will not affect the supply price or rent of land but will free land developers from any tax liabilities occasioned by land improvement. As a result, new construction will be stimulated. Additionally, proponents of the land tax often applaud the distributional effects of transferring all property taxes to the land-owner because land values are held to be products of external socio-economic forces rather than any efforts or productive activities on the part of the landowners.

Although these arguments are theoretically defensible they may be quite unrealistic, particularly in the short-run. Typically, in America, land and improvements are owned by the same party, either an owner-occupant or an absentee landlord. A shift to site-value taxation with no change in the total property tax revenue in a given taxing jurisdiction will result in an increase in the property tax liability of owners with properties having land-improvement ratios above the jurisdictional average and vice versa. When this occurs, it is difficult to argue that the users of properties with high land-improvement ratios, either owners or tenants, will not be faced with increased tax bills. In the case of rental properties, it might be argued that the absentee landlord rather than the tenants would be affected. However, the highly imperfect and oligopolistic nature of slum rental markets makes full-cost pricing quite likely. If so, the tax increases faced by most owners in a given slum area will result in a compensating general rent increase. Again, this is particularly apt to be the immediate and short-run effect of the tax increase.

The results reported here are those that would obtain under the assumption that the economic effects of any tax change rest mainly on the user of the property, whether owner-occupant or tenant. We computed the percentage change in taxes that would be occasioned in each MBA if, with no change

in total tax revenues or assessed valuations, land value became the sole base of the property tax. The percentages are determined by comparing the given MBA's share of total assessed property values (and thus its present tax share) with its share of total assessed land values (and thus its tax share following a shift to site-value taxation). Given the tax-incidence assumption specified above, analysis of the effects of site-value taxation may be made by comparing the characteristics of the MBAs in various tax-increase and tax-decrease categories.

In order to estimate the effect on different land-use types of a shift to site-value taxation, the following system was employed. The total property value in each MBA was multiplied by the percentages of the MBA's property in each of the four land-use types. The resulting figures formed estimates of the dollars of assessed value of each land-use type in each MBA. These figures were used as weights applied to the tax change percentages to determine a weighted average percentage tax change for each land-use type in the study area as a whole.

Due in part to the internal heterogeneity of the MBAs, the results are not terribly striking. Low-density residential uses would obtain a 0.9 per cent tax decrease, high-density residential uses would suffer a 1.1 per cent tax increase. Industrial uses would find their taxes reduced by 2.6 per cent. However, commercial uses would be faced with a tax change of somewhat more substantial magnitude. Their taxes would rise by 7.8 per cent.

The shift to site-value taxation has more pronounced differential effects in the case of households of different incomes. The 79 MBAs were divided into two groups—51 MBAs in which residential properties could in general expect to suffer a tax increase as a result of the shift to site-value taxation and 28 MBAs in which residential property taxes would in general be reduced. The tax-increase group consists of the 24 MBAs in which non-residential land uses occupy over 25 per cent of the land area plus all *other* MBAs in which taxes would rise following the shift to site-value taxation. This procedure is based on the argument that residential properties in areas with many non-residential uses may be expected to be situated on land with high alternative-use value. Such properties would have relatively high land-improvement ratios (and thus experience a tax-increase under site-value taxation) even though the MBA in which they are located, say a heavily industrialized area, would as a whole experience a tax decrease. The second group contains all those MBAs in the over-75 per cent residential category that would experience a tax decrease following the shift to site-value taxation.

The median incomes of the MBAs in the tax-increase group average $6,406, while in the tax-decrease group they average $8,196. This difference is significant at the one per cent level.[4] The same result, although much less emphatic, obtains when just the "residential" MBAs are compared. If we exclude the 24 MBAs in which non-residential land uses exceed 25 per cent of the total, the median incomes of the 27 remaining tax-increase MBAs average $7,422. This is still substantially below the $8,196 average income of the 28 tax-decrease residential areas but the difference is only significant at the 10 per cent level as a one-sided test.[5]

Summary and Conclusions

In this article we have examined 79 contiguous areas in Northern Alameda County,

[4] The t test was employed to test the significance of the difference between these two means. Calculations showed t = −3.56.

[5] In this case t = −1.28.

Effects of Property Taxation on **241**
Slums and Renewal: A Study of
Land-Improvement Assessment Ratios

California. The total assessed values of land and improvements in each area were known and were used to determine each area's overall land-improvement ratio. Data on land use, zoning and occupant characteristics were also compiled for each area.

The data were first examined for clues as to whether tax assessments tended to foster and perpetuate slums. It is argued that correct assessments and no "undertaxation" should obtain if land improvement ratios are higher in areas with relatively high incidences of old buildings, low-income residences, and potentially high reuse values. Although not terribly strong in every case, evidence was found to indicate that tax assessments were reflecting at least some of these tendencies. Particularly strong was the influence of old buildings and it is argued that, of the above factors, the presence of old buildings is the most likely to be associated with high land-improvement ratios if tax assessing is being done correctly.

A second use of the data was an investigation of some of the possible effects of shifting from the present property tax to one based only on land values. Apart from a 7.8 tax increase in the case of commercial properties, little differential effect was found between various major types of land users. Among the residential users, however, it was found that the shift to land taxes would, in general, raise taxes on properties occupied by lower-income groups and lower taxes on properties occupied by higher-income groups.

31

Controlling Urban Growth: The New Zealand and Australian Experiment

Robert O. Harvey
W. A. V. Clark

Reprinted with the permission of The Appraisal Journal and the American Institute of Real Estate Appraisers. Vol. 32, No. 4, October 1964, pp. 551–558.

THE RAPID peripheral growth of American cities in the postwar years has occurred in patterns which are often described as "sprawl." Sprawl is made up of scattered areas of urban character at the periphery of cities and is adjacent to, or surrounded by, agricultural uses and idle land. The sprawled area has a heterogeneous pattern with an over-all density less than that found in mature built-up areas of the city. There are at least three major types of sprawl: low-density sprawl—continuous developments containing extravagantly large lots; ribbon development—segments compact within themselves, strung out along highways, with the intervening areas undeveloped; and leap-frog development—a collection of discontinuous, although often compact, urban pockets.

Many observers of the urban scene looking at peripheral development on a short-term basis have decried the land use patterns called "sprawl" and have sought ways of ordering urban development into more compact, supposedly less wasteful, patterns. Four principal methods for influencing the

peripheral growth of cities have been advanced by planners and land economists critical of the growth process. Included among the major methods advocated for controlling or mitigating sprawl are the use of the land tax, planning and zoning, public acquisition of open land, and public control of the extension of utilities.

Advocates of the suggested techniques for sprawl prevention usually argue with more enthusiasm than evidence. The control devices are examined here to determine what might be accomplished given the conditions of sprawled areas and the political and metropolitan structure of American cities. A review of the experiences in Australia and New Zealand provides empirical evidence of the effectiveness of sprawl control in the urban scene.

Land Tax

The greater part of municipal revenues in the United States is derived from taxes levied against real property. In most urban areas in the United States, the property tax is based on assessment of the fair cash value of real property, that is, land and improvements. In some parts of the world, the real property tax is based on a levy against the earning power of real estate, and in other places land alone (excluding improvements) is taxed. The latter approach to property taxation (assessment) is called the land tax and is frequently advocated as an instrument to manipulate the development and redevelopment of urban areas.

The land tax, sometimes called the single tax, was originally advocated by Henry George, the late-19th century economist. George was interested in social questions and was concerned with the distribution of wealth and the contributions of society to individuals. He dedicated his classic, *Progress and Poverty,* "To those who, seeing the vice and misery that spring from the unequal distribution of wealth and privilege, feel the possibility of a higher social state and would strive for its attainment." (San Francisco, March, 1879). George's crusade has been carried on by many, and the concept of the single tax has been adopted by those who see in it an instrument which could compel the development or change in land uses in the urban scene.[1]

The arguments of the proponents of the land tax explain, and properly so, that taxes on the entire value of the improved urban real estate tend to prevent improvement, rehabilitation, or even change in the character of improved land uses. The argument is that if only the land were taxed, owners would not hesitate to improve urban land because the improvements would not be penalized. Furthermore, a tax imposed upon the "true" value of unused land would compel its use and thus be an instrument to thwart "socially undesirable speculation" in urban lands.

The advocates of the land tax are, in fact, pointing out the damage of any tax levied against real estate, and are arguing for a tax which does not change with a change in the character of the use of the land. However, values of unimproved land are based upon the productivity of the site under the use which is more realistically probable for that particular site. If the land tax were imposed on the basis of the actual values of the land as determined by the productivity released by the appropriate improvement on the site, land values, and therefore taxes, would rise with the identification of the "right" improvement to the land. As long as the land tax changes with changing land values, the results on the utilization of urban land and capital formation are not greatly different than under taxation of land and improvements.

The sudden imposition or major increase in the tax on a site which obviously is ripe for development may induce activity; but when large areas of land are available for partial conversion from one use to another, it is extremely difficult to measure which of the areas are appropriate for conversion and on

[1] Taxes on land are regarded as useful or appropriate for two main reasons. First, since land is primarily a social value which rises where people cluster together for exchange and social intercourse, it is particularly suitable for taxation, since taxation itself is a social phenomenon. Other things being equal, secondly, a tax on land value tends to lower the asking price for land, and thus to make more sites available for development, or at least at a lower price.

which the land tax should be increased. Further, if the land tax is increased with the maturity of the site, the tax during the ripening period merely serves to reduce the profitability of the existing use without necessarily hastening the appropriateness of the conversion. The rising land tax which presumably keeps pace with the maturing of the site would tend only to stimulate premature conversion in order to mitigate the burdens of the tax without allowing sites to ripen to ultimate highest and best uses when viewed from the social standpoint.

It is easy to recognize a mature site ripe for conversion in the heart of a city where a single site may be envisioned for a particular use. On the edge of the city where only a share of the available land is appropriate for conversion, it is a complex problem to identify the mature area among competing areas. To illustrate, the difference in area of circles with a three- and four-mile radius is about twenty-three square miles. A city expanding at its periphery rarely will be able to use all of the peripheral area at one time. There comes the choice of selecting which parcels shall be tagged as mature and subjected to increased land taxes. The evidence of which sites are appropriate for conversion is really found in the market. The subdividers precede the assessor and point the way. If the taxes rise, however, it is also possible that the rising taxes will be added to the supply price of the land, and in fact, delay the conversion of land from agricultural to urban uses.

The rising land taxes may, in fact, induce sprawl because as the taxes become a part of the costs of development in addition to the costs of acquisition, subdividers are inclined to choose other competing areas. Consumer choices for land are not restricted to the mere close-in areas.

The land tax is often advocated as a new device which presumably would curtail or mitigate the tendencies to sprawl and limit speculation, notwithstanding the fact that the real estate tax imposed upon rural or vacant property is essentially a land tax.

It is appropriate to ask if sprawl and speculation have been prevented in areas of the
world in which the land tax has long been
used. Australia and New Zealand have used
the tax on land for many years. For example,
in Sydney, Australia, the land tax is used
throughout the metropolitan area, and two-
thirds of the municipal councils in the
Melbourne metropolitan area have chosen
unimproved values as their tax basis. In
New Zealand, the opportunity for the land
tax was first established in 1896. However,
not all cities and counties in New Zealand
immediately took the opportunity. Of the
major cities, Wellington decided for the land

It would seem that the question of the land
tax versus the capital tax has had little or no
effect on the development of the urban form
in New Zealand. Moreover, the efficiency of
the tax system is questioned by city officials
who have experienced both systems:

> Frequently the basic fact that, whatever
> system you have, it is only a method by which
> the rate burden is distributed, is quite over-
> looked. It varies the incidence but not the
> total amount collected. Similarly, the fact that
> a new or different system will merely dis-
> tribute the same burden in a different way is
> also overlooked.
> The system of rating, no matter what it
> may be, does not affect the development of
> an urban area to any marked extent.[3]

It seems that speculation has been present
in all areas of urban expansion. Certainly, it

Table—1 Tax systems in use in New Zealand

| | CITIES, BOROUGHS, AND TOWN DISTRICTS | | COUNTIES | |
Rating System	Number	Population	Number	Population
Unimproved (land only)	129	1,134,250	64	472,950
Capital (land & improvements)	27	66,040	54	346,490
Annual (annual rent or annual earning capacity)	17	246,910	—	—

Source: New Zealand Official Year Book, 1960, Govt. Printer, Wellington, New Zealand, p. 844.

tax in 1901, Christchurch in 1902, and
Dunedin in 1954. Numerous smaller local
bodies and municipalities took up the system
during the half century from the inception of
the land tax. Both systems are in effect in
New Zealand today, as is shown in Table I.

Yet New Zealand's urban expansion can
be described in the following way:

> New Zealand cities have among the lowest
> densities in the world. The cult of the quarter-
> acre section is almost universal and this,
> combined with inability to finance purchases
> of existing houses which are in sound condi-
> tion and/or to provide the cost of rehabili-
> tating some of those which are not, is pro-
> ducing a very uneconomic, unsatisfactory
> urban pattern—a "sprawl"—which necessi-
> tates excessive expenditures for public services
> to reach the unnecessarily extensive suburban
> and fringe areas.[2]

2 Harold M. Mayer, "Some Urban Problems
in New Zealand," *New Zealand Geographer*
XVIII, April 1962, p. 18.

has been present in areas using capital value
systems and in areas using unimproved
rating systems.

> Perhaps the strongest arguments put for-
> ward against the Annual Value and similarly
> Capital Value Systems is that taxing on a
> basis related to improvements a property
> owner is penalized for his initiative and ex-
> penditure of capital; proper development is
> therefore discouraged and no adequate levy
> applies to vacant land which may be held for
> purely speculative purposes.
> I am inclined to the view that where land
> is held for purely speculative purposes this
> will tend to continue; to some extent at least,
> no matter what rating system is in force.[4]

3 Letters from the town clerk of Dunedin to
W. A. V. Clark, October 31, 1962, and to the
public relations officer, Timaru, New Zealand,
September 25, 1961.
4 C. M. Turner, "Rating Systems in New
Zealand," *Proceedings*, New Zealand Institute of
Town Clerks Conference, Dunedin, February,
1961, p. 70.

The reasons for the use of the land tax are interesting. The decision to use a capital or an unimproved tax is a decision made entirely by the voters in a public poll, which is, of course, dominated by self-interest. The land tax is adopted because the majority of voters believe the taxes on their real property will be reduced, through a shift in the burden of the tax to central city land owners.

In Australia, also, sprawling urban areas have been identified. One of the most forceful descriptions is of Sydney. The foreword to a publication by the Cumberland County Council, Sydney, closes with this sentence: "This report is presented as a challenge to sprawl and scatter and to the concept that increasing the scope for land subdivision is a solution to Sydney's housing problem." Excerpts from the report identify the sprawl character of the Sydney area:

In common with other metropolitan centres in Australia and overseas, Sydney has undergone a period of rapid growth during the past ten years (1947–1957). . . .
More than ninety-six percent of homes built during this period are single unit detached dwellings (cottages) and the bulk of population increases has been absorbed in outer suburban areas, located at distances between ten and twenty miles from the city. . . .
In retrospect, both form and direction of urban growth over the last decade are abundantly clear. There has been a process of low density "horizontal" expansion along the outskirts, reinforced by drift of population from the centre. . . .
Development within zone Living Areas has advanced to varying stages. In outer suburbs few areas can be regarded as fully built up, while large areas of land carry only scattered, partial development, in many cases less than 50 percent of their potential.

The existence of sprawl in New Zealand and Australia which have long had the land tax illustrates that the land tax does not necessarily prevent speculation or sprawl.

Advocates of the land tax have also suggested that it could be an instrument to attack blight and slums. A brief inquiry into the New Zealand experience indicates that the land tax as an instrument for the eradication of slums is as ineffective as its effect on sprawl. In answer to observers who report the absence of slums in New Zealand, there are the observations of Mayer:

The welfare state has gone a long way toward eliminating individual poverty. Nevertheless, there are slums and blighted areas in each of the four metropolitan cities of New Zealand, and in many other of its cities and towns. There are hollows in parts of Auckland, Wellington, Christchurch, and Dunedin which are as bad as anything in the world.

Pownall writes:

There is little doubt that no metropolitan community in New Zealand is alive to the fact that large numbers of low-value (poor quality) houses are already to be found within its older residential districts.[5]

Planning and Zoning

Planning and zoning would seem to be an effective method of preventing and/or treating sprawl. Indeed, attempts to use the planning weapons against sprawl are increasing. In the United States, there have been few strong efforts; but in Great Britain, New Zealand, and Australia, attempts via the Green Belt and new towns have been made to prevent sprawl and continuous urban expansion. Even planning, however, does not necessarily end sprawl.

As an example, Sydney, Australia, has extensive public programs devoted to sprawl treatment and prevention. A county plan was developed in 1947, the purpose of which was "coordination, consolidation, and conservation." It called for the arrangement of homes properly related to each other and to work and community facilities, the prevention of an unplanned mixture of uses. Consolidation required the compaction of already built-up areas before new land could be developed. Conservation extended to both the natural and man-made landscape.

To implement this wide-range plan, the main suggestion to prevent the "present sprawling development with all its economic and social disadvantages" was to put a limit

[5] L. L. Pownall, "Low Value Housing in Two New Zealand Cities," *Annals of the Association of American Geographers* L, no. 4, p. 460.

on the area of continuous living space by the development of the Green Belt.

In the County Planning Scheme Report 1948 the Green Belt is defined as: "a continuous belt of open country of uneven width surrounding the metropolitan area and lying generally on the outer fringe of existing development." The aims were threefold: to set a limit to the development of the urban areas, to prevent unnecessary subdivision, and to fill up yet unused lots in the urban area; or in more general terms, to prevent low density scatteration.

It is appropriate to examine the success of the Green Belt. In 1957 Winston wrote:

> The Green Belt is still substantially preserved and the County Council is now the sole authority for its administration. The ugly and uneconomic sprawl which characterizes Sydney's urban fringes is in many places giving way to a more marked definition between urban and rural development. This is particularly noticeable in some of the outer muncipalities which would otherwise have suffered widespread speculative subdivision, the destruction of amenities, and waste of agricultural land. The preservation of the Green Belt is giving a compactness to urban development which will result in many worthwhile economies and advantages.[6]

Thus, it was the plan which might be given credit for combating sprawl and speculation. Indeed, that these two factors were operating before the plan came into operation, and still may be, is clear. Much of the dead land which was a feature of the country before the plan was developed was produced by crude speculation; that is, notwithstanding the land tax, the purchase of land in anticipation of a change in valuation.

Moreover, an appendix in Winston describes the condition and extent of sprawl prior to the development of the plan:

> In 1947 only 41 percent of the present urban land in the County was sewered. . . . There were also thousands of residential lots with properly finished roads and full services

available, which were still vacant. . . . In 1947 the vacant land in the County with water and electricity could have supported a population of more than 250,000. . . .

There was a vast amount of vacant land in the county where public services were available but not used, while on the other hand there were many thousands of homes without sewerage and without paved access roads, footpaths, or curbs and gutters.

The plan was to replace the sprawl (notwithstanding the land tax) with compact living areas; but in 1959 an unprecedented *release* of Green Belt land took place. The areas within the Belt were not completely built up, so that a pattern was set for the release of Green Belt land and thus more urban sprawl.

An original intention had been to develop new towns beyond the Green Belt to take care of population expansion after the area within the Belt was built up. The administration of the Green Belt may encourage sprawl rather than prevent it. Speculation has certainly not been prevented.

> To most people the Green Belt is part of the stock exchange. You buy cheaply, await the release, and then collect your dividend.[7]

Even the planned Green Belt does not seem to have saved Sydney from the possibility of "a semi-planned sprawl to the foothills of the Blue Mountains. . . ."[8]

Public Acquisition of Land

One attempt to stop sprawl in conjunction with planning is through the public acquisition of land. In the case of Sydney, the county council had acquired approximately 2,000 acres at a cost of £700,000. Despite the rise in land values, several important scenic and recreation areas—harbor foreshores, for example—have been made. The county also has spent £300,000 resuming vacant land. However, this type of activity is limited by

[6] D. Winston, *Sydney's Great Experiment*, Sydney, 1957, p. 73.

[7] J. S. Emery, "Sydney—A Problem in Metropolitan Planning," *Monthly Bulletin*, Geographical Society of New South Wales, No. 3, July, 1962, p. 6.
[8] *Ibid.*

political decisions on the allocation of resources.

One argument for the public sector acquiring land at current agricultural prices is that the increased values will then accrue to the public in general. However, this activity is still essentially untried in the United States. Whether the public control of land is a socially acceptable answer to the American urban dweller is open to question.

The real question with respect to using public money to acquire vacant land is whether or not the vacant land "problem" is more demanding than other "problems" facing society. A public land acquisition program is in competition with expenditures for schools, unemployment compensation, national defense, fire protection, hospitals, and other public functions.

Capital Utilities and Control of Sprawl

It is also possible that utility programs may influence the extent and character of sprawl. Utilities are most influential if there are physical, practical, and legal limitations in the development of land. If land can be developed with substitutes for publicly required capital programs, then the utilities are not a major factor in limiting sprawl.

The inability of public utility groups to keep pace with urban growth oftentimes impels urban development to occur in regions outside the influences of the public utility agency. Sanitary sewer systems are a case in point. It is not uncommon for public sanitary agencies to be unable for monetary or physical reasons to extend their lines to new areas of development. Accordingly, developers of land faced with the installation of a septic tank system or the development of a private utility are not only free but also sometimes compelled because of physical factors to develop beyond the immediate periphery of the settled areas.

It appears that sprawl is least likely to occur under conditions in which sanitary, water, and power facilities are readily available at the edge of the settled area, provided that the type of facilities offered by the utilities are required for areas of typical urban densities.

Conclusion

It is likely that sprawl is a form of city growth which, at best, may be mitigated but not prevented. The various approaches to sprawl modification, including the land tax and the planning and zoning arrangements common in free societies, have not stopped sprawl. Utility requirements have been no more successful. It is probable that at any single moment a city experiencing growth and change will have sprawl on the fringe, and without the control possibilities found in a planned state it is unlikely that a free society can eliminate sprawl.

It is interesting that some controls designed to influence land use and prevent sprawl actually may have worked to promote sprawl. Whenever there exists within one housing market area both a controlled and an uncontrolled district, it is probable that sprawl limited within the controlled area simply may be cast outward to the uncontrolled area. It is doubtful that sprawl can be avoided in any other than a totally regimented state; and even then it is possible that administrators would not agree on the nature and form of urban compaction or estimate correctly the rate at which growth might occur. Sprawl could occur in the completely controlled state; in which case, the occupants of sprawl arrive there through political fiat and influence, as opposed to independent market decisions.

32

Taxation
and Development

Thomas J. Plunkett

This paper appeared originally in Planning 1962, pp. 96–101, *published by the American Society of Planning Officials, 1313 East Sixtieth Street, Chicago, Illinois 60637. Reproduced by permission.*

THERE ARE MORE implications arising from the subject of taxation and land development than can be disposed of in this article. My particular contribution will be limited to a consideration of the prospects of utilizing what is known as site value taxation in lieu of the real property tax which currently serves as the principal revenue source for municipalities in both the United States and Canada.

Interest in site value taxation has been increasing in recent years, particularly on the part of many who are concerned with problems of urban development and redevelopment. Despite this comparatively recent upsurge of interest in the subject, I would not want to suggest that site value taxation is a new or recent innovation. In simple terms, site value taxation means the imposition of a tax on the value of land only and not on the collective value of land and improvements as is presently the case. Interest in this form of taxation really goes back many years, indeed to the middle of the last century. It has been applied on a substantial scale in Australia, New Zealand, Denmark and the four western provinces in Canada. For some reason, the six eastern provinces in Canada have rarely been tempted to experiment with it.

The recent interest of urban administrators in site value taxation stems from the very real appeal of its supposed advantages. Advocates of site value taxation claim that its adoption would produce the following results: (1) Eliminate the evil of land speculation; (2) Stimulate the redevelopment of slum areas, by making continued ownership of slum properties uneconomic; and (3) Shift the burden of municipal taxation from home owners to the owners of other types of property in an urban community.

These are not the only advantages that would result from the introduction of site value taxation in the opinion of its most ardent advocates. However, these are the three claimed benefits that are very significant and appealing to those of us concerned with urban planning and development. Any system of taxation that would guarantee these results cannot be ignored. The real question confronting us is to assess whether or not the introduction of site value taxation will automatically produce the results that its devotees claim that it would. Inherent in this assessment, and of particular importance, are basic considerations of administrative and political practicability.

The first advantage claimed for site value taxation is that it would reduce land speculation by imposing a much heavier tax burden on unused land with the result that the unearned increment would largely disappear. This contention has a certain amount of validity but I am doubtful that it would eliminate speculation. There is no doubt, however, that the annual municipal tax on vacant land would be increased substantially with the introduction of site value taxation.

An example of what might happen to municipal tax rates is provided in a recent study. It was estimated that a particular city in 1959 which was required to raise $3,500,000 through the existing property tax would have needed a tax rate of $18.60 per $1,000 of assessed valuation of all taxable land and improvements within the municipality. If site value taxation was introduced, improvements would be eliminated from the municipal assessment and land alone would be taxed. This means that approximately 75 per cent of the tax base would be removed and the total tax burden carried on a base of land alone equivalent to one-quarter of the former base which included land and improvements. The new tax rate necessary to raise $3,500,000 on the assessment of land alone would need to be $72.30 per $1,000 of land value. There is no doubt that under site value taxation the owners of large tracts of vacant land would be faced with a much larger annual outlay in the form of municipal taxation. But would this eliminate speculation in land? The fact is that in a period of rising land values holding costs may be insignificant when land may need to be held for only a short period of time. In a paper presented to the 1961 Conference of the Canadian Tax Foundation, an appraiser-economist commented on this point as follows:

> The greatest boom in land values ever to occur in Western Canada took place during the years 1909–1913 when site taxation was at its zenith. The reason is not hard to find: profits from land speculation can be large in relation to holding costs and the tripling or quadrupling of land taxes, as might occur under a change to site taxation, could be a relatively minor consideration—especially where it is anticipated that the land will be held for only a short period of time.[1]

If land speculators were required to hold vacant pieces of land for any considerable length of time, the cost of holding would become prohibitive under site value taxation. In such circumstances, this might foster more rapid development. However, a lot of other people who hold vacant land and who are not necessarily speculators could be hurt in the process. It seems to me that it is possible for certain individuals and institutions to find it necessary to hold land for a long period of time without necessarily being regarded as engaging in economic piracy. For example, an industrial or commercial concern might hold land for future expansion. Similarly, a legitimate developer might be required to hold land for a long period of time because it is not propitious for him to undertake a particular type of development for many reasons. It seems to me that if we want to curb speculation in land that there are more effective ways of accomplishing this objective other than the use of site value taxation. To this end a steep capital gains tax or a deed transfer tax might have better results.

[1] D. H. Clark, "Site Value as a Basis for Local Taxation," *Report of the 1961 Conference of the Canadian Tax Foundation*.

The next important advantage that is supposed to result from the use of site value taxation is the effect that it would have in stimulating slum clearance and urban renewal. It is claimed, for example, that with the introduction of site value taxation, the tax burden that would fall on the owners of slum properties would be so heavy as to force them to redevelop their properties. I doubt that there is much the owner of a slum property could or would do, even under the stimulus of a drastically increased tax burden to redevelop or improve his property when he is completely encircled by ugly buildings. Certainly it is extremely doubtful that anyone could be attracted to make use of such an improvement if it still remains surrounded by ugly unimproved buildings. If we have learned anything about redevelopment of slum areas it is that we must, in order to be effective, redevelop an entire neighborhood. This means that whole blocks of properties have to be acquired and even though this might be done in a few cases by private initiative it will in the main require public direction, the use of the expropriation powers of the public authority, and some considerable use of public funds.

The last advantage claimed for site value taxation is that it would reduce the present burden of local taxation on private home owners. This is undoubtedly true, but it would also transfer the burden elsewhere. I suspect that the possibility of reducing taxes on private home owners is the real appeal of site value taxation. It certainly has substantial political attractiveness. In Australia and New Zealand where the use of site value taxation has been determined by local option, it was apparently the lure of reduced taxation that enabled residential property owners to sanction its introduction. While in general it may be said that site value taxation would result in a lower tax burden on residential homes, it is not absolutely clear that this would be the case for all types of homes. A number of owner-occupied homes where the improvement-land ratios are below the general average in a particular city would find that the introduction of site value taxation would probably mean an increase in taxes. The social consequences are not what would be desired inasmuch as most such homes belong to low-income people living in old homes on valuable land. On the other hand, the owners of residential property where the improvement-land ratio was higher than the general average throughout the city would benefit by reduced taxation. The owners of such homes are, of course, in the middle- to higher-income brackets.

In a number of other areas, site value taxation is open to question. The tax on improvements is supposed to be the great barrier to stimulating development. Proponents of site value taxation emphasize the point that it will bring about a reduction in the tax burden on improved property. If this is the case, and I'm not saying that it is, there is a possibility that it would have an important bearing on a fundamental principle of taxation, namely, ability to pay. Surely the quality of improvements erected on a particular site provide some evidence of ability to pay. For example, if there were two identical lots in the downtown area of which one supported a 15-story office building and the other a service station and garage. If we assume that the value of improvements in the case of the former is $8,000,000 and in the case of the latter $1,000,000, the ability to pay taxes is much greater in the case of the office building.[2] This fact is recognized under our present system of local taxation which is based on land and improvements, but this cannot be recognized under site value taxation.

In general, the application of site value taxation in a city causes certain shifts in the burden of taxation. The nature of these shifts can be determined to some extent by the ratio of improvements, i.e., the ratio of total property value to land value. Under this ratio method a vacant lot would have a ratio expressed as 1:1, that is, the total value of the property is equal to the land value. Lots with improvements might exhibit ratios such as 4.3:1, 3.1:1, 2.9:1, etc. An average ratio of

improvement can be worked out for the city as a whole. Using this method, it is not difficult to work out the improvement ratios of the various land uses in a particular city. This was done in a recent study in which the author made the following observations:

> The average ratio of improvement for the city as a whole becomes the pivotal point for determining whether a given property will pay more or less tax under (a) taxation on land and improvements at an equal rate, or (b) taxation of land only. Properties exhibiting improvement ratios above the average ratio for the city will pay higher taxes under case (a). Properties with ratios below the average for the city will pay high taxes under case (b).[3]

This is really another way of saying that the properties with the most valuable improvements would pay less taxes under site value taxation and that properties with the least valuable improvements would pay more.

This type of result under site value taxation does not seem to have much regard for another important principle of taxation and that is the relationship of the tax burden to the benefits received. Municipal services paid for through local taxation are really related to people more than property. Consequently, the number of people living in or working at a property is more closely associated with the value of the building than the land.

> Thus the cost of providing and maintaining roads, bridges, and public transportations for the thousands of people working in a downtown skyscraper can be enormous; surely the benefits received theory of taxation would require that a heavy tribute should be exacted from the owner of such a monster on a basis which would clearly differentiate between him and the owner of a property with a mere handful of persons in it.[4]

The present system of taxing land and improvements would seem to be more equitable in securing a proportionate tax return in accordance with benefits received than site value taxation.

One of the results of the introduction of site value taxation is a substantial change in the rate of taxation. To some extent this was implicit in the example I referred to earlier

---

[2] This is not necessarily always the case but would be in many instances.

[3] Clark, *op. cit.*
[4] *Ibid.*

where the former tax rate of $18.60 per
$1,000 of assessment of both land and im-
provements would have to be converted to
a rate of $72.30 per $1,000 when applied to
land only. This seems to me to raise a
psychological barrier that could have re-
percussions in terms of public reaction.

I think we can learn something from the
experience of the western Canadian provinces, all of which experimented with site
value taxation at the beginning of this
century. Between 1900 and 1915, the provinces of Manitoba, Saskatchewan, Alberta
and British Columbia experienced a period
of uncontrolled land speculation. In their
efforts to find a remedy for this situation, site
value taxation had a fascinating appeal.
Municipalities were enabled to apply site
value taxation either in whole or in part and
many of them did so. The spread of the use of
site value taxation has been described as
follows:

> The rural areas of Manitoba, Saskatchewan
> and Alberta removed all taxes from improve-
> ments, as did numerous other municipalities
> including Vancouver, Victoria, and New
> Westminster, in British Columbia and Edmon-
> ton, Medicine Hat and Red Deer, in Alberta.
> The increased taxes thus imposed on land
> values were insufficient to check the boom. In
> Edmonton, Alberta—an extreme example—
> land values increased from approximately
> $6,000,000 in 1904 to $196,000,000 in 1914.
> That year the boom burst. A large percentage
> of the municipalities found themselves virtually
> bankrupt. The financial position of even the
> provincial governments was impaired.[5]

By 1930, most Western municipalities had
had enough experience with site value taxation to convince them that it was inappropriate as a base for local taxation.
Since then, most have been engaged in
pushing the tax back on improvements.[6] In
the years following the collapse of the western
land boom, many cities and some of the
provinces fostered comprehensive investigations by Royal Commissions and reports by

[5] *Municipal Improvement and Finance as
Affected by the Untaxing of Improvements and the
Taxing of Land Values*, International Committee
on Real Estate Taxation, 1958.
[6] In many instances, improvements are not
taxed on 100 per cent of value but on a stated
percentage of the value of improvement.

economists and others. The vast majority of
the studies of site value taxation carried out
in western Canada were extremely critical of
its continued application. One report of an
inquiry in 1946, into provincial-municipal
relations in the Province of British Columbia,
contained this observation:

> The experience of British Columbia and of
> other western provinces has shown that on
> fiscal grounds alone the exemption of improve-
> ments is unsatisfactory....
> The argument that the exemption of im-
> provements stimulates building and penalizes
> the land speculator may have merit in the
> period of early development of a community,
> but it is not applicable to the later period when
> the community has been substantially de-
> veloped. Some of the effects of exempting
> improvements in developed communities are:
> 1. To restrict the tax base to the narrow and
>   unstable base which may have satisfied the
>   requirements of the community in its early
>   stages, but which cannot satisfy it in its
>   more developed stage. Municipalities which
>   wholly or largely exempt improvements now
>   recoup themselves out of utility profits
>   resulting from higher rates charged to the
>   consumers of the utility service.
> 2. To subsidize the holders of large improved
>   properties, commercial, industrial, and
>   residential, who in most instances have a
>   greater taxpaying capacity than the owners
>   of smaller properties or unimproved lands,
>   and whose properties require more municipal
>   services than do other properties.[7]

This report's reference to the practice of
certain municipalities in turning to utility
profits for additional revenue demonstrates
to a large extent the inadequacy of site value
taxation as applied in western Canada. Its use
by municipalities inevitably forces them to
turn to other sources of revenue. In western
Canada, it has meant a resort to the development of utility profits—a practice that has by
no means received universal public approba-
tion. In Australia and New Zealand, where
site valuation has been widely used, the
alternative to another source of revenue has
been found in restricting the range of local
government responsibilities. Consequently,
education and law enforcement in Australia

[7] H. Carl Goldenberg, *Provincial Municipal
Relations in British Columbia.*

have become responsibilities of the state governments which also have assumed major responsibilities for hospitals, public transportation, and water supply.

One gains the impression that the advocates of site value taxation apparently believe that the present system of taxing land and improvements is inherently inequitable. The only cure, therefore, is the adoption of site value taxation which will automatically right all wrongs in a single stroke. However, much of what we can complain about with respect to the taxation of land and improvements is really due to deficiencies in assessment practice, particularly with respect to the assessment of land. Most of us, I am sure, can provide innumerable examples of where our current assessment practice has exhibited seeming inability to attribute much more than a nominal value on certain land uses. There is little doubt, therefore, that these deficiencies in assessment practice would still exist, but in probably a more pronounced manner, under site value taxation.

Much has been accomplished in recent years in the improvement of assessment techniques and a great deal more remains to be done in this area. Site value taxation does not remove the need for improved assessment practice.

Site value taxation offers a sort of panacea approach to the problem of equitable local taxation. It may have a certain amount of appeal to a local electorate by holding out the hope of reduced taxation on residential homes. However, there is a tendency to overlook such important matters as: (a) the effect on the "ability to pay" principle of taxation; (b) the effect on the "benefits received" principle of taxation; (c) the apparent need for other sources of revenue when site value taxation is adopted; (d) the effects of shifts in the burden of taxation; and (e) the fact that some of the inequalities attributable to capital value taxation really are the result of poor assessment practice which would be continued under site value taxation.

LAND PLANNERS concern themselves with the relations among the uses to which independent private owners put their land. These private owners mostly seek to maximize their individual net welfare after taxes. Since taxes are a large fraction of all costs, after-tax welfare is quite different from before-tax welfare. So public land planners seeking to influence private landowners must perforce be tax planners.

Land planners generally have been tax planners in at least a passive sense: their expectation of private response to public initiative has been based on experience, which in turn reflects landowners' tax avoidance. Some planners have grumbled at individual tax avoidance, as though it were immoral and should go away—not a very realistic approach. Others have sweepingly condemned the entire market mechanism—a "rush to judgment" that might be tempered when we consider to what extent the malfunction of the market results from avoidance of ineptly imposed tax costs. Still others have supported land underassessment to relieve the pressure to develop suburban land— without, I believe, adequately considering that unused land lies among used parcels and disrupts their symbiotic interactions, which are the heart of public land planning and the essence of urban civilization. Yet others have foundered by expecting private landowners to respond to, and fill in, the empty niches in grand plans much more rapidly than the Great American Land Speculator is wont to do.

To be most effective, land planners must become positive tax planners. Collectively, they need to support national reform of the income tax as it bears on land development. Our theme here is what they can do locally through property tax laws and assessment procedures. Tax reform can help the market help the planner. What is good for the market is generally good for planning. Land planning amends and guides the market—it is not at war with the market. On the contrary, effective public land planning presupposes a well-oiled land market.

Planners and the Land Market

The planner, through his influence on

33

Land Planning
and the Property Tax

Mason Gaffney

This article appeared originally in the Journal of the American Institute of Planners, Vol. 35, No. 3, May 1969. Reproduced by permission.

zoning, street layout and other public constraints, presents each landowner with a sort of environmental challenge: he hopes the landowner will respond constructively. The planner provides avenues of linkage by which landowners may relate to one another: he hopes they will use those avenues. The market motivates them.

On the whole, the highest use of a site is that which most relates to and complements uses on other sites. This is what cities are all about. Planners are often preoccupied with minimizing conflicts between neighbors, which calls for minor departures from the most lucrative use; but conflicts must not blind us to the overriding value of symbiosis among neighbors. This is the first concern of land planning; it is also the first concern of the self-helping landowner. The worst nuisance a central landowner can commit is passive withdrawal of his land from the life of the city—right where it gets in everyone's way. The market, if he listens, tells him to participate instead. Taxation may be used to nudge the market a little this way or that, but the first concern of tax reform is to unleash the market to do its constructive work.

Capital and people compactly grouped, and with good mutual access provided by quality planning, interact synergistically to produce a large surplus above cost. The whole is greater than the sum of its parts: that is "synergism." Planning and the market work together to maximize synergism.

Another function of the land market is in the development of new areas, or redevelopment when new uses succeed old, to synchronize interdependent private investments that interact synergistically to produce a total community. Thus as a city expands, high land values at the perimeter put simultaneous pressure on all owners there to convert to urban use. Were this mechanism in good working order, planners could extend city services to compact increments of land, initially sizing utility lines and streets for ultimate demand, secure in the knowledge that the ultimate demand would be there in short order. Private builders could orient their plans to a more certain future, minimizing transition costs of, for example, shifting from wells and septic tanks to public water and sewers. Every private improvement could be less self-sufficient and more oriented to the prospect of a total community.

But the market is not in good working order. Taxation intercedes in every land use decision. Every piece of land is periodically mobile among uses—when there is some "sacrament" in its life, such as demolition and construction, sale, subdivision, or assembly. It is then in press among competing buyers, uses, densities, timings, parcel sizes, and so on. In every such press, taxation biases the choice of favor of the lighter taxed use. The real estate tax on building thus always favors old over new; gas stations over apartments; junk yards over factories; parking lots over parking structures; high income residences over low (high income residences are usually less intensive because of larger lots in neighborhoods of higher land value); billboards over offices; unused over improved land; waiting over acting. This bias has half-destroyed the market as an arbiter among competing land uses, and an agency promoting urban synergism. It has lowered the density, retarded renewal, and broken up integral linkages of the central city, fostering in their place random scattering of new buildings at the outskirts. It has so far impaired the city's function of linking small

independent industrial firms as to bear large responsibility for today's galloping merger movement in which a key word is—synergism! Firms seek through merger and vertical integration the access to services, labor, and supplies which in a well-ordered city they could get from independent firms through the market.

Tax Base Redefinitions

I do not propose that we eliminate taxes. The public needs money. I do submit that it is not necessary for real estate taxes to impair the market. The method is to modify the definition of the tax base.

It is not new that we can foster a particular thing by subsidizing it, or just leaving it alone when other things are taxed. It *is* new to note there is a way to tax something and not damage it. We can even tax something and, by taxing, foster and promote it.

Tax capital and you drive it away; tax land and you drive it into use. The technique is to redefine the real estate tax base as land value alone. Value at any time is what the land if bare would sell for. It is value in the best alternative use, the economists' "opportunity cost." It is independent of present use or ownership. It changes year by year, usually gradually as demands and neighborhoods change, or as anticipated public improvements, long since foreseen and discounted into values, are completed. It is very dependent on the things that planners plan and is in large part the product of good planning and implementation of planning—Alfred Marshall called it "the public value of land," in reference to its origin. A proper assessment of land changes in step with the outside determinants, ignoring the specific response that individual landowners make to the environmental challenge. They are taxed not for improving their opportunities, but for having and holding them; not for what they do themselves, but for the good things that planners do for them.

Private Renewal Problems

The real estate tax modified in this way would help planners with many problems that now seem intractable and foreboding. I will focus on one, the problem of slow urban renewal. Few would deny that the market has failed to renew our cities fast enough. For this the real estate tax, bearing differentially on new buildings, must shoulder much of the blame.

The economical time for an individual to clear and renew land is when the current cash flow from existing or "defender" use ceases to yield a fair return on the "scrap value" of the site in the most eligible succeeding use (the "challenger"). This scrap value is the present value of future income less the present value of future costs.

The land-based tax is neutral in this decision, because it is unmoved by renewal: it is the same on the defender as the challenger. The building-based tax is unneutral because it rockets upward when new succeeds old. It weakens the challenger vis-à-vis the defender by the amount of tax increase. Not only is the new building valued higher than the old: often assessors seize this occasion to reassess the land upwards, adding to the bias against renewal.

The general qualitative direction of the bias is clear—I have said that before. Quantitatively, the number of years during which building taxes retard site renewal depends, among other things, on how the cash flow from old buildings drops off. If it plummets steeply, then renewal dates are preordained by nontax factors, and tax policy is unimportant. If it tails off gradually, a substantial tax bias against new buildings retards the renewal of each site regarded individually; and of neighborhoods and school districts even more, as the nonrenewal of each site robs neighboring sites of their renewability, and suppresses competition from new buildings which would pull tenants from old defenders.

A number of time series showing historical income experience of commercial buildings have been compiled and published by Leo Grebler, Fred Case, and Louis Winnick. I have deflated them for price level changes. They are much affected by cycles of depression and war. The general time pattern and period of dropoff is clear enough, however. Real income from old buildings dwindles away slowly over many decades, in spite of depreciation and obsolescence. There is no sharp cutoff, no predestined date of demolition determined by technology or taste. Even when an old building has gone vacant, it may come back. After World War II, real income of many buildings rose sharply.

Another source of data is the Institute of Real Estate Management "Experience Exchange" among members of the N.A.R.E.B. In 1967, their 1,069 respondents reported on operating ratios (total expenses including real estate taxes divided by total actual collections) for apartment buildings classified by age groups. For elevator apartments the ratio rose gently from 45 per cent for 1961–1966 birthdays to 59 percent for all buildings over 47 years old, that is, pre-1920. For low-rise apartments it was from 41 per cent to 58 per cent; for garden apartments from 40 per cent to 48 per cent. In other words, almost half the gross collections from old apartments represents net income to the owner. A powerful factor helping hold down these operating ratios is that real estate tax expenses keep falling as a building ages.

Measured in years, therefore, the fiscal deterrent to urban renewal—the threat of increased taxes on new buildings—retards by decades renewal of the individual urban site. I could give you a precise number of years, using Milwaukee's present real tax rate of 4.0 per cent; but it would be a false precision, since it would be based on the individual site in isolation. Let us look at the extended effects on neighborhoods.

New Building Impacts

The renewal of one site speeds the renewal of nearby sites in at least three ways. First, it raises the renewal or challenger value of nearby land. One new building gives heart to potential builders of others, who naturally prefer new buildings for neighbors. Slum environs can virtually destroy the renewal value of land—a problem often noted. One or a few sound new buildings as inspiration can support supplementary and complementary renewal round about. The new GM building on 5th Avenue is reported by *Fortune* to have doubled floorspace rentals across the street. Once a new neighborhood or city or region gets well started, renewal snowballs, because people like to locate near their customers, contacts, suppliers, workers, and friends.

This, of course, raises the negative possibility that new buildings strengthen adjacent defender values as well as challenger values. There are frequent complaints that successful urban renewal projects, for example, raise the cost of nearby land for the next project. However, these higher land "costs" are merely *asking* prices and may be based on higher anticipated challenger values, plus the knowledge that federal funds are on tap to buy. They do not in general represent higher defender cash flow nearly as much as challenger values.

The reason is that new buildings pull tenants from old, in general weakening defenders. This is the second way that renewal reinforces itself. It is especially true when the new buildings are at higher density than what they replace—something which building taxes also discourage—and represent net new supply. Where tenants have a choice they move to newer quarters. The oldest defender filters down to be demolished. Its successor then pulls tenants from others, repeating the cycle. In the right conditions the reverberations from one new structure resound through several rounds of induced renewal.

Milwaukee's progress during the last eight years represents the ramifying effects that may flow from one new building. Through a series of historical accidents and legal technicalities, Wisconsin had an assessment freeze law that proved unconstitutional after being used essentially just once, in 1960, for the Marine Plaza—a high rise office and bank building. It was the first downtown building of consequence in thirty years. It pulled tenants from other buildings, forcing a wave of remodeling and renewal, still in progress, which has changed the face of downtown Milwaukee. By general account, this one new competitor set off the chain reaction. There is a multiplier the like of which few other

economic processes approach. Perhaps the time was unusually ripe, but that is mere hypothesis. The facts are there, and they speak volumes.

It is not that this one stroke alone was enough. The ripples are dying out, long before the job is done, but the point is if one original cause can ramify so far, even though every induced new building was fully taxed, twenty original causes would transform a city, if every induced new building were to be tax free.

A third way that renewal reinforces itself is through the higher income that it brings. Renewal means capital inflow, construction payrolls, material sales, new jobs, and so on. This pushes up local income levels. Now new buildings are "superior goods." The higher the local income, the greater the premium paid for new over old floor space, and the stronger are challengers relative to defenders.

So neighborhood and aggregate effects multiply the good done by each new building; conversely, of course, they multiply the damage from the present tax policy, which defers renewal.

But neighborhood effects are not the whole of the story of multiplied effects from taxing challengers more than defenders. Consider that most building is done on borrowed money. We live in a world of credit ratings, cash flows, front money, cash squeezes, and leverage—matters basic in business school but too often underweighed in economic analysis. A tax on new buildings, coupled with low taxes on old, weakens the credit of challengers and strengthens that of defenders. It adds to challengers' needs for front money and reduces defenders' needs for any money at all.

A tax on new buildings is at its maximum in the early years, the time of tightest cash squeeze. A high property tax rate today may take 30 per cent of gross income from a new building. If other expenses take 30 per cent, that is three-sevenths of the net operating income. If the entrepreneur is highly leveraged—and today, that is standard—most of the rest of net operating income goes to debt service. The net cash remaining for the entrepreneur then, especially during the early cash squeeze, is doubly leveraged, so a small rise in building taxes can wipe him out.

His credit rating in turn is leveraged by the prospects for his equity position. It is a familiar fact that a small rise of mortgage rates causes a large drop in building. Loanable funds rush out of building, not just because borrowers balk at higher rates, but because lenders lower everyone's credit rating because of lower equity income. Real estate taxes on new buildings add to costs in the same way as interest rates—that is, they are a fixed per cent of value. A 3 per cent-of-true-value property tax rate hits new building with the impact of a rise of mortgage rates from 4 per cent to 7 per cent; except that the real estate tax is worse because the tax rate applies to the whole value, while mortgage rates apply only to the debt. The tax not only defers renewal by its simple direct impact, but additionally by its leveraged effect on entrepreneur net cash flow and thence on credit ratings.

So it is powerful medicine to convert the real estate tax base to the site value basis. My current study comparing challenger and defender values in Milwaukee County is finding that a small rise of challenger values over defender values would cause 20 per cent of the central city area to be renewed forthwith; and that the large change resulting from a full exemption of buildings from real estate tax would cause some 50 per cent to be renewed —*if* the labor and money could be found to do it. Again, these results would be magnified by consideration of the neighborhood effects previously described.

They would be magnified again by consideration of the positive effect of cash squeeze on defenders. So far I have written only of exempting new buildings, but the land basis of real estate taxation does more than that. It raises taxes on defenders. The result is a potent cash squeeze effect. Today's real estate tax puts the squeeze on buildings. The proposed land tax puts it on defenders, holdouts, and preemptors of land.

So powerful is the medicine that, once it is understood, opposition may be expected, not from those who say it will not work, but from those who fear it will work too well: destroy historical antiquities, flood the market, jeopardize collateral values, lower rents, change the character of neighborhoods, sacrifice tradition to progress, overstimulate the economy, encourage immigration, spoil the labor, change voting patterns, weaken old ethnic ties, and generally frighten those who dislike change and abundance. There is also a concern for the welfare cases who inhabit old buildings and may have relocation problems. This is not the place to answer all those points; nor is this the place to answer those who would not have us do any good thing locally without first tracing its possible effects on the equilibrium of the whole world. They should reread *Candide*. But I do have a few words of conciliation and challenge for planners who might be concerned that the proposal to unleash the full force of the free market is also a proposal to substitute the market for planners.

Challenges for Planners

The unleashed market can solve some problems that now divert planners. It can bring urban renewal; group complementary land uses; promote low income housing; contain sprawl; attract an economic base; and weed out the worst generators of fiscal net deficits—old buildings. But on the whole, the land tax proposal implies more need for planners. Indeed, it gives planning so much more force and leadership as to make one ask whether planners are prepared to meet the challenge. Let us enumerate the ways that land value taxation supports and presupposes good public planning.

1. It gives planners a positive tool for influencing private land use, where now they largely have powers to say "Nay." When they designate an area for development, direct routes and utilities in it, and zone it for new use—up go land taxes, cash-squeezing the landowner into early attention to his new opportunities. Further, since high-use zoning is exploited quickly, there need be no great surplus scattered about, as it is today. It remains tight and retains its power to shape land use. This is also true for advantageous locations along public roads—which incidentally cost much more to produce than zoning, and if they are produced in surplus because half are unexploited (again as today),

they require the most egregious waste of public capital.

Some may even regard land taxation as a form of tyranny by planners over landowners. But note the limits to the planner's power. He does not direct a landowner to put his land to a specific use. Nor is there usually just one "highest and best" use of a given site, to which every landowner will be forced. Thriving cities are not characterized by monoculture and monotony, but by variety, constant change, and complementation. Whatever is the highest use in a neighborhood, say elevator apartments, is supplied in abundance until the need for another one is no greater than the need for some complement like a grocery store or parking structure. At any time an equilibrium generally prevails and affords each landowner several options. Within limits he may "do his own thing."

The land tax does not turn the planner into an overcentralized administrator or petty tyrant dictating specifics when he should be delegating authority. Rather, it sets a generalized performance standard, cutting off options beyond a certain degree of slothfulness and disregard for the public cost of giving land its latent value, but leaving wide latitude for individual discretion.

2. The land tax gives public investment great leverage over private investment. Today it is the reverse. Within limits, public roads, regulated utilities, the mailman, and school bus will follow you wherever you choose to locate. The regional planning commission uses traffic counts to plan bigger roads, following the lead of private emigres. These outreaching roads often seem to follow wealth and power.

The land tax lets public planners take the initiative—if they will. The city extends roads and sewers a reasonable way and then raises taxes on the land. The cash squeeze says: "Bring me roofs to match my roadways."

We have seen that individual buildings in new neighborhoods need synchronization because of synergistic interdependence. When the community of small independent entrepreneurs lacks synchronization, it is hard put to compete with giant developers of integrated centers and whole towns, who centrally control entire new communities. To compete, the public needs a community synchronizer. This the land tax affords. The planner does not try to play every instrument in the orchestra, but the land tax lets him set the tempo.

But how this puts the conductor on his mettle! The man with the baton had better set the right beat, for everyone knows who he is. From an objective view of administration, of course, that is very good. It may give stage fright to a profession still a stranger to the podium. Are planners ready?

3. The land tax gives planners some leverage over tax assessors. Now, assessors are preoccupied assessing building values. Then, they would assess site potential, the thing planners play such a role in determining.

4. Synchronized expansion lets planners plan for open space. Today, open space is a transitory byproduct of land speculation. In transition zones we undersize parks because there is so much open land and so few people. The private open space cannot be entered and supplies only visual amenities, and often not even that. When the landowner is ready for cash, the space is closed and a new load, often an overload, thrown on public land.

The land tax system lets transition be quick and orderly. Knowing the ultimate density, the planner can provide parks in optimal measured amounts and sizes so that settlement is not crowded, but unsprawled. By using tax pressure to assure early compact use of land between open spaces, he justifies the investment in open land and relieves the pressure to invade it. The public planner can work open space into an integrated pattern, just as large private developers can (and sometimes do) now.

With such power in hand, planners might even retain economists to measure the benefits and costs of open space. It is high time we introduce rational management and optimization into a topic now too freighted with hoarding, alarmism, sentimentality, camouflaged race prejudice, opportunistic tax-dodging and uncritical nature-worship.

5. The land tax system shortens the period

between site renewals. Every site renewal is another occasion to plan, and to plan ambitiously, excitingly, not just for rehabilitation but from the ground up. The public planner can go further. He can synchronize demolitions and replot the ground itself, something we had better get around to more often if our older city layouts are to avoid utter obsolescence.

6. The land tax system helps free planners from the constraint of "French equity." I allude to the concept of equity, characteristically French, that every man's share of land should be made equal, regardless of social cost, that the object of the institution of property is not good land use but distributive equity. In city planning that means what you do for Jacques' land you must also do for Pierre's.

Efficiency, on the other hand, calls for neighborhood specialization and differentiation, with high values for some and low for others. The land tax uses the fiscal and monetary mechanism to compensate the losers from the gains of the winners. Those who get the high unit values also get the high tax bills—*not* because of what they do for themselves, but for what the city planner does for them. Thus liberated from the tyranny of pettiness, the planners can relocate things and maximize net urban welfare on a much grander scale than now.

Equally important, the land tax gives city councils a better chance to be honest. Lincoln Steffens once remarked that the troublemaker in the Garden of Eden was not Eve, nor yet the serpent—but the apple! Taxing land values serves to dehydrate the apples of unearned increment which city councils dispense; and for which land developers vie when they contribute to campaigns, lobby, and otherwise influence officials. Keying the land tax to the provision of value-creating public works tempers the landowner's appetite by having him pay for his apples.

The planner can now put priorities in the capital budget with a clearer conscience and less fear of pressure.

7. Finally, the land tax system leads to demand for a greater variety of community facilities because it gives people better mutual access. It reduces the self-sufficiency of individual landowners. It obviates vertical integration by individual firms. It increases interdependence. It fosters more linkages of all kinds: social, commercial, industrial, political, cultural. It puts more load on the linkage mechanism—the sector of the city that planners plan.

To be sure, it greatly shortens the linkage network because orderly, unsprawled settlement lets people live closer, reducing the travel required for any given degree of linkage. Furthermore, it untaxes elevators and utility cores in private buildings and so lets private capital develop the third dimension of the linkage network, reducing the need for public capital. But the public capital released from lengthening the street grid and the planning talent liberated from this single-minded preoccupation have higher and varied uses. They can: replan interior areas and central lines; clean up air and water; perfect mass transit; sewer septic-tank suburbs and enlarge inadequate central lines; relocate buildings and lines to maximize synergistic gains from linkages; build a community house, a central mall and plaza, a Tivoli Gardens, a trade fair, an auditorium, stadium, art center, zoo, gymnasium, pool, theatre, marina, museum, library, playgrounds, park facilities, and so on without end.

Reviewing these seven challenges for planners, I must plead innocent of plotting their obsolescence and disemployment. Rather, I am moved to ask "How much boldness can you handle?"

34

Housing Rehabilitation and the Pittsburgh Graded Property Tax

David C. Harrison

This article appeared originally in 2 Duquesne Law Review, Summer 1964, p. 213. Reproduced by permission.

FEW PROPOSALS regarding the sticky problem of slums and taxes can be said to be new. Yet, one of the oldest ideas, that of shifting part of the real property tax burden from buildings to land as a means of eliminating city slums, has received recent endorsement from individuals whose aims and influence combine to give it, if not youth itself, a new lease on life.

Introduction: Rebirth of an Old Idea

Martin Meyerson, professor of city planning and Urban Research at Harvard University, Director of the M.I.T.-Harvard Joint Center for Urban Studies and past executive director and vice president of the American Council to Improve Our Neighborhoods, and Edward C. Banfield, Professor of Urban Government at Harvard, claim that:

The most serious defect of the real property tax is that it discourages new investment. As it stands, the tax offers property owners no incentive to tear down old houses, office buildings, stores, and factories and build better ones in their places. On the contrary, it actually penalizes efforts at modernization; a

new building is at a tax disadvantage as compared to an old one.

In a city like Boston, which has so many obsolete buildings, a tax system that works this way cannot be defended. . . .

The best way to remove the inhibiting effect of the property tax, however, would be to tax the land components of real estate relatively heavily and the building component relatively lightly. A tax on land is normally capitalized (that is, the price of the land changes to take the tax into account) while one on buildings is (except in a depression) normally passed on to tenants.

By taxing land heavily and buildings lightly the city would give owners an incentive to build on their land if it is vacant or to rebuild on it if it is already built upon, or else to sell it to someone who would build on it. In this way more might be accomplished by Federally aided housing and renewal programs.[1]

Professors Meyerson and Banfield are thus allied with descendants of Henry George's single tax reform movement, that flourished in this country and also in parts of Canada, England, Australia and New Zealand around the turn of the century. Among these is H. Bronson Cowan, who, in 1958, published a survey of the alleged beneficial economic and aesthetic effects of the "site-value" tax on cities in Australia and New Zealand. With his broad assertion that taxing the value of land while untaxing buildings is an effective economic weapon against urban slums, Mr. Cowan caught the attention of students of urban affairs here who not so long ago would have turned a deaf ear. They were—as many still are—committed to the belief that all proposed solutions to the problem of urban housing must wait upon the success or failure of the federal urban renewal program, financed and administered under the Housing Act of 1954.

Federal participation in urban redevelopment has its limitations, however, and as these are better understood other means are sought and ends are more closely defined. "A full range of housing opportunities outside the central cities for minority families, and for other low-income families who work there" was given top priority among renewal goals in the Report of the President's Commission on National Goals entitled *Goals for*

[1] Meyerson and Banfield, *Boston: The Job Ahead*, 1962.

Housing Rehabilitation and the **261**
Pittsburgh Graded Property Tax

"adequate supply of suitable housing for low
and middle-income families who need or
want to live in central areas, at low as well as
high densities." In reporting out the Housing
Act of 1954, moreover, the Senate Banking
and Currency Committee "made it quite
clear that a substantial improvement in
housing conditions was the intent of the
financial aid offered, and that cities would
not receive financial aid for community
facilities unless such improvement resulted."

Awareness of the housing problem was
further heightened by a series of studies
sponsored by the American Council to
Improve Our Neighborhoods (ACTION), on
the housing industry and community development, directed and edited by Professor
Meyerson. Professor Banfield was the co-
author with Morton Grodzins in the first
publication entitled *Government and Housing
in Metropolitan Areas*. The eighth and most
recent study, *Housing, People, and Cities* is
referred to below.

Omitted by the various authors in the
ACTION study, however, is discussion of the
Meyerson-Banfield tax reform proposal.
Such a tax, it is assumed, would benefit a
property-owner undertaking the rehabilitation of a run-down building. William W.
Nash's *Residential Rehabilitation: Private
Profits and Public Purposes*, third in the series,
deals with this subject. Limited assessments,
actual exemptions and other methods of tax
manipulation to further the purposes of
urban planning are considered, but Professor
Nash nowhere makes reference to the
feasibility of gaining differential rates on land
and buildings. Nor does Louis Winnick,
whose *Rental Housing: Opportunities for
Private Investment*, second in the series contains an indictment of unequal property tax
treatment of owners and renter-occupied real
estate discriminating against renters.

The omission of reference to a land-value
based tax in the ACTION series helps crystal-
lize the issues dealt with in the present study.
For the tax contemplated by Professors
Meyerson and Banfield is predicated on a
wide range of economic assumptions and to
some degree on a social philosophy that
requires examination of an equally wide
range of conditions, past, present and future.

Underlying the present examination into
some of these matters is the crucial question:
Why, at this juncture, has the land value tax
been brought back into public focus? Since
its enactment is specifically advocated for
Boston, the present study cannot contrive
an explanation. All that is offered is a framework for comparison.

The Graded Tax: A Means to What End?

In modified form, the single tax has been
in use in one major city in the United States
for nearly 50 years, and research into its
effects has been conducted. Dr. J. P. Watson,
of the University of Pittsburgh, concluded in
1934 that Pittsburgh's "graded tax," whereby
buildings are taxed at half the rate on land,
contained a "probable fallacy":

> There will be adjustments, upward and
> downward, of investment value and of assessed
> value until there is reached a capitalization in
> which allowance is made for the tax differential.
> ... In other words, the graded tax, really
> meant to be a classified property income tax,
> affects the valuation and, therefore, tends
> more or less to defeat itself.[2]

Taking note of the fact that the assessed
value of land within the city limits had declined almost every year since 1914 (the year
the graded tax was put into partial effect), as
a percentage of total assessed valuations,
while building assessments increased as a
percentage of this total, Dr. Watson felt it
likely that the tax differential had been at
least in part capitalized in tax valuations. It
followed then, that "To whatever extent this
has occurred, the rate differential has ceased
to constitute a current differential in tax
burden." The figures upon which he based
his calculations have since followed the same
pattern. In 1925 the split of the burden between land and buildings was 71 per cent—
29 per cent; by 1934 the relative burden on
land had fallen to 65 per cent of total yield

2 J. P. Watson, *The City Real Estate Tax in
Pittsburgh*, 1934, p. 33.

from real property taxes; and in 1962 the differential was further reduced to 51 per cent —49 per cent. The total valuation of taxable real property in Pittsburgh as of 1962 was $1.225 billion, of which $421.9 million, or 34 per cent, represented the assessed valuation of land, and $803.1 million, or 66 per cent, the assessed valuation of buildings. In contrast, land was valued at nearly twice the level of buildings in 1914.

This kind of information contributes either very much or very little toward proving the success or failure of the graded tax, depending on many circumstances, including the time of the attempted analysis. Dr. Watson seems convinced that because of the graded tax "building valuation has been marked up more than it would have been merely on account of new buildings and changes in the costs of building." Yet, in fairness, he admitted that as of 1934 there was no final answer to the question whether the graded tax differential had been wiped out as a current difference in burden, "with available data—probably not under any circumstances." Instead, he limits himself to the following observation, which raises issues more immediately calculable:

Consideration of the probabilities, however, is an essential step in an attempt to deal with the Pittsburgh real estate tax. This consideration hinges about the following factors: new building, transportation, rent and cost of building, and the change to the graded tax— none of which can be given more than tentative analysis here.

Since 1934, the building industry has undergone marked fluctuations. Rents and costs of buildings have soared, and the impact of the automobile on the whole of civilization needs no elaboration. Additional factors to be considered include: the flight to the suburbs; the revolution in municipal financing; the fortunes of Pittsburgh's economy; and, of course, urban renewal. Each by itself provides a framework of analysis radically different from the depression-oriented approach of Dr. Watson, just as the trends in the city's economy of the thirties

reflected a national economic upheaval that tended to invalidate fundamental theories and assumptions of a previous era.

In an attempt to formulate a more contemporary approach, in light of current goals and issues, Jerome P. Pickard recently studied specific land use effects of the graded tax in Pittsburgh. After consulting with ten of the leading participants in Pittsburgh's post-war *"Renaissance,"* Pickard reported that:

The evidence of the effects of this tax innovation was not conclusive as to specific land use effects; but our discussions led us to believe that there had been, and would continue to be, some definite effects of the graded tax in Pittsburgh not necessarily the effects claimed by the advocates of this type of tax.[3]

He recommended, that further study of the Pittsburgh situation be made, with the object of determining the desirability of a graded tax in relation, among other things, to "the prevention or amelioration of blight and slums and the encouragement of privately financed urban renewal and rehabilitation."

Since the question has been raised, and the material on the graded tax in Pittsburgh indicates that its effects, if any, are somewhat evanescent, it should be pointed out that the range of possibilities for fruitful research in this area is severely limited. Basically, the reason is that Pittsburgh has no graded tax. Since it applies only to the *municipal* property tax and not to school and county tax levies, the total property tax on improvements is levied at approximately 71 per cent of the rate on land, not at 50 per cent. Thus, the graded tax law affects only about one-half of the total combined tax levy on Pittsburgh real estate because the school district and county government combined now raise tax revenues from Pittsburghers approximately equal to that raised by the city itself. Moreover, with the tendency in Pittsburgh as well as other cities for building values to exceed land values, the reduction in the effective building tax rate is in fact much less than that envisaged by the early proponents of the tax.

Therefore, while assertions may go un-

3 Pickard, *Tax-Land Use Complexity in Allegheny County, Pennsylvania*, 1962, p. 96.

controverted that shifting part of the burden of the property tax from buildings to land will benefit homeowners, or that such a levy will discourage speculation in land and provide an incentive to the rehabilitation of deteriorated buildings, it is a matter of common sense that Pittsburgh's experience with the graded tax provides little, if any, visible evidence of their truth.

It would also seem that past thought on the subject has been unduly hampered by confusion and uncertainty. A general property tax having one purpose, the raising of revenue, but with it a multitude of unintended effects, cannot be weighed as an instrument of public policy except upon a scale of intended effects. Without doubt, the proponents of Pittsburgh's graded tax in 1913 had in mind the creation of a revolutionary instrument of public policy. According to Percy Williams, the intended effects were:

1. to encourage private improvements of all kinds through fuller development and redevelopment of urban land;
2. to check monopoly and land speculation that hinder the highest and best use of land;
3. to collect a larger share of the "unearned increment" of land values for public revenue as a matter of justice and equity; and
4. to reduce the tax burden on improved real estate particularly for the benefit of home owners but also including many other real estate owners, and indirectly their tenants.[4]

Given these aims, but with few identifiable effects, subsequent evaluations inevitably dismissed or accepted the tax on the merits of its theory alone.

With the passage of time even the aims of the tax lost something of their relevance in a world of changing needs. Confusion resulted when random effects were traced to an increasingly elusive cause. On a scale worthy of documentation this very confusion is the only measurable "effect" of the graded tax.

The following lines of inquiry are therefore established in order to relate newly defined ends with the graded tax as a proposed means. First, to what purpose within a framework of overall planning might the graded tax best be put to use? Second, which

among the ends suggested by Professors Meyerson and Banfield may be attainable by means of the graded tax in Pittsburgh? Third, by what other means are the same ends now approached? Fourth, to what extent are these and other factors barriers to the effectuation of a true "graded tax plan" in Pittsburgh?

Middle-Income Housing Rehabilitation

The existing stock of housing in American communities represents an investment whose protection and enhancement is a central concern of the owner, the mortgagor, the community, the government, and the housing industry. "From its bearing on the general welfare, in terms of the health, safety, comfort, and happiness of the people," Miles Colean points out in *Residential Rehabilitation: Private Profits and Public Purposes*, "its meaning is not surpassed by any of our other assets. In terms of the business generated through real estate and financing transactions and property repair and improvement, its importance is hardly less. It provides a large source of local tax revenues. It is at once the glory and the despair of our cities."[5]

There are four basic methods of rehabilitating the existing stock of housing: (1) voluntary rehabilitation by property owners; (2) higher housing code standards enforced through the police power; (3) public acquisition of property with private rehabilitation; and (4) public acquisition of property with public rehabilitation. Of these, the first involves no legal questions concerning property rights. Understandably, for this and many other reasons it is the most desirable alternative. Moreover, if improving the existing housing supply and adapting it to altered environmental conditions can make for good business "then we may point the way both to an important economic opportunity and to a means for reducing governmental burdens."

Faced with the need for rehabilitation, a

[4] Percy R. Williams, "Pittsburgh Experience with the Graded Tax Plan," *American Journal of Economics and Sociology*, 1964.

[5] Meyerson, Terrett, and Wheaton, *Housing, People, and Cities*, 1962, p. 179.

growing industry with considerable promise of serving that need, and the charge that, "few activities in the United States have become more dependent than housing upon governmental bulwarking, housing is in the industry capitalism forgot," planners contemplate "whether public policy should provide incentives to private rehabilitation and, if so, what form the incentives should take."

The graded tax proposal should be distinguished from attacks on the general regressivity of the real property tax. As a drag on private housing construction the real property tax has been criticized in *Housing Taxation*, by Walter A. Morton and in other works, such as *American Housing, Problems and Prospects*, by Miles Colean. But housing construction predominates in higher-income outlying suburban areas, where federal financing policies tend to neutralize the real property tax drag.

Since the focus here is upon housing conditions and the graded tax in Pittsburgh, another phase of the housing industry is excluded from consideration: "prestige rehabilitation" (e.g. Beacon Hill, Georgetown, Rittenhouse Square) is geared too much to the ability of the investor to pay a premium for a convenient location and social distinction to be of much significance in a weighing of increased tax costs in relation to other factors.

The benefits of the graded tax would seem to be greater in the case of middle-income rehabilitation.

Some of the best opportunities for the rehabilitation of housing for middle-income groups are to be found in the fringe development of a generation or more ago. Here the houses and apartments are larger than those closer to the downtown district and are rarely in as dilapidated a condition. Indeed, their loss of value is more often attributable to obsolescence and poor personal and municipal housekeeping than to serious structural defects or the intrusion into the neighborhood of deleterious commercial uses.

Many of the families that comprise the market for middle-income rehabilitation already own their homes in these areas, but as a rule the houses are deficient or obsolete on a number of counts. *If owners can obtain the*

necessary financing, they frequently are eager to bring their properties up to a higher level of maintenance, to rearrange interior space, and to install modern equipment. As they do the job themselves or turn to contract remodelers to do it for them, their expenditures make up the largest dollar volume of all rehabilitation.[6]

Whatever the character of a group within the middle-income bracket, whatever the nature of their preference, if they are in the market for rehabilitated housing, they are sensitive to fluctuations in costs.

The investor who operates in the middle-income field must scale his product with infinite care. His customers are the average families for whom most advertisements, Sunday supplements, and television programs are produced. They are heavily in the market for new equipment, more clothing, and even a second automobile, but they are in the market for more housing only when it gives them a favorable balance between convenient location and adequate space, modern equipment and easy financing.[7]

The prospect of increased costs owing to an upward revision of property assessments could clearly be a controlling factor in the investor's decision in this case. The best explanation might be that it is a matter of choice: investors in prestige rehabilitation are at comparative liberty to ignore marginal costs such as property taxes. But for the middle-income remodeler, preferences for convenient locations, adequate space, modern equipment and easy financing must be *balanced*.

The importance of marginal costs, including taxes, to middle-income rehabilitators is further enhanced by the fact that for lower-income groups the choice in housing accommodations is severely limited.

In a profit economy, the investment presumably will not be made unless it increases the marginal return on the property and unless the return on the new investment is equal to that available from alternative investment opportunities.

Under these circumstances, private rehabilitation, even when it takes place under the spur of housing code enforcement, can serve only limited purposes in the housing market for low-income families. Its chief function is to improve the quality of low-rent

6 *Ibid.*
7 *Ibid.* at 138.

dwellings which are *already* available to low-income families.[8]

Since private rehabilitation requires new capital investment and therefore almost invariably results in increases in the prices on rents of dwellings, it happens that "almost all rehabilitation for low-income families is linked to official programs of housing code enforcement. Indeed, only the spur of court action and penalties induces many owners to make improvements." Therefore, insofar as private rehabilitation of low-income dwellings is a goal, property taxes, lower or higher, could not make much difference.

Despite encouragement of the industry by the federal government, there is still little attraction for new investor money even in the middle-income field. The market for new housing generally, irrespective of special requirements for rental or rehabilitated housing, remains limited to the top 30 or 40 per cent of the population. The volume of public housing at the bottom was limited in 1959 to 2½ per cent of new construction. Prior to the Housing Act of 1961 it was believed that if interest rates on FHA-insured mortgages could be lowered by 2 per cent, the resulting 25 per cent lower monthly interest payments would let about 15 per cent of all American families into the potential market, "getting well into the middle-income group." It was also believed that adequate housing for low-income groups could be made available without resorting to heavily-subsidized new housing if enough vacancies could be created in the big supply of central-city moderate-quality homes to "free up the market, encourage normal mobility and permit the filtering process to operate effectively." According to this view, rehabilitation of central city residential areas is essential to an effective improvement in lower-income housing standards through the "filtering process," but only with "a great deal of middle-income construction . . . which is impossible with present costs and financial terms."

Pittsburgh's Renaissance: Means and Ends

The debate over whether and to what ex-

tent the local real estate tax should be manipulated to provide incentives for building improvements may go on forever, as it has already gone on for over half a century. In the meantime, Pittsburgh has the kind of tax—on the books, at least—that many feel should provide such incentives. If all that they expected of the graded tax had come about, Pittsburgh would contain scarcely a square foot of unused or unprofitably used space. There would be no blight, no dilapidation.

Anyone who has been there recently might even then get the impression, momentarily, that such is the case, for a face-lifting job of gigantic proportions has been done on the downtown section. But upon closer inspection it is evident that other forces have been at work over the years, and they have thrust upon the populace essentially the same dismal conditions prevailing in most big cities. Inadequate housing is as much a social disease in Pittsburgh as anywhere else.

But it is not so much a measure of the failure of an instrument of public policy—the graded tax, which for all practical purposes does not exist—as it is a reflection over a long period of time of the vagaries of the region's economy, the character of the inhabitants and the peculiarly erratic responses of the city's industrial and political leaders to their needs. All that has been done since the war to rebuild Pittsburgh has been accomplished within a framework of knowledge and expectations about the regions past and its future that by now has been welded into a highly rational, if flexible, formulation of specific goals. The premise upon which these goals are based is that Pittsburgh's main industries have ceased to expand.

With the fall-off in industrial activity came demographic changes and with these changes came the necessity for decisions as to whether and how old land uses might be replaced by new. Those who made the decisions contemplated the further alternative of non-use, but they worked instead for full-scale re-use and urban redevelopment. This fact must be given precedence over all other factors in discussing conditions in Pittsburgh today.

[8] *Ibid.* at 190.

For those who do the planning in Pittsburgh have a stake in the outcome. They have invested much in the city that belonged to them; they may, with some justification, regard the return on the investment as theirs.

Under any system of effective planning and leadership, legal tools for the implementation of social policy and the ideals they represent will gather dust without the support of the leaders. The graded tax, of course, is both used and supported—to the extent that it is noticed at all. More worthy of attention are the ends and means adopted by the generation of civic leaders who undertook the "Renaissance" of Pittsburgh after the Second World War.

In 1944 "Pittsburgh . . . was a filthy, worn-out plant, having served as the production guts of two world wars. . . . Pittsburgh, whatever the reasons, was not a fit place in which to live and work and raise a family." To make it a fit place in which to live became the first goal. Planners elsewhere may start with the proposition that it is their task to make their city a *better* place in which to live. But because Pittsburgh was indeed notoriously "filthy" and "worn-out" and scarcely "a fit place in which to live," the fact of second importance is that planning in Pittsburgh remains principally motivated by this single objective.

It was possibly more of a hindrance to the attainment of this end than a stimulus that the region's economy at the time was, and had been for over thirty years, on the decline. The Pittsburgh regional population growth rate fell rapidly after 1914, partly because World War I disrupted international travel, cutting off the flow of European emigration which had fed Pittsburgh's labor demands, and possibly because Congress in 1924 imposed a quota severely restricting alien immigration. It has been suggested, however, that in any case the flow of migration to Pittsburgh, which had accounted for a spectacular 41 per cent population growth rate in Allegheny County in 1880–1890, a 34 per cent rate of increase in 1890–1900 and 34 per cent in 1900–1910, would have dried up at about that time because local demands for

labor were satisfied. As to why local demands for labor were satisfied a number of reasons may be given but the most significant one was that Pittsburgh's export specialities— primary and fabricated metals, coal and glass,—even during the national prosperity of the 1920's, were meeting competition from other products and from producers closer to western markets, and the 1930's Depression only increased these difficulties. Whatever the ultimate explanation, Pittsburgh *as a city*, "a place in which to live, work, and play," urgently needed overhauling. It would therefore add nothing to a full appreciation of the aims behind the city's renaissance to insist that the needs of industry and industry alone were to be served, any more than it would be realistic to ignore the role played by industry in shaping the course of the renaissance.

Thus, the removal of the "three greatest impediments to rejuvenation," smoke, floods and "a complete lack of anything approaching an effective rapid mass transit system," was begun in 1944 as the first steps toward creating a city fit to live in. Beyond this point goals tend to blend in with means. Industry needed refurbishing, because without it the city wouldn't exist; but people had to be attracted—people with skills to contribute to the community's main enterprises—so that the economy would not flounder for lack of manpower; and appearances everywhere, including the city's natural setting—the hills, rivers and landscape,—had to be restored, to encourage people to remain in Pittsburgh or to move there for reasons other than opportunities for employment.

Redevelopment in the years immediately following the war proceeded without benefit of a comprehensive plan. That it proceeded at all has widely been attributed to the will of one man, Richard K. Mellon, president of T. Mellon and Sons. His influence in the selection of means that have been utilized in the course of redevelopment cannot be stressed too heavily, for essential to the mechanics of urban renewal is the organization and financing of agencies to formulate effective solutions to the problems posed. And it was largely by virtue of the concentration of capital and industrial leadership he represented that the Allegheny Conference for Community Development came into being in 1944, a year before the enactment of Pennsylvania's Urban Redevelopment law authorizing the creation of Urban Redevelopment Authorities.

The importance of the Allegheny Conference to Pittsburgh's renewal, encompassing a multitude of projects financed and administered directly or indirectly at every level of government and by a number of private groups cannot be precisely estimated. But neither can it be doubted that other groups played an important role. Edward J. Magee, executive director of the ACCD, stated:

> To imply . . . that the Allegheny Conference alone is responsible for all this activity and record of accomplishment would be considerably less than honest. To one degree or another we have been involved in all these projects and I think . . . our participation has been helpful in every instance and in some cases essential. . . .

In brief, the goal chosen was the "renaissance" of the city; the means utilized—the collaboration of private groups and public agencies, through channels already made available by the market economy and channels fashioned by law. Since the time of the passage of the graded tax law an unprecedented combination of political and industrial power has concentrated in Pittsburgh and overshadowed all other efforts, by whatever means, to plan for its welfare.

The Will To Rebuild

Better housing is both a means and an end in the lexicon of urban planning. As an end in itself it must compete with other ends, and quite frequently, as the history of urban renewal in the United States indicates, it comes off second best. As a means to an end, much depends on the weight of importance attached by the authorities to the end it serves. This will determine whether or not it is to be provided for.

In Pittsburgh today better housing is high on the list of priorities. A review of ten redevelopment and renewal projects undertaken by the Urban Redevelopment Authority, shows that nearly 4500 families have been or will be removed from deteriorating

and slum areas. In the Lower Hill project alone over 1500 families were affected. These are not very many people in comparison with the total city population, but "unless we have some satisfactory place to which they can move, this whole program will eventually stall, if for no other reason than the fact that Federal assistance, in whatever degree, will be cut off."

Much of the burden, of course, is placed on the City and County Public Housing Authorities, but these authorities do not account for the families who choose not to relocate in public housing; nor do they account for the families who inhabit some of the 27,500 dwelling units within the Standard Metropolitan Statistical Area (SMSA) designated as "dilapidated" by the 1960 Census Bureau Housing report. The four-county SMSA contains 765,800 occupied housing units, according to the Census bureau, of which 78.2 per cent are structurally sound. The remaining 18.2 per cent, or approximately 140,000 dwelling units are "deteriorating" but presently "safe and adequate."

These statistics only substantiate a commonly known fact, that housing conditions are not what they ought to be in Pittsburgh, urban renewal notwithstanding. Renewal projects in planning or under way will affect only 16 per cent of the deficient housing in the county. Urban renewal is, in fact, frequently criticized for creating conditions worse than those it was designed to eliminate. In this sense it has proven more of a failure than the graded tax, a pitifully meager tool by comparison.

What is needed instead is an effective measurement of demand, that can be counted upon to respond to incentives. In that context the salient features of the housing situation in Pittsburgh are (1) ACTION-Housing, Inc. a non-profit citizens' organization:

> Established to initiate, coordinate and help to effectuate, in cooperation with other private, civic and public institutions and agencies, a program of good housing in good neighborhoods for moderate income families, and the elimination of slums and blight in Allegheny County.

and (2) the make-up of the housing market served by ACTION-Housing.

(1) ACTION-Housing was organized as the direct result of a survey of local housing needs undertaken by the Pennsylvania Economy League, Inc. (Western Division) for the Allegheny Conference on Community Development. "This survey of the Conference came to the conclusion that a non-profit, representative citizens' organization with a professional staff should be formed to move effectively against the obstacles hindering housing progress." ACTION-Housing has a 44-member Board of Directors, six officers and a staff of six including two attorneys. In the five-year summary report published in September, 1962, Executive Director Bernard E. Loshbough cited one major accomplishment as deserving special attention:

> This is the establishment of the Pittsburgh Development Fund of ACTION-Housing, Inc. The Pittsburgh Fund is a revolving loan fund which has as its fundamental purpose the providing of intermediate equity capital—seed money—for the construction of privately financed privately built and privately operated sales and rental housing for moderate income families, *as well as the stimulation of large-scale home modernization*. The emphasis is on private participation.
>
> The fund was launched in September, 1959, and given impetus toward its goal of $2 million by grants totaling $350,000 from the three Mellon Foundations. Subscriptions to the Fund now total nearly $2 million in interest-bearing loans and grants from 31 local companies, corporations, department stores, utility companies, foundations and banks.
>
> The Fund serves to backstop lending institutions and the home building industry, and is a source of working capital that could not be obtained otherwise. Its funds are to be used in four ways:
>
> 1. Loaning intermediate capital to builders for development of new housing.
> 2. *Supplying intermediate equity capital to modernizers for restoring run-down housing.*
> 3. Acquiring land sites available only for total cash purchases, for resale to developers.
> 4. Providing large scale demonstrations of new housing materials, design, technology and production.
>
> The availability of loans from the Development Fund depends upon the merit of the

individual proposal, the responsibility of the developer, his willingness to conform to high standards of design, cost limitations and other criteria.

The first privately financed housing to receive a loan from the Pittsburgh Development Fund of ACTION-Housing is the $20 million East Hills Park project.

ACTION-Housing's list of accomplishments is impressive in the field of housing and neighborhood betterment. But with just the facts given it is evident that Pittsburgh's "power hierarchy" has undertaken the task of refurbishing Pittsburgh on a large scale. According to Bernard Loshbough, ACTION-Housing's executive director, and Seymour Baskin, Special Counsel to ACTION-Housing, the graded tax did not enter into their calculations in completing the East Hills Park project. Their views are scarcely startling; more revealing is their indifference to the tax. What to the graded tax group are goals to the others are achievements.

(2) The market for home modernization should be more promising in Pittsburgh than could be expected in nearly any other major American metropolis. Besides great quantities of "dilapidated" and "deteriorating" dwelling units the city contains within its limits a population whose patterns of living place them squarely in the market for an improved existing stock of housing. Of first importance is the fact that the metropolitan area as a whole has virtually ceased growing. Each decade since 1920 the Region has suffered a net loss by migration both in absolute and percentage terms. In Allegheny County net losses in migration began in the 1930's and have increased in the 1940's and 1950's. In the decade 1950–1960 the net loss by migration in Allegheny County was 86,000, a large part of it brought about by the exodus of young males. The Region's population growth rate as a whole has increased from 6.2 per cent in 1940–1950 to 8.7 per cent in 1950–1960, but unquestionably any growth at all since the 1920's is due entirely to natural increases.

The population is presently composed of age groups whose numbers and preferences will have visible bearing on the housing market. More than half the Region's population loss through migration fell within the age bracket of 15–29 years; in all, 83 per cent were within the economically productive years of 15–64. The percentage of young adults in the Pittsburgh SMSA in the 20–29 age bracket declined since 1940, when they were 18.4 per cent of the total to 10.8 per cent in 1960; 30–44-year-olds reached their peak in 1950, when they made up approximately 23 per cent of the total, by 1975 they are expected to decrease to 15 per cent. The age group of 45–64-year-olds usually permanently settled in their own homes, with their mortgages paid off, moved up from 16.7 per cent of the SMSA total in 1930 to 21.4 per cent in 1960.

A fair conclusion to be drawn from these facts is that the market of the 60's will contain fewer families setting up housekeeping for the first time, as compared with the 1950's. But there will be more potential customers in older age-brackets ready to move into better houses.

At the height of industrial expansion in Pittsburgh immigrants of a great variety of national and ethnic origins were attracted by the opportunities for work. They were herded en masse into jerry-built tenements near the mills and mines, paid low wages and exploited economically and politically by the established order. Possibly the one remaining vestige of those conditions, however, is the fact that Allegheny County and Pittsburgh still prove the most attractive to minority groups within the four-county region. Allegheny County contains 82 per cent of all Negroes in the Region and only 63 per cent of the total population. Pittsburgh has 23 per cent of the Region's population and 60 per cent of all Negroes. Moreover, the pressures of congestion have diminished within the city limits not only because of the general population decline, characteristic of several other urban core areas in the United States, but because of Pittsburgh's decline since 1930 as a destination of Negro migration—a decline unparalleled by the experience of other northern and western metropolitan areas where economic opportunities are more abundant. Given the facts that "the vast majority of choices of housing are made from the already existing supply, comprising houses and neighborhoods built some time in the past for other people with other needs and incomes, and under conditions differing

from those of today, and the fact that minority groups are restricted in their selection of housing not only by low incomes but also by "special barriers to settling in the suburbs," it would seem that incentives for housing rehabilitation fairly abound simply on the basis of demographic trends.

Not the least of these trends is Pittsburgh's affinity for single family detached houses. Among the 4 largest SMSA's in the nation in 1960, occupied units in apartment structures accounted for an average of 15.3 per cent of all units. For the four-county Pittsburgh SMSA the corresponding figure is only 7.6 per cent. Corresponding figures for other cities are: New York, 51 per cent; Philadelphia, 7.8 per cent; Buffalo, 8.2 per cent. While cities such as Philadelphia and Buffalo do not appear to offer a much greater percentage of apartment accommodations, it has been pointed out that they compensate by offering small multi-family structures in large numbers—e.g. 56 per cent in Philadelphia as compared with 27 per cent in Pittsburgh. On the other hand, Pittsburgh resembles rapidly growing SMSA's in the West and South in that the number of renter-households far exceeds the number of apartment units available to the extent that 29 per cent of all renters occupy single family houses. The market in Pittsburgh is also exceptionally well supplied with older single-family structures set close together—a factor which very likely depresses the market for apartments and discourages investment in new and larger structures. In any event the market for rental units of all kinds has narrowed a good deal throughout the nation since 1940, when home ownership constituted 40.6 per cent of all households in the Pittsburgh SMSA as compared with 65.4 per cent in 1960. Apparently the trend of residential arrangements in the Pittsburgh region is in the direction of single family detached houses owned by their occupants; rental tenure is becoming increasingly rare.

It would be misleading to infer from these sources that Pittsburgh's housing differs from that of other cities in the Northeastern and North Central states. The point emphasized is that several among the multifarious factors that go into the making of highly congested disease-ridden slums in cities like New York, Philadelphia and Chicago are missing from Pittsburgh. If it is acknowledged that "the economics of slum property deters extensive replacement, modernization or even maintenance of the antiquated housing," then it must also be questioned whether without a steady influx of ethnic minority groups forced to congregate at high densities on rental property and a high incidence of rental tenure in dilapidated tenements Pittsburgh is comparatively unaffected by barriers to housing rehabilitation present in other cities.

To make housing rehabilitation possible "the effectiveness of different sanctions or incentives will depend on local economic conditions, forms of tenure and the ephemeral *sine qua non* for any program, Community spirit." The ordinary residents of the city, like the prime movers of its renaissance, have a stake in its future, much as any inhabitant of a blighted area must care for the welfare of his community if, despite the attractions of alternative locations, he elects to stay where he is. As a city at the end of the war the whole of Pittsburgh was a slum. It was a place not to be in, a place not to go to, a place to get out of. Even today its charms pale beside the brilliance of San Francisco, New York, Boston, Chicago and other older American cities whose relative appeal to most city dwellers has never waned. But the fact that Pittsburgh has charms, in addition to an economic base capable of supporting over a million and a half people, attests to the earnestness of those who have gone about restoring their city. It also serves as an indication of their willingness to invest in the rehabilitation of their homes.

The Outlook in Pittsburgh: Old Issues and New

Assuming that a graded tax provides incentives to housing rehabilitation, what are the barriers to its effective enactment? What reasons may be given as to why it should not be made effective?

Several have already been suggested. In the main they amount to the fact that in Pittsburgh, planning has proceeded without regard to the tax. It has neither been relied upon nor subverted. It would appear to be significant only to the extent that in its operation or by its very existence it cuts across the purposes of others.

More concretely the first obstacle in the way of its effective enactment—so that it begins to make itself felt—is the law. Article nine, section one of the Pennsylvania State Constitution decrees that:

> All taxes shall be uniform upon the same class of subjects, within the territorial limits of the authority levying the tax.

Assessors must assess or value all objects of taxation whether for county, city, township, town, school, institutional district, poor or borough purposes:

> *According to the actual value thereof,* and at such rates and prices for which the same would separately bona fide sell. . . . [S]uch selling price, estimated or actual, shall be subject to revision by increase or decrease to accomplish equalization with other property within the taxing district.

Where it is impossible in assessing property for taxation to secure both the statutory standard of true value and the constitutional standards of uniformity and equality, those latter requirements are to be preferred as the just and ultimate purposes of law.

The uniformity requirement does not prohibit classification of property for taxation purposes but classification must be proper under the due process and equal protection requirements of the 14th Amendment to the Federal Constitution; its validity, moreover, depends upon whether there exists such a difference between the entities taxed and the ones not taxed as justifies the legislative classification.

These are the legal hurdles. In the case of the graded tax, in 1913, the law had to be satisfied that classification of land and buildings as separate taxable entities was reasonable, and that in the valuation of real estate by boards of assessment the imposition of a different rate of taxation on buildings from that imposed on land was not in violation of constitutional uniformity requirements. Although they cannot specify the effects of the graded tax there are those in Pittsburgh who feel, as Mayor Joseph G. Armstrong felt in 1914, that the classification of buildings as a separate taxable entity was unjust, and that "in approaching the single tax theory . . . in this way the economic relationship of one property to another seems to have been overlooked." This "economic relationship of one property to another" can perhaps best be defined functionally. The owner of a building is also the owner of the land upon which it stands. Thus, to real-estate brokers and investors, a separate levy upon land and buildings is a separate—and senseless—levy upon two distinct but necessarily economically interrelated components of the same "package." As to how the General Assembly in 1913 was persuaded to permit this classification, it may be noted that prior to the graded tax Pittsburgh had been levying property tax rates on an almost exactly opposite system of classification. "Built up" lands were required to pay "full rates," "suburban or rural" lands paid two-thirds; and "agricultural" lands were taxed at one-half the full rate. The inequities of such a tax in its impact on a growing city may have neutralized much potential opposition to the graded tax."

The reasonableness of the separate classification of land and buildings hinges upon the extent to which it adheres to or infringes on the uniformity requirement. Thus, assessors are at pains to assess real property uniformly so long as there remains any question as to the economic difference between any two given classes. Since in Pittsburgh buildings and land are legally subject to different levies, but at the same time the actual tax burden borne by any given parcel may vary in relation to other parcels according to the size and value of the building, property owners are apt to feel that they have been treated unfairly. This is only to say that the graded tax adds to assessors' fears that their judgment will be questioned in court, and to that extent it raises administrative problems not likely to be discounted in considering extension of the act.

Prospects for more widespread acceptance

of the graded tax in the United States are further diminished by the fact that time has not favored the economic trends which joined in Pittsburgh in 1913 to fashion the "graded tax plan." The original land assessment under the graded tax law in 1914 came to $480.9 million, and buildings were valued at $282.1 million. By 1956 land values according to Board of Assessment figures had fallen to $403.8 million. Since then there has been a modest increase, to $421.9 million in 1962. Building values, meanwhile, have shot up to $803.1 million in 1962. The coming of urban renewal in 1945 added up to a net *decrease* in Pittsburgh land values of approximately $500,000, from 1946 to 1962 —although from a low in 1956 of $403.8 million assessments reached a post-war high of $424.7 million only four years later. Building assessments gained by about 50 per cent in the same period—an increase of $262 million. On its face, a proposal to shift more of the tax burden from buildings to land would appear to pose a serious threat to city revenues where it would not have half a century ago.

That the graded tax in 1914 *failed* to cut into real estate revenues is one of the strongest arguments *against* its enactment now, if Pittsburgh is representative of many American cities. The real property tax yield increased from $5.1 million in 1915 to $8.2 million in 1916 after the first step had been taken in the gradual 10-year shift to the graded tax. Rates on land were 9.4 mills and 8.46 on buildings. By 1925, the first year of full operation for the tax, the total yield from land and buildings had mounted to approximately $14.9 million—$10.6 million from land and $4.3 million from buildings. Land assessment had gone up to $547.4 million and buildings to $441.4 million; but even with the strengthened tax base in both classes and the reduced differential between land and building assessments, rates now stood at 19.5 mills on land and 9.75 mills on buildings. The cost of municipal services was going up. Efforts to meet costs with new sources of revenue have since overshadowed whatever intentions there might have been to redistribute the tax load. It is largely for that reason that although "the untaxing of improvements appears to be the most valid part of the graded tax program, . . . there seems no likelihood that this can be accomplished unless substitute revenues are found."

The search for substitute revenues leads in many directions in Pennsylvania, as elsewhere. The graded tax has by no means been dated by the facts adduced, for as recently as 1951 the General Assembly—by a vote of 50-0 in the Senate and 184-1 in the House—passed a bill enabling third class cities to adopt the graded tax. No explanation appears in the literature on land value taxation as to why third class cities have so far not used the tax.

Further mention is made of a bill introduced in the General Assembly in 1945 to reduce the rate on buildings from one-half to three-tenths of the rate on land. At the same time the "Essential value and also the political popularity of the graded tax plan was clearly indicated when in 1945 some of the real estate interests began again to talk about the possibility of repealing the law or placing a legal limitation of the tax rate to handicap its operation. . . . The City Council unanimously adopted a resolution endorsing the graded tax plan."

The drive to improve municipal financing in Pennsylvania has also produced the "tax-anything law," whereby the whole field of taxation not devoted to state purposes was opened to most political subdivisions. Pittsburgh as a result now imposes a mercantile tax and taxes on personal property, amusements, earned income and deed-transfers, in addition to real property. The total income dollar in 1961 was made up of a $50.2 million "general fund" and an $8.1 million "water fund." Where in 1945 the real estate tax had accounted for 67.5 per cent of the General Fund, by 1961 it accounted for only 50 per cent. Whether it will fall below this ratio in the future is debatable, although in 1955 it had already fallen to 48.4 per cent. In any case local governments remain dependent upon the real property tax and to that extent the financing of local governments will continue to exert an unrationalized influence on consumer choices in a number of ways, including choices between rehabilitated and deteriorated housing.

The thought that a grade tax would tend to counteract ill effects of the real estate tax meets an insurmountable obstacle in the likelihood that it would hurt central commercial areas. The fall in urban center land values and the rising costs of government are a minor fraction of the changes cities have undergone in the last half century, and almost every change has meant more trouble for the older commercial centers. An understanding of the nature of their ills and the importance planners attach to them is essential to a well-reasoned valuation of the graded tax.

Since land may be privately held for investment certain lands acquire more investment value than others. For a while, in the nineteenth and early twentieth centuries, cities contained considerable quantities of open land strategically located for investment purposes. Like corporate stock, it was held until its sale netted the owner a profit. The days of in-city open land investment came to an end, however, not only when most or all of the open land had been sold but when the uses to which land was put became more diversified. Locational requirements for industry, new preferences for spacious living and an increased mobility of the population as a whole combined with a multitude of other pressures to scatter site values all about the metropolitan area. Cities in the nineteenth century, it has been said, grew after the fashion of a sand-pile poured from an overhead spout, while more recently they spread out like poured molasses. As a consequence in-city land values dropped; their attractiveness as investment opportunities faded, just as corporate stock loses its appeal in a falling market.

But unlike corporate stock, "down-town" represents more things to people than a piece of paper with a certain trade-in value. It has a value all its own. When it was no longer the sought-after commodity it had once been in the days of Henry George, downtown lost its luster, not only as a place to invest in but as a place in which to live.

The normal functioning of the market economy threatened to lay waste much that it alone was responsible for and with it the pride of an entire civilization. For the individual investor the loss was perhaps regrettable. But for civilization it was too much to bear. Enormous supplies of tangibles and intangibles essential to the restoration of all that the market had abandoned had to be replenished. As a means to this end the very same incentives for investment and profit previously wielded by the invisible hand were employed. As before, some would profit and some would take a loss. And there would be risks to the individual. The difference now was that the city was using the market to further its own ends. The market had been rationalized.

Against this crude historical backdrop it will be seen that the decisions on how land in Pittsburgh should be used are not arrived at in the same fashion today as they were 50 years ago. Different people with different intentions plan for its future, and certain effects weigh heavily on their decisions. The survival of the central business district—"downtown," the heart of the city—is the ultimate end.

The Pittsburgh Regional Planning Association has forged a master plan of Pittsburgh's "Golden Triangle" summarizing the results of intensive studies of the Triangle and outlining suggested reuses of land to be completed by 1980. The importance of the revival of the Triangle is stressed in the following language:

> The Golden Triangle is the heart of the Pittsburgh region. This triangular piece of real estate . . . covers approximately 374 acres. Within this small area—less than one-one-thousandths of the total land in the county—there are more than 30 million square feet of commercial floor space with a total assessed value of over $300 million, 8.4% of the county. Of all the people employed in the metropolitan area, 11.8% or about 100,000 persons, work in the Triangle. Along with shoppers and other visitors, they spend some $333 million during a year in Triangle establishments. From these facts the appropriateness of the name Golden Triangle becomes evident. *It is also evident that the future growth (or decline) of this small but important area will strongly influence the development of Pittsburgh, Allegheny County, and the surrounding urban region.*

In comparison with the central business districts of Philadelphia, St. Louis, Cleveland, Baltimore, Cincinnati, Milwaukee, Kansas City and Denver.

> Pittsburgh has proportionately more offices and banks and less manufacturing . . . the average per cent of space used for office uses in the nine cities is 32% as compared to 44%, for the Triangle. In manufacturing the average is 14%, while in the Triangle it is less than 3.9%.
> . . . 61.8% of all CBD employees work in offices.
> The dominance of office employment reflects the role of the Triangle as a national and regional office center.

Because office activities represent the largest and most important uses in Pittsburgh's Triangle "projections indicate that they will be the strongest part of the future downtown. . . . The projection of 3,000,000 to 3,500,000 square feet of new office construction over the next 20 years provides ample opportunity for developing a fine office complex."

Businesses must be encouraged to invest in such property; they must be convinced among other things that locating office facilities downtown will not overburden them with costs in comparison with other sites. Property taxes in Pittsburgh, as in many other cities, are a major source of complaint among office building owners. In 1961 the National Association of Building Owners and Managers reported that while an upward trend in costs and a downward trend in profits had been arrested in the cities tabulated, and average occupancy levels were generally satisfactory, the controlling increase in the rise in general operating accounts was in "fixed charges over which management has little or no control." The most highly resented among total fixed costs seems to be real estate taxes:

> Local taxes increased 2 cents per square foot, from 55.5 cents to 57.5 cents, an increase of 3.6 per cent. The ratio of taxes to total income increased from 14.4 per cent to 14.7 per cent another way of saying that real estate taxes consumed 14.7 cents of every dollar of income.

The resentment does not stem from any significant change in the proportional relation of real property taxes paid to other fixed costs, such as fire and other insurance, personal property assessments and depreciation. Figures compiled by the Building Owners Association show a drop in percentage of real estate taxes paid in relation to other fixed charges, from 59 per cent in 1924 to 49 per cent in 1956 and 47 per cent in 1961. Total fixed costs increased 123 per cent from 1935 to 1961 while in the same period the real estate tax cost component increased by only 110 per cent. Thirty-five per cent of the rise in total fixed costs occurred in 1956-1961, when realty tax costs climbed just 30 per cent.

Building owners argue simply that they pay more than their fair share of the city real estate tax. Complaints of Pittsburgh building owners are perhaps justified by the fact that real estate taxes there take 16.3 per cent of their gross receipts—more than in any other city except Boston and New York.

An unusually high ratio of assessments to actual market values is thought to be the controlling factor. Pittsburgh Regional Planning Association data regarding the sales price and assessed values of 139 properties sold within the Triangle from 1955 to 1961 reveal that:

> 84 of these properties (approximately 60%) sold for more than their assessed values, while 55 (40%) sold for less than their assessments. The total assessment a percentage of sales price ranged from 19% to 532%, with the average property selling for slightly less than its assessed valuation. The average property had an assessment of $252,600 and sold for $250,000.
> It was further found that properties tend to be assessed higher in relation to their market values in what is generally considered to be the retail and office core of the Triangle than in the fringe area. In the core area 60% of the properties sold for less than assessed values.... Properties tend to be assessed higher in the retail and office core of the Triangle than in the fringe areas.

PRPA based its findings in part on a market study of the Golden Triangle which concluded that, so far as the graded tax was concerned:

> A general observation is that such a graded tax system works least well in these areas and at those times when the market does not support a high level of investment. Since many areas of the Pittsburgh SMSA are experiencing a high level of real estate activity the graded method of taxation does not have the same impact as it does on downtown real estate. If there is any future large-scale adjustment made on real estate taxation it would be more practical to restudy the assessment ratio on individual properties and locales than amend the graded taxing system.

The same study weighed the various factors that might account for building owners' complaints about the high level of taxation, including the graded tax and high levels of assessment. It found that:

> A strengthening of the market for Triangle purposes and for rental space, within the properties would alleviate the relatively high tax load, because of the greater income levels to support the taxation. Therefore it is perhaps more appropriate when describing existing property assessment and taxation to state that the market is weak rather than that the land assessments and taxes are high. If the market within the Triangle improves, taxes will decrease as a percentage of total income; if the market does not improve, then the existing complaint of high land assessments and taxation will be alleviated.

Planners are therefore well aware of the disproportionate tax load borne by downtown properties, which "undoubtedly accounts in part for the lack of new buildings and improvements in the central area in recent years." Moreover, they are aware that an effective graded tax—if it exerted any influence at all—would be detrimental to their stated purpose of strengthening the downtown market, and hence rejuvenating the city of Pittsburgh.

The graded tax has come to a new pass. Generally conceded to be helpful to residential rehabilitation it is also conceded, by friend and foe alike to be a hindrance to redevelopment in the central business district. It tends to discourage investment where investment is most needed. In residential sections regional economic trends repressed the incentives it was supposed to have nourished. A good part of its job was preempted by local, state and federal powers whose might and precision eclipsed whatever feeble surge it might have sparked.

So hopeless, indeed, is the outlook for the graded tax that the only real possibility of its widespread *and* effective enactment lies in the degree to which urban patterns of growth, planning and land-use specialization have already physically separated residential from business and commercial uses, and will continue to do so. For them might it not be feasible, within the limits of uniformity and equality, to apply the tax to that part of the jurisdiction where it does the most good, without extending it to that part where it does the most harm? Could the law not then be persuaded that with the accomplished separation and isolation of economically divergent classes of property taxing jurisdictions might accordingly be re-formed, to devise means of raising revenue best suited to the preservation of its source? How unorthodox is such a solution, in any case, when by means of lower assessment rates on residential properties and higher ratios on business and commercial properties the existing real estate tax already takes the separation into account?

True, time has not favored the combination of economic trends that fashioned the graded tax in 1914. But, more important, it has preserved its ideological origins. At one time property could be put to any use its owner wished, within the . . . limits of a system of law dedicated to the sanctity of private property. Land-use planning today is predicated upon the proposition that the use of land is within the public province— whether or not the "public" is so convinced. Single taxers and land-use planners agree that land is a resource whose supply is fixed, and for the public good its use should not be dictated by ordinary laws of supply and demand but by a rational system of allocation. They are further agreed that taxation wields sanctions and incentives which, in the interest of a planned economy, ought to be controlled; and that the administration of the local real estate tax could encourage housing improvements if all or part of the tax on buildings, separately classified, could be shifted to land.

Their differences lie in the extent of their ambitions. Single taxers intended only that land be used. Perhaps it was to this end that they sought the nationalization of land. In any case they posed no serious threat to the institution of private property, and it cannot be said that in their immediate purpose they were enemies of the law.

Land-use planners, on the other hand, intend that land be used in certain ways, by certain people and in certain places. Their basic assumption is that land will be used, and if in their opinion vacant land is a "use" they have means at their disposal— including laws revolutionary by standards of less than 20 years ago—to assure its perpetuation. Vacant land is as much to them a remedy for blight as it was a cause to single taxers.

The question of who is wreaking havoc with property rights or challenging fundamental notions of equality and justice is thus somewhat fuzzy. In answer to the question of why a land value based tax has been brought back into focus at this juncture it can only be said that now, as before, the issues raised are equally fundamental and equally troublesome.

Selected References

References to Chapters 26–34

Advisory Commission on Intergovernmental Relations, The, *Measures of State and Local Fiscal Capacity and Tax Effort*, U.S. Government Printing Office, Washington, D.C., October 1962.

Becker, Arthur P., ed., *Land and Building Taxes*, University of Wis. Press, 1969.

Caldwell, Bernard L., "Tax Factors Which Affect Real Estate Values," *The Appraisal Journal*, October 1964.

Heilbrun, James, *Real Estate Taxes and Urban Housing*, Columbia University Press, 1966.

Hodge, Patricia Leavey and Hauser, Philip M., *The Federal Income Tax in Relation to Housing*, Research Report No. 5, Washington, D.C., 1968.

Lindholm, R. W., "Land Taxation and Economic Development," *Land Economics*, Vol. XLI, No. 2, May 1965.

Morton, Walter, *Housing Taxation*, The University of Wisconsin Press, 1955.

National Commission on Urban Problems, *Hearings Before the National Commission on Urban Problems*, Vol. 1, May-June 1967, Baltimore, New Haven, Boston, Pittsburgh; Vol. 5, October 1967, Detroit, East St. Louis, St. Louis, Washington, D.C.; U.S. Government Printing Office, Washington, D.C., 1968.

Netzer, Dick, *Economics of the Property Tax*, The Brookings Institution, Washington, D.C., 1966.

Netzer, Dick, *Impact of the Property Tax*, Research Report No. 1, National Commission on Urban Problems, Washington, D.C., 1968.

Stocker, Frederick D., "Assessment of Land in Urban-Rural Fringe Areas," in A. D. Lynn, Jr., ed., *The Property Tax and Its Administration*, University of Wisconsin Press, Madison, Wisconsin, 1969.

Urban Land Institute Publications
1. Beck, Morris, *Property Taxation and Urban Land Use in Northeastern New Jersey*, Research Monograph No. 7, Washington, D.C., 1963.
2. Beeman, William J., *The Property Tax and Spatial Pattern of Growth Within Urban Areas*, Research Monograph, No. 16, Washington, D.C., 1968.
3. Pickard, Jerome, *Changing Urban Land Uses as Affected by Taxation*, Research Monograph, No. 6, Washington, D.C., 1962.
4. Rawson, Mary, *Property Taxation and Urban Development*, Research Monograph, No. 4, Washington, D.C., 1961.

Index

Abbott, Edith, 166, 169
Abrams, Charles, 222-26
ACTION (American Council to Improve Our
    Neighborhoods), 169, 261, 267-68
Adamec v. *Post,* 190
Addams, Jane, 166
Administration
    achieving compatibility and, 97-98
    of building codes, 139, 165*n*
    discretionary power of, 13
    enforcement of zoning process and, 121-22
    entrapment by, 78-79
    of general elimination program, 99
    of housing codes, 165*n*, 189
        procedures to enforce housing codes,
            188-89
    improvement of, 117-19
        taxation and procedural improvements
            in, 219-20
    incompetence of, 124-25, 128
    of new Chicago zoning ordinance, 107-9
    rent withholding by, 195, 196-98
    residential zoning control by, 78-80
    review of zoning by, 13-14
Administrative Requirements for Building
        Codes A55, Sectional Committee on,
        139
Advertising signs
    action against offensive, 83-86
    incompatibility of uses and, 93
    removal of
        Illinois, 109
        Los Angeles, 94
Advisory Committee on Government Housing
        Policies and Programs, President's, 194
Aesthetics
    beauty defined, 87-88
    court and

aesthetic values and, 89, 90
    aesthetics in housing codes and, 181-83
    court support for, 101*n*
    incompatibility of uses and, 93
    in performance standards, 72
    in residential performance standards,
        76-77
    zoning for objective in, 83-91
Age of improvements, 238
Agle, Charles, 81-82
Aid for Families with Dependent Children
        (AFDC), 195, 196
Allegheny Conference for Community
        Development, 266
Amendments
    of new Chicago zoning ordinance, 108
    as part of a discretionary system, 115
American Council to Improve Our
        Neighborhoods (ACTION), 169, 261,
        267-68
American Federation of Labor-Congress of
        Industrial Organizations (AFL-CIO),
        198, 199
American Housing, Problems and Prospects
        (Colean), 264
American Public Health Association, 188
American Standards Association, 134
Amortization
    basis for, 119-20
    compatibility and, 99
    compulsory, 94-96
    in new Chicago zoning ordinance, 105-6
    normal period for, 119
Appeals
    in housing codes, 188
    residential zoning and, 78, 79-80
Architectural zoning, 77
Area enforcement in housing codes, 194

Area-variance, as harassment, 120; *see also* Variances
Armstrong, Joseph G., 271
Assessment practices, 233-34
Aurora v. *Burns* (1925), 105
Australian experiment, 242-47

Babcock, Richard F., 2, 100-9
Baltimore Plan, 157-63
  pilot program, 160-63
  structure of enforcement program, 158-60
Banfield, Edward C., 260, 261
Banking and Currency Committee, Senate, 261
Barnhart, Gilbert R., 132, 140-45
Beauty, defining, 87-88;*see also* Aesthetics
Bellone, Christopher J., 201-5
Bentham-Edgeworth sum of the individual utilities, 25-26
Berman v. *Parker* (1954), 101, 126, 182, 183
Billboards, *see* Advertising signs
Bonvallet, G. L., 66
Brennan v. *City of Milwaukee,* 187
Bright v. *Evanston,* 107
Brownlow, Louis, 168, 170
Building Code Committee (Department of Commerce), 134
Building codes, 131-48
  conservation of Chicago's housing supply and, 164-76
  defined, 165n, 177n-78n
  enforced waste and, 148-49
  existing buildings and, 140-45
  preparation and revision of, 133-39
  stages in elaboration of, 64-65
Bureau of Family Service (Department of Health, Education and Welfare), 197
Bureaucratic entrapment, 78-79; *see also* Administration
Business, fines as expense of, 168n
Business area, economic incompatibility factors in, 93
Business districts in new Chicago zoning ordinance, 101-4
Business space, inelastic demand for, 61-62
Business uses
  economic compatibility and, 103
  in new Chicago zoning ordinance, 101-4

California cases on monopoly rule, 21
California laundry cases (1890s), 5, 59, 96
Canadian Tax Foundation, Conference of (1961), 249
Capital utilities, control of sprawl and, 247
Cars, abandoned, 202-3
Census Bureau, 1960 census of, 267
Central city, progress in renewal of, 4-5; *see also* Rehabilitation; Renewal
Central Savings Bank v. *City of New York,* 193
Certificate of occupancy, 141-42, 146-47
Chapin, F. Stuart, Jr., 56
Charles Center (Baltimore, Md.), 128

Chicago (Ill.), new zoning ordinance of, 100-9
Chicago City Homes Association, 166
Chinese laundry cases (1890s), 5, 59, 96
Churches, rehabilitation and, 164n-65n
Circle Lounge and Grille, Inc. v. *Board of Appeal,* 20
Cities
  broadening tax base of large, 220
  controlling urban growth, 242-47
  demand for (1960-2020) urban land, 57
  expansion of metropolitan area, 49-50
  housing codes in
    enforcement of codes, 150-63
    renewal and, 177-84
    See also Housing codes
  industrial development desired by, 52-53
  land suitable for industry in, 51, 52
  land value tax and control of growth of, 242-45
  program in renewal of, 4-5; *see also* Rehabilitation; Renewal; Slums
  public acquisition of land to control growth of, 246-47
  racial changes in, 4, 5
  zoning to control growth of, 245-46
  See also Local government
Cities and Villages Act, 107
Citizens' Committee to Fight Slums, 166
City and County Public Housing Authorities, 267
City planning, early pioneers of, 3; *see also* Cities; Planning
Civic Center development (Baltimore, Md.), 128
Clark, Colin, 56
Clark, W. A. V., 242-47
Colean, Miles, 264
Commentaries in the Law of Municipal Corporations (Dillon; 1911), 182
Commerce, *see* Business
Commission on National Goals, President's, 260-61
Community, effects of building codes on, 136
Community development, housing quality and, 150-51
Community interests, industry's needs in conflict with, 56-63
Community objectives, classification of aesthetic, 86-89
Community relationships, industrial site and, 52
Compatibility standards, achieving, 92-99
Compensation principle, 27-28
Competition
  among landowners, 113
  zoning as control of, 19-23
Comprehensive Amendment (to Chicago Zoning Ordinance; 1957), 100-9
Comprehensive zoning principle, 93-94
Compulsory amortization, 94-96
Condemnation
  criteria for repair and demolition, 142-43; *see also* Demolition; Repair
  emergency, 144-45

Condor, John, 200
Connery, Robert, 7
Conversion, defined, 172n
Cook, Lorned, 232
Corruption, overly rigorous codes and, 169
Courts
  advertising signs and actions of, 83-86
  aesthetics and
    aesthetic values and, 89, 90
    aesthetics in housing codes and, 181-83
    court support for, 101n
  approval of exclusive zoning in, 63
  community aesthetic objectives and, 86-89
  competition factors and, 19-23
  emerging zoning legal issues and, 110-22
  granting variances, 33-38
  municipal housing codes and, 185-94
    retroactive housing code measures and,
      180
    zoned housing codes and, 184
  new Chicago zoning ordinance and, 100-9
  nuisance abatement doctrine and, 96-98
  original view of zoning in, 102
  in review of zoning regulations and
    administrative officials, 14-17
Cresskill v. Dumont (1953), 99, 117

Davis (economist), 169
Davis, Otto A., 41-50
Delogu, Orlando E., 209-16
Democratic process, 47
Demolition
  building codes and, 140-45
  failure to comply with order for, 192
  housing codes and order for, 191-92
  liens for cost of, 193-94
Density
  floor area ratio control of, 100-1
  lot area regulation of, 100, 101
  noise and residential area, 76
  specifying employment, 71
  zoning of low density urban residential
    areas, 81
Density measurements, transportation, 71-72
Depreciation, cost of building and deductible,
  223-24
Design plan, described, 128-29
Development
  economy and land, 218-19
  housing code enforcement and local, 150-63
  housing quality and community, 150-51
  income tax and, 231
  increasing public, favored, 11
  industrial
    city desired, 52-53
    city land suitable for, 51, 52
    municipal services needed for, 58
    needs of industry in conflict with
      community, 56-63
    in new Chicago zoning ordinance, 104-5
    prohibited industries and, 60-62
    tax base and, 53
    See also Industrial zoning
  of industrially zoned districts, 59-60

plan for, for undeveloped land, 127
process of suburban, 227-35
taxation and, 217-21, 227-35
  land value taxation and, 248-52
  zoning inadequate for, 123
Development Plan absorbs zoning, 127-28
  defined, 126-27
Dillon (judge), 182
Dirt, performance standards and, 67-68
Discretionary system, 13, 115
District of Columbia v. Little, 188
Districts
  development of industrially zoned, 59-60
  Euclid zoning and, 111; see also Euclid
    zoning
  new Chicago zoning ordinance and
    manufacturing, 104-5
  new Chicago zoning ordinance and
    residential, 100-1
  principle of progressively inclusive, 61, 62
  profit maximization and, 113
Doebele, William A., Jr., 3-9
Douglas, William O., 182
Dukeminier, J. J., Jr., 83-91
"Dumping," 99
Dust
  incompatibility of uses and, 93
  in performance standards, 67-68

Easement purchases, 211-12
Economic compatibility, commercial uses
  and, 103
Economic effects of industrial zoning, 56-63
Economic elements in municipal zoning
  decisions, 41-50
Economic incompatibility factors in
  commercial areas, 93
Economic theory underlying Euclidian and
  non-Euclidian zoning, 113-14
Economics, welfare, 26-27
Economics of Housing, The (Kingsbury),
  229
Economics of Real Property (Turvey), 232
Economy, land development and, 218-19
Education, government units responsible for,
  118
Effluent changes, 214, 215
Elimination, administration of program of
  general, 99; see also Condemnation
Eminent domain
  achieving compatibility by, 98
  compatibility and, 99
  police power and, 186
Employment, specifying density of, 71
Enforced waste, building codes and, 148-49
Enforcement
  avoiding, 168-69
  of Baltimore Plan, 158-60
  of housing codes
    administration, 188-89
    area enforcement, 194

housing codes providing for, 178, 179
local development and, 150-63
need for, in zoning process, 121-22
police power for, *see* Police power
English development plan, 112
English planning practices, 22
Euclid v. *Ambler* (1926), 74, 92, 93, 110, 128
Euclidian zoning
abandoning, 112
defined, 111
economic theory underlying, 113-14
introduced, 59, 62
lip service paid to, 115
Exceptions, as part of discretionary system,
115; *see also* Variances
Exit requirements, 171
Exposure, fire and safety hazards and, 69

Federal Housing Administration (FHA), 224,
265
Chicago codes and, 173, 175
Federalism, new type of three-tiered, 6-7
Feiss, Carl, 16, 123-29
Fines
as business expense, 168*n*
for failure to comply with repair or
demolish order, 192
Fire
housing quality and, 165-66
incompatibility of uses and, 93
performance standards and, 68-69
requirements judging, 173
in residential performance standards, 76
Fire insurance ratings, 69
Fischer v. *Bedminster Township* (1952), 117
Free market, land competition in, 54

Gaffney, Mason, 253-59
Gans, Herbert, 5
General welfare, 25-28
hardship and, *see* Hardship
individual welfare and, 25-26
George, Henry, 207, 229, 242
Givner v. *Comm. of Health,* 187, 189
Glare
incompatibility of uses and, 93
in performance standards, 68
Goals for Americans (report), 260-61
Golden Triangle (Pittsburgh), 127, 273
*Government and Housing in Metropolitan
Areas,* 261
Graft, as normal fees, 168*n*
Grazia, Victor R. de, 200
Grodzins, Morton, 261
Guandolo, Joseph, 132, 177-84
Guiding Metropolitan Growth (publication),
229

Haar, Charles M., 110-15
Hadacheck case, 97

Hardship, 33-40
new Chicago zoning ordinance and, 107-8
repair and alter order and, 187-90
self-created, 36
uniqueness of, 36-38
unnecessary, 31-35
variance upon others and, 38-40
Harrison, David C., 260-75
Harvey, Robert O., 242-47
Hearings on violations, 188
Heat, performance standards for, 68
Height control, 123
Hoffman, Nicholas von, 198
Horack, Frank E., Jr., 74-80, 110, 115-22
House and Home (magazine), 229, 231, 232
Housing
building codes, housing codes and
conservation of Chicago's supply of,
164-76
community development and quality of,
150-51
control of design of, 89-90
deductible depreciation and cost of, 223-24
fire and safety hazards and building
construction, 69
impact of new, 255-56
lots and changes in style of residential, 75-76
See also Rehabilitation; Renewal
Housing Act (British; 1936), 177*n*
Housing Act (1937), 177
Housing Act (1949), 131, 164, 177
Housing Act (1954), 131, 260, 261
Housing Act (1961), 265
Housing Codes, 131, 150-205
conservation of Chicago's housing supply
and, 164-76
courts and municipal, 185-94
retroactive housing code measures and,
180
zoned housing codes and, 184
criticism of, 194
defined, 165*n*, 177*n*-78*n*
enforcement of
administration, 188-89
area enforcement, 194
housing codes providing for, 178, 179
local development and, 150-63
standards and, *see* Standards—of housing
codes
urban renewal and, 177-84
Housing and Home Finance Agency (HHFA),
177
Housing Taxation (Morton), 264
Hozek, 115
Hull House, 166
Hutchinson, Theodore, 7

Imprisonment for failure to comply with repair
or demolish order, 192
in lieu payments, 207
Incentives, tax, 218-19
Income tax
development and, 231
modifying, 233-34

Incompatibility
  classified, 98
  elimination of, 92-99
  See also Nonconforming uses
Incompatibility principle, 105-6
Indices of slum conditions, 237
Individual welfare, 24-25
  general welfare and, 25-26
Individuals, architecture and equilibrium of, 89
Industrial developer, zoning and, 51-55
Industrial development
  city desired, 52-53
  city land suitable for, 51, 52
  municipal services needed for, 58
  needs of, in conflict with community, 56-63
  in new Chicago zoning ordinance, 104-5
  prohibited industries and, 60-62
  tax base and, 53
  See also Industrial zoning
Industrial land, demand for, 57-59
  relative elasticity of demand for, 61-62
Industrial zoning, 51-73
  developer and, 51-55
  economic consequences of, 56-63
  performance standards in, 64-73
Inspection
  constitutionality of, 188
  of existing buildings, 141
  in Irish Channel program, 204-5
Internal Revenue Code, 207
Intrazone restriction, 74
Irish Channel Action Foundation (ICAF),
    201-5
Irish Channel program, 201-5

Jacobs, Jane, 5
Jones v. *Los Angeles,* 97
Journal of Housing (magazine), 195-200
Journal of Property Management (magazine),
    200
Judiciary, *see* Courts

Kaukas v. *City of Chicago* (1963), 170, 171
Keogh (Representative), 233
King, Dr. Martin Luther, Jr., 198, 199
Kingsbury, Laura, 229
Krumbiegel, E. R., 184

Land-improvement assessment ratios, study of,
    236-41
Land market
  competition in free, 54
  planners and, 253-54
Land prices (1950s-1960s), 231
Land speculation, 228-31
Land tax, *see* Land value taxation
Land value taxation, 207-8, 229, 248-75
  advantages of, 248-52
  controlling urban growth and, 242-45
  development and, 248-52
  effects of a shift to, 239-41
  land planning and, 253-59
  rehabilitation and, 260-75
Law and Contemporary Problems (magazine),
    194

Lawrence, David L., 232
Leach, Richard, 7
Legal issues, emerging zoning, 110-22
Legislative permit, achieving compatibility
    and, 97; *see also* Variances
Lehman, Warren W., 132, 164-76
Licensing
  compatibility and, 99
  of nonconforming uses, 98
  of residential builders, 78-79
Licensing business, zoning power and, 20
Liens for cost of repair or demolition, 193-94
Lionshead Lake, Inc. v. *Wayne Township*
    (1953), 117-18
Local government
  courts and municipal housing codes, 185-94
  economic elements in zoning decisions of,
    41-50
  elimination of incompatible uses by, 98
  enforcement of housing codes and, 150-63
  fragmentation of, 4, 6
  intelligent planning and, 117-18
  original view of zoning in, 102
  parochial zoning regulations and, 12
  rebuilding, 6-8
  taxation and, *see* Taxation
Logue, Edward, 6-7
Los Angeles v. *Gage,* 106
Loshbough, Bernard E., 268
Lot area, regulation of density by, 100, 101
Lot of record, zoning lot distinguished from,
    100*n*
Lot sizes, prices of, 225
Lots, changes in residential, 75-76

McQuillin, 187-88
Magee, Edward J., 267
Maudelker, Daniel R., 12, 19-23
Manufacturing districts in new Chicago zoning
    ordinance, 104-5; *see also* Industrial
    development
Map Book Area (MBA), 237-41
Masonic Fraternity Temple Association v.
    Chicago, 190
Master plans, coordinating zoning ordinances
    with, 56-57
Materials, building codes and new, 138-39
Measuring
  industrial sewage waste, 70
  of performance standards, 64-73
Mellon, Richard K., 266
Merrifield, Lewis B., III, 24-40
Methods, building codes and new, 138-39
Metropolitan area, expansion of, 49-50
Metropolitan common market, 7, 8
Metropolitan federalism, abandoning, 7
Metropolitan government
  abandoning, 6
  need for, 15
  See also Local government
Meyerson, Martin, 260, 261

Middle-income housing rehabilitation, 263
Miller v. *Schoene* (1928), 183*n*
Minimum wage for women, 111
Moerdler, Charles G., 199
Morals, incompatibility of uses and, 93
Morton, Walter A., 264
Municipal government, *see* Local goverment
Municipal services, industrial need for, 58
Municipal zoning, economic elements of, 41-50
Murphy, Inc. v. *Westport,* 84

Nash, William, 169, 261
National Association of Building Owners and
   Managers, 273, 274
National Building Code (Board of
   Underwriters), 171
National Bureau of Standards, 134
National Commission on Urban Problems, 131
National Industrial Zoning Committee, 71, 73
Negroes, excluded from suburbs, 5
Netzer, Dick, 230, 232
New York Health Department v. *Dassori,* 191
New York State Department of Commerce,
   146-47
New Zealand experiment, 242-47
Noise
   incompatibility of uses and, 93
   new Chicago zoning ordinance and, 104
   performance standards for, 65-66
   in residential performance standards, 76
Noncombustible external structures, 172
Noncombustible wall requirements, 171-72
Nonconforming uses
   frequency of cases involving, 110
   inability to remove, 125
   licensing of, 98
   in new Chicago zoning ordinance, 105-6
   present standards and, 119-20
Notice of violations, 188
Noxious gases
   new Chicago zoning ordinance and, 104
   in performance standards, 68
Nuisance abatement
   achieving compatibility by, 96-97
   building code and, 144
   commercial police power and, 185-86
   courts and, 96-98
   new Chicago zoning ordinance and, 104

Occupancy
   certificate of, 141-42, 146-47
   fire and safety hazards and, 69
O'Donnell, James, 233
Odors
   incompatibility of uses and, 93
   in performance standards, 67
O'Harrow, Dennis, 51-55, 64-74, 77, 119
Oil and gas depletion allowances, 215-16
Open land, as expendable, 124
Orton, Lawrence M., 93
Osgood, Harry, 169

Oster, Robert M., 185-94
Overt zoning, defined, 44*n*
Over-zoning problem, 44-50

Paretian criteria, 26-27
Parking, incompatibility of uses and, 93
Parking bays, 81
"Patio plan," 111
Performance basis of building code, 138
Performance code, as stage in building code
   elaboration, 64, 65
Performance standards
   compatibility and, 97-98
   emergence of, 112
   in industrial zoning, 64-73
   nonconforming use and, 119-20
   principle behind, 104-5
   in residential zoning, 74-80
Philadelphia Housing Survey of 1951, 157
Philadelphia Real Property Survey of 1934,
   157
Pickard, Jerome P., 262
Pittsburgh (Penna.), graded property tax in,
   260-75
Pittsburgh Regional Planning Association, 273
Placarding, 192-93
"Planned irregularity," 111-12
Planning
   controlling urban growth by, 245-46
   property tax and land, 253-59
   taxation and achieving purposes of, 222-26
   zoning absorbed by, 123-29
Plumkett, Thomas J., 248-52
Police power
   aesthetic objectives and, 83, 84
   building code justified by, 136
   defined, 185
   housing demolition and, 191-92
   as legal basis of housing codes, 185-86
   limitations on, 186-87
   property destruction and, 183*n*
   standards for housing codes and, 180-81
Political model, assumptions of, 43-44
Powell (professor), 111
Power, discretionary, of administrative
   officials, 13; *see also* Police power
Pownell, L. L., 245
Primitive stage of building codes, 64, 65
"Prisoner's dilemma," 176*n*
Profit
   depreciation and, 223-24
   traditional land use and maximum, 113
   unnecessary hardship and reasonable, 33-35
Progress and Poverty (George), 242
Progressively inclusive districts principle, 61,
   62
Prohibited industries, 60-62
Property taxation
   altering, 232-33
   checking erosion of, 220
   effects of, on slums and renewal, 236-41
   goals of reforming, 219-20
   land planning and, 253-59

rehabilitation and graded, 260-75
See also Taxation
Property Taxation and Urban Development
    (publication), 232
Proposed Housing Ordinance, 188
Provisions of Housing Codes in Various
    American Cities, 178
Psychological effects
    incompatibility of uses and, 93
    in performance standards, 72-74
    in residential performance standards, 77-80
Public acquisition of land, controlling urban
    growth and, 246-47
Public assistance, 195; *see also* Welfare
Public benefit rule, granting variances and,
    35-36
Public development, increasing, favored, 11
Public policy, taxation and, 234-35
Public welfare in housing codes, 181, 182

Queenside Hills Realty Co. v. *Saxl,* 189

Racial changes of central cities, 4, 5
Rank correlation coefficients cross-
    classification (table), 239
Rational enactment of zoning ordinances,
    47-49
Rationales for zoning variances, 29-31
Rawson, Mary, 232
Rear yards, 76-77
Reconstruction and Production, Senate
    Committee on, 133
Recreation space, 203
Regional Science Association, 230
Rehabilitation
    Baltimore Plan, 157-63
        pilot program, 160-63
        structure of enforcement program, 158-60
    building codes, housing codes and housing,
        164-76
    current housing codes and workable
        program for, 177
    graded property tax and, 260-75
    See also Renewal
Renaissance (Pittsburgh, Penna.), 262, 265-67
Renewal
    effects of property tax on, 236-41
    housing codes and urban, 177-84
    private, 254-55
    progress in central city, 4-5
    See also Rehabilitation
Rent, improvements and increase in, 171
Rent strikes, 195, 198-99
Rent withholding, 195, 196-98
*Rental Housing: Opportunities for Private
    Investment* (Winnick), 261
Repair
    building codes and, 140-45
    liens for cost of, 193-94
Repair and alter orders
    challengers to, 189-90
    failure to comply with, 192
    housing code and, 189
Reps, John W., 10-18

Requirements
    extent of building code, 135-36; *see also*
        Building codes
    housing code standards and technical,
        152-57; *see also* Housing codes;
        Standards
    for rehabilitation, 173-74
Residential area
    noise and density of, 76
    zoning of low density urban, 81
Residential districts in new Chicago zoning
    ordinance, 100-1
Residential lots, changes in, 75-76
Residential performance standards, aesthetics
    in, 76-77
*Residential Rehabilitation: Private Profits and
    Public Purposes* (Nash), 261
Residential zoning, performance standards in,
    74-80
Retroactive measures in housing codes, 179-80
Retroactive zoning, defined, 98
Ribicoff, Abraham, 195, 198
Richards v. *City of Columbia,* 187, 189
Riis, Jacob, 166
Rodgers v. *Churchill,* 112
Rosellini (Governor of Washington), 7

Safety hazard
    incompatibility of uses and, 93
    performance standards for, 68-69
St. Louis Gunning Advertising Co. v. *St. Louis*
    (1911), 83-84, 86
Schaaf, A. H., 236-41
Schorr, Alvin L., 195
Segregation, reasons for, 59-60
Segregation principle, 43, 44, 46
Self-determination, industrial zoning and, 53
Sert, Dean, 111
Setback, 79-84, 123
Sewage wastes, industrial, 70
Shelter allowances, 195-96
    rent withholding and, 196, 197
Shenkel, William M., 56-63
Side yards, 76-77
Single tax, *see* Land value taxation
Site value taxation, *see* Land value taxation
Slayton, William, 16, 191, 192
Slums
    effect of property taxation on, 236-41
    indices of conditions in, 237
    See also Rehabilitation; Renewal
Slums and Social Insecurity (Schorr), 195
Smoke
    incompatibility of uses and, 93
    new Chicago zoning ordinance and, 104
    in performance standards, 66
    transportation smoke, 71
Social Security Act, 195-96, 198
Soderfelt v. *Drayton,* 191
Southern Christian Leadership Conference,
    198, 199

Spann case, 182
Special assessment tax therory, 214-15
Special permit, achieving compatibility by,
    97-98
Special uses, defined, 109
Specification standards, 74
    of building codes, 64
    in residential zoning, 78
Spiegel law (1962), 196, 197
    amendment to (1965), 199
Spooner, William, 171
Spot zoning, 99
    by Chicago City Council, 108
    new Chicago zoning ordinance and, 107
Standard Metropolitan Statistical Areas
        (SMSA), 267, 269
Standard State Zoning Enabling Act, 3, 15
Standards
    compatibility, 92-99
    enforcement and changing, 187
    of housing codes, 152-57
        aesthetics in standards, 181-83
        criticism of housing code, 194
        current minimum standards, 180-81
        fixing standards, 178
    housing demolition and minimum, 191-92
    mandatory statewide, 195-200
    performance
        compatibility and, 97-98
        emergence of, 112
        in industrial zoning, 64-73
        noncomforming use and, 119-20
        principle behind, 104-5
        in residential zoning, 74-80
    specification, 74
        of building codes, 64
        in residential zoning, 78
State enabling acts
    nonconforming buildings and, 94
    zoning variances and, 29
State ex rel. Saveland Park Holding
        Corporation v. Wieland, 193
State Land Use Commission (Hawaii), 234
Statutory basis for zoning variances, 31
Stein, Clarence, 94
Strauss, Jay J., 200
Structures, elimination of incompatible, 92-99
Suburbs
    characteristics of, 6
    middle-class exodus to, 4, 5
    process of development of, 227-35
Sum-of-the-individual-utilities theory, 25-26
Sutherland, George, 92, 111, 112

Tarrytown floating zone case, 112
Tax base
    broadening large city, 220
    industry as, 53
Tax exemption, growth in use of, 223
Tax systems in New Zealand (table), 244
Tax theory, special assessment, 214-15

Taxation, 207-75
    for achieving planning purposes, 222-26
    archaic system of, 7
    development and, 217-21, 227-35
        land value tax and, 248-52
    income
        development and, 231
        modifying, 233-34
    as land use control device, 209-16
    land value, 207-8, 229, 248-75
        advantages of, 248-52
        controlling urban growth and, 242-45
        development and, 248-52
        effects of a shift to, 239-41
        land planning and, 253-59
        rehabilitation and, 260-75
    property
        altering, 232-33
        checking erosion of, 220
        effects on slums and renewal, 236-41
        goals of reforming, 219-20
        land planning and, 253-59
        rehabilitation and graded, 260-75
    public policy and, 234-35
Taxing power, as land use control device,
    209-16
Taxing units, logical, 219
Tenant unions, 195, 199-200
Tenants
    rent strikes by, 195, 198-99
    responsibility of, 201-5
Tennessee Valley Authority, 117
Territorial planning and zoning units, 118
Tests for building codes, 136-38
Thompson, George N., 133-39
Time problems in zoning, 54
Town and Country Planning Act (1947), 112
Traffic
    incompatibility of uses and, 93
    large store and congested, 102-3
    in performance standards, 70-72
Transition problem, 42-50
Transportation, performance standards for,
    70-72
Turvey, Ralph, 232

Under-Utilization Index, 238
Ultra vires, control of competition, 20
Unconstitutional control of competition, 20
Undeveloped land, development plans for, 127
Uniqueness of hardship, 36-38
United Auto Workers, 199
United States Census of Housing (1940), 157
United States Census of Housing (1950),
    151, 157
Unnecessary hardship, 31-35; see also
        Hardship
Urban land, see Cities
Utilization, rate of, for industrial land, 57-59

Vacation order, 192-93
Values, implementation of aesthetic, 89-90
Valley View Village v. Proffett (1955), 184n

Variances, 28-40
  achieving compatibility and, 97-98
  administrative changes toward, 118
    courts and granting of, 33-38
  criticized, 75
  frequency of cases involving, 110
    in new Chicago zoning ordinance, 107-8
  as part of a discretionary system, 115
  as weakest link in zoning, 120
Village of Euclid v. *Ambler Realty Company*
    (1926), 74, 92, 93, 110, 128

Walker, Mabel, 217-21
Washington Post (newspaper), 198
Waste-load surcharges, 215*n*
Wastes
  incompatibility of uses and, 93
  industrial sewage, 70
  in residential performance standards, 76
Watson, J. P., 261, 262
Welfare
  general, *see* General welfare
  individual, 24-25
    general welfare and, 25-26
  public, in housing codes, 181, 182
Welfare economics, 26-27
Welfare families, 195-200
  housing for, 195
Welton v. *Hamilton,* 107
Whinston (economist), 169
Whitewashing, 181*n*
Widnall, William B., 198
Williams, Percy, 263
Winnick, Louis, 261
Winston, D., 246
Wolfe, Myer R., 227-35
Wiener, Paul, 111
Wooton, 115

Zoned codes, 183-84
  problems of, 174-76
Zoning, 1-130
  to achieve compatibility, 93-96
  for aesthetic objectives, 83-91
  for control of competition, 19-23
  controlling urban growth by, 245-46
  definition of, 11-12
  economic elements of municipal decisions
      on, 41-50
  emerging legal issues in, 110-22
  industrial, 51-73
    developer and, 51-55
    economic consequences of, 56-63
    performance standards in, 64-73
  judicial review of, 14-17
  new Chicago ordinance, 100-9
  performance standards in
    compatibility and, 97-98
    emergence of, 112
    in industrial zoning, 64-73
    nonconforming use and, 119-20
    principle behind, 104-5
    in residential zoning, 74-80
  planning absorbs, 123-29
  purpose of (1920s), 3-4
  variances in, *see* Variances
Zoning boards (boards of appeal or
    adjustment), 124-26
Zoning lot, lot of record distinguished from,
    100*n*
Zoning ordinances, defined, 177*n*-78*n*
Zoning principles, comprehensive, 93-94
Zwerner, A. H., 169